Study Guide

Social Psychology

Study Guide

SABINI
Social Psychology

Maury Silver
ST. FRANCIS COLLEGE

W • W • Norton & Company
New York   London

Cover art: Colleen Browning, *Encounters* (1975), ACA Galleries, New York City.
Courtesy of the artist.

W. W. Norton & Company, 500 Fifth Avenue, New York, NY 10110
W. W. Norton & Company Ltd., 10 Coptic Street, London WC1A 1PU

ISBN 0-393-96202-4

1 2 3 4 5 6 7 8 9 0

Contents

prejudice
perception

Preface

This study guide is intended to help you understand and remember what you read in John Sabini's *Social Psychology.* A study guide helps with a text but is not a substitute for it. If you try to use it as a substitute you will quickly become confused, bored, and not learn very much at all. What then is the use of this study guide? It will allow you to concentrate on the arguments in the text, puzzle about human nature, and enjoy Sabini's humor without having to break the flow of your reading by memorizing definitions, experimental details, names of important experimenters, and the like. How? Read a section of the text to understand the arguments. Then turn to the study guide. Just about every point that you might need to remember, indeed almost every point in the text, will be handled from one to three times, as a multiple-choice question, a fill-in, or as a series of statements that outline what you should have come away with in that section. Since the text is rather dense it may be helpful for you to read a section or two of text, review those sections in the study guide, and then return to the text. It will be relatively easy to go back and forth from the study guide to the text: The answers to the multiple-choice questions (Self-Test) refer back to the page in the text that the question was derived from, the statements that outline what you should know (Learning Objectives) have the same headings and subheadings as the text, so that once you've read the material in the text you can review the material under the same subheading in the study guide. I regret that the fill-in section (Programmed Exercises) does not reproduce all the headings of the text, but it has the most important of them so you should not have much difficulty using it.

Now for some specifics about the use of the study guide. Each chapter of the text is covered by a chapter of the study guide divided into four sections. As I've already mentioned the Learning Objectives, Programmed Exercises, and Self-Test sections independently cover most points made in the text; the fourth section—Thought Questions and Exercises—is not a review but an attempt to prick your curiosity and get you to think about and even investigate issues raised by the text. It also might be used as a source of possible term papers and term projects. Why does this, and most study guides, have three separate review sections? Each section has a slightly different task. The Learning Objectives section contains a straightforward list, in statement or question form, of what you should know if you've mastered a part of the text. You should go through the learning objectives, mentally checking off what you remember, what you don't remember and what you sort of remember but are shaky on. Then go back to the text (unless you recall everything, of course). The Programmed Exercises (fill-ins), on the other hand, go further into the details of the experiments and studies and arguments of the text. These are the sort of details that some instructors like to put on tests. These fill-ins will be helpful to you in two ways. As a review: The words to fill in the blanks are right next to the sentence so that you can use the fill-ins as a brief, condensed (and much less interesting) version of the points in the text. And the fill-ins ask you to produce from memory the answers and not just to pick the best alternative, so they are a good test of whether you have mastered a section. The Self-Test (multiple-choice questions) is probably the most popular exam format. The multiple-choice questions are a good way to test yourself to see whether you are ready for an exam. I've written lots of multiple-choice questions, most chapters have from sixty to eighty, covering most points in the text. As with most multiple-test questions, there is usually one best answer, but occasionally an alternative specifying "all of the above" or two alternatives is correct. For example, if I ask you:

If you are having any trouble with a text at all it is best to:

    a. reread the text
    b. read only the study guide
    c. read a Batman comic
    d. a and b

I hope you put "d" the alternative specifying two alternatives, a and b. I sympathize with you if you put down answer "c" but I'd still mark it wrong. If you get a question wrong, before you turn back to the text to review (right?), try to figure out why you selected the wrong answer you selected. My multiple-choice questions may be less tricky (I hope) than some that you have encountered. My intention is to use the multiple-choice test questions to help you learn the material, review for exams, and see how well you are doing—not to test you. But if you can get my questions right, you should be well prepared for a course exam.

The Sabini text is enjoyable and thought provoking. It's my hope that this study guide will allow you to relax with the text and do the drudgery with me. I hope this study guide will make the drudgery pay off.

Maury Silver
June 1992

CHAPTER 1

Introduction

Learning Objectives

1. Be able to explain the difference in emphasis among social psychologists, anthropologists, historians, and sociologists. Use the case of romantic love to illustrate this difference. Many chapters in the text treat aspects of, or issues related to, romantic love. Give some examples.

METHODS OF SOCIAL PSYCHOLOGY

The Experimental Method
2. Be able to describe the function of experiments.

Brainstorming
3. Discuss what brainstorming is and what it is used for. In brainstorming the solution of a problem is separated into two distinct phases. What are they? What is the point to doing this?
4. According to its proponents following brainstorming instructions *causes* more creative solutions than would have been the case without the brainstorming instructions, meaning a group would do better if it used brainstorming rather than another method. How can this be experimentally tested? In an experiment contrasting brainstorming and standard instructions, what would be "the experimental group," "the control group," "the independent variable," "the dependent variable"? If the brainstorming group (experimental group) produced more creative ideas than the standard group (control group) what could you conclude?

5. Explain why it would be a deadly flaw in an experiment for the subjects to choose which condition they wanted to be in. (Remember the example of creative people choosing to be in brainstorming groups.)
6. Review the evidence that brainstorming groups do better than the same number of individuals given brainstorming instructions but working alone. When this hypothesis was experimentally investigated what was found? Did the difference between groups and pooled individuals become smaller or larger as group size increased?
7. Understand the difference between an experiment that examines *whether* something works and one that determines *how* something works.

How Groups Interfere with Productivity
8. Be able to name the two sorts of reasons proposed by Steiner that groups do not measure up to the individuals who comprise them. Describe the experiment that attempted to show that a group's difficulty is one of coordination. What is the importance of the condition in which individuals work alone but can only speak their ideas through a microphone that only works when someone else is not using it? In what way is this condition like being in a group?
9. Strictly speaking, to whom are the conclusions of an experiment limited? When is it prudent to generalize the results of an experiment to a broader group than that of the original subjects? The subjects in the brainstorming experiments were students. How does this limit the generality of the findings?

THE CORRELATIONAL METHOD

10. Be able to describe the two sorts of information provided by correlation coefficients. What would it mean if the correlation between wealth and happiness were +1, –1, or 0? Explain why in the social world correlations are rarely above .5.

11. Correlation coefficients tell the degree and direction of relations between two variables. What don't they tell us?

12. If A and B are correlated then there are three possible causal relationships that might account for this. What are they?

Programmed Exercises

1. Social psychology differs from anthropology or sociology in that it places more emphasis on the _____ than they do.

   individual

METHODS OF SOCIAL PSYCHOLOGY

The Experimental Method

2. Experiments are the best tools to determine _____ relations.

   causal

3. According to Osborn brainstorming is a way to maximize _____ in groups.

   creativity

4. Brainstormers are forbidden to hold back _____ no matter how trivial or silly they may seem.

   ideas

5. Brainstormers separate the solution of a problem into two distinct phases: generating possible solutions and _____ the solutions that have been generated.

   evaluating

6. It is logically impossible to assess what would happen if we had done otherwise (since we didn't do otherwise); the _____ is a practical way around this problem.

   experiment

7. In an experiment we compare subjects treated in _____ ways.

   two

8. In an experiment on brainstorming we would compare a group of subjects given brainstorming instructions, the _____ group, and a group of subjects following standard instructions (i.e., "only contribute if you think your idea is good"), the _____ group.

   experimental

   control

9. Whether or not a subject gets the brainstorming instruction is called the _____ variable.

   independent

10. The number of creative ideas produced by each of the two groups is called the _____ variable.

    dependent

11. If the brainstorming group produces more creative ideas than the standard group then we have reason to believe that brainstorming _____ the group to produce more creative ideas.

    causes

12. In a properly conducted experiment the _____ group is the surrogate for how the experimental group would have acted if it had other (non-brainstorming) instructions. This is the case if and only if subjects were _____ assigned to condition.

    control

    randomly

13. _____ assignment to control and experimental conditions is the crucial element of an experiment.

    Random

14. It would be a deadly flaw in an experiment for the subjects to _____ which condition they wanted too be in.

    choose

15. If subjects could choose their condition, creative people, for example, might prefer to try the brainstorming condition. If the brainstorming condition resulted in more creative ideas we would not know whether it was due to the _____ or just that the group had more creative people to begin with.

    instructions

16. Groups of students using brainstorming or standard instructions had to come up with brand names that would appeal to male students. The brainstorming group produced _____ brand names than the standard group.

    more

17. When an undergraduate panel rated how much each idea appealed to them in the brand-name experiment, there was _____ difference in the number of excellent ideas produced by the two groups.

    no

18. The undergraduate panel did not know whether an idea came from the brainstorming or the regular group. This was done to avoid _____ caused by the panelists' beliefs in favor or against brainstorming. This is known as keeping the panelists _____ to the experimental condition.

    bias

    blind

19. The number of solutions to a problem produced by brainstorming groups or by the same number of individuals working alone (and pooling their product) was compared. _____ produced the most solutions. The larger the group, the _____ the difference between individual and group production of solutions.

    Individuals

    greater

20. The brainstorming experiments examined so far tell us _____ brainstorming works or not. Experiments are also used analytically to tell _____ something works, what about something leads it to have the _____ _____ it has.

    whether

    how

    causal effect

21. According to Steiner there are two reasons why groups do worse than the equivalent number of individuals. One reason concerns failures of _____, people work less hard in a group; the other concerns failures of _____.

    motivation

    coordination

22. The same number of subjects had to figure out ways to reduce unemployment in a brainstorming group, individually, or in a condition in which each subject worked alone but had to speak his ideas into a microphone (and only one mike was alive at a time). The microphone and brainstorming groups both contributed about as many ideas; both produced _____ ideas than the same number of people working alone.

    fewer

23. The above experiment suggests that the reason brainstorming groups do less well than individuals has something to do with being _____ in one's speech.

    interrupted

24. Experimentation as in the above example allows for the isolation of the "active ingredient" that _____ an outcome.

    causes

25. Strictly speaking the results of an experiment are valid only for the subjects that _____ in it.

    participated

26. Psychologists attempt to _____ these results to much broader groups.

    generalize

27. Most of the brainstorming experiments were done with undergraduates so it would be safer to generalize these results to _____ than to octogenarians.

    undergraduates

28. Unfortunately these experiments did not take a _____ sample of undergraduates, hence even generalization to this population is uncertain.

random

29. Experimental results that derive from a more broadly _____ subject pool are more worthy of attention than those that use a narrow one. It is most noteworthy when the results of several instances of the same experiment with different types of subjects _____.

representative

converge

30. Experiments take place in a particular culture in a particular moment in time, yet psychologists usually wish to make universal, timeless _____.

generalizations

31. It would be ethically and practically prohibitive to _____ assign people to many of the conditions we would like to randomly investigate. (For instance, what are the effects of being raised in poverty or wealth, or being married to an attractive or unattractive partner?)

randomly

THE CORRELATIONAL METHOD

32. A "correlation coefficient" tells us the degree of _____ between two variables.

relation

33. A correlation of +1 means that two variables are perfectly related in the _____ direction, when one goes up so does the other, when one goes down so does the other.

positive

34. A correlation of −1 means that the two variables are perfectly related in the _____ direction, when one goes up the other goes down.

negative

35. If wealth and happiness were perfectly positively correlated, a correlation of +1, then for everyone studied the more the wealth the _____ the happiness, and nothing else would affect happiness.

more

36. If the correlation between pain and happiness were −1, then the more the pain the _____ the happiness for every person studied, and nothing else would affect happiness.

less

37. If the correlation between variables x and y were 0, then there would be _____ relation between the variables.

no

38. If the correlation between attractiveness of husbands and satisfaction of wives were _____, then for the group as a whole attractive husbands would have neither happier nor less happy wives than would ugly husbands.

0

39. In the _____ world, correlations are rarely above .5 because any variable is related to many other variables.

social (real)

40. Correlation coefficients tell the degree and direction of relations between two variables, but they do not tell us directly about _____.

causality

41. If there is a positive correlation between judgments of pleasant personality and attractiveness, it may be because genuine attractiveness biases us to see the person as pleasant, or because having a pleasant personality biases us to see the person as _____.

attractive

Self-Test

1. Social psychology differs from anthropology or sociology in that it
    a. studies topics such as romantic love, which is not of interest to anthropology.
    b. always uses experiments.
    c. is only concerned with individuals and not how they relate to a culture.
    d. places a greater emphasis on the individual's relation to culture than do the other fields.

2. An experiment is best suited to
    a. determine correlations.
    b. determine causal relations.
    c. determine regression coefficients.
    d. determine only the neural or chemical aspects of behavior.

3. Brainstorming is intended to maximize
    a. creativity in groups.
    b. abreaction at therapeutic sessions.
    c. deep feelings.
    d. an illusion of intimacy.

4. Brainstormers separate the solution of a problem into two distinct phases:
    a. thinking about ideas and then telling them to the group
    b. screaming and crying and then resting from the brain storm
    c. making fun of other people's ideas and promoting your own
    d. generating possible solutions and evaluating the solutions that have been generated

5. In an experiment on brainstorming, which would be the experimental and which would be the control group?
    a. Subjects with the brainstorming instructions would be in the experimental group, and subjects following standard instructions would be in the control group.
    b. Subjects with the standard instructions would be in the experimental group, and subjects with the brainstorming instructions would be in the control group.
    c. subjects with brainstorming instructions would be in both the experimental and the control groups.
    d. all of the above (depending on the details of the experiment)

6. A good dependent variable in a study of brainstorming would be
    a. number of criticisms of other people's ideas.
    b. number of complaints against people in the group.
    c. number of creative ideas.
    d. any of the above, depending on the type of brainstorming.

7. If the brainstorming group produces more creative ideas than the standard group, then we have reason to believe that brainstorming
    a. is only correlated with creativity.
    b. causes the group to produce more creative ideas.
    c. is only accidentally related to the production of creative ideas.
    d. may or may not cause more creative ideas; now correlational analysis is needed to determine causality.

8. We are entitled to use the control group as a surrogate for the experimental subjects treated with control instructions only if the subjects are assigned
    a. carefully.
    b. according to their own choice.
    c. randomly.
    d. nonrandomly.

9. If the subjects were allowed to choose the condition they were in then
    a. it would be easier to decide causality than if subjects were randomly assigned.
    b. they could more truly identify with the condition they were in and a correct experimental result would be more likely.
    c. it would not be possible to decide whether the experimental result was due to the difference between experimental and control instructions or a difference between the sort of person who chose a particular condition.
    d. it would sometimes be easier and sometimes more difficult to make causal conclusions.

10. Groups of students using brainstorming or standard instructions had to come up with brand names that would appeal to male students. The brainstorming group produced
    a. more brand names than the standard group.
    b. more creative brand names than the standard group.
    c. no more creative ideas than the standard group.
    d. a and c

11. In the previous experiment excellence of the brand names was determined by a panel. To prevent distortion of results
    a. the panelists should be carefully informed whether a brand name idea came from the brainstorming or standard group.
    b. the panelists should know where the ideas came from but this should not be greatly stressed.
    c. the panelists should not know whether the brand name idea came from the brainstorming or standard group.
    d. the panelists should each be given the choice of whether they wish to know the origin of an idea or not.

12. The number of solutions to a problem produced by brainstorming groups or by the same number of individuals working alone (and pooling their product) was compared. Which produced the most solutions?
    a. the brainstorming groups
    b. the individuals
    c. sometimes the brainstorming groups and sometimes individuals, depending on whether the brainstorming group was compatible or not
    d. the brainstorming groups 70 percent of the time

13. According to Steiner the reason(s) why groups do worse than the equivalent number of individuals is that
    a. people try too hard in groups and tend to "choke."
    b. people are less motivated in groups.
    c. effort is wasted in coordinating the efforts of members of the group.
    d. b and c

14. The same number of subjects had to figure out ways to reduce unemployment in a brainstorming group, individually, or in a condition in which each subject worked alone but had to speak his ideas into a microphone (and only one mike was alive at a time). The microphone and brainstorming groups contributed about as many ideas; both produced
    a. many more ideas than the "group" of individuals working alone.
    b. about the same number of ideas as the "group" of individuals working alone.
    c. fewer ideas than the "group" of individuals working alone.

    d. many more ideas than the "group" of individuals when they were highly motivated, but fewer when they were not.

15. The previous experiment suggests that the advantages of hearing others' ideas generally
    a. are less than the disadvantage of having one's own thoughts interrupted.
    b. balance the disadvantage of having one's own thoughts interrupted.
    c. are much greater than the advantages of hearing one's own ideas.
    d. are either greater or less than the disadvantage of having one's thoughts interrupted, depending on the personality of the individual.

16. Strictly speaking the results of an experiment are valid
    a. for all people in all places at all times.
    b. only if the results are in accord with our own intuition.
    c. only if advanced instruments and statistical methods are used.
    d. only for the subjects who participated in it (although we generalize to other people who are similar to the subjects in relevant ways).

17. It is best to generalize the results of an experiment when
    a. there are other studies with different subjects whose results converge with this one.
    b. the experiment used correlational methods.
    c. several variants of the experiment give different results and (after the results are in) the experimenters give an explanation of why this is the case.
    d. experimental intuition supports generalization.

18. If an experiment is done properly and obtains results then
    a. one can generalize from the experimental results to all people.
    b. one can generalize from the experimental results to all cultures.
    c. one can generalize from the experimental results to all periods, past, present, and future.
    d. one can generalize only to groups, cultures, and time periods that are similar to that of the original culture.

19. If we know that wealth and happiness are *perfectly positively correlated* then
    a. for everyone studied the more wealth the less happiness and nothing else would matter.
    b. for everyone studied the more wealth the more happiness and nothing else matters.
    c. for some people studied wealth is important for happiness, but for other people it is not very important.
    d. for everyone studied the more wealth the more happiness, but there are many other factors that are very important to happiness.

20. If pain and happiness were *perfectly negatively correlated* then
    a. the more pain the more the happiness.
    b. the more pain the less the happiness and nothing else would matter to happiness.
    c. the more the pain the less the happiness, but there are many other factors that are relevant to happiness.
    d. some people with pain would be happier than some others without it, depending on their attitudes.

21. If the correlation between attractiveness of husbands and marital satisfaction were 0 then
    a. for the group as a whole attractive husbands had neither happier nor less happy wives than did ugly husbands.
    b. for the group as a whole attractive husbands had happier wives than did ugly husbands.
    c. for the group as a whole attractive husbands had less happy wives than did ugly husbands.
    d. for some people attractive husbands had happier wives than ugly husbands, but for other people the attractiveness of husbands wasn't very important for marital satisfaction.

22. What strength correlations are typically found in the social world?
    a. 1
    b. 0
    c. from .7 to .9
    d. rarely more than .5

23. Correlations
    a. give the degree of relation between two variables.
    b. give the direction of the relations between two variables.
    c. do *not* tell us directly about causality.
    d. all of the above

24. If there is a positive correlation between judgments of pleasant personality and attractiveness it may be because
    a. how attractive a person is influences our judgments of his personality.
    b. people with pleasant personalities appear more attractive.
    c. a third factor (e.g., favorite children are more likely to become attractive adults and have pleasant personalities) could be responsible for the correlation.
    d. all of the above

25. Threat of severe shock produces anxiety, which produces a desire to affiliate (compared to threat of negligible shock). When would we be confident in concluding that *anxiety* produces a desire to affiliate?
    a. If the study were repeated with different groups of subjects.
    b. If several studies using independent variables that had nothing in common with each other except that they produced anxiety all produced a desire to affiliate (such as embarrassment, a failing grade, an operation).
    c. If the number of subjects in the experimental and control group were increased.
    d. all of the above

Answer Key for Self-Test

1.	d (p. 1)	14.	c (p. 9)
2.	b (p. 4)	15.	a (p. 9)
3.	a (p. 4)	16.	d (p. 10)
4.	d (p. 4)	17.	a (p. 10)
5.	a (p. 5)	18.	d (p. 10)
6.	c (p. 6)	19.	b (p. 12)
7.	b (p. 6)	20.	b (p. 12)
8.	c (p. 6)	21.	a (p. 12)
9.	c (p. 6)	22.	d (p. 12)
10.	d (p. 7)	23.	d (p. 12)
11.	c (p. 7)	24.	d (p. 13)
12.	b (p. 8)	25.	b (p. 13)
13.	d (p. 9)		

Thought Questions and Exercises

1. The text distinguishes social psychology from anthropology, sociology, and history. Literature also analyzes life. How would you distinguish between the insights about human nature and social life derived from literature and those derived from social psychology?

2. The text illustrates the experimental method by considering "brainstorming." It would be helpful for you to take an issue you are interested in and attempt to plan out how you could study it experimentally. Assume you have access to a hefty budget and can get around merely practical difficulties. What is your independent variable and how can you experimentally vary it? What is your dependent variable? Remember your dependent variable must be specific, measurable, and yet capture the effect you are interested in. You may have difficulty finding such a dependent variable. So do most psychologists. What are your experimental and control groups? Why do you always need a control group? You will have to assign subjects to the experimental and control groups randomly. Why? Let us say that you get the result you predicted. Since it is an imaginary experiment that should be easy. You wish to generalize your results to more than just the people who participated in your experiment. To which groups would it be safer to generalize?

3. Why is it not strictly possible to generalize from the results of the experiments on brainstorming that used students at a particular university to the undergraduate population as a whole? Why

do social psychologists have more confidence in a finding when they get the same results from different samples (for example, army personnel and undergraduates)? Experiments are bound to a particular culture at a particular moment in time. Yet, experimenters often wish to talk of people in general. When is the time and culture-bound nature of an experiment least likely to matter? When is this most likely to matter?

4. Are there some issues that cannot be approached experimentally (for practical or moral rather than logical reasons)? Why?

5. What is a correlational study? Under what circumstances would it be better to do a correlational study than an experiment? What would it mean to say that there was a perfect negative correlation between hitting people on the head and being liked. What would it mean to say that there was a perfect positive correlation between running and heart rate? If two variables are correlated at 0, what is the relation between them? Remember that when two variables A and B are correlated, A might be the cause of B, B might be the cause of A, or a third factor C might cause both A and B. There is a moderate correlation between amount of ice cream consumed (on a particular day) and drownings (on that day). Why might this be the case?* What are three possible interpretations of the correlation of +.3 between judgments of pleasantness of pesonality and attractiveness? There is a large correlation between a child's shoe size and his knowledge of the world. Explain.

---

* Roughly. On hotter days we eat more ice cream and on hotter days we are more likely to go swimming and drown. Ice cream doesn't cause drowning, and presumably the drowned don't consume ice cream. Rather, hot weather and the desires that go with it are a cause of both.

CHAPTER 2

Social Influence

Learning Objectives

CONFORMITY

1. Be able to explain what is meant by "conformity," "compliance," and "internalization."

The Asch Experiment

2. Describe the Asch experiment from the point of view of a naive subject. What is the conflict for the subject in the Asch experiment? In what way is the position of a subject in the Asch experiment like that of the emperor, or even the townsmen, in Andersen's "Emperor's New Clothes."

3. Know what percent of Asch's subjects, college students, went along with the clearly wrong majority in the Asch experiment. What proportion of the subjects remained independent and never erred? What percent of the trial judgments were in error? If subjects were tested alone, what percent of their judgments were in error?

Why Do People Conform?

Conformity and Objectivity

4. Explain why all of Asch's subjects (whether they conformed or not) were so upset? Why is it important to be able to assume that you are seeing and acting in the same world as everyone else? Why didn't the subjects realize that the people who gave the wrong answer were in reality confederates?

Conformity and Embarrassment

5. Describe the difference between "informational" and "normative" pressure. Describe the experiment in which subjects listened in on the Asch experimental group, wrote down the group's and their answers and gave it to the experimenter, but did not state their judgment aloud before the group.

Conformity and Ambiguity: The Sherif Experiment

6. In Sherif's experiment subjects had to judge how far a point of light moved in a dark room. Give two reasons why this was a difficult task. How did the subjects handle this difficulty? What happened to a subject's judgments over the course of judging movement a hundred times? Was there any consistency between subjects in their judgments? Why not? In the next phase of the experiment Sherif took the separate subjects and brought them together. The subjects were now to call out their individual judgments in front of each other. What happened? What did Sherif intend this experiment to demonstrate?

7. Understand the difference between judging a very ambiguous stimulus in the Sherif experiment and a very clear one in the Asch experiment. What is the importance of this difference? Give two reasons why it was more difficult to compromise in the Asch than in the Sherif experiment.

8. Contrast how the Sherif and Asch subjects reacted to finding that the others in the experiment disagreed with them. What is the reason for the difference in their reactions?

9. Describe the difference in the responses of Asch subjects later retested alone and Sherif subjects retested alone a year later. Explain what accounts for this difference.

What Reduces Conformity?

10. Explain how understanding *why* others might be disagreeing with an obvious judgment reduces conformity in an Asch-type situation. Describe the Ross study and why his subjects conformed less.

Conformity and Preferences

11. Understand the effect of conformity pressures on objective issues and on issues of taste. How did Crutchfield's subjects judge popular and less-popular drawings? Why should the same subjects be independent in this situation and conformist in the original Asch experiment? How do the results of this experiment show that subjects are less concerned about being different and more concerned about looking crazy?

The Lone Dissenter

12. Describe the power of a lone dissenter. Does having a partner who does not give the wrong answer reduce the rate of conformity? When a confederate disagrees with the group by being even more wrong than they are, does the rate of conformity change? Does the group's power in the conformity studies derive from the power of majority rule or unanimity?

Minority Influence

13. Explain how a minority can lead a majority to reexamine its position. What happened in the variant of the Asch experiment in which nine confederates gave the wrong answer in the presence of eleven naive subjects?

14. Understand the difference in the kind of influence exerted by minorities as opposed to majorities. Describe Moscovici's experimental procedure. In what way does Moscovici's choice of stimuli make the phenomenon he is studying quite different from that of Asch? Describe the first and second phases of the Moscovici experiment. Was there any difference in the amount of social influence shown in the first and second phase?

15. Describe whether minority or majority arguments produced more public compliance, more private attitude change, or more counterarguments in the study examining attitudes toward gay rights.

THE RISKY SHIFT

16. Describe what the "risky shift" is. Does this phenomenon go against common-sense beliefs?

Explanations for Risky Shift

Risky Shift as Social Comparison

17. Describe the two central ideas of social comparison theory. How does Brown use social comparison theory to explain the risky shift phenomenon?

18. Describe the evidence in support of risk taking as a value. Do people generally see themselves as riskier than most? What did Teger and Pruitt discover about the relation between endorsing risk before a discussion and the amount of risky shift in the discussion? Is the mechanism of the risky shift group *discussion* or is it just knowing others' initial judgments (allowing social comparison)? The Teger and Pruitt experiment demonstrates that social comparison is sufficient but not necessary for the risky shift to occur. Explain.

Social Comparison vs. Persuasive Arguments

19. Understand the fundamental similarity between the Brown theory and persuasive argument theory. Do these theories agree or disagree on the issue of whether risk taking is a value? What are the two different aspects of social comparison focused on by the two theories?

The Demise of Risky Shift

20. Describe what will produce a conservative shift. In McCauley's race-track study, what kind of shift was produced among bettors after their bets were placed?

Group Polarization

21. Describe what is meant by "group polarization." Does the work on risky shift and the shift toward conservatism support or refute the notion of group polarization?

BYSTANDER INTERVENTION

22. Thirty people watched out of their apartment windows and saw Kitty Genovese being murdered. What did they do?

Ambiguity of Emergencies

23. Describe Latané and Darley's explanation for why bystanders failed to act at the time of the Genovese murder. How did it differ from the press' explanation. How did the ambiguity of the situation affect their reactions?

Pluralistic Ignorance

24. Describe what "pluralistic ignorance" is. Explain

how pluralistic ignorance may have contributed to the passivity of the onlookers at the time of the Kitty Genovese murder. Explain the role of social influence in this situation.

Diffusion of Responsibility
25. Describe what "diffusion of responsibility" is. How might diffusion of responsibility have affected the bystanders at the time of the assault on Kitty Genovese?

Experimental Findings

Where There's Smoke There's Fire
26. Describe the "where there is smoke" experiment (include the subject alone condition, the subject and two confederates condition, and the three naive subjects condition). Why was the subjects' behavior in the experiment not an example of apathy? Which of the conditions was most like the Kitty Genovese situation?

Helping and Epileptic Seizures
27. Describe the "epileptic fit" experiment. What happened when subjects believed that they were alone with the victim, when they believed that there was someone else present who could help, when they believed that there were four others present who could help? Do these results support the notion of diffusion of responsibility?
28. Explain how the results of the Latané and Darley experiments are confirmations and extensions of Sherif and Asch's work on social influence.

Social Impact Theory
29. Explain Latané's formal theory of social influence as a multiplicative function.

OBEDIENCE

The Asch Experiment and Human Significance
30. Explain the main weakness of the Asch experiments. What did Milgram decide to do to give the experiment human import? Why did Milgram not carry out this experiment?

Eichmann in Jerusalem
31. Describe what is meant by the phrase "the banality of evil." Who was Adolf Eichmann? Was he extraordinary? How did Eichmann explain his part in the Holocaust?

The Milgram Experiment
32. Describe the Milgram experimental set-up. Include how subjects were recruited, the justification for the setup, what the roles of teacher

and learner appeared to involve, how the learner was supposedly selected, the "learning procedure" (including the apparent punishment for an error), the appearance of the shock generator, and other details of the setting that Milgram used to make the situation appear credible.
33. Describe the difference between the predicted and actual results of the Milgram experiment. What were the expected results? Out of forty male subjects, how many actually went all the way to the end? Are women less likely to shock to the end?

Explanations for Obedience
34. Be able to answer the two questions raised by the results of the Milgram obedience experiment: Why did so many people obey the experimenter? Why did no one expect them to obey?

Slippery Slopes
35. Describe the slippery slope explanation of the obedience in the Milgram experiment.

The Objectivity of the Experiment
36. Describe how the experimenter in the Milgram experiment acted. Give parallels between Asch's experiment and Milgram's. What is the role of objectivity in each experiment?

Reducing Obedience

Disagreeing Experimenters
37. Describe how disagreeing experimenters will affect a subject's obedience in the Milgram experiment.

Rebelling Peers
38. Describe how confederates who disobey the experimenter affect the obedience of a naive subject.
39. Describe Gamson's research on the social dynamics of groups resisting unjust authority. In what way was the group dynamics of successfully resisting groups different from that of obedient groups?

Obedience and Embarrassment
40. Describe whether the presence or absence of the experimenter is relevant to his informational influence. What is the would-be disobedient subject's problem in confronting the experimenter directly?

Distance from the Victim and Disobedience
41. Describe the effect on the rate of obedience in the Milgram experiments of moving the subject

closer to the victim or even requiring the subject to hold the victim's hand to a shock plate. What is the reason for the greater disobedience in the close conditions?

Subjects' Justifications for Their Obedience

Legitimacy

42. Subjects often explained that their obedience was due to the prestige and respectability of Yale University (where the experiments were conducted). Milgram reran the experiment in a rundown office building in Bridgeport. What were the results? What does this demonstrate about the subjects' belief that they only obeyed because they trusted Yale?

Fairness

43. Some subjects explained their obedience by saying that the experiment was fair. In what sense could this experiment be fair?

Obedience and Responsibility

44. When the experimenter "accepted responsibility" it made it easier for some subjects to continue shocking. Why?

45. Describe what Hamilton discovered about people's beliefs about the assignment of responsibility in hierarchies. What did she find about people's beliefs about the assignment of responsibility in the Milgram experiment? How are subjects able to see the experiment as fair, and the experimenter as bearing responsibility for the learner's suffering?

Social Influence and Arendt's Questions

46. Explain how the Milgram experiment is relevant to the question of whether an ordinary person could become a mass murderer like Adolf Eichmann.

Ethics of the Social Influence Experiments

Long-Term Impairment

47. Milgram had a psychiatrist follow up forty of his subjects. Was there evidence of long-term harm as a result of participation in the experiment?

Short-Term Stress

48. Describe the ethical issues raised by the Milgram study. Is it ethical to expose subjects to intense short-term stress? What are the three ethical issues?

BRUTALITY

The Zimbardo Experiment

49. Describe how the set-up of the Zimbardo experiment was intended to test the effect of prison on ordinary people.

Prisoners and Guards

50. How did Zimbardo make his prison experience as much like real prisons as possible? What were some of the things that Zimbardo did to degrade his "prisoners"? Why did he do this? In what ways were the guards treated like real guards?

The Results of the Zimbardo Experiment

51. Give examples of ways the guards degraded the prisoners. Did the guards become more and more brutal over time? How did the prisoners react? When was the experiment terminated? Why?

Explanations of the Brutality

52. Give some reasons why the guards might have wanted to punish the prisoners. Why aren't knowing these reasons a sufficient explanation for why the guards were brutal? What is the difference between our assumptions concerning appropriate force in our everyday lives, and in prisons and mental hospitals?

53. Explain how the guards in the Zimbardo experiment slipped down a slippery slope from reasonable force to brutality. Is this similar to what happened to subjects in the Milgram experiment? How?

Degradation

54. Describe how the degradation inflicted on the prisoners facilitated the slide on the slippery slope? How did Stengl, the commandant of the Treblinka extermination camp, explain why they humiliated prisoners before killing them?

Moral Drift

55. Explain why the "bad guards" had a disproportionate influence causing the escalating brutality. What was the ambiguous issue faced by the guards in the Zimbardo experiment? Why didn't all the guards compromise their original views? Contrast the influence in the Sherif experiment with that in the Zimbardo experiment.

56. Explain why only the "bad guards" expressed their views. Did the good guards accidentally contribute to a pluralistic ignorance (of the kind seen in Latané and Darley's experiments)? Why didn't the good guards just tell the bad guards that they were acting immorally?

Programmed Exercises

1. A fundamental cause of social influence is that we expect to see the same world as everyone else and so are _____ by the perceptions of other people. Just letting on that we see things differently risks our showing ourselves to be _____.

   influenced

   foolish

CONFORMITY

2. When we _____ our actions are at odds with what we believe to be true, best, or proper.

   conform

3. When we change our mind because we have _____ a group's position we have been persuaded and really accept the group's position as correct.

   internalized

4. When we change our position by _____ with others, although we go along with the group we do not believe that they are correct; behavior is changed but private belief is not.

   complying

The Asch Experiment

5. In the Asch experiment a naive subject faces a conflict between what obviously seems to be a right answer and a contrary _____ judgment of six people.

   unanimous

6. In the Asch experiment about _____ of the subjects, college students, erred along with the clearly wrong group on a majority of the trials and _____ were always independent.

   one-third

   one-quarter

7. If subjects judge alone only _____ percent of the judgments are incorrect.

   2

8. The rate of conformity in the Asch experiment is slightly _____ for women than for men.

   higher

Why Do People Conform?

9. All subjects, even the completely independent ones, felt _____ by the majority's wrong answers and experienced _____.

   pressured
   anxiety

10. Asch's subjects were upset because they were forced to doubt two things that they could not doubt: their own _____ and that they see the _____ world that everyone else sees.

    senses
    same

11. The group (except for the subject) was composed of _____. If the subjects had realized this it is likely that they would have given _____ right answers.

    confederates (actors)
    more

12. What bothered the subjects was not that they were behaving differently from the others but that they were perceiving the _____ differently.

    world

13. Subjects may have feared that they would look _____ and be laughed at if they did not conform.

    foolish

14. In a variant of the Asch experiment a confederate gave the false answer when he was a part of a group of six naive subjects. The group _____ at the confederate making the wrong response.

    laughed

15. To the extent that subjects are influenced by others because they see them as sources of information they are responding to _____ pressure.

informational

16. To the extent that subjects change their minds from fear of group ridicule or harm they are responding to _____ pressure.

normative

17. Subjects listened in on the Asch experimental group, wrote down the group's and their own answers, and gave it to the experimenter. They did not state their judgment aloud in front of the group. These subjects did not have to be afraid that the group would _____ at them.

laugh

18. If subjects conformed under these circumstances it would demonstrate _____ conformity.

informational

19. In the above experiment subjects gave _____ wrong answers than when they were tested alone, but fewer wrong answers than if they had been answering aloud in the _____.

more

group

20. Subjects gave the wrong answer, both because of the fear of being laughed at, _____ conformity, and because they were confused, _____ conformity.

normative,
informational

21. In the Sherif experiment subjects separately judging a very ambiguous stimulus produced consistent responses that were _____ from each other.

different

22. When Sherif took the separate subjects and brought them together, they were now to call out their individual judgments in front of each other. Their judgments quickly _____.

converged

23. Sherif intended this experiment to illustrate how social interaction leads to the creation of _____.

norms

24. Social influence in the _____ experiment derives from the subjects' belief that there was a right answer. It can be demonstrated that the same is true of the _____ experiment, since if one tells the subjects that the movement of light is an _____ then their judgments do not converge.

Asch

Sherif
illusion

25. In the Asch experiment the stimulus is clear; in the Sherif experiment the stimulus is _____.

ambiguous

26. In the Sherif experiment since everyone realizes that they are in the same position judging an ambiguous stimulus, it is sensible to _____, but in the Asch experiment the right answer is seen as obvious so subjects realize everyone should have the _____ answer.

compromise

same

27. Once the subjects in the Asch experiment learn that the other "subjects" were confederates they are typically upset by their conformity and _____ how much they conformed.

underestimate

28. When the Sherif experiment subjects are told of the nature of the experiment they are _____ upset since they had acted reasonably.

not

29. When conforming subjects in the Asch experiment are retested they give the _____ answer; when subjects in the Sherif experiment are retested alone a year later they give the _____ judgment.

right
group's

30. A minority has _____ influence in the Sherif experiment than in the Asch experiment.

more

What Reduces Conformity?

31. Ross created a version of the Asch experiment in which subjects believed that others would be getting bonuses if particular answers were correct. Subjects could interpret others' disagreement as their foolishly playing long shots. This version of the Asch experiment substantially _____ conformity as compared to the standard condition.

    reduced

32. The Ross experiment demonstrates that it isn't disagreement per se that causes the pressure to conform but the belief that the disagreement indicates real differences in perception, and more particularly the assumption of a _____ _____.

    single world

33. Crutchfield repeated the Asch conformity experiment using tasks such as judging the areas of geometric figures, the meaning of words, etc. He found a considerable degree of _____. He then showed subjects two simple drawings and asked which they preferred. Subjects were _____ in this situation. They treated the question about which drawing they preferred as _____.

    conformity
    independent

    subjective

34. Subjects are less concerned about merely being _____ and more concerned about looking crazy by disagreeing about a clear, objective matter.

    different

35. A devil's advocate is always appointed by the Catholic Church in canonization proceedings in order to discover possible discrediting facts and to relieve _____ pressures on other members of the proceedings. The presence of the devil's advocate can liberate others to express their own _____.

    conformity
    perceptions (beliefs)

36. In a variant of the Asch experiment one of the confederates did not give the wrong answer. Having a partner reduced the rate of conformity by _____.

    three-quarters

37. In another variant of the Asch experiment one of the confederates disagreed with the group by being even more wrong than they were. In this case conformity was _____ than when there was a unanimous majority.

    less

38. Social influence in conformity studies derives from _____ rather then from majority rule.

    unanimity

39. In a variant of the Asch experiment in which nine confederate gave the wrong answer in the presence of eleven naive subjects the naive subjects _____ conformed.

    never

40. When there was just one dissenting confederate all the subjects _____ at him; this did not happen when there was a dissenting group.

    laughed

41. Moscovici's experimental procedure, like Asch's involved subjects making a judgment in the presence of a group, but unlike Asch he used a somewhat _____ stimulus, a color that is almost always called blue, but that could also be sensibly seen as green.

    ambiguous

42. In the Moscovici experiment a naive majority is faced with a united minority that gives a _____ but plausible answer, green. Naive subjects were substantially _____ likely to say "green" than when judging alone.

    wrong
    more

43. In the second phase of the Moscovici experiment subjects were shown a series of colors in the blue-green range and asked to draw the line between blue and green. Subjects who had been exposed to the consistent minority, even those

who had not called any blues "green," _____ the point at which
they cut the spectrum, calling more blues "green" (as compared to a control
group).
shifted

44. Subjects were exposed to arguments for and against gay rights. These
arguments supposedly came from a minority or a majority. The majority
source produced more public _____ than the minority source; the
minority source produced more private _____ _____.
compliance
attitude change

THE RISKY SHIFT

45. It used to be assumed that group decisions would be more conservative than
the prior judgments of the individuals comprising the groups. Stoner found that
some group decisions were _____ than individual decisions. This is
called the _____ _____.
riskier
risky shift

Explanations for the Risky Shift

46. According to social comparison theory risky shift arises when people are
confused about _____ _____ and _____-
_____.
shared reality,
self-evaluation

47. Since risk taking is a value in our culture individuals will usually believe that
they are _____ willing to take risks than the average person. When
they enter the group discussion they find they are in fact not likely to be more
daring than the _____ group member. Social comparison then leads to
a shift in the culturally valued direction, toward _____.
more

average
risk

48. According to Brown the mechanism of the risky shift is not group _____,
rather it is just knowing others' initial _____.
discussion
judgments

49. In the Teger and Pruitt experiment there was a condition in which subjects did
not discuss the issue but merely learned of each others' positions. The risky
shift was _____ (although present) than in discussion conditions. This
demonstrates that social comparison is _____ but not necessary for the
risky shift to occur.
smaller
sufficient

50. Burnstein and Vinokur found that the number of subjects favoring a risky
course was _____ closely associated with the risky shift than was the
number of arguments favoring risk. They also found that the _____ of
the arguments used was related to the risky shift.
less
persuasiveness

The Demise of Risky Shift

51. McCauley intercepted bettors at the $2 window after they had placed their bet.
He created groups of three bettors and told them he would place a bet on
whatever horse they would agree upon. There were _____ long shots
placed by individuals than by groups, showing a shift toward _____.
more
conservatism

52. Groups do not necessarily become more risky or more conservative, but they
do become more _____, more extreme.
polarized

BYSTANDER INTERVENTION

Ambiguity of Emergencies

53. The press saw the bystanders to the Kitty Genovese murder as uncaring and

apathetic, but Latané and Darley argued that they were _____, which inhibited their action.

confused

54. Latané and Darley argued that the onlookers saw that no one else was intervening and misread the _____ of others as a sign that everyone believed that nothing was wrong.

passivity

55. _____ _____ is a state in which a group of people misinterprets what each other believes, and then uses that misinterpretation as evidence about what must be true.

Pluralistic ignorance

56. Even when people decide that there is an emergency and that *someone* should act they do not know that they, as opposed to someone else, should act; this is the logic of _____ ___ _____.

diffusion of responsibility

57. Latané and Darley argue that if there had been only one person watching the assault that person would have known that it was her place to do something; there would have been no _____ ___ _____.

diffusion of responsibility

Experimental Findings

58. While subjects filled out a questionnaire _____ in an office, smoke began to pour in. Almost all subjects left the room within two minutes. While a subject and two confederates filled out a questionnaire in an office, smoke began to pour in. The confederates did not react to the smoke. Very _____ subjects left the room within two minutes. In this experiment the subjects' own lives were on the line; if they did not respond it could not have been because they were _____.

alone

few

apathetic

59. In another condition that was closest to the situation in the Kitty Genovese murder three naive subjects were filling out a questionnaire when smoke began to pour in. These subjects responded _____ than in the condition with two confederates but _____ than subjects in the alone condition.

faster
slower

60. A subject in a cubicle is having a conversation with a confederate in another cubicle through transmitters. They are the only two "subjects" present. The confederate begins to have an epileptic fit. _____ percent of subjects in this condition come to the aid of the "victim"; the average time to respond was under a _____. But when the subject believes that there are four other people who could come to the aid of the victim _____ percent come to the rescue.

85

minute
31

Social Impact Theory

61. According to Latané, social influence is a multiplicative function of _____, _____, and _____ of people exerting the influence.

strength, immediacy, number

62. Strength of influence is determined by an agent's _____, _____, and _____.

status, expertise, power

OBEDIENCE

The Milgram Experiment

63. When subjects came to the Milgram experiment they met the experimenter and another subject. It was (apparently) determined by lot that the other "subject" would be the _____ and the subject would be the _____.

learner, teacher

64. The teacher was to give the learner a 15-volt shock for his first wrong answer and was to increase the shock by _____ volts every time he made a mistake (the shocks were not real, but the learner thought they were real).

15

65. At 150 volts the learner screamed, refused to cooperate with the teacher, and demanded to be _____.

released

66. By 300 volts the learner refused to answer but the experimenter instructed the teacher to treat "no answer" as a _____ answer.

wrong

67. The point of the Milgram experiment was to determine the factors that control our willingness to obey a(n) _____ commands that go against strongly held moral sentiments.

authority's

68. In the beginning Milgram and others believed that _____ subjects would continue shocking the victim until 450 volts.

few

69. Out of forty male subjects _____ went all the way to the end.

26

70. Women are _____ likely to shock to the end as are men.

equally

Explanations for Obedience

71. To understand the forces displayed in the obedience experiments it is necessary to understand not only why so many people went to the end but also why no one _____ them to.

expected

72. Although obedient subjects wind up giving incredibly intense levels of shock, they start with completely _____ levels.

harmless

73. The shock increases by very _____ amounts, making it difficult to decide at just what point the innocuous turns into the evil; this is the _____ _____ from harmless to lethal.

small

slippery slope

74. Part of the experimenter's power derives from his presenting himself as an unbiased, _____ party whose only role is to interpret the experiment's requirements for the subject.

disinterested

Reducing Obedience

75. In an experimental variant where there are two experimenters, one telling the subject to stop at 110 volts and the other telling him to continue, _____ subjects stop. Disagreement between authorities calls into question whether they can provide the definitive interpretation of the _____ requirements of the situation.

all

objective

76. Not only a dissenting experimenter but dissenting fellow _____ can cause a subject to doubt the experimenter's interpretation and refuse to continue.

subjects

77. When the experimenter is absent, the level of obedience in the Milgram experiment is greatly _____.

reduced

78. The difficulty in refusing to continue for moral reasons is that it implies a _____ of the experimenter for ordering the subject to continue. This is _____ to do.

criticism
embarrassing

79. Reducing the distance between the victim and the subject, or even requiring the subject to hold the victim's hand to a shock plate, greatly _____ obedience.

reduces

80. Reducing the distance between the subject and victim does _____ alter the *moral* issue of whether the subject should obey or not.

not

81. People find screams aversive; it is likely that the more obvious pain cues produced by closeness made it more difficult to administer the _____.

shock

Subjects' Justifications for Their Obedience

82. Milgram reran the experiment in a rundown office building in Bridgeport rather than in the elegant interaction laboratory at Yale. Obedience _____, but only modestly. No *special* signs or symbols of _____ were needed to produce obedience in the Milgram experiments.

declined
legitimacy

83. Some subjects explained their obedience by saying that the experiment was _____, that the teacher and learner had both volunteered for the experiment, and that either could have been made the victim.

fair

84. In a variant of the obedience experiment the experimenter agrees to stop the experiment if the learner demands it; at 150 volts the learner demands to be released and the experimenter orders the teacher to continue; _____ of 40 subjects continue to shock to the end.

16

85. People not in the Milgram experiment see the subject as _____ for the learner's suffering even though many subjects in the heat of the action do not see themselves as _____ because this is the interpretation that the _____ offers.

responsible

responsible
experimenter

BRUTALITY

86. Commonsensical reasons to expect prisons to be violent and degraded are that prisoners are more likely to be _____ people to begin with and there should be more sadists among the guards than in the population as a whole.

violent

The Zimbardo Experiment

87. Subjects in the Zimbardo prison experiment were college students selected to screen out those with a criminal past or _____ disorders.

psychological

88. Subjects were assigned at _____ to be prisoners or guards.

random

89. Zimbardo had his "prisoners" stripped and deloused, made to wear stocking caps to conceal their hair, and made to wear dress-like gowns without underwear. This was to _____ the subjects in an analogous way to what happens in prisons.

degrade

90. Over the six days until the experiment was terminated the behavior of the guards became more and more _____ and degrading to the prisoners.

brutal

Explanations of the Brutality

91. In everyday life we usually assume that violence is almost _____ appropriate. In mental hospitals and prisons the rule is different: Use the "minimal" force necessary, but it is difficult to know how much force is _____.

never

enough

92. Guards in the Zimbardo experiment slid down the slippery slope from reasonable force to _____.

brutality

93. There were three types of guards in the Zimbardo experiment: good guards, _____ guards, and average guards.

bad

94. In the Zimbardo experiment, like in the Sherif experiment, the subjects face an
    _____ issue.   ambiguous

95. The ambiguity in the Zimbardo experiment is just how much force is
    _____.   appropriate

96. In the Zimbardo study the experimenter did _____ solicit the subjects'   not
    opinions and not all opinions were shown; the bad guards' actions were most
    obvious so they exercised the _____ influence.   most

97. When one of the guards turned a fire extinguisher on the prisoners he did
    two things at once: he assaulted the prisoner and he also expressed his
    _____ view of such behavior.   moral

98. Remaining silent in the face of immoral action _____ to immorality   contributes
    since our disapproval never gets entered into the social _____.   consensus

Self-Test

1. According to the text a fundamental cause of
   social influence (for people in general) is that
   a. some people have low self-esteem.
   b. people are generally sheep; they like to be
      influenced by others.
   c. people are influenced by bribes.
   d. people expect to see the same world as
      everyone else does and so are influenced by
      the perceptions of others; also if they admit
      to seeing the world differently they may look
      like fools.

2. When we change our mind because we are
   genuinely persuaded by a group's position we
   are conforming because of
   a. internalization.
   b. compliance.
   c. catheterization.
   d. infibulation.

3. When we change a position because of a bribe
   or through fear, our conforming is due to
   a. internalization.
   b. recreation.
   c. obfuscation.
   d. compliance.

4. In the basic Asch experiment a naive subject
   faces a conflict between what seems obviously
   to be a right answer and a contrary judgment of
   a. one other person.
   b. three people in a group of five.
   c. a unanimous group of six people.
   d. an eccentric but amiable ex-military man.

5. In the Asch experiment
   a. almost no one conformed (except those who
      had been previously tested as having a deep
      need for social approval).
   b. one-quarter of the subjects were completely
      independent.
   c. one-third of the subjects conformed to the
      clearly wrong group on a majority of the
      trials.
   d. b and c.

6. In the Asch experiment the completely
   independent subjects felt
   a. pressured by the majority's wrong answers
      and were confused and upset.
   b. amused by the majority's wrong answers
      and would sometimes break out laughing at
      a particularly silly response.
   c. contempt for the majority.
   d. no pressure from the majority and did not
      later remember that the majority had
      disagreed with them.

7. In the Asch experiment what particularly
   bothered the subjects was not that they were
   behaving differently from the others but that
   they were
   a. surprised that their eyesight was so much
      worse then the rest of the group.
   b. afraid that the group would be unfriendly to
      them after the experiment since it was a
      group of people they had wanted to be
      friendly with.
   c. perceiving the world differently than others.
   d. afraid that the experimenter would be angry
      at them for giving deviant responses.

8. In a variant of the Asch experiment in which one confederate (actor) gave the false answer when he was a part of a group of six naive subjects the group
   a. seriously considered the confederate's response.
   b. laughed at the confederate making the wrong response.
   c. changed their responses to be in accord with the confederate's.
   d. did not notice that the confederate gave a different answer.

9. Subjects listened in on the Asch experimental group, wrote down the group's and their own answers, and gave it to the experimenter. They did not state their judgment aloud in front of the group. Subjects
   a. gave no wrong answers.
   b. subjects gave more wrong answers than when tested alone but fewer than when tested with the group.
   c. gave as many wrong answers as they did when tested with the group.
   d. changed the group's answers so that the group's response would be the same as their own.

10. The results in the previous question demonstrate that
    a. subjects gave the wrong answer because of both the fear of being laughed at (normative conformity) and because they were confused (informational conformity).
    b. subjects gave the wrong answer only because of their fear of being laughed at (normative conformity).
    c. subjects gave the wrong answer only because they were confused (informative conformity).
    d. subjects gave the wrong answers because of ophthalmological problems.

11. In the Sherif experiment why was it so difficult to judge the movement of the point of light in the dark room?
    a. There was no frame of reference.
    b. The darkness prevented comparing the extent of movement of the light with the size of familiar objects.
    c. Because the light really didn't move, its apparent movement was an optical illusion, the autokinetic effect.
    d. all of the above

12. The answers of a subject judging alone over the course of one hundred trials
    a. become more and more consistent although they are often quite different from the responses of other subjects judging alone.
    b. become more and more variable.
    c. display a fatigue effect.
    d. become over time almost identical to the responses of other subjects even though they are not responding in each other's presence.

13. After the subjects developed consistent responses while judging alone they were brought together. They were instructed to call out their individual judgments in front of each other. Their judgments
    a. stayed the same since they were overlearned.
    b. became much more variable.
    c. converged to a single group average.
    d. varied from group to group; some groups converged and others became much more variable.

14. Social influence in the Sherif experiment depends on the subjects' belief that there was a right answer. What is the evidence for this?
    a. When the subjects lack self-confidence they are more likely to go along with the group.
    b. If the subjects are told that the movement of the point of light is an optical illusion then the judgments do not converge.
    c. If the subjects are told that the movement of the point of light is an optical illusion then they are much more conformist and convergence is extremely rapid.
    d. Subjects refuse to believe that the movement of the point of light is an optical illusion.

15. The Asch and Sherif experiments are *similar* in that
    a. the stimuli in both experiments are ambiguous.
    b. in both experiments the subjects believed that the others were in the same position as they were to answer a question that had an objective, correct answer.
    c. subjects in both experiments are nervous and confused when they discover that others disagree with them.
    d. in both experiments the subjects realize that it is quite difficult to make out the correct answer.

16. The Asch and the Sherif experiments are *different* in that
    a. in the Asch experiment the right answer is obvious while in the Sherif experiment it is ambiguous.
    b. In the Asch experiment the subject knows the right answer but in the Sherif experiment she is unsure.
    c. in the Sherif experiment it is reasonable for the subject to take into account the answers of others while in the Asch experiment it is not.
    d. all of the above

17. What happened when the subjects in the Sherif and Asch experiments were informed about the true nature of the experiments?
    a. Both the Asch and the Sherif subjects were upset by their conformity.
    b. Asch subjects were upset by their conformity and underestimated the extent they had conformed, but Sherif subjects were not upset.
    c. Sherif subjects were upset by their conformity and underestimated the extent they conformed, but Asch subjects were not upset.
    d. Neither Asch nor Sherif subjects were upset by their conformity since it took place in the context of an experiment.

18. When subjects in the Sherif experiment are retested alone a year later they give
    a. the group's compromise judgment and not their original response; the same occurs with the Asch experiment's subjects.
    b. the group's compromise judgment and not their original response; the same does not occur with the Asch experiment's subjects.
    c. their original judgment before they entered the group; subjects in the Asch experiment also give the answer they would have given if they had not been in the group.
    d. very variable answers as do subjects in the Asch experiments.

19. Ross created a version of the Asch experiment in which subjects believed that others would be getting bonuses if particular answers were correct. Subjects could interpret others' disagreement as their foolishly playing long shots. This version of the Asch experiment
    a. substantially increased conformity as compared to the standard condition.
    b. did not affect the rate of conformity.

c. substantially reduced the conformity as compared to the standard condition.
    d. brought out the gambling streak in the naive subjects and caused them to act in wild and unpredictable ways.

20. The Ross experiment demonstrates that
    a. once a gambler always a gambler.
    b. that some people just enjoy conforming.
    c. that it is disagreement with others per se that causes conformity.
    d. that conformity pressures only arise when disagreement indicates real differences in the perception of a single world.

21. Crutchfield repeated the Asch experiment but asked the subjects which of two simple drawings they preferred. The group unanimously preferred what was known to be the less popular drawing. Subjects in this experiment
    a. conformed to the group at a slightly higher rate than did those in the original Asch experiment.
    b. conformed to the group at a much higher rate than did those in the original Asch experiment.
    c. did not conform to the group.
    d. asked to take the drawings home.

22. In the Crutchfield experiment subjects treat the question of "preferred drawings"
    a. as a subjective one where disagreement in tastes is to be expected.
    b. as a subjective one in which everyone ought have the same preference.
    c. as an objective one that does not require agreement.
    d. as an implicit offer to sell them the drawings.

23. In an experiment subjects were to play the role of admissions officers. Some subjects were told that they had sufficient information to make a good estimate of the chances of an applicant, while other subjects were told that they did not have sufficient evidence for such a judgment. Subjects were allowed to compare their judgments to similar or dissimilar others.
    a. When subjects knew there was insufficient information to make a decision, they preferred to compare their judgments to those of similar others.
    b. When subjects knew that there was sufficient information to make a decision,

they wanted to compare their judgments to those of dissimilar others.
c. Subjects who knew that the issue was decidable attempted to correct for their own bias.
d. all of the above

24. A devil's advocate
a. tries to invent a damning case even if it means inventing facts.
b. is a member of a cult that worships the devil.
c. is a type of tax lawyer.
d. attempts to make sure that discrediting facts are not overlooked and by doing so relieves the pressure on members of an investigation to just find evidence of virtue.

25. In a variant of the Asch experiment one of the confederates did not give the wrong answer. Having a partner (in effect a devil's advocate)
a. increased conformity slightly.
b. increased conformity but only among Catholics.
c. decreased conformity slightly.
d. decreased conformity substantially.

26. In a variant of the Asch experiment one of the confederates disagreed with the group by being even more wrong than they were. In this case conformity was
a. increased greatly.
b. less than when there was a unanimous majority.
c. the same as when there was a unanimous majority.
d. slightly increased since subjects did not want to be identified with the obviously deficient confederate.

27. Moscovici in his experiment on minority influence used
a. stimuli that were as ambiguous as those of Sherif.
b. stimuli that were as clear-cut as those of Asch.
c. stimuli that were more ambiguous than those of Asch but less than those of Sherif.
d. stimuli that had covert sexual and aggressive associations.

28. In the Moscovici experiment a naive majority is faced with a united minority that gives
a. the correct answer.
b. a wrong and implausible answer.
c. completely irrelevant answers.
d. a wrong, but plausible answer.

29. In the second phase of the Moscovici experiment, after subjects had been exposed to a unanimous minority labeling a blue slide "green," they were shown a series of colors in the blue-green range and asked to draw the line between blue and green. Subjects who had been exposed to a consistent minority shifted the point at which they cut the spectrum, calling more blues "green" (as compared to a control group). This effect
a. only occurs with subjects who conformed in the first part of the experiment.
b. occurs even with subjects who did not conform in the first part of the experiment.
c. occurs in less than 1 percent of the subjects.
d. occurs only in liberal and environmentally concerned subjects.

30. In the Moscovici experiment the minority had a substantial influence only when
a. it really believed in itself.
b. it was sincere and showed that it appreciated variety.
c. it was unanimous and consistent.
d. all of the above

31. In a Moscovici-type situation Nemeth found that if the minority consistently called the brighter blue "green" and the duller blue "blue" then their influence over the majority
a. was greater than if they had used "green" or "blue" at random.
b. was less than if they had used "green" or "blue" at random.
c. would completely disappear and the subjects would even laugh at the minority.
d. would entirely disappear but the majority would treat the minority respectfully.

32. Subjects were exposed to arguments for or against gay rights. These arguments supposedly came from a minority or a majority. The majority source produced more public compliance than the minority source; the minority source produced
a. no private attitude change.
b. ridicule for those making the argument.
c. more private attitude change than the majority source.
d. less private attitude change than the majority source.

33. The greater risk taking of groups after a discussion than of the individuals comprising them is called the

a. gambler's fallacy.
b. risky shift.
c. bad company effect.
d. massacre of the innocents.

34. According to social comparison theory
    a. when people are confused about the world they use other people's opinions to orient them.
    b. we use other people's opinions for independent sources to compare our judgments against.
    c. since many virtues and vices are relative we need to compare ourselves to others to see where we stand.
    d. all of the above

35. Since risk taking is a value in our culture people will want to see themselves as
    a. riskier than the average person.
    b. less risky than the average person.
    c. very risky in all ways and at all times.
    d. less risky than most people.

36. If risk taking is a value, and a person finds that she is less risky than the average member of the group, what is she likely to do, and how will this affect the group's riskiness average?
    a. She should shift to a riskier position, which will shift the group average to greater risk.
    b. She should shift to a riskier position, which will shift the group average to less risk.
    c. She should shift to a more conservative position, which will shift the group average to less risk.
    d. She should shift to a more conservative position, which will shift the group average to greater risk.

37. One important difference between what happens in the Sherif experiments and what happens in the risky shift studies is that
    a. Sherif subjects believe that there is one non-relative right answer; for this reason their answers converge.
    b. risky shift subjects believe that the answer is relative to that of the group and answers shift.
    c. in the risky shift experiments subjects try to outdo each other while in the Sherif experiment subjects are just trying to get something right.
    d. all of the above

38. Teger and Pruitt found that there was a substantial correlation between average risk endorsed by subjects before a discussion and the degree of shift toward
    a. hedonism found in the discussion.
    b. conservatism found in the discussion.
    c. risk found in the discussion.
    d. daydreaming about mountain climbing and other adventures found in the discussion.

39. Which plays a role in causing the risky shift?
    a. knowledge of the other group members' position on risk.
    b. discussing risk in the group and the number of arguments favoring risk produced in group discussion.
    c. the persuasiveness of the arguments produced in the group discussion.
    d. all of the above

40. McCauley intercepted bettors at the $2 window after they had placed their bet. He created groups of three bettors and told them he would place a bet on whatever horse they would agree upon. There were more long shots placed by individuals than by groups, showing a shift toward
    a. insolvency.
    b. a paradigm.
    c. risk.
    d. conservatism.

41. Groups do not necessarily become more risky or more conservative. It depends on the issue discussed; however, after a discussion people's opinions always become
    a. more extreme (polarized).
    b. more open.
    c. more interesting.
    d. less political.

42. Thirty people watched out of their apartment windows while Kitty Genovese was murdered. The press saw these bystanders as uncaring, apathetic, but Latané and Darley argued that they were
    a. sadistic.
    b. inattentive.
    c. confused and that confusion inhibited their action.
    d. afraid and they did not help because of their fear.

43. In their interpretation of why bystanders did not help in the Genovese murder Latané and Darley argued that the onlookers saw that no one else was intervening and
    a. decided that it was too dangerous to help.
    b. misread the passivity of others as a sign that the others believed that nothing was wrong.
    c. were "infected" by the apathy of the others.
    d. all of the above

44. What is the term that describes a state in which a person misinterprets what others believe, and then uses that misinterpretation as evidence about what must be true?
    a. pluralistic responsibility
    b. diffusion of responsibility
    c. bystander intervention
    d. pluralistic ignorance

45. Even when people know that someone should act they do not know that they, as opposed to someone else, should act, hence it is tempting to wait for someone else to do something. This is called "diffusion of responsibility." What logically follows from this notion?
    a. The more the onlookers, the greater the chance of being helped.
    b. If there is only one onlooker there will be a greater chance of being helped.
    c. Personality rather than numbers is the important factor.
    d. An intermediate number of onlookers would maximize "diffusion" and the probability of helping.

46. When a subject and two confederates fill out a questionnaire in an office, smoke begins to pour in. The confederates do not react to the smoke. How do subjects react in this condition as compared to the condition in which they are alone?
    a. Subjects feel encouraged by the presence of others and react much more quickly to the smoke than they would if they were alone.
    b. Few subjects respond within two minutes; the presence of the confederates greatly inhibits responding to the smoke as compared to the alone condition.
    c. Some subjects are helped by the presence of confederates and other subjects are hindered. All in all the average time of responding to the smoke is the same as when subjects are in the alone condition.
    d. "Hysterics" are calmed by the presence of the confederates and are more likely to respond than in the condition in which they are alone.

47. The above "where there's smoke there's fire" experiment most directly *refutes* one hypothesis about why people do not respond in emergencies. Which hypothesis?
    a. That people are apathetic.
    b. That people are conformist.
    c. That people are attentive; few subjects notice the smoke.
    d. That people care for their own lives; many subjects did not respond to the fire.

48. Three naive subjects filled out a questionnaire in an office when smoke began to pour in. These subjects responded
    a. slower than in the condition with two confederates but faster than subjects in the alone condition.
    b. faster than in the condition with two confederates but slower than subjects in the alone condition.
    c. as fast as the condition with two confederates but slower than subjects in the alone condition.
    d. faster than in the condition with two confederates and equally fast as subjects in the alone condition.

49. By using transmitters, a subject in a cubicle is having a conversation with a confederate in another cubicle. The subject believes that there are four additional people present. The confederate has an epileptic fit. How likely is the subject to come to her aid as compared to a condition in which he believes he is alone with the epileptic?
    a. much more likely
    b. considerably less likely
    c. just as likely
    d. the number of people present is irrelevant; it's personality that counts

50. The experiment with the epileptic fit illustrates
    a. pluralistic ignorance.
    b. diffusion of responsibility.

c. both a and b
d. neither a nor b

51. According to Latané and social impact theory social influence is a multiplicative function of
    a. strength.
    b. immediacy.
    c. number of people exerting influence.
    d. all of the above

52. The point of Arendt's book *Eichmann in Jerusalem: The Banality of Evil* was that
    a. the Nazis were monsters totally unlike other people.
    b. Eichmann, one of the Nazis most involved in the killing of millions, was a banal, pretty-minded bureaucrat, and yet he was responsible for horrible evil.
    c. if banal, ordinary people can cause horrible evil, then the possibility of evil is there for all people.
    d. b and c

53. In the Milgram obedience experiments, a "teacher" was to give a learner (a confederate) a 15-volt shock for his first wrong answer and was to increase the shock by 15 volts every time he made a mistake. At 150 volts the learner screamed, refused to cooperate, and demanded to be released. The experimenter ordered the teacher to continue. What did subjects do?
    a. All subjects broke off at this point.
    b. Ten percent of the subjects continued as long as the experimenter ordered them to.
    c. One percent of the subjects continued until the experimenter told them to stop.
    d. More than half of the subjects continued until the experiment ended at 450 volts.

54. In a variant of the Milgram experiment conducted with women it has been found that
    a. women are willing to shock to the end moderately less often than men.
    b. women are much more likely to obey the experimenter and go to the end than are men.
    c. woman never go to the end.
    d. women are no more, nor less, likely to go to the end than men.

55. Milgram asked a sample of psychiatrists, graduate students, and faculty members what percent of the subjects would continue until the end and what they themselves would do.

a. They predicted that 45 percent would go to the end; 30 percent of the sample said that they themselves would go to the end.
b. They predicted that less than 3 percent would go to the end; everyone in the sample said he would not go to the end.
c. They predicted that 90 percent of the people would go to the end since it was an acceptable way to work off hostile impulses; 80 percent of the sample said that they would go to the end.
d. They predicted that none of the subjects would go to the end, but 20 percent of the sample said that they themselves would since they placed a very high value on science.

56. In the Milgram experiment the shock the subject is ordered to give increases from trivial to lethal by very small amounts, making it difficult to decide at just what point it is no longer legitimate. The subject may be described as being on a
    a. slippery slope.
    b. roller coaster.
    c. big jump.
    d. wave.

57. In the Milgram experiment part of the experimenter's ability to get the subject to continue shocking had to do with the way he acted, which was
    a. in a threatening manner.
    b. as if he were very excited.
    c. as if he were enjoying the subject's pain.
    d. in a disinterested manner as if he were only interpreting the objective requirements of the situation to the teacher.

58. Which of the following are parallels between the Asch and the Milgram experiments?
    a. In both experiments people enter with clear-cut beliefs about what it is proper to do and to say.
    b. In both experiments either the group or the experimenter undercuts the subjects' beliefs about what is proper to do.
    c. In both experiments the disagreement between the subject's entering beliefs and what he is pressured to do causes great stress.
    d. all of the above

59. In a variant of the Milgram experiment where there are two experimenters, one telling the

subject to stop at 110 volts, and the other telling him to continue, how many subjects stop?
a. none
b. 50 percent
c. 65 percent
d. all

60. In a variant of the Milgram experiment there are two confederates and a naive subject involved in giving shocks. At some point one confederate refuses to pull the lever and the experimenter orders the other "subject" to do so. Soon he too refuses. The experimenter then orders the real subject to take over delivering the shock. What percent of the subjects continue to the end?
a. 100 percent
b. 60 percent
c. 10 percent
d. 77.2 percent

61. Gamson studied the social dynamics of groups resisting unjust authority. Groups were led to create testimony against their own beliefs and ultimately asked to perjure themselves by signing an affidavit that their testimony was true. How common was resistance?
a. Almost half the groups unanimously resisted the authority.
b. None of the groups unanimously resisted authority but all groups had some individuals who did so.
c. About 80 percent of the groups resisted authority.
d. About 20 percent of the groups resisted authority.

62. When the experimenter is absent and communicates his orders through a tape recorder or over a phone
a. obedience in greatly increased since the subjects feel more comfortable with the experimenter not looking over their shoulder.
b. obedience is greatly decreased.
c. obedience is the same as in experimenter-present conditions.
d. no subject even starts the experiment.

63. Subjects experience difficulty in telling the experimenter that they will not continue because they think it is wrong to shock the learner against his will. This is because
a. it doesn't occur to the subjects to try to get the experimenter to stop.

b. most subjects who continue are not really concerned about the rights and wrongs of the issue.
c. telling the experimenter is a moral reproach and would be embarrassing.
d. they know that the experimenter will start shocking them if they protest.

64. Reducing the distance between the victim and the subject or even requiring the subject to hold the victim's hand to a shock plate
a. greatly reduces obedience.
b. makes the subject realize that the learner is in pain.
c. shows the subject that it is wrong to shock the learner.
d. all of the above

65. Milgram reran the experiment in a rundown office building in Bridgeport rather than in the elegant interaction laboratory at Yale. Obedience
a. increased in the more depressing, less respectable atmosphere of Bridgeport.
b. declined but only modestly.
c. was reduced to less than 10 percent.
d. completely stopped.

66. The Bridgeport variant of the Milgram experiment demonstrates that
a. the prestige of an institution like Yale is not necessary for the subject's obedience.
b. that even though subjects often explained their obedience by citing their trust in Yale this trust is not necessary for the obedience.
c. no *special* signs or symbols of obedience are necessary for the obedience.
d. all of the above

67. In a variant of the Milgram experiment the experimenter agreed to stop the experiment if the learner demanded. At 150 volts the learner demanded to be released, but the experimenter ordered the teacher to continue. How many out of forty subjects continued to the end?
a. twenty-six
b. none
c. sixteen
d. four

68. The above experimental variant shows that
a. the perception of fairness is irrelevant to whether subjects obey or not.
b. the perception of unfairness has some but not a predominant effect on obedience.

c. people enjoy victimizing others.

d. fairness is the central issue by which subjects decide whether to obey or not.

69. When the experimenter "accepts responsibility" it makes it easier for some subjects to continue shocking. But when the issue of responsibility is considered by people not in the experiment

a. they tend to pass responsibility up the ranks of hierarchies, but 82 percent still feel that the subjects in the Milgram experiment had a responsibility for delivering the shocks.

b. they tend to pass responsibility up the ranks of hierarchies, and for that reason they feel that the subjects in the Milgram experiment had no responsibility for delivering the shocks.

c. they believe that Milgram's subjects were just following orders and should not be held responsible.

d. they believe that responsibility can never be passed up the ranks of a hierarchy.

70. The subjects see the experiment as fair and legitimate and themselves as not responsible because

a. this would be obvious to anyone in or out of the experiment.

b. this view derives from deeply entrenched personality variables.

c. this is the interpretation that the experimenter offers.

d. they fully realize that they are doing wrong and are trying to find an excuse.

71. Commonsensical reasons to expect prisons to be violent and degraded are that prisoners are more likely to be violent people to begin with and there should be more sadists among the guards than in the population as a whole. Zimbardo in his mock prison experiment tried to show that a prison environment could be degrading even without its typical population. He attempted to show this by using

a. only people who had been to prison for white-collar offenses.

b. college students who had never been arrested and who were screened against mental illness.

c. sadists as both prisoners and guards.

d. ex-convicts as both prisoners and guards.

72. Zimbardo had his "prisoners" stripped and deloused, and made them wear stocking caps to conceal their hair and dress-like gowns without

underwear. This was to

a. make the "prisoners" feel at home.

b. make it easier and pleasanter for the "prisoners" to adapt to their role in the experiment.

c. degrade the subjects in an analogous way to what happens in prison.

d. follow the identical procedure followed in a prison.

73. Over the six days until the Zimbardo prison experiment was terminated the behavior of the guards became

a. more and more brutal and degrading to the prisoners.

b. progressively less tense.

c. more boring for both the prisoners and the guards.

d. almost pleasant as everyone adjusted to the prison routine.

74. One reason for guards' slip into brutality in the Zimbardo experiment is that

a. many of the guards had a prior history of sadism.

b. the guards were so provoked by the prisoners that anyone would have responded with violence.

c. in everyday life we have an almost absolute prohibition against violence, but in prisons it is necessary to have a "minimal force necessary rule" and what minimal force should be is ambiguous.

d. there were no "good guards" to give an example of restraint.

75. The degradation that was inflicted on the prisoners in the Zimbardo experiment

a. aroused sympathy for the prisoners and made it harder for the guards to be violent.

b. aroused sympathy for the prisoners which made the guards more violent by reaction formation.

c. did not have any relation to the ease or difficulty the guards had in brutalizing them.

d. inhibited empathetic and sympathetic responses and made it easier to be brutal to them.

76. The reason that Zimbardo subjects unlike the Sherif subjects did not reach a consensus and instead became more and more violent is that

a. they were a very different group of people.

b. the experimenter did not solicit the opinions

of all the subjects, nor did anyone else, so that not all opinions were shown for a consensus.

c. the subjects were much too argumentative.

d. violence is much more fun than playing nice.

77. "Bad" guards showed by their behavior that they believed violence was right. Good guards
    a. were not violent, but they said nothing against the violence.
    b. did not show whether they were not violent because they believed the violence was wrong, or because they just didn't happen to feel like being violent that day.
    c. always confronted and reproached the violent guards.
    d. a and b

78. In what way is the behavior of the guards in the Zimbardo experiment like the behavior of subjects in some of Latané and Darley's experiments?
    a. Both involved apathy.
    b. Both involved pluralistic ignorance caused by subjects not taking a stand and having their lack of action misinterpreted.
    c. Both involve degradation.
    d. all of the above

Answer Key for Self-Test

1. d (p. 18)	21. c (pp. 28–29)	41. a (p. 42)	60. c (p. 55)
2. a (p. 20)	22. a (p. 29)	42. c (p. 43)	61. a (p. 56)
3. d (p. 20)	23. d (p. 30)	43. b (p. 44)	62. b (p. 57)
4. c (p. 21)	24. d (p. 30)	44. d (p. 44)	63. c (p. 57)
5. d (p. 22)	25. d (p. 30)	45. b (p. 45)	64. a (p. 57)
6. a (p. 22)	26. b (p. 30)	46. b (p. 46)	65. b (p. 59)
7. c (pp. 22–23)	27. c (p. 32)	47. a (p. 46)	66. d (p. 59)
8. b (p. 23)	28. d (p. 32)	48. b (p. 46)	67. c (p. 59)
9. b (p. 24)	29. b (pp. 32–33)	49. b (p. 47)	68. b (pp. 59–60)
10. a (p. 24)	30. c (p. 33)	50. b (p. 47)	69. a (p. 60)
11. d (pp. 24–25)	31. a (p. 33)	51. d (p. 47)	70. c (p. 60)
12. a (p. 25)	32. c (p. 34)	52. d (p. 50)	71. b (p. 62)
13. c (p. 25)	33. b (p. 36)	53. d (p. 53)	72. c (p. 63)
14. b (p. 25)	34. d (p. 37)	54. d (p. 53)	73. a (p. 63)
15. b (p. 26)	35. a (p. 38)	55. b (p. 53)	74. c (p. 64)
16. d (p. 26)	36. a (p. 38)	56. a (p. 54)	75. d (p. 64)
17. b (pp. 26–27)	37. d (p. 38)	57. d (p. 54)	76. b (pp. 65–66)
18. b (p. 27)	38. c (p. 39)	58. d (p. 54)	77. d (p. 66)
19. c (p. 27)	39. d (p. 40)	59. d (p. 55)	78. b (p. 66)
20. d (p. 27)	40. d (p. 42)		

Thought Questions and Exercises

1. There has been a thread running through the many analyses of social influence presented in this chapter: We expect to see the same world as everyone else does, and for this reason we are influenced by the perceptions of other people. Because we expect that we will see the same world as others, and we know that others have the same belief, we fear that we will look foolish, incompetent, stupid if we let on that we don't see the same world. Take the various different ways that each of them is affected by a belief in a shared world. You may also want to review the various ways that embarrassment and fear of embarrassment magnify social influence.

2. One reason that subjects conformed in the Asch experiment was because they were confused. Is confusion a sufficient explanation for the subjects' behavior? Why not? Influence in the Asch experiment derived from the subjects' belief that there was a right answer. This was also true of the Sherif experiment. How can you demonstrate this?

3. The Asch and Sherif experiments demonstrate two poles of social influence. (For instance, the stimulus is ambiguous in Sherif and clear-cut in Asch; subjects internalize in Sherif but comply in Asch; subjects are relaxed in Sherif and tense

in Asch.) The Latané and Darley, Milgram, Moscovici, and Zimbardo paradigms may be seen to be between the two poles of Sherif and Asch. For each paradigm show what aspects of the experimental set-up and subjects' behavior reflect each pole.

4. If Brown is right about people valuing risk taking, should there be phenomenon analogous to the risky shift for other values? Values are necessarily abstract. Explain. People believe that they ought to be considerate of their neighbor but just what considerateness involves in a particular situation may be difficult to decide. Give some examples. How might gossip help to translate abstract principles into concrete stories of transgression? In what sense does the group discussion of the risky shift function in the same way as gossip (in regard to making abstract norms concrete)?

5. In the original risky shift study Stoner found that there was usually a shift to more risky positions after group discussion but not always. Presumably this had to do with the particular values discussed and whether it was more esteemed to be to the "left" or the "right" of the group average. Think of some examples of things that should produce a conservative shift (people should want to be conservative for some things even in terms of risk and investment— for example, you are charged with investing an old retired couple's savings). Get a group to discuss two different topics (one after another), one topic that you predict will produce a risky shift and the other a conservative shift (to do it right you will need two groups, one with topic A first and B second, and the other with B first and A second). (Remember to get each member's assessment of acceptable risk before the group discussion.)

6. Think back to the last time that you witnessed an emergency. Were you a participant, a bystander, the injured? If you were a bystander did you help? Did you walk away? Does Latané and Darley's model (pluralistic ignorance and diffusion of responsibility) describe the behavior you witnessed or performed? What does their

model particularly capture and what does it leave out?

7. What does the Milgram experiment tell us about the potential of basically good people to go along with evil? How might you educate people so that they would not so easily follow evil authority? Would it be self-defeating to teach people to reject all authority? Remember it is very easy to see the Milgram situation as immoral when you are outside looking in. The goal of education would be that people would be able to summon and act on their moral perceptions when they are *inside* the situation. Just about none of us believes that we would go to the end in the Milgram situation. Yet most of us are wrong, since people like us do go to the end. Is there some way to inoculate ourselves against giving in to Milgram-type pressures?

8. Do you think it was ethical to conduct the Milgram experiments once it was known that the subjects would experience intense short-term stress? Why or why not? Milgram argued that as long as the great majority of the subjects were happy to have participated in the experiment, the experiment was ethical notwithstanding the fact that the subjects had been deceived and had suffered intense short-term stress. Do you agree with Milgram? Your text argues that the issue of deception could be gotten around if the subjects were warned about stress and given some very general idea of what might happen in experiments. Note that the information would have to be very vague; the experiment would be ruined if the subjects knew beforehand what it was about. Do you agree with Sabini's position? Why or why not?

9. There are several parallels between the Milgram experiment and the Asch experiment. Describe some of these parallels, including why stress and confusion are created in both experiments.

10. The text explains the escalation of brutality in the Zimbardo experiment by the concept of "moral drift." Can you think of other examples of moral drift (gangs, groups of kids egging each other on, etc.)? Is the moral drift explanation illuminating?

CHAPTER 3

Groups and Task Performance

Learning Objectives

1. You should be familiar with how various types of groups differ from each other. What is a primary group? Define "co-actors." What is the crucial element that co-actors lack that more developed groups have? How does an ad hoc group differ from an enduring group? Understand what is meant when we say that enduring groups differ in cohesiveness.

SOCIAL FACILITATION

2. Understand how the presence of others can affect an individual's performance. What are the two effects that are produced by arousal in the presence of others? Given the dual effect of arousal, would you have different recommendations about taking an exam alone or in company for a student who did not know the material well than for a student who knew it fairly well? How did Zajonc experimentally test his proposition?

Explanations of Social Facilitation
The Mere Presence Explanation
3. Describe what "social facilitation" is. What is Zajonc's very simple explanation for social facilitation? Why is it called the "mere presence account"?

The Evaluation Apprehension Explanation
4. Describe Cottrell's explanation for Zajonc's social facilitation effect. What were the three conditions set up by Cottrell in his experiment to test social facilitation? What were the results of Cottrell's experiment?

5. Explain what Marcus meant when she said that the issue was whether the presence of others is *sufficient* to cause arousal. How did Marcus explain the fact that the blindfold condition (in Cottrell's experiment) produced no more social facilitation than the alone condition? Describe Marcus's experiment (involving shoe untying and lab coat tying) to test her claims. What were the results? Describe the computer experiment testing the mere presence hypothesis.

Four More Sources of Social Facilitation
6. Describe how "distraction" can be a source of arousal and can account for social facilitation in the presence of others.

The Aids to Cognition Explanation
7. According to Berger, when we are alone and faced with a task we use aids such as counting on our fingers, mumbling the item to be memorized, etc. In the presence of others we do not use them from fear of looking foolish. How can this be used to account for social facilitation?

The Social Monitoring Explanation
8. According to Guerin and Innes, it is not mere presence per se that is arousing. What is? According to this account, should the social facilitation effect be more likely when the confederate sits behind the subject or when the confederate is in view?

The Evaluation Apprehension and Embarrassment Explanation
9. According to Bond, how are evaluation apprehension and embarrassment implicated in the social facilitation effect? Bond embedded a single

complex task in a set of simple tasks. He also embedded a single simple task in a set of complex tasks. What did he predict about the social facilitation effects of the two embedded tasks? Why? If people expect to fail, then the presence of an audience should have what effect? If they expect to do well, then the presence of an audience will have what effect?

Weighing the Results
10. According to the evidence, is the mere presence of others sufficient to produce the social facilitation effect? What other factors contribute?

LEADERSHIP

Contingency View of Leadership
11. Explain how the contingency view of leadership came to dominate research on leadership. What is Fiedler's theory of effective leadership? What is meant by an overall situation being favorable or unfavorable for a leader? Is there a different leadership style called for in situations of high, low, or intermediate favorability to a leader?

Consistency in Leadership
12. Some researchers believe that there are unspecified traits related to leadership in all situations. How could one gather evidence for this statement? Describe the "round robin" procedure.

Power
13. Describe French and Raven's conception of social power.
14. Describe what is meant by a "legitimate power"? Give some examples of legitimate power. Give some sources of legitimate power. Is legitimate power typically limited in scope? Is surveillance necessary if someone is following orders strictly because she believes that they are legitimate?
15. Define "reward power." Is it limited in scope?
16. Define "coercive power." Does it require surveillance for its enforcement?
17. Define "referent power." Does referent power require more or less surveillance for its exercise than do reward or coercive power?
18. Define "expert power." Do we sometimes treat an expert in one domain as if she were particularly knowledgeable in others?

SOCIAL LOAFING
19. Explain what "social loafing" is. What did Ringelmann find about how hard people pull a load when alone versus when they are pulling

together? What did Latané find when he had individuals cheer alone or in groups of two or six? Latané tried to distinguish between coordination losses and motivational losses by having subjects cheer in "pseudogroups," wearing earphones so they could not tell they were the only ones cheering. What did he find using this procedure? Does social loafing only apply to physical effort? Name three conditions in which social loafing does not take place. What conditions maximize social loafing?
20. Tasks differ according to how members' contributions are combined. What is an "additive combination rule?" Give an example. What is a "disjunctive task"? Give an example. What is a "conjunctive task"? Give an example. What is a "compensatory task"? Give an example. If you are in a group doing a disjunctive task but you are not good at this sort of thing, is there any point in trying hard? What if it is a compensatory task? Should you always try your best on an additive task, whether you are good at that sort of thing or not?

GROUP COHESIVENESS

21. Understand how group cohesiveness can be a source of motivation. Explain why German soldiers continued to fight at the end of World War II even after it was obvious that the war had been lost.

Factors Affecting Cohesiveness
Attractiveness of a Group
22. Describe some factors that contribute to a group's attractiveness to its members.

Costs and Cohesiveness
23. List some of the costs associated with being a member of a group.
24. Explain what Thibaut and Kelley meant by "opportunity costs." How does the comparison level for alternatives determine the attractiveness of a group?

Cohesiveness and Cognitive Dissonance
25. Explain how the high cost of being a member of a group can lead to greater attraction to the group. Describe the results of Staw's study on the effect of lottery number on ROTC members' satisfaction with the ROTC. How did whether or not they had already signed the contract to take a commission as an officer affect their satisfaction with the ROTC? When were the men's

attitudes and behavior rational and when were they irrational?

Cohesiveness and Loyalty
26. Describe how loyalty leads to group cohesiveness.

Consequences of Cohesiveness
27. Describe the effect of group cohesiveness on the attitudes of the group members. Festinger proposed that groups are particularly likely to pressure their members to conform to group standards under certain conditions. What are they? How is pressure brought to bear on deviant members?

Uniformity of Attitudes
28. Understand how cohesive groups differ from less-cohesive groups in resolving differences of opinion. In Back's experiment, what was the difference between how cohesive and less-cohesive groups resolved their differences about the stories?
29. Schachter examined how groups communicated to members who did not hold the modal position on an issue. He introduced several confederates into the discussion—the mode, the slider, and the deviant. Describe the role of each of these confederates. Describe the patterns of communication to the slider and to the deviant (both for groups where this discussion was very relevant or less relevant). Did the group reject any of the confederates?

Groupthink
30. Define "groupthink." Describe how groupthink could lead to foreign policy fiascos. What are some of the symptoms of groupthink? What are two ways that a leader can prevent groupthink from emerging among her advisers? Tetlock looked at the public statements of policymakers involved in fiascos and successes. What did he find about the quality of thinking of those involved in fiascos? Did they tend toward group overevaluation? What is the evidence that avoiding groupthink correlates with favorable outcomes?

The Contagion of an Eating Disorder in a Cohesive Group
31. Describe how groupthink can lead to an eating disorder in a cohesive group. What did Crandall find about the association of binge eating and popularity in two college sororities?

32. Define the relation between being uninvolved with cohesive familial, religious, and political groups and the likelihood of suicide.

GROUPS vs. INDIVIDUALS
33. Knight had a group of people attempt to guess the temperature in a room without a thermometer. Which was better, the mean judgment of the group or the judgment of a single randomly chosen individual?

Group Judgment and Bias
34. Does the Knight experiment show that group discussion yields more accurate results than individual judgments? Why not? Explain why a pooled judgment (without individuals knowing each other's positions) is likely to be better than that of a randomly selected member of a group. To show that group discussions are productive one must show that they are better than the results of pooling the judgments of the same number of individuals. Explain.

Communication Networks and Group Performance
35. Describe Leavitt's experiment (using a technique developed by Bavelas) that studied the effect of group communication on group performance of a simple task. What were the results of the experiment? Which of the structures had the greatest group satisfaction? Are the results the same when the group task is complex? Why not?
36. Shaw proposed that structures can be characterized by two features, degree of centralization and degree of saturation. What is meant by "saturation" and "centralization"? What is the relation between the degree of saturation and the efficiency of a centralized network?

Group Performance on Cognitive Tasks
37. Be able to identify tasks in which groups outperform individuals. What is a "preference task"? What is an "intellective task"? What is a "demonstrable" answer? What are the two features of Eureka problems? How do groups tend to handle preference problems?
38. Groups perform with different effectiveness depending on whether they are attempting to solve intellective problems with high or low demonstrability. What are the differences between groups attempting to solve these two types of problems?

JURY TASK PERFORMANCE

39. Describe the two major problems that psychologists who try to study juries encounter. Give examples of some "mock" jury procedures. What does even the most realistic mock jury set-up lack?

Juries and Judges

40. Compare how judges and juries decided whether to convict or acquit a defendant in the Kalven and Zeisel study. How often were the judge and jury in agreement? When the judge and jury disagreed was it more likely for the jury to convict or free the defendant? Was the evidence similar for civil cases? How did the judges interpret their disagreement with the juries? What is the difference between a jury as trier of facts and a jury as an interpreter of law as well as facts? In real trials do juries generally convict or acquit defendants?

41. According to the law, do juries have to have twelve members?

42. According to the law, do juries have to convict unanimously? One cannot ask whether a unanimous jury or a twelve-person jury gets the verdict right more often than a non-unanimous or six-person jury. But what questions might be profitably asked?

Initial Juror Opinion and Final Jury Verdicts

43. Kalven and Zeisel interviewed jurors in 225 cases (twelve-person juries, unanimous rule). What did they find about the relation between first ballot vote and the final verdict? What is James Davis's position (social decision theory) on how juries decide cases? According to these positions, should there be a large difference between juries using a unanimous or a majority rule? What is the difference between the deliberation of these two kinds of juries?

The Death-Qualified Jury

44. Explain why death-qualified juries might be biased against defendants with regard to the question of guilt or innocence. Why might people who are in favor of capital punishment be more likely to convict on the same evidence than people who are not? What were Moran and Comfort's findings about the characteristics of death-qualified jurors? Why are these leanings of death-qualified jurors particularly troublesome to fair capital trials?

Programmed Exercises

1. A _____ group is one that meets face-to-face at least on occasion.   primary

2. People doing something in each others' presence but without substantial communications are called _____.   co-actors

3. Co-actors, unlike people in a more full-fledged group, lack a _____ _____.   common goal

4. An _____ _____ group, unlike an enduring group, is created for a single, temporary purpose, and when that purpose is fulfilled the group disbands.   ad hoc

5. _____ concerns how tightly connected to a group its members are; it is primarily an attribute of enduring groups.   Cohesiveness

SOCIAL FACILITATION

6. If you had a choice of being alone or with others when taking an exam in a subject you knew fairly well, according to Robert Zajonc, you should choose to take it with _____.   others

7. According to Zajonc, the mere presence of others is _____.   arousing

8. Arousal has two very different effects. It _____ the performance of well-learned, or simple tasks, and it _____ the performance of poorly learned, novel, or complex tasks.   enhances
inhibits

9. If you had a choice of being alone or in a group when taking an exam in a subject you did not know well, you would do better to take the exam _____. This is because performance on a poorly mastered task, such as your knowledge of the subject matter on the exam, is _____ by the arousal caused by the presence of other students.

alone
inhibited

10. Observers who sit and watch an experiment without comment will _____ performance on well-practiced tasks and inhibit performance on little-practiced tasks.

enhance

11. _____ _____ is the facilitation of dominant responses by an audience.

Social facilitation

12. To determine in the face of conflicting results whether a phenomenon is real one combines the results from all of the studies into a single analysis called a _____-_____.

meta-analysis

13. By using combined, single analysis it has been concluded that there is a reliable but _____ tendency for well-learned tasks to be facilitated by the presence of others and poorly learned ones to be inhibited by the presence of others.

small

Explanations of Social Facilitation

14. Zajonc's view is called the _____ _____ account because it holds that we are aroused by the presence of others no matter what they are doing.

mere presence

15. Cottrell argued that social facilitation is caused by the fact that people watching us can _____ us.

evaluate

16. Marcus argued that Cottrell was right that the anticipation of _____ caused social facilitation, but she claimed that although mere presence was not necessary for social facilitation it was _____ for it.

evaluation
sufficient

Four More Sources of Social Facilitation

17. According to Baron and Saunders, the presence of others is _____.

distracting

18. Distracted subjects try _____ than other subjects in order to overcome the effects of the distraction.

harder

19. There are two effects operating in opposite directions: trying harder _____ performance and distraction _____ performance.

facilitating,
inhibiting

20. According to Baron and Saunders on simple tasks the facilitation from greater effort is _____ than the inhibition from distraction, while on complex tasks the facilitation from greater effort is _____ than the inhibition from distraction.

greater
less

21. According to Berger, when we are alone and faced with a task, we use aids such as counting on our fingers, mumbling the item to be memorized, etc. Complex, difficult tasks are helped by using such habitual aids, but over-learned, simple tasks are _____ with.

interfered

22. In the presence of others we do not use these "aids" from fear of looking _____. Hence, performance of complex tasks is _____, and performance of simple tasks is improved.

silly, hurt

23. According to Guerin and Innes, it is not mere presence per se that is arousing, rather it is the presence of others who might be _____.   dangerous

24. A stranger, especially one who is difficult to _____, should be most arousing.   monitor

25. According to this account the social facilitation effect is more likely when the spectators sit _____ the subject than when they are in view.   behind

26. According to Bond, people do better on simple tasks if they are before an audience because they want to _____ them.   impress

27. In the presence of others we try harder, but if the task is difficult we may notice that we are beginning to fail and become _____ before the audience and do even worse.   embarrassed

28. If people expect to fail then the presence of an audience will _____ performance; if they expect to do well then the presence of an audience will _____ performance.   hurt

help

LEADERSHIP

29. The relationship between various personality traits and leadership has been found to be _____.   weak

30. The _____ view of leadership holds that there is no single trait that effective leaders share. Effective leadership requires _____ traits depending on the circumstances.   contingency
different

31. A situation in which a leader has great authority and a good relationship with her group, and in which there is a well-specified task, is one in which the overall situation is _____ to the leader. A situation in which a leader has no authority, in which the members don't get along with each other or the leader, and in which the task is poorly specified is one in which the overall situation is _____ to the leader.   favorable

unfavorable

32. According to Fiedler, in both extremely favorable and unfavorable circumstances a _____-_____ leader will be most effective. In intermediate circumstances a leader focused on _____ relationships will do better.   task-focused
interpersonal

Consistency in Leadership

33. The round robin procedure (in which the person who becomes the leader of one group is shifted into another group with a different task) provides evidence that there is a trait, or traits, associated with _____, but not what these traits are.   leadership

Power

34. French and Raven see social power as the ability to _____ another person's behavior, thoughts, and feelings.   influence

35. One has legitimate power over another to the degree that one has the _____ to give orders, and the other has the _____ to obey them.   right, obligation

36. Legitimate power is typically _____ in scope.   limited

37. If someone follows an authority strictly because she recognizes the authority's legitimacy, then compliance will occur without _____.   surveillance

38. _____ power involves making a desirable outcome contingent on a person's doing something.   Reward

39. Coercive power is the power to _____.   punish

40. Both reward and coercive power require _____ for their enforcement.   surveillance

41. _____ power is the power you have over someone because that person likes you, respects you, or wants to be like you. It is _____ in need of surveillance than reward or coercive power.   Referent
less

42. Expert power derives from _____, usually in a specific domain. We sometimes treat experts in one domain as if they had expertise in _____.   knowledge

others

SOCIAL LOAFING

43. Ringelmann discovered that an agricultural laborer pulls a load with _____ force when alone than when in a team.   more

44. The lessened force of an individual in a team my be due to _____ losses or to lessened motivation.   coordination

45. In a replication of the Ringelmann findings confederates appeared to be pulling on a rope but were not, this eliminated or lessened _____ effects. Individuals in groups still pulled _____ hard than individuals alone.   coordination
less

46. Latané had individuals cheer and clap alone, or in groups of two or six. He found that being part of a group _____ the effort that each person contributed. This phenomenon has been called _____ _____. It applies to _____ effort as well as to physical effort.   reduced
social loafing
cognitive

47. It was found that while people in groups put out less effort than when they are alone, this effect does not occur when the members of the group believe that _____ performance is being monitored. Social loafing also does not occur when subjects have a clear idea of how well they are doing individually in comparison with a _____ _____ (even if the experimenter does not monitor their performance).   individual

social standard

48. On a _____ _____ only the worst performance in each group matters.   conjunctive task

49. On a _____ _____ only the best performance in a group matters.   disjunctive task

50. In an additive task _____ member's contribution counts.   every

51. In a compensatory task members' errors can _____ each other out.   cancel

52. It would be rational in a disjunctive task for the _____ player on the team to loaf, and on a conjunctive task for the _____ player on a team to loaf. Subjects in fact behave in this manner.   worst
best

53. Social loafing on a group task mainly occurs when people can't see the fruits of their own efforts, on not very _____ tasks, and especially where their individual effort is not _____ to the group's success.   challenging
important

GROUP COHESIVENESS

54. In World War II the reason the German army continued to fight at the end of the war was not ideology but because of small group _____.

    cohesiveness

55. Personal liking of other members, the prestige of the group, and the practical utility of being a member of the group all contribute to the _____ of a group to its members.

    attractiveness

56. Some groups have unpleasant people in them, negative prestige, or dues or fees. These are some of the _____ of being part of a group.

    costs

57. The _____ _____ of being a member of a group are the costs associated with *not* being a member of an alternative group.

    opportunity costs

58. Sometimes an attraction to a group is born of the _____ cost one has paid to be a member.

    high

59. In Staw's study of the ROTC, if people's attraction to a group were wholly a rational matter, then those in ROTC who discovered that they would have been drafted should have been _____ satisfied than those who wouldn't have been drafted.

    more

60. Students in the "to be drafted" category who had not yet signed the contract with the army did stay in the ROTC _____ than those in the "not to be drafted" category. These students' attitudes toward ROTC were affected by the alternative level of _____.

    more

    comparison

61. Those students who had already signed the contract to be an officer and who had then discovered that they would *not* have been drafted rated themselves as _____ satisfied with the ROTC than those who would have been drafted.

    more

62. Satisfaction with ROTC varied with draft status in a rational fashion for those who were not yet _____, but varied in an irrational fashion for those who had already committed themselves.

    committed

63. _____ _____ involves trying to make regrettable decisions more palatable.

    Cognitive
    dissonance

64. Loyalty is the sense of _____ one has to members of a group just by virtue of having a shared history with them. It is one factor leading to the _____ of a group.

    obligation

    cohesiveness

Consequences of Cohesiveness

65. Festinger proposed that groups are particularly likely to pressure their members to conform to group standards when the group is _____, and the issue is directly _____ to the group.

    cohesive
    relevant

66. According to Festinger, the pressures brought to bear on members are in the form of communications toward the _____ members in order to bring them back into line.

    deviant

67. In an experiment by Back, pairs of subjects had to create stories. Cohesiveness of the pairs was manipulated in three different ways. The more cohesive pairs pressured each other and accepted pressure _____ than the less cohesive pairs; their stories changed _____ than those of the less cohesive pairs.

    more
    more

68. Schachter studied groups discussing how to handle a juvenile delinquent. He introduced several confederates into the discussion—the mode, the slider, and the deviant. The _____ took as his own the group's modal position on the issue; the _____ took a very different position from the group and stuck to his position; the _____ started out deviant and moved to the group's average position.

mode
deviant
slider

69. Communication to the slider started _____ and declined as he came closer to the group's mode. In groups where the discussion of delinquency was very relevant, communication to the deviant started _____ and then fell off, but in groups where the discussion was less relevant the communication remained _____. The _____ was rejected by the group, while the _____ and _____ were not.

high
high
high, deviant
mode, slider

70. The groups where the discussion of delinquency was very _____ reduced talking to the deviant because they had given up on him.

relevant

71. Groupthink occurs when the task demands on a decision-making group are overwhelmed by the social demands to reach _____.

consensus

72. Among the symptoms of groupthink are: an overestimation of the value and _____ of the group, group _____ for the defective policies, reliance on _____ of the enemy rather than accurate conceptions, and the _____ of doubts in the name of loyalty to the group, causing an illusory belief in a unanimous consensus.

morality,
rationalizations
stereotypes
suppression

73. In order to prevent groupthink from emerging a leader should avoid _____ of policymakers. Second, the leader should attempt to get all sides of an issue aired and avoid prematurely signaling his own _____.

isolation
opinion

74. Cradall found that binge eating was _____ with popularity in two sororities. Each sorority had a different standard for appropriate binging that the popular members conformed to.

associated

75. Durkheim found that people without significant attachments to cohesive groups are more likely than those with cohesive ties to commit _____.

suicide

GROUPS vs. INDIVIDUALS

76. Knight had a group of people attempt to guess the temperature in a room without a thermometer. The mean judgment of the group was found to be _____ than the judgment of a single randomly chosen individual.

better

Group Judgment and Bias

77. The reason why _____ judgments are better is that there is one factor, temperature, influencing all their judgments; the other, idiosyncratic, factors will tend to cancel each other out.

pooled

78. To show that group discussions are productive, one must show that they are _____ than the results of pooling the judgments of the same number of individuals.

better

79. Pooling the judgments of people who share a bias is likely to lead to an answer _____ from the truth than one would get by asking just one of them.

further

Communication Networks and Group Performances

80. Leavitt studied the effect of group communications on group performance of a simple task. His structures for communication in a five-person group included the circle in which each person could only communicate with his _____, or the wheel in which each member could communicate only with the person in the _____ _____.

neighbor

central position

81. The wheel functioned best on Leavitt's simple task. But because only one person in the network does the thinking the wheel should become _____ efficient as the task becomes more complex.

less

82. For a relatively complex task Shaw found that the decentralized circle was _____ than the centralized wheel.

faster

83. Shaw proposed that group structures are characterized by their degree of _____, the degree to which a communication channel is _____ with information, and degree of _____.

saturation, overloaded

centralization

Group Performance on Cognitive Tasks

84. In a preference task the group attempts to _____ its own satisfaction.

maximize

85. In intellective tasks there are _____ answers, the solution is not a matter of preference.

right

86. Many intellective problems are _____ in that one can demonstrate the right task.

demonstrable

87. A Eureka problem, such as a good riddle, is difficult to figure out but when the answer is given it is immediately, intuitively, _____.

obvious

88. On preference problems the group solution is the preferences of the majority or _____, when one or the other exists.

plurality

89. On Eureka problems a group immediately adopts the _____ answer when someone proposes it.

right

90. On less _____ problems, the groups adopted the correct answer if it was proposed and endorsed by other members of the group. The less _____ a solution the more group support it needed for it to become the group answer.

demonstrable
demonstrable

JURY TASK PERFORMANCE

Juries and Judges

91. Kalven and Zeisel obtained the judge's opinion of the proper verdict while the jury was deliberating and compared it with the jury's verdict for over 3,000 criminal cases. The judge and jury _____ over 75 percent of the time.

agreed

92. When the judge and jury disagreed in only about _____ percent of the cases the judge was for acquittal and the jury for conviction, but in over _____ percent of the cases the judge was for conviction but the jury acquitted.

2
16

93. Judges interpreted the reasons for judge-jury disagreement as relating to the differences in the interpretation of the facts, differences in the interpretation of law, and the tendency of juries to be _____ by personal characteristics of the defendant.

overinfluenced

Initial Juror Opinion and Final Jury Verdicts

94. Kalven and Zeisel interviewed jurors in 225 cases (twelve-person juries, unanimous rule). They found that if the jurors were _____ on the first ballot vote, then that decision became the verdict.

    unanimous

95. If only one to five jurors voted guilty on the first verdict then there was an over _____ percent chance of a not guilty verdict.

    90

96. If the first ballot vote was split then there was a _____ percent chance of either a guilty or a not guilty verdict.

    50

97. Kalven and Zeisel suggest that most of the work of a jury is done _____ the first ballot.

    before

98. In a study of mock juries by Nemeth it was found that unanimous and majority rule juries reached the same verdict, but that the unanimous juries' deliberations were characterized by greater _____.

    conflict

The Death-Qualified Jury

99. In the *Witherspoon* case, it was argued that the death-qualified jury is _____ likely to convict given the same evidence than a jury including people who were against the death penalty.

    more

100. Moran and Comfort in a study involving over 500 jurors found that death-qualified juries are more likely to be politically conservative and _____.

    authoritarian

Self-Test

1. Which of the following definitions or descriptions are *not* correct?
   a. A primary group is one that meets face to face.
   b. Co-actors do not share a common goal nor do they communicate much with each other.
   c. An ad hoc group is an enduring group that fulfills more than one goal for its members.
   d. A cohesive group has members who are tightly connected to the group.

2. According to Zajonc the mere presence of others is
   a. arousing.
   b. annoying.
   c. not noticeable unless they start to do something.
   d. all of the above

3. Arousal has two very different effects. What are they?
   a. Arousal disrupts the performance of simple or well-learned tasks and enhances the performance of complex tasks.
   b. Arousal disrupts the performance of complex tasks and enhances the performance of simple and well-learned tasks.
   c. Arousal increases daydreaming but disrupts conversation.
   d. Arousal inhibits sociability but enhances solitary pursuits.

4. If you had a choice of taking an exam alone or with others, according to Zajonc you should choose to
   a. take the exam alone.
   b. take the exam with others.
   c. take the exam alone if you don't feel sociable and with others if you do.
   d. take the exam with others if you have really mastered the material and alone if you have not.

5. Social facilitation is the facilitation of dominant responses by
   a. an audience.
   b. intense aloneness.
   c. drugs.
   d. any source.

6. The social facilitation effect is reliable and
   a. quite large.
   b. accounts for most interpersonal behavior.
   c. small.
   d. inconsistent.

7. Zajonc's account of social facilitation is that
   a. the anticipation of interaction is arousing.
   b. knowing that others are present and might evaluate us is arousing.
   c. we are genetically endowed to be aroused by the mere presence of others no matter what they are doing.
   d. we are genetically endowed with a fear of the dangers caused by the presence of unknown others.

8. Cottrell believed that social facilitation was due to "evaluation apprehension" and not "the mere presence effect." Which of the following results would be predicted by Cottrell but not by Zajonc?
   a. Subjects who performed alone did worse on a simple task than subjects performing before spectators.
   b. Subjects who performed in the presence of blindfolded people did no better on a simple task than subjects who performed alone.
   c. Subjects who performed in front of spectators did better than subjects who performed alone.
   d. Subjects who performed in the presence of blindfolded people did better on a simple task than subjects who performed alone.

9. Marcus argued that evaluation apprehension was sufficient for social facilitation but not
   a. necessary.
   b. prudent.
   c. interesting
   d. reliable.

10. Marcus believed that there was no difference in the blindfolded and alone conditions in the Cottrell experiments because
   a. the groups wanted to do well in both cases.
   b. the groups thought that the blindfolded people were peeking at them.
   c. both groups knew that the experimenter would be aware of their performance.
   d. the experiment was sloppily conducted.

11. In order to test this hypothesis Marcus had subjects take off their shoes (a habitual action) and get into a tricky lab coat (a nonhabitual action) either alone or in the presence of a "repairman" who was not looking at them. Marcus found
   a. that the presence of the repairman caused people to take off their shoes faster and put on the lab coat slower than they did in the alone condition.
   b. that the subjects' behavior was not affected by the presence of the repairman.
   c. that the presence of the repairman caused subjects to take off their shoes more slowly than in the alone condition.
   d. that the presence to the repairman did not cause subjects to put on the lab coat more slowly than in the alone condition.

12. Marcus's experiment
   a. supported the evaluation apprehension interpretation of social facilitation.
   b. supported the mere presence hypothesis.
   c. showed that social facilitation does not exist.
   d. showed that habits are inhibited by social anxiety.

13. According to Baron and Sanders, the presence of others is distracting and
   a. people try to overcome the effects of distraction; this works for simple tasks but not for complex tasks.
   b. people try to overcome the effects of distraction and thus do better than nondistracted people on all tasks.
   c. people do not try to overcome the effects of distraction; thus they do worse on all tasks than people who were not distracted.
   d. distraction has no effect on simple task performance.

14. According to Berger, when we are alone and faced with a task we use aids such as counting on our fingers, mumbling the items to be memorized, etc. In the presence of others we do not do this because we don't want to look foolish. Complex difficult tasks are helped by using these habitual aids, but over-learned simple tasks are interfered with. For these reasons
   a. the presence of others should prevent our using aids on complex tasks (where they are helpful) and inhibit performance (compared to when we are alone).

b. the presence of others should prevent our using aids on simple tasks (where they are distracting) and enhance performance (compared to when we are alone).
c. both complex and simple tasks should be facilitated by the presence of others.
d. a and b

15. Which of the following have(has) been offered as explanation(s) for the social facilitation effect?
a. It is not the mere presence of people per se but the presence of strangers that causes the arousal in social facilitation.
b. People try harder in the presence of an audience and thus usually do better on simple tasks; on complex tasks they notice that they are faltering and become embarrassed. This embarrassment inhibits performance.
c. It involves the distraction caused by the presence of others.
d. all of the above

16. The contingency view of leadership holds
a. that there is a single trait that all effective leaders share.
b. that effective leadership requires different traits in different circumstances.
c. that effective leaders are best at handling contingencies.
d. that effective leaders have no traits.

17. According to Fiedler, a situation in which a leader has great authority, a good relationship with his group, and in which the group task is clear-cut is most effectively handled by
a. a leader who is focused on interpersonal relationships.
b. a leader who is focused on only his own ideas.
c. a leader who is task-focused.
d. a leader who rejects her leadership role.

18. According to Fiedler, a situation in which a leader has moderate authority, a decent although not excellent relationship with his group, and in which the group task is somewhat ambiguous is most effectively handled by
a. a leader who is focused on interpersonal relationships.
b. a leader who is focused on only her own ideas.

c. a leader who is task-focused.
d. a leader who rejects his leadership role.

19. In the round robin procedure, the person who becomes the leader of one group is later shifted into another group with a different task and different members. Using this procedure, it has been found that
a. different people keep emerging as leaders depending on the nature of the group task.
b. the same person is unlikely to be a leader in two consecutive groups.
c. leadership in one group is negatively correlated with leadership in another group.
d. the same people keep emerging as leaders.

20. If one has legitimate power over another, then
a. the other has an *obligation* to obey, typically within a delimited scope.
b. one will obey only with surveillance.
c. one will obey only if paid well.
d. one will obey only if convinced that the order is a good idea.

21. In the Milgram obedience experiments, subjects cheated in the experimenter's absence. This shows that
a. there is no such thing as legitimate power.
b. that subjects were sociopaths.
c. that legitimate power was not the only force causing obedience in this situation.
d. that the subjects wanted to hurt the victim.

22. Reward power involves
a. doing something in order to get a reward.
b. doing something in order to avoid punishment.
c. doing something because you like and respect the person giving the orders.
d. doing something because you realize that what the other says derives from her knowledge of the situation.

23. Coercive power involves
a. doing something in order to get a reward.
b. doing something in order to avoid punishment.
c. doing something because you like and respect the person giving the orders.
d. doing something because you realize that what the other says derives from her knowledge of the situation.

24. Referent power involves
    a. doing something in order to get a reward.
    b. doing something in order to avoid punishment.
    c. doing something because you like and respect the person giving the orders.
    d. doing something because you realize that what the other says derives from her knowledge of the situation.

25. Expert power involves
    a. doing something in order to get a reward.
    b. doing something in order to avoid punishment.
    c. doing something because you like and respect the person giving the orders.
    d. doing something because you realize that what the other says derives from her knowledge of the situation.

26. Exercising _____ power would require the least surveillance.
    a. reward
    b. coercive
    c. legitimate or referent
    d. reward and coercion operating together

27. Ringelmann discovered that an agricultural laborer pulls a load with more force when alone than when in a team. Which of the following statements is *not* true of this phenomenon?
    a. Work in a group can reduce individual motivation.
    b. Coordination losses reduce the per individual expenditure of energy.
    c. This phenomenon is called "social loafing."
    d. This phenomena only occurs with physical labor and not with mental labor.

28. Latané found that in a "pseudogroup" of six (that is, one subject wearing earphones who cannot tell that the other five group members, confederates, are not cheering) each person produced
    a. slightly more sound than he would have alone.
    b. less sound than he would have alone.
    c. roughly the same amount of sound that he would have alone.
    d. at first more sound and then considerably less sound than he would have produced alone.

29. Social loafing does *not* occur when
    a. subjects have a clear idea of how well they are doing individually in comparison with a social standard or if they realize that their performance is being monitored.
    b. subjects are in two- or three-person groups.
    c. the work is intellectual and not physical.
    d. no one knows how much effort each individual is contributing to the group task and there is no clear standard against which to compare the group's performance.

30. Subjects were given the easy task of finding uses for a knife, or they were given the challenging task of finding uses for a detached doorknob. They were to work alone; some were to be evaluated on their own work, but some were told that the uses they found would be combined with the answers of nine other subjects and that only the ten-person group would be evaluated. The social loafing effect
    a. did not occur.
    b. occurred for both tasks.
    c. only occurred for the easy task.
    d. only occurred for the challenging task.

31. On which type of task is the *worst* performance in a group the one that matters?
    a. a conjunctive task, for instance, the last member of a team to cross the finish line determines the team's score
    b. a disjunctive task, such as a team quiz game
    c. an additive task
    d. a compensatory task

32. On which type of task is the *best* performance in a group the one that matters?
    a. a conjunctive task, for instance, the last member of a team to cross the finish line determines the team's score
    b. a disjunctive task, such as a team quiz game
    c. an additive task
    d. a compensatory task

33. On which type of task would it be rational for the *best* players on a team to loaf, and do subjects behave in this manner?
    a. disjunctive tasks; subjects do behave in this manner
    b. disjunctive tasks; subjects do not behave in this manner

c. conjunctive tasks; subjects do behave in this manner

d. conjunctive tasks; subjects do not behave in this manner

34. On which type of task would it be rational for the *worst* players on a team to loaf; do subjects behave in this manner?
    a. disjunctive tasks; subjects do behave in this manner
    b. disjunctive tasks; subjects do not behave in this manner
    c. conjunctive tasks; subjects do behave in this manner
    d. conjunctive tasks; subjects do not behave in this manner

35. Social loafing on a group task mainly occurs
    a. when people can't see the fruits of their own efforts.
    b. on not very challenging tasks.
    c. when individual effort is not important to the group's success.
    d. all of the above

36. Personal liking for other members, the prestige of the group, and the practical utility of being a member of the group all increase the
    a. attractiveness of a group.
    b. extent of social loafing in a group.
    c. interest of members in finding even more attractive groups.
    d. feeling of being disconnected from the group.

37. The "opportunity costs" of being a member of a group are the costs associated with
    a. the dues required by many groups.
    b. *not* being a member of an alternative group.
    c. the price individuals in a group pay for the opportunities the group affords them.
    d. all of the above

38. Staw examined the attitude toward ROTC of ROTC members who had just discovered that the "draft lottery" ensured that they would almost certainly be drafted, or almost certainly not be drafted. He also looked at how this draftability interacted with the effect of having, or not having, signed a contract to take a commission as an officer. He found that

a. among students who had not yet signed a contract with the ROTC, those in the to-be-drafted category stayed in the ROTC almost twice as often as those who knew that they would probably not be drafted. This is an example of rational behavior.

b. among students who had already signed the contract to be with the ROTC, those who discovered that they would *not* have been drafted were more satisfied with the ROTC than those who discovered that they would probably be drafted.

c. satisfaction with ROTC varied with discovered draftability in a rational fashion only for those who were not yet committed (signed up) but varied in an irrational fashion for those who had committed themselves by already signing up.

d. all of the above

39. Loyalty
    a. is not involved in group cohesiveness.
    b. is the sense of obligation one has to members of a group just by virtue of having a shared history with them and is for this reason a factor leading to group cohesiveness.
    c. is a political issue irrelevant to social groups.
    d. only keeps an individual in a group until a more attractive one is found.

40. According to Festinger, groups are most likely to pressure members to conform to group standards when
    a. the group is not quite cohesive.
    b. the group is barely holding together.
    c. the group is cohesive and the issue is directly relevant.
    d. the issue is not directly relevant to the group.

41. Schachter studied groups discussing how to handle a juvenile delinquent. He introduced several confederates into the discussion—the mode, the slider, and the deviant. Which of the following is *not* true about the roles of these confederates?
    a. The mode took as his own the group's modal position on the issue.
    b. The slider took a very different position from the group and stuck to that position.

c. The deviant took a very different position from the group and stuck to that position.

d. The slider started with a very different position than the group and moved to the group's modal position.

42. Communication to the slider
   a. started high and remained high throughout the group discussion.
   b. started low and remained low throughout the group discussion.
   c. started high and declined as he came closer to the group's mode.
   d. started high and declined only in those situations in which the discussion was very relevant to the group.

43. Communication to the deviant
   a. always started high and remained high throughout the group discussion.
   b. started low and remained low throughout the group discussion.
   c. started high and declined over time if the discussion was not very relevant to the group.
   d. started high and declined only in those situations in which the discussion was very relevant to the group.

44. In the above experiment which of the confederates was rejected by the group?
   a. the slider
   b. the mode
   c. the deviant
   d. the penitent

45. Groupthink occurs when
   a. the task demands on a decision-making group are overwhelmed by the social demands to reach consensus.
   b. the task demands on a decision-making group are too minimal to engage the focused attention of the group.
   c. group members underestimate the value and morality of their group.
   d. members of a group are unafraid to speak out even if they hold dissenting opinions.

46. Which of the following is *not* a symptom of groupthink?
   a. The group produces rationalizations for defective policies.
   b. The group overestimates the value and morality of the group.

c. The group is not concerned with the symbols and rituals of their country, such as reciting the pledge of allegiance.
d. The group relies on stereotypes of the enemy.

47. In order to prevent groupthink from emerging, a leader
   a. should avoid isolating the policymakers.
   b. should attempt to get all sides of an issue aired.
   c. should not make her preliminary opinion known until the members of her staff have presented their opinions.
   d. all of the above

48. Tetlock looked at the public statements of American policymakers involved in fiascos and successes. He found that policymakers involved in fiascos were
   a. more likely to make anticommunist statements than successful policymakers.
   b. more likely to be simplistic in their analyses, and more likely to praise the United States in their statements than did successful policymakers.
   c. less likely to be simplistic in their analyses and also less likely to praise the United States in their statements than did successful policymakers.
   d. usually deliberate or unconscious traitors.

49. Crandall found that binge eating was associated with popularity in two sororities. What was the association?
   a. Each sorority had a different standard for appropriate binging that the popular members conformed to.
   b. Only the least popular members in either sorority binged.
   c. Initially popular members who binged lost their popularity.
   d. In each sorority the members who binged most were the most popular.

50. Durkheim found that people without significant attachments to cohesive groups are more likely than those with cohesive ties to
   a. binge eat.
   b. become devoted to rock and roll.
   c. commit suicide.
   d. become members of the Young Republicans.

51. Knight had a group of people attempt to guess the temperature in a room without a thermometer. The mean judgment of the group was found to be
    a. worse than the judgment of a single randomly chosen individual.
    b. better than the judgment of a single randomly chosen individual.
    c. inconsistent, not comparable with the judgment of a single randomly chosen individual.
    d. the same as the judgment of a single randomly chosen individual.

52. Knight's experiment does *not* show that group discussion is better than an individual's judgment since
    a. pooling individual responses (without any discussion) is also more accurate than a randomly selected individual judgment.
    b. the group Knight used was atypically good at judging temperature.
    c. Knight's experiment has not been replicated.
    d. all of the above

53. To show that group discussions are productive one must show that
    a. the group result is better than the result of a randomly selected group member.
    b. the group comes up with good productive ideas.
    c. the group result is better than the results of pooling the judgments of the same number of individuals.
    d. the members of the group are satisfied with their performance.

54. Pooling the judgments of people who share a *bias* is likely to
    a. result in a much better decision than that of a randomly chosen group member.
    b. result in a slightly better decision than that of a randomly chosen group member.
    c. result in about the same quality decision as that of a randomly chosen group member.
    d. result in an answer further from the truth than one would get by asking a randomly chosen group member.

55. In the Stasser and Titus experiment in which groups had to decide on the appropriate candidate for a political office, each member of a group had partial information (favoring candidate B), but collectively the group had the complete information favoring candidate A. Who did the groups usually decide on?
    a. candidate A
    b. candidate B
    c. the groups were deadlocked between the two candidates
    d. Harold Stassen

56. Leavitt studied the effect of group communications on group performance of a simple task. His structures for communication in a five-person group included the circle, in which each person could only communicate with his neighbor, or the wheel, in which each member could communicate only with one person in the central position. What did Leavitt find?
    a. When only the fastest trials of the groups were compared the circle was slowest and had the most errors.
    b. Subjects communicating in a circle were most satisfied.
    c. On the fastest trials the wheel functioned best although it gave the least satisfaction for a simple task. The hub person on the wheel becomes overwhelmed on more complex tasks.
    d. all of the above

57. According to Shaw, the more a channel is overloaded with information
    a. the more efficient centralized structures such as the wheel are liable to be.
    b. the less efficient centralized structures such as the wheel are liable to be.
    c. the more people will enjoy a centralized structure.
    d. the less people will enjoy a circle network as compared to a wheel.

58. A "Eureka" problem, such as a good riddle, is difficult to figure out, but when the answer is given it is
    a. puzzling.
    b. a shaggy dog story.
    c. immediately, intuitively obvious.
    d. a disappointment.

59. A group is likely to
    a. go along with the preference of the majority of its members, if there is one, on a task involving deciding between individual preferences.
    b. adopt immediately a sensible proposed

answer when the group is working on a Eureka problem.

c. adopt the correct answer for a nonobvious problem if it is proposed and endorsed by various members of the group; the less demonstrable a solution the more group support is needed.

d. all of the above

60. One difficulty in studying jury positions is that we are rarely in a position to be certain as to whether the jury's decision
a. was unanimous.
b. was fair.
c. was correct.
d. was for a guilty or innocent verdict.

61. Psychologists have a group of people who are on jury duty, but not called for a case, listen to a real trial and make their judgment. The psychologists are using a
a. jury.
b. control group.
c. mock jury.
d. mock turtle.

62. Kalven and Zeisel obtained judges' opinions of the proper verdict while the jury was deliberating and compared it with the jury's verdict for over 3,000 criminal cases. The judge and jury were
a. rarely in agreement.
b. almost always in agreement.
c. in agreement over three-quarters of the time.
d. in agreement 47.6 percent of the time.

63. Kalven and Zeisel found that when the judge and jury disagreed
a. the jury was more likely to be for conviction than the judge.
b. the jury was more likely to be for acquittal than the judge.
c. in only 2 percent of the cases was the judge for acquittal and the jury for conviction.
d. b and c

64. In some states juries are supposed to be triers of fact while the judge is to interpret the law; in other states juries are supposed to be both triers of fact and interpreters of law. To some degree juries in all states tend to see themselves as
a. interpreters of law as well as triers of fact.
b. only triers of fact.

c. incompetent for the task facing them.
d. only following a judge's orders.

65. Judges believe that one reason that juries and judges disagree is that juries are overinfluenced by
a. expert testimony.
b. the personal characteristics of the defendants.
c. mood, weather, and other extraneous factors.
d. bias.

66. Kalven and Zeisel interviewed jurors in 225 cases (twelve-person juries, unanimous rule). They found that if the jurors were unanimous on the first ballot vote, then that decision
a. became the verdict.
b. was a starting point for discussion but that often after further deliberation the jury changed its decision.
c. was uncorrelated with the first ballot vote.
d. was rarely the final decision.

67. If one to five jurors voted guilty on the first verdict then
a. there was an under 48 percent chance of a not guilty verdict.
b. there was an over 50 percent likelihood of a hung jury (undecided).
c. there was an over 90 percent likelihood of a not guilty verdict.
d. the five jurors voting guilty were likely to convince the others to vote guilty (62 percent of the time).

68. If the first ballot vote was split then there was a
a. 50 percent chance of either a guilty or a not guilty verdict.
b. most juries wound up voting for acquittal.
c. most juries wound up voting for conviction.
d. there was a 60 percent likelihood of a hung jury.

69. If the majority voted to convict on the first ballot then there was a
a. 40 percent chance of acquittal.
b. a certainty that the jurors would vote for conviction.
c. 86 percent chance of a guilty verdict and a 5 percent chance of an innocent verdict.
d. a 40 percent likelihood of a hung jury.

70. Kalven and Zeisel suggest that these data show that most of the work of a jury is done
    a. right before the last vote.
    b. in discussions about the case with fellow jurors.
    c. before the first ballot.
    d. during lunch break

71. In a study of mock juries by Nemeth it was found that unanimous and majority rule juries reached the same verdict but that the unanimous juries' deliberations were characterized by greater
    a. harmony, less disagreement.
    b. conflict, suggesting that the juries aired the issues more thoroughly.
    c. disregard of the evidence.
    d. selectivity.

72. The evidence from Nemeth and Kalven and Zeisel suggest that
    a. there would be a great difference between juries using a unanimous or a majority rule as to verdict reached.
    b. there would be no difference between juries using a unanimous or majority rule.
    c. there would be little difference between majority and unanimous rule juries in regard to verdict reached, but that unanimous rule juries would air the issues more thoroughly.
    d. a majority rule jury is likely to disregard totally the rights of the defendant.

73. In a death-qualified jury any juror who expresses categorical opposition to the death penalty during the voire dire (jury selection) is excluded. In a study involving over 500 jurors Moran and Comfort found that death-qualified juries are more likely to be
    a. conservative and authoritarian.
    b. conservative and libertarian.
    c. liberal.
    d. inattentive to the arguments presented in court.

74. Pennington and Hastie argue that having a death-qualified jury would increase the probability of a guilty verdict over a representative jury made up of supporters and opponents of the death penalty. According to the authors approximately
    a. 40 percent of defendants would be convicted by a death-qualified jury who would not have been convicted by a representative jury.
    b. 3 percent of defendants would be convicted by a death-qualified jury who would not have been convicted by a representative jury.
    c. 10 percent of defendants would be convicted by a death-qualified jury who would not have been convicted by a representative jury.
    d. 1 percent of defendants would be convicted by a death-qualified jury who would not have been convicted by a representative jury.

Answer Key for Self-Test

1. c (pp. 69–70)
2. a (p. 71)
3. b (p. 71)
4. d (p. 71)
5. a (pp. 72–73)
6. c (p. 73)
7. c (p. 73)
8. b (p. 74)
9. a (p. 74)
10. c (p. 75)
11. a (p. 76)
12. b (p. 77)
13. a (p. 77)
14. d (p. 78)
15. d (pp. 77–80)
16. b (p. 81)
17. c (pp. 81–82)
18. a (pp. 81–82)
19. d (p. 82)
20. a (p. 82)
21. c (p. 84)
22. a (p. 84)
23. b (p. 84)
24. c (p. 84)
25. d (p. 85)
26. c (p. 84)
27. d (pp. 85–87)
28. b (p. 86)
29. a (p. 87)
30. c (p. 88)
31. a (p. 88)
32. b (p. 88)
33. c (pp. 88–89)
34. a (pp. 88–90)
35. d (p. 90)
36. a (p. 91)
37. b (p. 92)
38. d (pp. 93–94)
39. b (p. 94)
40. c (p. 95)
41. b (p. 96)
42. c (p. 96)
43. d (p. 96)
44. c (p. 97)
45. a (p. 98)
46. c (pp. 98–99)
47. d (p. 99)
48. b (p. 100)
49. a (p. 102)
50. c (p. 102)
51. b (p. 103)
52. a (p. 103)
53. c (p. 104)
54. d (p. 104)
55. b (p. 106)
56. d (p. 107)
57. b (p. 108)
58. c (p. 108)
59. d (pp. 109–110)
60. c (p. 110)
61. c (p. 111)
62. c (p. 112)
63. d (p. 112)
64. a (p. 113)
65. b (p. 113)
66. a (p. 116)
67. c (p. 116)
68. a (p. 116)
69. c (p. 116)
70. c (p. 116)
71. b (p. 117)
72. c (p. 117)
73. a (p. 118)
74. c (p. 119)

Thought Questions and Exercises

1. You can replicate some of Latané's studies of social loafing (pp. 86–87) by having your subjects wear a walkman playing a rock tape loud enough so that they will not be able to tell that your confederates are not singing. Vary the number of confederates and see if you get the social loafing effect. See what the effect on social loafing is when it is apparent to the subject that you are monitoring his performance in particular. Can you think of a way to allow the subject to monitor his own performance without your being present? Do you think that self-monitoring will be effective? More than no monitoring? As effective as your monitoring him?

2. Have you ever been a member of a group that you feel was very cohesive? Have you ever been a member of a group that could hardly keep itself together? Try to account for the difference between the two groups (it may happen that the same group at different moments can provide you with your two examples). Bring up both practical and "personal" factors insofar as they are relevant. Is the concept of "opportunity costs" of any use in your analysis (see p. 92)?

3. Loyalty, the sense of obligation to others one has just by virtue of having a shared history with them, is one factor leading to group cohesiveness. Loyalty in informal groups usually comes about slowly and unannounced—friends rarely take blood oaths. Think of your relationship to some more formal group—for instance, a church group, a club, etc.—that is important to you, and also to a group of your friends. How much of the cohesion that you feel in both of these groups is due to loyalty? When does loyalty become an issue? When were you first aware that you had an obligation to the group or to your friends rather than or in addition to merely shared practical and social interests?

4. Can you think of some public policy decision—local or national—that you believe was a result of groupthink (see pp. 97–102)? Which of the symptoms of groupthink applies to this decision?

5. Using the round robin technique (p. 82) the same individuals have been found to tend to lead in different groups even on different tasks; yet a single leadership trait has not been found. One possibility is that the same individual may act differently, appear to have different traits, depending on the requirements of particular groups. Do you know anyone who is a leader, that is, leads in several different groups? Try to see if the way she acts, especially her sociability and task orientedness varies with task and group. (This, of course, is not a substitute for an experiment but it might be the first step in developing your hypothesis on the way to an experiment.)

6. Psychologists often study mock juries and not the real thing. Yet, as you have seen, the mock juries that they have formed are as close as possible to the real thing. If you were a Supreme Court justice trying to assess evidence as to whether a six-person jury was as fair as a twelve-person jury would you use the evidence from mock juries? Why or why not? If you would use it, how much weight would you give the evidence?

7. It appears from the work of Kalven and Zeisel that most of the work of a jury is done before the first ballot, before the jury discusses the issues. Does this mean that the jury is closed-minded? That it doesn't really debate the issues? Why or why not?

8. Pennington and Hastie argue that because 17 percent of all potential jurors are excludable from capital cases based on their opposition to the death penalty and because death-qualified jurors are perhaps 20 percent more likely to convict a defendant than are other jurors that more defendants are convicted by death-qualified jurors than would have been convicted by more representative jurors. What percent more? What are some possible remedies to the problem caused by the bias introduced by the death qualification?

CHAPTER 4

Prejudice

Learning Objectives

WHAT IS PREJUDICE?

1. Be able to distinguish between "prejudice" and "discrimination."

Discriminatory Behavior

2. Define "discrimination." Is discrimination always the result of a prejudiced attitude? What is "institutional racism"? Give an example. Does prejudice always result in discrimination?

Prejudiced Attitudes

3. Give some definitions of a "prejudiced person." What are some different measures of prejudice? Do they intercorrelate? What does the notion of stereotype suggest?

Sources of Prejudice

4. Describe three accounts social psychologists give of prejudice.

THE CULTURAL VIEW

Realistic Conflict Theory

5. According to realistic conflict theory, what is the source of prejudice? What are the specific changes that a group undergoes in the face of conflict?

The Robbers Cave Experiment

6. According to Sherif, what are the four major effects of a conflict on the groups in conflict? How might hostility be overcome? What is a superordinate goal?

7. Describe the set-up of the Robbers Cave experiment. Include in your description the sort of boys selected, how many boys in each group, the way the counselors were to run the camp, and how the two groups were formed. What was the reaction of the groups to each other when they "accidentally" met? How did Sherif introduce material conflict between the groups? What was the effect of this conflict on the groups? Were these effects the ones Sherif had predicted? How did Sherif demonstrate that ingroups overestimate their group relative to the outgroup? What did Sherif do to reduce conflict between the groups? Did just bringing the groups together reduce the level of conflict? What is the evidence that having a superordinate goal reduces conflict between groups? What were the superordinate goals in this study? What were the measures of conflict reduction?

8. A problem with the experiment is that the hostility slightly anticipated the conflict. Why is this important?

Integration of the Military

9. When black platoons were incorporated into white companies in the Second World War conflict between blacks and whites was not sparked. Rather the attitude of white officers and men became much less anti-black. Why? In what way do these findings support realistic conflict theory?

Minimal Group Research

10. Tajfel does not believe that competition is for the development of ethnocentrism. What is necessary? What is a "minimal group" and how is it created?

Ethnocentrism in Minimal Groups

11. Give the evidence that people will assign (as a first impression) more favorable traits to, remember more favorable information about, and vote to reward more members of their minimal group as against members of another group.

Explanations for Ingroup Bias

12. Describe social identity theory's explanation for the minimal group effect. Subjects in a minimal group are allowed to divide points between their group and another, or to read a newspaper. Did members of the minimal group show ingroup bias in the distribution of points? Was there a difference in self-esteem between the point assigners and the newspaper readers? How does social identity theory explain these results? In what sort of situation will bias against a group member reverse? Describe the "black-sheep" effect.

MOTIVATION APPROACHES

13. Understand how frustration-aggression theory is derived from Freud's theories.

Frustration-Aggression Theory

Some Evidence for a Frustration-Aggression Theory of Prejudice

14. Hovland and Sears found an inverse correlation between the price of cotton and the number of lynchings of blacks in the South (between 1882 and 1930). Explain why this supports frustration-aggression theory. Were frustrated counselors more likely to use favorable terms for minorities before or after they had been frustrated? What was the drawback of this study? Berkowitz conducted a study to get around this drawback. Describe the study (remember there were three variables that had to be accounted for: insult vs. no insult; anti-Semitic vs. not anti-Semitic; "Jewish" vs. "Christian" confederate).

Frustration-Aggression Theory: An Assessment

15. What does frustration-aggression theory contribute to our understanding of prejudice?

The Authoritarian Personality

The Syndrome of Authoritarianism

16. The authors of *The Authoritarian Personality* believed that a person's personality *caused* her prejudice, that because of childhood experiences people *seek out* prejudiced attitudes. Explain.

17. Describe the Anti-Semitism Scale (A-S Scale).

Give examples of some items. How was the scale scored?

18. What was the Ethnocentrism Scale (E Scale) designed to measure? Why was a subscale on "patriotism" included in the E Scale? How was the E Scale scored? Adorno and his collaborators selected eighty subjects tested on the E Scale and interviewed them in depth. How were these subjects selected? Were the coders of the interviews told whether an interview was from a high or low E subject?

19. What is the California F Scale? What was it supposed to measure? Give some examples of items from this scale. What correlation was found between the F Scale and the E Scale. According to the evidence in *The Authoritarian Personality*, was it an historical accident or was there some connection between the Nazis' suppression of modern art and their attempt to exterminate homosexuals?

20. The coders did not know whether an interview was high or low E but the interviewers did. What possible problem does this lead to?

21. All of the items in the F, E, and A-S scales are keyed in the same direction and written in the same clichéd style. What problems do these facts create for the interpretation of the scales? In order to address this problem a questionnaire measuring prejudice was constructed that did not rely on clichés. What was its correlation with the F Scale?

Development of Authoritarianism

22. What did Adorno and his colleagues believe to be the basic cause of authoritarianism? According to the Freudian view, in what way would a child who has been *harshly* punished for aggressive and sexual impulses handle her impulses differently from one who has been mildly punished? Show how the conventionalism, antisexuality, and hostility toward the outgroup of an authoritarian derives from the harsh child-rearing practices she had been subjected to.

Authoritarianism: Culture or Personality?

23. Describe the different perspectives of the theorists with a personality focus and those with a social focus on the relation between authoritarianism and prejudice.

24. Let us say that parents of prejudiced people treated them more harshly than parents of unprejudiced people. Is this enough to determine whether harsh child-rearing practices cause prejudice? Why or why not?

25. In a survey of attitudes people in the South were found to be more prejudiced against minorities and have higher F scores than those in other areas. Is this fact consistent with the cultural view, the personality view, or both?

26. The correlation between F and ethnocentrism is about the same in all regions. What does this suggest about the role of history and culture, and the role of personality in determining prejudice? It is possible that a Southerner who is less racist and less authoritarian than average for her region might be more racist than a Northerner who is considerably more racist than average for his region. Explain. If this were so, what would you predict about the difference in the F scores between the Southerner and the Northerner?

Prejudice and Ambivalence

27. Describe Myrdal's "conflicted motive" analysis of American race relations.

Explicit Values and Underlying Feelings

28. Using a questionnaire, Weitz assessed the attitudes of white students to blacks. She then had them interact with a black confederate. Some students who rated themselves as sympathetic on the questionnaire were ill at ease during the conversation. How did Weitz analyze this discrepancy? According to Weitz, what were the subjects' overt values, and what were the subjects' unconscious values? Under which circumstances will the overt values guide behavior, and under which circumstances will the unconscious values? What experimental evidence does she have for her analysis?

Ambivalence and Response Amplification

29. Katz and Glass argue that many Northern whites have egalitarian values, feelings of hostility, and also feelings of sympathy for blacks. In ambiguous circumstances either hostility or sympathy will be expressed. What will result from the conflict between sympathy for and hostility by a white toward a black? Describe an experiment that shows that whites will help a black confederate more than a white confederate after injuring him. What would happen if the situation were one to provoke hostility and not sympathy?

30. Katz and Haas argue that white Americans' attitudes of sympathy and hostility toward blacks derive from a conflict of two core values. What are they? What is the correlation between the score on a scale measuring humanitarianism and attitudes toward blacks? What is the correlation between the score on a scale measuring support for the work ethic and attitudes toward blacks?

Ambivalence Research Considered

31. One factor affecting whether someone's race will affect behavior toward him or her is whether or not race is an explicit issue in the interaction. When race is *not* an explicit issue, white reactions to blacks are complex. Explain and give examples from the studies presented.

COGNITIVE APPROACHES

What Are Stereotypes?

32. According to the cognitive approach prejudice is a matter of beliefs and fallible memory. Explain.

33. Describe what "stereotypes" are. What is the problem in using stereotypes?

34. If someone says that a trait is characteristic of a group, for instance, x's are overly fond of y, does he mean that every single member of x has this weakness? What is a more sensible interpretation of what people are asserting when they use a stereotype?

Why Do Stereotypes Develop?

35. Describe the three accounts proposed to explain why stereotypes develop. Does the shared distinctiveness account of the development of stereotypes see stereotypes as coming from motivational or informational processes? What is the outgroup homogeneity account of the development of stereotypes? What is the cultural view of the development of stereotypes? How is it different from the cognitive view?

The Shared Distinctiveness Account

36. Explain how the shared distinctiveness account can be used to explain racial prejudice. What is an illusory correlation? How could illusory correlations give rise to stereotypes? Describe Hamilton's attempt to show the role of illusory correlations in the development of prejudice.

The Outgroup Homogeneity Account

37. When does it make sense to generalize from the characteristics of one or a few members of a group to members of the group as a whole? According to outgroup homogeneity theory, in what way does our belief that an outgroup is homogeneous and our own group is heterogeneous affect the development of stereotypes? Does competition between groups have any

effect on the likelihood of seeing the outgroup as homogeneous?

The Cultural Account

38. Describe how LeVine and Campbell account for the stereotypes of Jews and blacks.

How Are Stereotypes Maintained?

39. Describe how once a stereotype is formed "illusory correlations" might play a part in its maintenance.

Differential Remembering and the Illusory Correlation

40. Describe what happens when people selectively forget cases that clash with their stereotypes. Do people better remember stereotype-consistent information than stereotype-inconsistent information? Give an example of a study showing that bias takes effect at the point of encoding and one that shows that it can also occur at the point of recall.

Typicality of Exemplars

41. Let us say that you meet, contrary to your beliefs about academics, a professor who is not absent-minded. When will you be most likely to revise your opinion of professors—when the professor is typical of professors in other ways or atypical?

42. Describe Wilder's experiment in which students pleasantly or unpleasantly interacted with stereotypical or atypical members of a rival school. Which interactions improved their views of their rivals?

43. Stereotypes aren't easily upset by a few counterexamples since people can decide that the counterexamples are just exceptions. What is needed to upset a stereotype? Note the footnote discussing when the segregation of atypical instances is irrational or not.

The Accuracy of Stereotypes

44. In 1936 LaPiere solicited stereotypes of the Armenian community. What were they? How accurate were they? Describe the 1978 study of the accuracy of stereotypes that whites had of blacks. How accurate were they? In what direction?

Prejudice and the Use of Stereotypes

45. People often find it distressing to learn that some elements of stereotypes are true. Why? Is prejudice evidenced by believing certain stereotypes, or by using them unfairly or harmfully?

46. Sometimes using stereotypes, even accurate ones, demonstrates prejudice and sometimes it does not. What is the difference between the two uses? Do people in a culture, even those who are unprejudiced, know the stereotypes current in the culture? Are they sometimes unconsciously influenced by these stereotypes.

The Immoral Use of Correct Information

47. It is sometimes morally wrong to act on the basis of stereotypes, *whether accurate or not.* Explain. Present the text's example of a personnel manager having to decide between a black and a white applicant. Explain why it is wrong to use group data to make the decision, even correct group data, when it is possible to check the particular case.

Stereotypes and the Attribution of Responsibility

48. Ethnocentrism may not show up as much in the content of stereotypes as in the assessment of responsibility for having the stereotyped characteristic. Give an example. In the study of Hindus how did they handle the reported good acts and bad acts of Hindus and Moslems? Were the results of this study replicated with Malays and Chinese in Malaya? In Singapore?

PREJUDICE RECONSIDERED

An Assessment of the Cognitive Approach

49. The essential aspect of stereotypes is that they are perpetually reinforced, not by contact with their targets, but through contact with other people, especially those we love and trust, who believe them. What is the implication of this approach for the strong form of the cognitive position?

An Assessment of the Motivational Approach

50. Describe the two essential unresolved questions about the authoritarian personality.

An Assessment of the Cultural Approach

51. The attractiveness of the cultural approach is that we don't pick the target of our prejudice ourselves. We are taught whom to hate and fear. Give some examples from different societies. What are the weak and strong forms of the cultural approach? Which is more plausible?

Programmed Exercises

WHAT IS PREJUDICE?

1. Prejudice is distinguished from discrimination in that prejudice is a matter of _____, and discrimination a matter of behavior.

attitudes

Discriminatory Behavior

2. Discrimination is _____ always the result of a prejudiced attitude.

not

3. Institutional racism is the result of institutional pressures rather than a direct result of _____ attitudes.

prejudiced

4. Discrimination is _____ treatment regardless of cause.

unfair

Prejudiced Attitudes

5. Prejudice may refer to beliefs, impulses, or _____.

evaluations

6. A _____ person believes in the inherent inferiority of some group, or evaluates people negatively just on the basis of their belonging to a group, or wishes to attack someone just on the basis of their belonging to a group.

prejudiced

7. The various measures of prejudice have been found to _____ to a reasonable degree.

correlate

8. The notion of "stereotype" suggests a belief about a group that is _____, inaccurate, and difficult to change.

unfavorable

Sources of Prejudice

9. Social scientists have three sorts of approaches to the origins of prejudice. They are the _____, the _____, and the _____ approaches.

cultural, motivational, cognitive

THE CULTURAL VIEW

Realistic Conflict Theory

10. According to realistic conflict theory, a conflict over _____ is at the heart of prejudice.

resources

11. When an ingroup comes into conflict with an outgroup, first the relations between competitors become hostile; then they begin to _____ the other group; then they begin to act toward the other group in ways they had previously seen as immoral. Finally, the loyalty of the group to itself, the ingroup, becomes _____.

stereotype

greater

12. According to Sherif, conflict between groups leads each group to adopt a _____ internal structure. Conflict also leads the groups to feel _____ to their own group and hostility to the outgroup. Further, conflict causes each ingroup to think of the outgroup in a stereotyped, _____ way and to _____ the performance of the ingroup relative to the outgroup.

hierarchical
loyalty

derogatory,
overvalue

13. If two groups share a _____ goal, then neither group can reach the goal alone, but both groups can attain the goal if they work _____.

superordinate
together

14. Sherif proposed that _____ between groups can be overcome if, and only if, the groups found that they had a _____ goal.

hostility
superordinate

15. Twenty normal boys randomly divided into two groups for a "summer camp" "accidentally" met each other and were somewhat _____.

hostile

16. In the second stage of the experiment Sherif introduced _____ by creating a competitive tournament in which the winning team would receive a nice jackknife.

conflict

17. Sherif found, using counselors ratings, that the leadership hierarchies in each group became more _____ with conflict.

rigid

18. Both groups negatively _____ the outgroup as could be seen by the insults they used and by their reactions on a trait checklist; they very favorably characterized their own group.

stereotyped

19. The groups of campers were brought together socially (noncompetitively) seven times. The conflict _____.

escalated

20. Sherif arranged for the two groups to have a _____ goal: to cooperate in fixing a water supply, or pulling a truck out of the mud. This reduced conflict between the groups as can be seen by the decline in name calling and a reduction in the assignment of _____ traits to the outgroup.

superordinate

negative

21. For adults, conflict between groups is especially likely to be reduced if each group has a distinct _____ in achieving the shared goal.

role

22. The Robbers Cave experiment is a full-bodied realization of a theoretical point since it was not done in a _____, where people are on guard, or with strangers, or with artificial independent variables.

laboratory

23. One problem with Sherif's interpretation of his experiment is that the _____ occurred before material conflict was introduced. It is possible that conflict _____ hostility but is not necessary for it.

hostility
increases

24. Aronson's jigsaw classroom technique involves giving small multi-ethnic groups a joint task to perform with each member of the group having a necessary component for the task's _____. This forces the groups to participate together in the pursuit of a _____ goal.

solution
superordinate

25. Using the jigsaw classroom technique reduces inter-ethnic hostility; this _____ Sherif's realistic conflict theory.

supports

Minimal Group Research

26. Tajfel argues that competition is not necessary for ethnocentrism, rather the mere formation of two groups on a trivial basis will be _____ to produce ingroup favoritism.

sufficient

27. People will assign (as a first impression) more favorable traits to, remember more favorable information about, and vote to reward more members of their _____ _____ as against members of another group.

minimal group

28. Social identity theory claims that subjects in minimal groups overfavor their own group to enhance their own _____ and _____-_____.

status, self-esteem

29. According to social identity theory, in order to enhance their status group members may evaluate an *unlikable* member of their group more _____ than an equally unlikable member of another group. This is called the _____-_____ effect.

negatively
black-sheep

THE MOTIVATIONAL APPROACHES

Frustration-Aggression Theory

30. According to Freud, the chronic frustrations of childhood produce a chronic hostility toward the parents which is _____ onto safer targets.

displaced

31. Hovland and Sears found an inverse correlation between the price of cotton and the number of _____ of blacks in the South (between 1882 and 1930). The frustration-aggression account of this correlation is that as the Southern economy worsened white Southerners took their _____ out on a safe and available target.

lynchings

frustration

32. Frustration-aggression theory best explains why ethnocentrism will be incited in _____ economic periods, but since the effects of frustration on prejudice are general, it does not explain why specific groups become targets; it also does not account for the glorification of the _____.

bad

ingroup

The Authoritarian Personality

33. Adorno and colleagues believe that the basic cause of authoritarianism is harsh _____-_____ practices.

child-rearing

34. According to Freud, if a child is severely punished for aggressive behavior he will deny that he has aggressive desires and _____ these disapproved desires onto others.

project

35. According to Adorno and colleagues, harsh discipline has the additional effect of creating an attachment to, and _____ of, powerful figures.

fear

36. The *correlation* between authoritarianism and ethnocentrism is approximately the _____ for all regions of the country. This suggests that the difference in prejudice between areas is determined by _____ and _____. On the other hand, F scores are related to how prejudiced a person is in _____ to other people in the same area.

same
culture
history
comparison

Prejudice and Ambivalence

37. In *The American Dilemma*, Gunnar Myrdal analyzed American race relations in terms of _____ motives. Northern prejudice in particular was torn between a belief in the equality of all people and _____ toward blacks.

conflicted
hostility

38. Weitz assessed the attitudes of white students to blacks using a questionnaire, and then had them interact with a black confederate. Some students who rated themselves as _____ on the questionnaire were ill at ease during the conversation.

sympathetic

39. Weitz suggested that this discrepancy was due to a conflict between explicit _____ and hidden _____.

values, feelings

40. Weitz claimed that sympathy will be more likely to be expressed when the situation makes clear what fairness demands, but when the appropriate standard in a situation is less clear then _____ will show.

prejudice (hostility)

41. The helping behavior of liberal white students in an emergency was studied. Either a white or a black confederate participating in the experiment with them had an accident in another room. There was _____ difference in response to a victim of either race when the subject believed that she was alone

no

with the victim. Subjects were _____ likely to help victims of either
race when they believed that someone else could also help. The decrease in
helping for the black Confederate in this situation was _____ than the
decrease in helping for the white confederate.

    less

    greater

42. According to Katz and Glass, the conflict in Northern whites between
sympathy and hostility toward blacks will cause whatever response is
expressed to be _____.

    amplified

43. Subjects who believed that they had injured a confederate, regardless of the
confederate's race, helped _____ than those who hadn't injured the
confederate. If the injured confederate was black, white subjects helped
_____ than if he was white.

    more

    more

44. In conditions where the situation is designed to produce hostility, whites are
_____ hostile to blacks than they are to whites.

    more

COGNITIVE APPROACHES

What Are Stereotypes?

45. According to the cognitive approach, at root, prejudice is a matter of beliefs
and fallible _____.

    memory

46. _____ are preconceptions that oversimplify and treat individuals as if
they only were members of a group.

    Stereotypes

47. People who affirm stereotypes rarely believe that all members of the stereotyped group have a certain characteristic, rather they believe that members of
the group are _____ likely to have the characteristic. To hold a stereotype is to believe that there is a _____ between being a member of an
ethnic group and having certain traits.

    more
    correlation

Why Do Stereotypes Develop?

48. According to the _____ _____ account, the development of
stereotypes is due to information-processing bias rather than motivational bias.

    shared
    distinctiveness

49. The _____ _____ account sees stereotypes as deriving from
merely dividing people into ingroups and outgroups.

    outgroup
    homogeneity

50. According to the cultural account, the _____ of a culture determines
the particular content that various stereotypes have.

    history

51. In certain circumstances if two distinctive events sometimes occur at the same
time people will come to believe that there is a correlation between them, that
they generally go together. This is called an _____ _____.

    illusory correlation

52. If and only if we believe that a group is _____ does it make sense to
generalize from a few members to the group as a whole.

    homogeneous

53. According to outgroup homogeneity theory, people are likely to see outgroups
as _____ and ingroups as _____.

    homogeneous
    heterogeneous

54. Competition between groups _____ the tendency to see the outgroup
as homogeneous.

    heightens

How Are Stereotypes Maintained?

55. If people expect there will be a _____ between two things, then they are more likely to see it even if there is none in reality.

correlation

56. If people tend to forget cases that clash with their stereotypes but remember cases that conform to their stereotypes, then they will perceive an

_____ _____.

illusory correlation

57. People are more likely to remember _____-_____ information than _____-_____ information.

stereotype-consistent
stereotype-inconsistent

58. If one discovers an exception to a stereotyped class one is more likely to modify the stereotype if the exception is in other ways _____ of the class. Stereotypes are not upset by a few counterexamples since they can be perceived as _____ of the class.

typical

atypical

The Accuracy of Stereotypes

59. In 1936 LaPiere solicited stereotypes of California's Armenians. They were believed to be much more likely than the average Californian to have been on welfare and in trouble with the law. In fact Armenians were much _____ likely to have been on welfare or to have had trouble with the police.

less

60. In a 1978 study subjects were asked to estimate such things as the percentage of adult black Americans and Americans in general who were on welfare, who were born out of wedlock, who had not completed high school, and so forth. On about one-half of the measures the subjects _____ the difference between blacks and whites.

underestimated

61. Prejudice may be shown by _____ bringing up, emphasizing, or talking about even an accurate stereotype. What is prejudicial is how the talk is used.

unfairly

62. Sometimes just having a stereotype available, even for an unprejudiced person, _____ attitudes.

influences

63. It is morally wrong to do something to an individual on the basis of even *accurate* stereotypes about his group if there is better information about her in _____ at hand.

particular

64. If blacks have a 49 percent high school graduation rate and whites have a 51 percent graduation rate, and a high school diploma is required for a job, then it would be rational, if the above information were the only information you had to go on, to hire a _____ each time there was a choice between a white and a black. This rational policy would wind up with _____ whites and _____ blacks hired.

white
all
no

65. One reason why this rational policy is unfair is that there is in fact a better source of making an estimate of the educational level of the applicant than referring to the average educational level for his group. You can easily find out from the _____ whether he graduated from high school.

applicant

66. Ethnocentrism may not show up as much in the content of stereotypes as in the assessment of _____ for having the stereotyped characteristic.

responsibility

67. In a study in South India, Hindus were presented with stories of desirable or undesirable acts committed by Hindus or Muslims. Hindus found _____ for the Hindus' undesirable acts and reasons to deny credit for the Muslims' _____ acts.

excuses

desirable

PREJUDICE RECONSIDERED

An Assessment of the Cognitive Approach

68. The essential aspect of stereotypes is that they are perpetually reinforced, not by contact with their targets, but through contact with other people, especially those we love and trust, who _____ them.

believe

69. The cognitive defects that the cognitive approaches point out help support these _____ and make them harder to shake.

distortions

An Assessment of the Motivational Approach

70. Two not-yet-resolved questions about the authoritarian personality are what is the _____ of the syndrome and how the syndrome relates to childhood.

essence

71. The text suggests that the heart of authoritarianism is an attachment to a society's _____ beliefs. When the society is prejudiced against a particular group, the authoritarian will be prejudiced; when it is not, he will not be prejudiced.

conventional

An Assessment of the Cultural Approach

72. Realistic conflict theory suggests that groups become prejudiced against other groups when competition over _____ _____ or _____ is provoked.

material resources, status

73. At the least, conflict is an important contributor to prejudice; cross-cultural evidence is needed to determine whether the strong form of the cultural hypothesis, that conflict is necessary and _____ to produce prejudice, is correct.

sufficient

Self-Test

1. Prejudice is distinguished from discrimination in that prejudice is a matter of attitudes and discrimination a matter of
   a. feelings.
   b. thoughts.
   c. neurosis.
   d. behavior.

2. Discrimination
   a. is always a result of prejudice.
   b. is always personal and never institutional.
   c. is unfair treatment regardless of the reason for the treatment.
   d. is only against racial groups.

3. A prejudiced person may
   a. believe in the inherent inferiority of some group.
   b. evaluate people negatively just on the basis of their belonging to a group.
   c. wish to attack people just because they belong to a group.
   d. all of the above

4. The notion of "stereotype" suggests a belief about a group that is
   a. unfavorable, inaccurate, and difficult to change by evidence.
   b. unfavorable, inaccurate, but easy to change by evidence.
   c. just unfavorable.
   d. specific and flexible.

5. Realistic conflict theory holds that
   a. psychological conflict is at the heart of prejudice.
   b. conflict over resources causes prejudice.
   c. faulty cognitive processing causes prejudice.
   d. all of the above

6. According to realistic conflict theory, when a group comes into conflict with an outgroup what happens?
   a. The group becomes hostile to the competing outgroup.
   b. The group begins to stereotype the other group.
   c. The loyalty of the group to itself, the ingroup, becomes greater.
   d. all of the above

7. A pattern of hostility to an outgroup and intense loyalty to an ingroup is called
   a. being a groupie.
   b. loyalty.
   c. ethnocentrism.
   d. common sense.

8. According to Sherif, entering into conflict with another group will have all the following effects but one. Which of the following is *not* a result of group conflict?
   a. The group will adopt a more hierarchical structure.
   b. The group's authority relations will become more flexible.
   c. Loyalty to the ingroup and overvaluing of their achievements will increase.
   d. Negative stereotyping of, and hostility toward, the outgroup will increase.

9. Sherif proposed that hostility between two competing groups could be overcome if
   a. they studied religion.
   b. they channeled their competition to sports.
   c. they needed to cooperate on a goal that neither group could reach without the help of the other.
   d. if they were not incited by outsiders but allowed to act in the way they wanted to.

10. In Sherif's Robbers Cave experiment, two groups of randomly selected boys in the setting of a summer camp competed for a prize. According to ratings of their counselors
    a. the boys' leadership hierarchy became less rigid after the competition began.

b. the boys had fewer negative stereotypes of boys in the other group after they got to know them through competition.
    c. they were more realistic about the virtues and failings of members of their own team after competition began.
    d. the leadership hierarchy became more rigid, and there was more negative stereotyping of the outgroup and positive stereotyping of the ingroup.

11. In Sherif's Robbers Cave experiment, there was a contest involving which group could pick the most beans. After the contest, each boy's collection of beans (in reality the same number of beans) was projected on a screen and everyone had to estimate the amount. Each group
    a. underestimated its performance relative to the other.
    b. correctly estimated its own performance, but overestimated the other group's performance.
    c. overestimated its performance relative to the other group.
    d. misestimated its performance but correctly estimated the other group's performance.

12. In the Robbers Cave experiment, after the two groups had become hostile noncompetitive contact between the two groups was introduced. What was the result?
    a. Hostility between the two groups was reduced.
    b. Hostility between the two groups increased.
    c. At first there was no change in the level of hostility, but after a day the hostility greatly decreased.
    d. There was no change in the level of hostility.

13. In the Robbers Cave experiment, it was arranged that the two groups of campers had to cooperate in fixing a broken water tank and pulling out a truck stuck in mud. Having these superordinate goals
    a. reduced hostility.
    b. increased name calling.
    c. increased competition.
    d. increased the use of unfriendly or nasty traits to describe the outgroup.

14. Adults in competing groups who come to have a superordinate goal are particularly likely to reduce hostility if each group
    a. has nicknames for the members of the other group.

b. has no distinct role in achieving the superordinate goal.

c. has a distinct role in achieving the superordinate goal.

d. has some way to reintroduce competition into their relationship.

15. A drawback of the Robbers Cave experiment as a confirmation of realistic conflict theory is that

a. the two groups of boys did not become hostile to each other.

b. the boys had been selected from a population of delinquents.

c. the boys became aggressive toward each other immediately upon their discovery of each other (before competition was introduced).

d. the counselors constantly prodded the boys into becoming aggressive, and the two groups were not allowed noncompetitive contact.

16. Although white American soldiers were initially hostile to having platoons of black soldiers fight near them, after the forced integration the reaction of the white soldiers was strongly positive. Does this finding support or refute realistic conflict theory?

a. It supports realistic conflict theory since there was a superordinate goal, fighting the enemy, and the officers, who according to the theory, command greater respect in situations of conflict, supported integration.

b. It refutes realistic conflict theory since hostility between blacks and whites did not increase.

c. It is irrelevant to realistic conflict theory since there were no conflicts inherent in the situation.

d. It refutes realistic conflict theory since if the officers had not supported integration there probably would have been considerable hostility expressed by the men.

17. In the "jigsaw classroom," multi-ethnic class groups are each given a piece of a joint task. The contribution of all members of the group is necessary to solve the task. This is an application of Sherif's concept of

a. a disordered goal as a means to reducing intergroup tension.

b. a superordinate goal as a means of increasing intergroup tension.

c. a superordinate goal as a means of reducing intergroup tension.

d. competition as a means to increase intergroup friendship.

18. In Tajfel's experiments, if one is a member of a "minimal group" one believes that there is some minor basis for assignment to that group although

a. the basis for assignment takes into account very important personal characteristics.

b. assignment to a group is really random.

c. assignment to a group is based on religion.

d. assignment to a group is based on the minimal number of important personality traits sufficient to distinguish one personality type from another.

19. A member of a minimal group will

a. reward ingroup members more than outsiders.

b. will rate the characteristics of ingroup members higher than those of outgroup members.

c. remember more favorable behaviors of ingroup members than of members of the outgroup.

d. all of the above

20. Social identity theory claims that subjects in minimal groups over-favor their own group to enhance their own

a. pleasure and long-term happiness.

b. material rewards.

c. status and increase their self-esteem.

d. anger and increase righteous indignation.

21. Subjects in minimal groups either were allowed to divide up points between their group and another, or they had to read a newspaper. Subjects who divided up points showed more ingroup bias and also showed

a. less self-esteem than newspaper readers.

b. more self-esteem than newspaper readers.

c. more self-questioning than newspaper readers.

d. less self-directed anger than newspaper readers.

22. When group members show the "black-sheep effect"

a. they evaluate an unlikable member of their own group more negatively than an equally unlikable member of another group.

b. they evaluate an unlikable member of their

own group more positively than an equally unlikable member of another group.

c. they "pull the wool over the eyes" of a gullible member of their own group.

d. they are attempting to decrease the status of their own group.

23. Social identity theory's emphasis on status best illuminates what fact about prejudice?
    a. Prejudice is most intense in periods of economic hardship.
    b. Prejudice against an outgroup occurs when there is a conflict between groups over material rewards.
    c. Some personalities are more "open" to prejudice than others.
    d. Prejudice is strongest in the lowest class.

24. According to Freud, the chronic frustrations of childhood produce a chronic hostility toward the parents which
    a. is displaced onto safer targets.
    b. completely disappears with age.
    c. causes people to physically attack their parents as soon as they are able.
    d. all of the above

25. According to the "frustration-aggression hypothesis," frustration always causes
    a. aggression or anger against some convenient outlet.
    b. sublimation.
    c. a desire to create great art.
    d. sadness.

26. Hovland and Sears found an inverse correlation between the price of cotton and the number of lynchings of blacks in the South. The frustration-aggression account of this correlation is that as the economy worsened white Southerners
    a. believed that blacks were the cause of the economic hard times.
    b. took out their frustrations on a safe and available target.
    c. were not frustrated; they lynched blacks just because they were racist.
    d. all of the above

27. Camp counselors were frustrated by being made to take tedious tests instead of going to a show that they expected to attend. How did they rate minorities both before and after the frustration?
    a. They used more favorable trait terms after they were frustrated.

b. They used the same number of favorable trait terms before and after they were frustrated.

c. They used fewer favorable trait terms after they were frustrated.

d. They refused to fill out the rating scales because the tests were too tedious.

28. What may be concluded from the above study?
    a. Frustration increased prejudice to minorities but did not increase general hostility.
    b. Frustration may have increased hostility in general and may, or may not, have increased hostility to minorities in particular.
    c. Frustration increased hostility to minorities but decreased hostility in general.
    d. Frustration had different effects on different people.

29. Berkowitz insulted female college students who had measured high (or low) on anti-Semitism and had them work with a Jewish (or non-Jewish) confederate. What were the results?
    a. Insulted anti-Semitic students were more hostile to Jewish but not Christian confederates (than non-anti-Semitic students).
    b. Insulted anti-Semitic students were more hostile to both Jewish and Christian confederates (than non-anti-Semitic students).
    c. Insulted anti-Semitic students became more withdrawn (than non-anti-Semitic students).
    d. Insulted anti-Semitic students became friendlier (than non-anti-Semitic students).

30. Frustration-aggression theory best accounts for
    a. why a particular group is targeted for hostility.
    b. why some people are more prejudiced than others (assuming frustrations are held constant).
    c. the glorification of the ingroup.
    d. when ethnocentrism will be incited.

31. According to the authors of *The Authoritarian Personality*,
    a. prejudice derives from conflict between groups.
    b. prejudice is a matter of personality; people who were spoiled as children tend to be prejudiced.
    c. susceptibility to prejudice is a personality trait with roots in a child's early experience with harsh discipline.
    d. prejudice is merely a means to advance economic self-interest.

32. The studies in *The Authoritarian Personality* employed scales to measure anti-Semitism (A-S Scale), ethnocentrism (E Scale), and susceptibility to fascism (F Scale). The following is likely to be an example from which scale: "Anyone who employs many people should be careful not to hire a large percentage of Jews."
    a. the E Scale
    b. the A-S Scale
    c. the F Scale
    d. the A & P Scale

33. The studies in *The Authoritarian Personality* employed scales to measure anti-Semitism (A-S Scale), ethnocentrism (E Scale), and susceptibility to fascism (F Scale). The following is likely to be an example from which scale: "The main threat to basic American institutions during this century has come from foreign ideas, doctrines, and agitators."
    a. the E Scale
    b. the A-S Scale
    c. the F Scale
    d. the P Scale

34. The studies in *The Authoritarian Personality* employed scales to measure anti-Semitism (A-S Scale), ethnocentrism (E Scale), and susceptibility to fascism (F Scale). The following is likely to be an example from which scale: "Obedience and respect for authority are the most important virtues children should learn."
    a. the E Scale
    b. the ABC Scale
    c. the F Scale
    d. the A-S Scale

35. The correlation between the E Scale and the A-S Scale was
    a. almost zero.
    b. quite high.
    c. low to moderate.
    d. inconsistent.

36. All of the items of the F, E, and A-S Scales are written in the same manner; that is, they are clichés written so that agreement will count as ethnocentrism, anti-Semitism, etc. The problem with this is
    a. prejudice people who do not like clichés will not come off as prejudiced as they really are.
    b. gullible, but not particularly prejudiced, subjects might agree with the statements because of their form, and they might appear to be prejudiced.

    c. gullible, prejudiced people will appear less prejudiced than they really are.
    d. all of the above

37. The biased manner of phrasing questions was corrected on a new questionnaire to measure prejudice. The correlation between prejudice, as measured by the new questionnaire, and the F Scale was
    a. negative.
    b. much lower.
    c. slightly lower, but still quite high.
    d. zero.

38. Counselors were given the F Scale, and their scores were computed. At the end of the season, campers were asked to rate how authoritarian their counselors were. There was
    a. almost no relation between a counselors' scores on the F Scale and campers' judgments of their authoritarianism.
    b. a moderate correlation between counselors' scores on the F Scale and campers' judgments of their authoritarianism.
    c. an almost perfect relation (+.97) between counselors' F Scale scores and campers' judgments of their authoritarianism.
    d. no consistent correlation.

39. The authors of *The Authoritarian Personality* believed that the authoritarian's projection of aggressive and sexual desires, and attachment to and fear of powerful figures (resulting in conventionality) derived from which cause?
    a. being spoiled as a child
    b. being poor
    c. being the victim of harsh child-rearing practices
    d. not being breast-fed

40. Those who focus on personality and development believe that prejudice is attractive to authoritarians because of how they were treated as children; those with a *social* focus believe that
    a. those parts of society that are prejudiced are also likely to be authoritarian, but that one does not cause the other.
    b. only overindulgence in childhood causes authoritarianism.
    c. prejudice is not attractive to authoritarians except for prejudice against sexual minorities.
    d. being brought up in an unprejudiced family that does not use harsh discipline will cause a child to become an authoritarian.

41. People in the South (as of 1964) were found to be more prejudiced against minorities and have a higher F score than people in other areas. This is
    a. only consistent with the personality view of prejudice.
    b. only consistent with the social view of prejudice.
    c. consistent with both the social and the personality views of prejudice.
    d. consistent with neither the personality nor the social views of prejudice.

42. The correlation between authoritarianism and ethnocentrism is approximately the same for all regions of the country even though some regions have a higher absolute level of prejudice. This suggests that
    a. absolute level of prejudice is determined by the history of an area, but that F scores show personality, or at least, how prejudiced a person is in comparison to others in her area.
    b. history and culture have nothing to do with the level of prejudice in an area.
    c. prejudice is purely a matter of history and culture; everyone in an area is prejudiced to approximately the same degree.
    d. F scores are unrelated to prejudice.

43. Weitz assessed the attitudes of white students to blacks using a questionnaire, and then she had them interact with a black confederate. Some students who rated themselves as sympathetic on the questionnaire were ill at ease during the conversation. Weitz suggested that this discrepancy was due to a conflict between
    a. explicit values and explicit interests.
    b. implicit values and covert selfishness.
    c. explicit values and hidden feelings
    d. hidden values and strident fears.

44. According to Weitz, sometimes a person's explicit values and sometimes her hidden fears will determine how she will act. Explicit values dominate in situations where the demands of fairness are clear. When will hidden fears dominate?
    a. when the standards of fairness are clear but unenforceable
    b. when it is unclear what fairness demands in a particular situation
    c. when the person knows that they can get away with being prejudiced
    d. all of the above

45. The helping behavior of liberal, white students in an emergency was studied. Either a white or a black confederate participating in the experiment had an accident in another room. There was
    a. less helping of whites than blacks, both when the subject believed that she was alone with the victim and when she believed that someone else could also help.
    b. more helping of whites than blacks, both when the subject believed that she was alone with the victim and when she believed that someone else could also help.
    c. equal helping of whites and blacks when the subject believed that she was alone with the victim, but the black was helped less when the subject believed that someone else could also help.
    d. there was almost no helping of either whites or blacks in either condition.

46. Katz and Glass argue that the attitude of many Northern whites to blacks is complex. The attitude derives from
    a. egalitarian values.
    b. feelings of sympathy for blacks.
    c. feelings of hostility to blacks.
    d. all of the above

47. According to Katz and Glass the conflict between sympathy and hostility will cause whatever response is expressed to be
    a. reduced.
    b. eliminated.
    c. amplified.
    d. insincere.

48. White subjects read a harsh personality description to a black or white confederate who was supposedly upset by it. The confederate then requested the subject's assistance on a boring task. Subjects who believed that they had injured a confederate, regardless of the confederate's race, helped
    a. more than those who hadn't injured the confederate, and helped the black confederate even more than the white.
    b. less than those who hadn't injured the confederate.
    c. more than those who hadn't injured the confederate, but helped the white more than the black.
    d. more than those who hadn't injured the confederate; the black and white confederates were helped equally.

49. In experimental conditions designed to make whites hostile to a black or white confederate, whites react with
    a. less hostility to a white confederate than to a black confederate.
    b. more hostility to a white confederate than to a black confederate.
    c. fear and loathing.
    d. with equal hostility to both the black and white confederate.

50. According to the "cognitive approach," prejudice is a matter of
    a. conflicting interests.
    b. personality.
    c. irrationality.
    d. beliefs and fallible memory.

51. Stereotypes
    a. are preconceptions.
    b. simplify reality.
    c. treat individuals as if they were only members of a group.
    d. all of the above

52. To hold a stereotype is to believe that being a member of an ethnic group and having certain traits are
    a. correlated.
    b. unrelated.
    c. dependent on the particularities of the individual.
    d. perfectly related for every member of the group.

53. According to the shared distinctiveness account of the development of stereotypes, stereotypes derive from
    a. motivational bias.
    b. practical conflicts.
    c. information-processing bias.
    d. a diet poor in vitamin L.

54. According to the outgroup homogeneity account of stereotypes, stereotypes derive from
    a. merely dividing people into groups.
    b. a history of conflict between groups.
    c. harsh child-rearing practices.
    d. an economic conflict.

55. According to the shared distinctiveness account, in certain circumstances, if two distinctive events sometimes occur at the same time people will come to believe that there is a correlation between them, and that they generally go together. This is called an
    a. illegitimate inference.
    b. a spasmodic comment.
    c. an illusory correlation.
    d. an inverted matrix.

56. Hamilton has experimentally shown that in a situation where there is no correlation between group membership and unfavorable acts subjects will over-assign rarer undesirable acts to the
    a. smaller group.
    b. larger group.
    c. Rotarian group.
    d. group without powerful members.

57. Hamilton's thesis is too broad since
    a. there are some rare positive events that occur with infrequent negative events, but we don't associate them.
    b. it would hold that, since being a heroine is uncommon and injecting cocaine mixed with turpentine is uncommon, we should believe that heroines inject cocaine mixed with turpentine.
    c. there are no cases in which distinctive events occurring at the same time cause people to form an illusory correlation.
    d. a and b.

58. It only makes sense to generalize from a few members of a group to a group as a whole if we believe that the group is
    a. unpopular.
    b. dangerous.
    c. unusual.
    d. homogeneous.

59. According to the outgroup homogeneity account, people are likely to see
    a. outgroups as heterogeneous and ingroups as homogeneous.
    b. outgroups as violent and ingroups as peaceful.
    c. outgroups as prejudiced and ingroups as fair.
    d. outgroups as homogeneous and ingroups as heterogeneous.

60. In an experiment in which Rutgers and Princeton students had to decide what percent of students in each institution would do the same as a sample student presented on videotape, students believed that those who were from the opposing institution were
    a. more homogeneous in their choices than those in their own institution.

b. less homogeneous in their choices than those in their own institution.

c. more variable in their choices than those in their own institution.

d. neither more nor less homogeneous in their choices than those in their own institution.

61. Competition between groups does what to the tendency to see the outgroup as homogeneous?
a. It reduces this tendency.
b. It heightens this tendency.
c. It has no effect on this tendency.
d. It reverses this tendency.

62. According to LeVine and Campbell the typical stereotypes of Jews are stereotypes of _____ dwellers held by rural dwellers, and some of the stereotypes of blacks are stereotypes that urban people have of _____ people.
a. rural, urban
b. urban, rural
c. cave, strange
d. none of the above

63. To calculate a correlation, say, between being wealthy and being a doctor involves four pieces of information: the number of wealthy doctors, the number of poor doctors, the number of wealthy non-doctors, and the number of
a. wealthy chiropractors.
b. poor optometrists.
c. poor non-doctors.
d. doctors who don't cheat on income tax.

64. The more cases of wealthy doctors and poor non-doctors
a. the higher the correlation between wealth and being a doctor.
b. the lower the correlation between wealth and being a doctor.
c. the more likely that doctors cheat on income tax.
d. the more likely that non-doctors are oppressed.

65. If you were selectively to forget cases of poor doctors and wealthy non-doctors, you would incorrectly perceive the correlation between being wealthy and being a doctor to be
a. lower than it really is.
b. about what it really is.
c. higher than it really is.
d. zero.

66. If people tend to forget cases that clash with their stereotypes but remember cases that conform to their stereotypes they will perceive
a. clearly.
b. illusory correlations.
c. the world as more threatening than it really is.
d. all of the above

67. Subjects who were told that a group was particularly friendly remembered more information about the group that was consistent with
a. friendliness than was consistent with, say, intelligence.
b. arrogance than was consistent with humility.
c. suspiciousness than was consistent with openness.
d. vice than was consistent with virtue.

68. If one discovers an exception to a stereotyped class, one is more likely to modify the stereotype if the exception is in other ways
a. atypical of the class.
b. an exception to the class.
c. typical of the class.
d. nicer than the class.

69. Women from rival colleges had a pleasant or unpleasant interaction with a confederate who was quite typical or atypical of the stereotype for students from the rival college. The pleasant interaction improved the students' impression of their rival school only with the confederate who was
a. atypical of the stereotype of the school.
b. typical of the stereotype of the school.
c. smarter than the average member of her school.
d. more athletic than the average member of her school.

70. For a stereotype to be eroded it is better to have
a. a few large deviations from the stereotype rather than many small deviations.
b. a few small deviations rather than a few large deviations.
c. many small deviations rather than a few large deviations.
d. many small deviations rather than many large deviations.

71. Even when a stereotype is correct it sometimes shows prejudice if one
a. brings it up repeatedly in the wrong circumstances.

b. mentions it.

c. believes it.

d. all of the above

72. Sometimes just having a stereotype available, even for an unprejudiced person, can
   a. cause a person to unfairly discriminate.
   b. can subtly influence attitudes.
   c. make a person less susceptible to prejudiced thinking.
   d. make a person a racist.

73. It is morally wrong to do something to a person on the basis of even accurate stereotypes about his group if there is
   a. better information about the person at hand.
   b. known to have been past discrimination against his group.
   c. known to have been inaccurate stereotypes held about the group in the past.
   d. all of the above

74. If blacks have a 49 percent high school graduation rate and whites have a 51 percent graduation rate, and a high school diploma is required for a job, then it would be rational (maximize the number of hired high school graduates), if this were the only information to go on to hire
   a. only blacks.
   b. only whites.
   c. a black and then a white.
   d. 21 percent blacks.

75. The above rational policy would be unfair because
   a. too few blacks would be hired.
   b. too few whites would be hired.
   c. too few Asians would be hired.
   d. there was a better source of information available (than the stereotype)—the applicant himself.

76. There is a possible additional source of unfairness in the above example:
   a. Fewer than 49 percent of blacks might be hired.
   b. Fewer than 51 percent of whites might be hired.
   c. A high school diploma might not really be necessary for the position, and yet serve to screen out blacks.
   d. Blacks are said to have a lower graduation rate than whites.

77. Subjects who were acting as personnel managers had to judge the severity and likelihood of recurrence of a transgression. When the transgression appeared typical of the employee's ethnic group, then the punishment recommended was severer and the probability of recurrence was believed to be
   a. higher than when the transgression was stereotype-inconsistent.
   b. lower than when the transgression was stereotype-inconsistent.
   c. about the same as when the transgression was stereotype-inconsistent.
   d. zero.

78. Someone who is ethnocentric will not only hold negative stereotypes of an outgroup but will also
   a. believe it is not the fault of the outgroup for having the stereotyped characteristics.
   b. blame the outgroup for having the stereotyped characteristics.
   c. try to excuse the outgroup for having the stereotyped characteristics.
   d. try to show how the stereotyped characteristics are not as negative as they appear to be.

79. In a study in South India, Hindus were presented with stories of desirable or undesirable acts committed by Hindus or Muslims. Hindus found excuses for the Hindus' undesirable acts and reasons to deny credit for the Muslims'
   a. neutral acts.
   b. nasty acts.
   c. desirable acts.
   d. high-wire acts.

80. According to the text, the essential aspect of stereotypes is that they are perpetually reinforced, not by contact with their targets, but
   a. through reports of scientific studies.
   b. through careful investigation.
   c. through reading what the stereotyped group has to say about itself.
   d. through contact with other people, especially those we love and trust, who believe the stereotype.

81. The text holds that the cognitive, the motivational, and the cultural approaches
   a. are mutually contradictory.
   b. are all completely wrong.
   c. all have something to tell us about different aspects of prejudice.
   d. really are saying the same thing.

Answer Key for Self-Test

1.	d (p. 124)	42.	a (p. 146)
2.	c (p. 124)	43.	c (p. 147)
3.	d (p. 124)	44.	b (p. 147)
4.	a (p. 125)	45.	c (p. 149)
5.	b (p. 127)	46.	d (p. 150)
6.	d (pp. 127–128)	47.	c (p. 150)
7.	c (p. 128)	48.	a (p. 150)
8.	b (p. 128)	49.	a (p. 150)
9.	c (p. 128)	50.	d (p. 152)
10.	d (p. 129)	51.	d (p. 152)
11.	c (p. 130)	52.	a (p. 154)
12.	b (p. 129)	53.	c (p. 154)
13.	a (p. 131)	54.	a (p. 154)
14.	c (p. 131)	55.	c (p. 154)
15.	c (p. 132)	56.	a (p. 155)
16.	a (pp. 132–133)	57.	d (p. 155)
17.	c (p. 133)	58.	d (p. 156)
18.	b (p. 133)	59.	d (p. 156)
19.	d (p. 134)	60.	a (pp. 156–157)
20.	c (p. 135)	61.	b (p. 157)
21.	b (p. 135)	62.	b (p. 157)
22.	a (p. 135)	63.	c (p. 158)
23.	d (p. 136)	64.	a (p. 158)
24.	a (p. 137)	65.	c (p. 158)
25.	a (p. 137)	66.	b (p. 158)
26.	b (p. 137)	67.	a (pp. 158–159)
27.	c (p. 137)	68.	c (p. 160)
28.	b (p. 138)	69.	b (p. 160)
29.	b (p. 138)	70.	c (p. 162)
30.	d (p. 138)	71.	a (p. 164)
31.	c (pp. 139, 146)	72.	b (p. 165)
32.	b (pp. 139–140)	73.	a (pp. 165–166)
33.	a (pp. 140–141)	74.	b (p. 165)
34.	c (p. 142)	75.	d (pp. 165–166)
35.	b (p. 142)	76.	c (p. 166)
36.	b (p. 143)	77.	a (p. 167)
37.	c (p. 144)	78.	b (p. 168)
38.	b (p. 144)	79.	c (p. 168)
39.	c (p. 144)	80.	d (p. 169)
40.	a (p. 145)	81.	c (p. 170)
41.	c (p. 145)		

Thought Questions and Exercises

1. Has prejudice ever touched you? Have you ever felt looked down upon, excluded, discriminated against because you were "not the right sort"? When? Describe the occasion. Have you ever felt that people were not reacting to you according to what you did, but rather according to "what" you were? Describe the occasion. Do you sometimes feel prejudice—have immediate prejudiced reactions, whether you act on them or believe in them? Describe when. Do you sometime feel that people assume that you are (must be) prejudiced and react to you on the basis of that assumption? After answering these questions for yourself, ask your friends and classmates to answer them. You may be surprised at how many different sorts of people have been, or feel they have been, the target of prejudice or the target of the assumption that they must be prejudiced.

2. Social scientists usually emphasize cultural, motivational (personality), or cognitive causes of prejudiced attitudes, but they recognize that all three are involved in prejudice. Think of some instances of prejudice that you have observed and consider ways that culture, personality, and habits of thought may have been involved in these instances.

3. Attempt to apply realistic conflict theory to some ethnic or racial conflict currently occupying the news. What do you think this theory handles best about the conflict? What do you think are the important elements that it leaves out?

4. Can you think of any instances of conflict that you have read about where intergroup hatred was reduced by the discovery of a superordinate goal? Why isn't this solution to group conflict used more often?

5. One possible limitation to the Sherif experiment is that it may only apply to American culture. Explain.

6. Personality scales are rather tricky instruments. The form of the scale itself—whether it is keyed in one direction and whether it contains seductive clichés—influences the answer given, independent of what the subject really believes. Make up a list of questions about some current issue of concern. Invent two forms of your list, each of which contains the same points, asks about the same issues. The difference between the forms will be that one is keyed in one direction and uses glib generalizations and clichés; the other form should not use clichés and should

not be keyed in one direction. It should have as many "no's" as "yeses" that indicate agreement with the concept you are interested in. For instance, a "yes" to "I think teachers are fair" and a "no" to "teachers are usually unfair" would both indicate the same belief in the fairness of teachers and would not be keyed in the same direction. Present each list to a group of people (flip a coin to determine which list a person gets) and see if the way the questionnaire is formed makes a difference.

7. Look at the sample questions for authoritarianism, F, in your text (the F Scale). The study was done after the Second World War and some of the questions may not capture a modern authoritarian spirit. The text presents what the researchers believed the characteristics of the authoritarian personality are. Invent a list of questions that you think might better capture the present-day authoritarian.

8. The correlation between authoritarianism and ethnocentrism is approximately the same for all regions of the country, even the South. The South, however (at least circa the 1960s), was more prejudiced against minorities and had a higher F score. Why would the South have both higher prejudice and higher F and yet the correlation between F and prejudice was the same in the South as in the North? Correlations are about relations. If the relation were perfectly positive, then the most authoritarian person would be the most prejudiced and the least authoritarian the least prejudiced and a person average on authoritarianism would be average on prejudice. On the other hand, the South's average prejudice (and authoritarianism) was higher than average prejudice in the rest of the country. For this reason, even with the correlation between F and prejudice being identical and perfect in the North and the South, the South still would have a higher level of F and prejudice than other regions. Explain how it would be possible for a Northerner who was more prejudiced than average for his region to be less prejudiced than an average Southerner. Would it be likely that this Northerner was more or less authoritarian than the average Southerner?

9. It has been suggested that ambivalence of whites to blacks rather than unremitting hostility characterizes the attitudes of many whites to blacks in the North (and some whites to blacks in the South). Can you give some examples from your experience or readings of the sorts of ambivalence that the text discusses?

10. What is a stereotype? Can a stereotype be true? The text discusses several ways that a stereotype might be true and yet it would be prejudiced to apply it. What are they? Attempt to give several other ways that it might be unfair to apply a true stereotype. In your opinion, should the employment interviewer described in the text have expended effort to get the information about the utility of high school graduation for a position?

11. If and only if we believe that a group is homogeneous does it make sense to generalize from a few members to the group as a whole. Explain. Have you ever experienced another's surprise when she discovered that you were a member of some group and yet didn't have the presumed characteristics of the group? How did you feel? How would you (did you) feel if the group characteristics mentioned were positive and the other person assumed that you must have the positive characteristics?

12. Experiments have shown that discovering an exception to a stereotype class will cause one to modify the stereotype only if the exception is in other ways typical of the class. Why is this so? Think of the "exceptions" you have encountered. When did they modify the generalizations you held about their groups? Does your experience accord with the experimental findings?

CHAPTER 5

Person Perception and Social Cognition

Learning Objectives

FORMING IMPRESSIONS

Asch's Studies of Impression Formation

1. Be able to discuss Solomon Asch's studies of impression formation. What was Asch's central concern? Describe how Asch attempted to determine how people's impressions of others cohere, are integrated, and are transformed.

Central and Peripheral Traits

2. Asch gave subjects two identical lists of trait words (for example, "intelligent" and "cautious"). The lists were identical except that one list had "warm" and the other "cold." What effect did this difference have on people's impressions of the person the traits were supposed to describe? Why did Asch call "warm" and "cold" central traits as opposed to peripheral traits?

Drawing Inferences about Traits

3. You should be able to explain what it means to say that we "infer" that a person has a trait (rather than directly observe that he has the trait). Do all traits allow the same breadth of inference? Why does Asch believe that we all have an implicit theory of personality? Asch used people's patterns of inferences to support his notion of an implicit personality theory. Other researchers have examined correlations among traits people give in descriptions of acquaintances. Are the results essentially the same?

4. Some theorists argue that implicit personality theories are inherent in our language; others argue that traits really do go together. Explain.

Traits and Behavior

5. Asch considered traits to be the building blocks of our understanding people. Did he answer the question of how our impressions of traits are derived from actual behavior?

6. Be able to describe how both the work of Asch and the work of Heider derive from Gestalt psychology. Heider's conception of how we understand others comes from the idea of "object constancy" in the study of visual perception. What is "object constancy"? How is our perception of our friend's personality like our perception that his or her body remains the same even though we see it from different perspectives?

7. You should understand the contributions of both dispositions and situations to a person's behavior. We must always interpret a person's behavior in light of the situation she is in. Explain. Are some situations more revealing of personality than others?

ATTRIBUTION THEORY

Jones and Davis's Correspondent Inference Theory

8. Jones and Davis's attribution theory is concerned with intentions and dispositions. Be able to define each. Give an example of someone, working back from the effects of an act to the intentions and then to the dispositions of the actor. Would it be easier to infer intentions and

dispositions if each act had many effects or just one effect? What is the goal of correspondent inference theory? Why would Beth's choice of a job in Philadelphia be a better guide to her dispositions toward Bob than would be her choice of a job in San Francisco? When do we make a personalized "internal" attribution?

Research on Jones and Davis's Attribution Theory

9. Present in your own words the submariner/astronaut experiment. Why were people more likely to believe that the applicant was gregarious when he described himself as gregarious in the astronaut interview than when he described himself as gregarious in the submariner interview?

Kelley's Covariation Theory

10. Understand in what sense Kelley sees us as reasoning like a scientist in our ordinary lives. If we are trying to understand why Claire is laughing at a comedian, how would we try to determine the *causes* of her behavior?

11. Explain what it means to say that "the discovery of covariation is essentially a statistical matter" (remember the importance of frequencies). To determine whether A causes B is it enough to see how often A occurs in the presence of B? What else do you need to know?

12. Kelley believes that we focus on three kinds of information about causes of behavior: distinctiveness, consistency, and consensus. Define and give an example in your own words of a person showing high and low distinctiveness in her behavior. Define and make up an example of high and low consistency in behavior. Define and give an example of high and low consensus. Use the notions of distinctiveness, consistency, and consensus to explain when we would infer that a person's behavior was most externally caused, and when it was most internally caused.

Causal Schemata

13. Describe when we are unable to rely on the principle of covariation. What do we use in its place? What is the "model of multiple sufficient causes"? Give examples illustrating the difference between an event having multiple necessary causes and multiple sufficient causes. A donor may give money because he is generous or because of a gun pointing at him. Knowing that there is a gun aimed at the donor allows us to "discount" generosity as a cause of his behavior. Explain.

Research on Kelley's Attribution Theory

14. McArthur gave one group of subjects behavioral descriptions of people and another group information about the degree of distinctiveness, consistency, and consensus of their behavior. Did this second sort of information affect the certainty with which subjects attributed behavior to the person or the situation? Which type of information was found to have the least effect?

A Comparison of Jones and Davis's model with Kelley's Model

15. Jones and Davis's model is focused on intentional behavior while Kelley's model focuses on reactions. Give an example of each. Be able to describe how the models are similar.

ATTRIBUTIONAL ERRORS AND BIASES

16. Describe what "descriptive models" are. Describe what "normative models" are. Be able to explain the difference between a normative model and a descriptive model. How do you tell the two sorts of models apart? (Hint: How do theorists react to behavior that goes against the model?) Are Jones and Davis's and Kelley's models normative or descriptive? What are normative models used for?

Actor-Observer Differences

17. Be sure you understand what is meant by the "actor-observer difference" in attribution. Give some examples of internal causes and external causes. When we observe someone else's behavior are we more or less likely to attribute internal causes to them than when we think about our own behavior? According to Jones and Nisbett what are two important causes of the actor-observer difference in attribution?

Experimental Results

18. Give some examples of research that supports Jones and Nisbett's theory. Give some examples of research that is not as supportive of their theory.

Salience and Attribution

19. Explain how visual salience can account for the apparent asymmetry between actor and observer. In Storms's experiment some subjects saw a videotape of an interaction between two people from an observer's point of view and other subjects saw a videotape of the same interaction from a participant's perspective. When given a questionnaire, how did seeing each type of video affect subjects' situational versus dispositional

attributions? How did this contrast with people who saw videos only from their own point of view, or who did not see a video? What does this experiment tell you about the importance of salience and recency?

The Fundamental Attributional Error

20. Subjects read an essay supposedly written by another student. The essay either supported or opposed Castro. The subjects were told that the essay writer had been assigned either to a supporting or opposing position. What did the students conclude about the genuine opinions of the writer of the pro-Castro essay? Might this be a failure to "discount"? Jones argued that the subjects made the mistake of taking behavior to be closer to its face value than they should. What is this error called? How is this error related to the actor-observer difference?

Investigating the Fundamental Attributional Error

21. Ross, Amabile, and Steinmetz had some college students make up difficult general knowledge questions and ask them to other students. The experimenters were concerned with how the askers and the answerers would view themselves. Both groups of students rated themselves and the others on their general knowledge. What were the results? Why is this an example of the fundamental attributional error?

Limits of the Fundamental Attributional Error

22. Miller gave subjects the results of the Milgram experiments on obedience to malevolent authority (most subjects in the Milgram experiment obeyed the experimenter) and asked subjects what particular "teachers" would do. How did the predictions of these subjects differ from those of subjects who were not told the results of the Milgram experiment? Miller also asked subjects to describe the traits of a person who gave very high levels of shock. Were these ratings affected by the subjects' knowledge about how likely it is for people to obey the experimenter?

23. Give two examples of things that the person being judged can do to lessen the fundamental attributional error. People discover that Rob wrote an essay supporting a controversial position either because he was assigned to do so or because he was trying to ingratiate himself to someone to get a job. What do people perceive Rob's true beliefs to be in each of these cases?

What do the results of this study suggest about people's ability to discount?

Base Rates and the Fundamental Attributional Error

24. Understand what base rates and diagnostic facts are. Imagine that seventy personality descriptions of lawyers and thirty of engineers are put into a box. What are the odds of your drawing from the box a description of an engineer? Let's say you draw a description that really sounds like that of an engineer. To decide whether it really is an engineer being described you have to keep in mind two sets of facts. What are they? What is the fact about "base rates" in this example? What is the diagnostic fact?

25. Explain the importance of the diagnostic ratio. How is the diagnostic ratio calculated? What have Kahneman and Tversky found about how people handle problems like the one above?

26. Describe how Kahneman and Tversky's finding that people underestimate base rates could help to explain why subjects in the Jones and Harris study believed that people who were forced to write a pro-Castro essay supported Castro. Can the fundamental attributional error be seen as a failure to take base rates into account? When should subjects be more likely to use base-rate information?

Ethnocentrism and Consensus

27. Describe the "false consensus effect." Give some experimental examples of this effect. How do Jones and Nisbett explain the false consensus effect? How might the fact that our own evaluation of a situation is more easily recalled than someone else's also explain this effect? (Remember that people sometimes confuse how easy something is to remember—how available it is—with how common it is.)

Self-Serving Biases in Social Perception

28. Understand what a "self-serving attribution" is. Self-serving attributions look motivational, but they may be cognitive. Explain. What is the role of intentions to succeed and expectations of success in self-serving attributions? Describe the experiment that demonstrated a motivational role by showing that "ego-involved" subjects made more external attributions for failure on a task than did non-ego-involved subjects.

Confirmation Bias

Candidate Causes and Testing Hypotheses

29. Understand how confirmation bias may lead to

errors in testing hypotheses. Hansen proposes that to save time people follow a simple procedure in thinking about the causes of an event. What is this procedure? How do people come up with candidates for causes? Do people generally look for evidence both for and against their hypotheses?

Confirmation Bias in the Social Domain

30. Understand how confirmation bias may affect social judgments. Either subjects were told that they had to find out if someone was an introvert or they were told they had to find out if he was an extravert. How were the questions they asked affected by whether they were set to find out about introverts or extraverts? How does this illustrate confirmation bias? What's wrong with using confirmation bias here? What did observers listening to the same person answering either the "introvert questions" or "extravert questions" conclude?

ATTRIBUTIONAL CRITICS

31. Attribution theory is based on several assumptions. One assumption is that when we ascribe traits to someone we are reporting a particular internal cause of that person's behavior. How has this assumption been criticized? Another assumption is that we find the cause of something by determining what covaries with what, but this requires eliminating all causes but one or two. Explain. What would Kelley rejoin to this point?

Social Knowledge Structures

32. Be able to explain how Schank and Abelson believe our knowledge of the world is organized. Describe our social knowledge structures for restaurants. What is a "script"? Give examples of some things that would fit in the "slots" of a restaurant script. What other sorts of "knowledge structures" are there?

33. Describe the difference between "actions" and "occurrences." What are the three types of occurrences? Why don't "occurrences" and "actions" need the same sort of explanations? Is attribution theory more suitable for explaining actions or occurrences?

Causes and Responsibilities

34. Some critics of attribution theory argue that when we claim that the cause of our failing the test was external, we are not trying to locate causes. What are we doing? What is the

importance of "a reasonable standard" of exam difficulty in our account? Show how the internal-external distinction as used in explaining a failure on an exam can be reconstructed in terms of who is to blame for the failure. How is this an example of the common-sense actor as a lawyer rather than a scientist?

"Man the Lawyer" and the Attributional Errors

35. Explain why the "man the lawyer" view says that we tend to ignore base rates. How does our focus on moral judgments involving responsibility help to explain the results of Miller's experiment?

Egocentric Bias

36. Describe what "egocentric bias" is. Does the "poorly printed textbook" example demonstrate that evaluations can be as certain as perceptions—that it is often reasonable for us to expect everyone to make the same judgment we make? If it is often sensible to believe that others will evaluate as we do, then are we "egocentric" for giving weight to our own reactions in deciding what others will do?

Attributions and Pragmatics

Pragmatics

37. Understand the role of language in making attributions. What is "pragmatics"? Why is it funny to say "I saw Dan Quayle today and he was sober"? What does this statement presuppose? What does it mean to say that this sentence "carries the implication" that Quayle drinks too much, without stating it?

38. Grice articulated "maxims" of conversation, rules that speakers try to observe. What is the maxim of quantity? Give an example of someone violating this maxim. A maxim must be applied to a particular case by keeping in mind what the hearer needs to know. Explain. Give an example. Give examples of the maxims of quality and relevance. How might pragmatics be used to explain the fundamental attributional error, specifically, subjects' judgment that people who wrote pro-Castro essays under constraint were pro-Castro?

Cause and Consideration

39. You say that you are attracted to your girlfriend because she is warm and that your friend is attracted to his girlfriend because he likes warm women. It has been said that this is a difference in attributing external or internal causes to

behavior, but is there a causal difference between your choice and your friend's? How might this merely be a difference determined by pragmatic considerations?

COGNITIVE PROCESSES

Preconceptions and Evaluations

40. Kelley described a guest lecturer as either "warm" or "cold" and then had students evaluate him on a variety of trait scales. What were the results? Did the warm-cold difference affect all the traits evaluated to the same extent?

41. Explain what a schemata is. Describe the differences in how a first-timer and a fan look at a baseball game by referring to the three functions of schemata: "controlling attention," "integrating information," and "guiding memory."

Activation of Schemata

42. Subjects read a list of adjectives describing a fictional character. The list included extravert traits for one group of subjects and introvert traits for another group. Later the subjects were given a new list and asked which of the words had appeared on the old list. How did having read extraverted or introverted traits affect subjects' recognition memory? How can these results be explained by saying that the subjects had formed an introvert or extravert schema?

Sensitivity to Incongruent Material

43. Explain how the activation of a schema can make people particularly sensitive to incongruent material. Give an example. When is our memory more likely to focus on consistent information and when is it likely to focus on inconsistent information?

Priming of Schemata

44. Explain how activating a schema can affect subsequent thought even when the original activation has nothing to do with the behavior being encoded.

Chronic Activation

45. People differ as to which of their schemata are chronically activated. What does this mean? Subjects whose "inconsiderateness" schema was chronically activated were primed with the word "inconsiderate." They were then asked to judge an ambiguously inconsiderate behavior. How did chronic activation and priming affect judgments?

Encoding Behavior

46. Subjects were primed with stories of the helpful behavior of a carpenter—stories that stressed personal or situational causes of the helpfulness. Did this priming cause people to guess word fragments semantically related to "helpful" more quickly? Did it matter whether the priming story stressed internal or external causes?

47. Describe the experiment that shows that priming matters only when one is communicating to targets with neutral opinions. How does this experiment show that our purposes in encoding have a greater effect than accidental priming?

The Organization and Representation of Impressions

Impressions and Memory

48. Explain why attempting to form a unified impression of a person rather than memorizing a list of traits leads to better recall. Why did people remember better when they are given information about someone and then told that they are about to meet the person?

Overall Impressions and Recall of Specific Facts

49. Explain what "dual representation theory" is. Give an example from your own experience. What are the two things we do when we begin to form an overall impression of someone? Can a specific behavior have an impact on our evaluation of someone even after we have forgotten about it? Why? Why does this suggest that there should be a "primacy effect" for evaluations and a "recency" effect for specific behaviors?

50. Subjects were given an "overall impression" set. Other subjects were given a "comprehension set." Which group should form an evaluation on line? Why should this produce a disjunction between overall evaluations and behavioral recall?

51. Subjects were given information about someone and told that specific pieces of the information were in error and should be disregarded. Were they able to do so? What would this experiment predict about the effect of presented "inadmissible evidence" on juries? What has research with mock juries shown?

Programmed Exercises

FORMING IMPRESSIONS

Asch's Studies of Impression Formation

1. Asch read to his subjects a list of personality _____ and then gave them an additional list of pairs that were also supposed to be like the person.

   traits

2. Some trait words such as "warm" or "cold" are called _____ and have a large effect on our overall impression of personality; other traits called _____ have a smaller effect.

   central

   peripheral

3. We draw _____ about aspects of personality that we do not know directly.

   inferences

4. Our ability to make trait inferences shows that we have an _____ theory of personality.

   implicit

Traits and Behavior

5. When we move, the image on our retina changes shape, but the perceived object doesn't change shape. This is called _____ _____.

   object constancy

6. Someone's behavior constantly changes, yet we see an _____ _____ behind their changing behavior.

   enduring
   personality

7. _____ are properties of a person that give rise to the person's behavior. They are the fixed, enduring _____ of a person.

   Traits
   dispositions

8. Some situations reveal and other situations _____ our real dispositions.

   conceal

ATTRIBUTION THEORY

Jones and Davis's Correspondent Inference Theory

9. Jones and Davis's attribution theory is concerned with inferring _____ from intentional actions.

   dispositions

10. Their correspondent inference theory shows how people reason from actions to intentions to dispositions when the actions have _____ effects.

    multiple

11. If someone has a number of reasons for her behavior than an observer is _____ confident about her dispositions and intentions than if she has only one reason.

    less

12. When subjects heard the applicant for the submariner position describe himself as gregarious, they were _____ likely to believe him than they were to believe the applicant for the astronaut position who described himself as gregarious.

    less

13. This is because the submariner applicant had _____ reasons to describe himself as gregarious than did the astronaut applicant.

    more

Kelley's Covariation Theory

14. Kelley argued that when we perceive behavior we are reasoning much as _____ reason.

    scientists

15. When we try to understand someone we are trying to find the _____ of her behavior by the principle of _____.

    causes
    covariation

16. There are three sources of information about the causes of behavior. They are information about _____, _____, and _____.

    distinctiveness,
    consistency,
    consensus

17. We use these three sources of information to tell if the causes of behavior are _____, in the person, or _____, in the environment.

    internal, external

18. If Claire laughed at this and only this clown, then the clown is highly _____ in producing the laughter and Claire's behavior is _____ caused.

    distinctive
    externally

19. If Claire always laughs when she sees this clown, then the clown is highly _____ in producing laughter and Claire's behavior is _____ caused.

    consistent,
    externally

20. If not only Claire but everyone else laughed at this clown, then there is a high _____ on the effect of the clown, and laughing at him is _____ caused.

    consensus
    externally

21. Claire went to see *King Lear*. She cried during the performance; she always cries at tragedies. No one else in the audience cried. The cause of Claire's crying is _____.

    internal

22. When we observe only a single instance of behavior we _____ apply the principle of covariation.

    cannot

23. For some events we believe that several causes must occur at the same time for the event to happen. When this is the case the model of multiple _____ causes applies.

    necessary

24. For some events we believe that any of several causes would be enough for the event to happen. When this is the case the model of multiple _____ causes applies.

    sufficient

25. If we know that there are several *sufficient* causes of a behavior then we are _____ sure about which event caused the behavior. This is called the principle of _____.

    less
    discounting

26. In McArthur's study, while distinctiveness, consistency, and consensus information did affect the certainty with which subjects attributed information to internal or external causes, _____ was the weakest source of information.

    consensus

A Comparison of Jones and Davis's Model with Kelley's

27. Jones and Davis's model is focused on _____ _____ while Kelley's focuses on _____.

    intentional behavior
    reactions

28. Both models place an emphasis on _____, on weakened faith in one cause if other causes are present.

    discounting

ATTRIBUTIONAL ERRORS AND BIASES

29. A _____ model states how people ought to use information; a _____ model states how people do use information.

    normative
    descriptive

30. It has been found that the Kelley and the Jones and Davis models are in fact
    _____.   normative

31. The function of a normative model is to direct attention to where people
    _____ from what they should do.   deviate

Actor-Observer Differences

32. According to Jones and Nisbett, people are more likely to attribute
    _____ causes to themselves and _____ causes to others.   external; internal

33. This difference is called the _____-_____ _____.   actor-observer
                                                                                difference

34. If this is so then people deviate from _____ models, which require normative
    that information apply in the same way to everyone.

35. One reason that actors are more likely than observers to give external causes of
    their behavior is that actors are mainly attending to properties of the
    _____.   environment

36. Another reason is that actors typically know a lot _____ about   more
    themselves than do observers.

37. Male students were asked to explain why they and their best friend chose their
    majors and girlfriends. Subjects made more _____ attributions when situational
    writing about themselves than when writing about their friends.

38. Subjects are _____ likely to use "it depends on the situation" when more
    rating themselves than when rating their friends.

39. Dormitory resident assistants were rated by students on their floor who did not
    know them very well and by their friends who did know them quite well.
    Friends used _____ trait words in describing the assistants than did more
    students on their floor.

40. This finding contradicts the Jones and Nisbett position since friends who know
    the person well should use _____ trait words and more _____ fewer, situational
    attributions than acquaintances do.

41. When subjects were asked to describe themselves and their spouses using a
    checklist of desirable and undesirable traits the actor-observer difference
    _____.   disappeared

42. These same subjects were asked to assign responsibility to either the situation
    or the person. Jones and Nisbett believe that situational and dispositional
    attributions are highly _____ correlated, but the correlation was only negatively
    slightly negative.

43. The evidence for the actor-observer difference is _____.   mixed

44. Something that is _____ is the center of attention.   salient

45. In Storms's experiment, actors who saw a videotape of their interaction from
    the perspective of an observer responded to a questionnaire in the same way as
    an _____; that is, they made more _____ attributions than did observer, internal
    actors who had not seen the video.

The Fundamental Attributional Error

46. Subjects read pro-Castro essays that they knew students had been required to write. They judged these students to be _____ pro-Castro than the average student. These subjects made the mistake of taking behavior to be _____ to its face value than they should have. This is an example of the _____ _____ _____.

    more

    closer
    fundamental
    attributional error

47. Some subjects made up difficult questions and other subjects tried (and usually failed) to answer them. Subjects who had to answer the questions saw themselves as significantly _____ knowledgeable than their peers. This is an example of a failure to _____ sufficiently.

    less
    discount

48. People who knew that most subjects go to the end in the experiments on obedience to malevolent authority, nonetheless _____ the likelihood that any particular subject would go to the end.

    underestimated

49. When people who knew the results of this experiment were asked to describe the traits of someone who shocked at a high level, they described him just as _____ as did someone who didn't know the results of the experiment.

    negatively

50. When subjects were read an essay and were asked about the writer's opinion, they made the fundamental attributional error even when they knew that the essay writer was _____ arguments to use by the experimenter.

    given

51. If the essay writer in the essay states that she is writing under constraint the fundamental attributional error is _____.

    lessened

52. If observers believe that a controversial essay was written for an ulterior motive, to get a job, then they _____ _____ attribute the attitude expressed in the paper to its author and they do not make the _____ _____ _____.

    do not

    fundamental
    attributional error

53. If you pick a description that sounds like that of an engineer from a box that mainly contains descriptions of lawyers and you have to guess the person's occupation, you must bear in mind both how much the description sounds like an engineer, the _____ fact, and the fact that most of the descriptions are of lawyers, the _____ _____.

    diagnostic
    base rate

54. The _____ _____ is the proportion of how diagnostic the sketch is of a engineer versus how diagnostic it is of a lawyer.

    diagnostic ratio

55. _____ _____ gives the likelihood of the sketch's being that of an engineer by multiplying the diagnostic ratio by the base rate.

    Bayes's Theorem

56. According to Kahneman and Tversky people pay too much attention to _____ _____ and too little attention to _____ _____ when dealing with tasks like the one just described.

    diagnostic ratios,
    base rates

57. Kahneman and Tversky believe that students who were forced to write a pro-Castro essay were judged to be pro-Castro because observers didn't pay attention to the _____ _____ of student anti-Castro sentiments.

    base rate

58. Students were given information about the positive relation between IQ or family income and grades and were asked to predict someone's Grade Point Average. Students used the base-rate _____ information, but they ignored the base-rate family _____ information.

    IQ
    income

59. This was because the students saw a _____ relation between IQ and grades but not between family income and grades.   causal

Egocentrism and Consensus

60. When people misestimate the base-rate information and predict that others will behave as they did, they are showing the _____ _____ effect.   false consensus

61. People's overestimating the typicality of their own behavior is an example of _____ bias, a false consensus effect.   egocentric

62. One possible explanation for egocentric bias is that our own evaluations are more _____, easier to remember, and people confuse how common   available
something is with how _____ it is to recall.   easy

Self-Serving Biases in Social Perception

63. A _____-_____ attribution makes you look better (or less   self-serving
bad) than you really are. This leads to a pattern of _____ attributions   internal
for success and _____ attributions for failure.   external

Confirmation Bias

64. In the study of people trying to determine the rule generating 2-4-6...,
subjects guessed _____ numbers and would not test their hypothesis   even
with an _____ number.   odd

65. The tendency not to look for disconfirming evidence for one's hypothesis is called _____ bias.   confirmation

66. Observers who heard a person answering questions put to her by someone with an extraversion hypothesis saw the person as an extravert; when they heard her questioned by someone with an introversion hypothesis they saw her as an

_____.   introvert

67. If a person has a clearly stated _____ _____ in mind she is   alternative
less likely to be biased in hypothesis testing.   hypothesis

ATTRIBUTIONAL CRITICS

68. One assumption of attribution theory is that when we attribute a trait to a person we are reporting a particular internal _____ of her behavior.   cause

69. The problem with attributing the cause of a particular behavior—for example, crossing the street to get a cup of coffee—is that there are very _____   many
possible causes.

Social Knowledge Structures

70. According to Schank and Abelson we have _____ for many different   scripts
types of activities stored in memory. They specify what will happen in
_____ terms, but leave _____ to be filled in.   general, particulars

71. Read argues that when we search for causal explanations of an event we call up the script and focus on the empty _____.   slots

72. The most important slot for understanding the cause of an action is the one specifying the _____.   goal

73. Actions, under the control of the will, are explained by _____.   goals

74. _____ are behaviors we can't will, such as emotions and _____ .

Occurrences
reflexes

75. Attribution theory focuses on _____ and not actions.

occurrences

Causes and Responsibilities

76. When we argue with our teacher that the exam was too hard we might not be attempting to find causes but to assign _____ .

responsibility

77. To claim that it was the test and not you that was the cause of your failure is to claim that your instructor is at _____ .

fault

78. Claiming that a test is too hard is in comparison to a _____ _____ for an appropriate test.

reasonable
standard

79. One reason that subjects make attributional errors is that they don't have much practice treating each other as a _____ might.

scientist

80. Base rates are not important to _____ judgments.

moral

81. According to the moral view, just because a lot of people do something does not make it _____ .

right

82. People may ascribe traits to others not in order to make predictions but to make _____ judgments.

moral

83. This may be the reason why informing people about the results of the Milgram experiments _____ _____ change the negative traits they assigned someone who went to the end.

did not

Attributions and Pragmatics

84. Pragmatics is concerned with aspects of language use that are _____ .

implicit

85. "Dan Quayle is sober today" presupposes that Quayle is not usually _____ .

sober

86. According to Grice, speakers attempt to follow certain _____ , principles of talk.

maxims

87. An acquaintance says "how are you" and you give him a five-minute account of the state of your health. You are violating the maxim of _____ .

quantity

88. The Dan Quayle joke works by making use of the maxim of _____ .

relevance

89. Subjects believed that students who were required to write a pro-Castro essay were more pro-Castro than they indeed were. This has been explained as due to the fundamental attributional error, but it may instead be due to subjects' belief that the experimenter was following the maxim of _____ in showing them the essay.

relevance

91. Subjects' errors in predicting that people volunteered due to altruism rather than for money might be due to _____ and not to observers' fondness for attributing internal causes.

politeness

Preconceptions and Evaluations

92. _____ control attention, integrate information, and guide memory.

Schemata

93. People who had heard a lecturer described as _____ were more likely   warm
to direct attention to evidences of warm behavior, to attempt to integrate
"warmth" with other behaviors, and to remember warm behaviors.

Activation of Schemata

94. Subjects read a list of adjectives describing someone. The list included
extraverted traits. They later falsely believed that they had read other
_____ traits that were not on the list.   extraverted

95. Subjects misremembered because the original lists and the new words were
part of their extraversion _____.   schema

96. When one is forming an impression, behaviors that are _____ with   congruent
what we already know about the person are easier to recall; when one has a
firm impression of someone, however, then behaviors that are _____   incongruent
are easier to recall.

Encoding Behavior

97. If we are told to remember a description in order to pass it on, we are likely to
use _____ words in writing down our impressions.   trait

98. If subjects are primed with stories of helpful behavior they are more likely to
guess word fragments related to _____ behavior.   helpful

99. People tend to slant their description _____ the opinions of the people   toward
they will be talking to.

100. People who believed that they would communicate an impression of a person
to someone who *disliked* him remembered more _____ information.   negative

The Organization and Representation of Impressions

101. When we form an overall evaluation of someone based on her behavior, we
separately store the behavior and the evaluation in memory. This notion is
called _____ _____ _____.   dual representation
theory

102. A behavior, even after it has been forgotten, may influence our overall
impression, since it affected the _____ _____ of our   starting point
evaluation.

103. Early information will have greater impact on overall evaluations; this is called
a _____ effect. Later information will have greater impact on the   primacy
recall of specific behaviors; this is called a _____ effect.   recency

104. Subjects asked to form an overall impression of someone from a list of
behavioral descriptions and then asked for a recall of the descriptions and an
evaluation are more likely to have a _____ between description and   disjunction
evaluation than those who had been asked merely to attend to the behaviors.   (discrepancy)

105. Subjects were given information about someone and told that specific pieces of
the information were in error and should be disregarded. Subjects' overall
impressions after trying to disregard the evidence were _____ from   different
the impressions of those subjects who had never heard the evidence.

106. In courts of law juries can successfully _____ evidence they are told is   disregard
inadmissible.

Self-Test

1. If changing just one particular trait word in a list of seven describing a person has a large effect on the overall impression of the person then
   a. the particular trait is a peripheral trait.
   b. the particular trait is a central trait.
   c. trait perception is unorganized.
   d. trait perception is additive.

2. Our ability to make trait inferences shows
   a. that we have an implicit personality theory.
   b. that we do *not* have any expectations about which traits go together.
   c. that our understanding of people's personalities is basically unstructured.
   d. that various traits are not related to each other.

3. Heider compared our perception of other people to the notion of "object constancy" in the study of visual perception. His point was that
   a. people and visual objects more generally are unchanging.
   b. people but not other visual objects are seen to endure despite changing stimulation.
   c. visual objects are seen as the same despite changes in illumination and orientation; personalities are seen as different with the smallest changes.
   d. both personality and visual objects seem to be the same despite differences in their momentary appearance.

4. Which of the following is *not* true of Heider's view of traits?
   a. Traits are properties that give rise to behavior.
   b. Traits are dispositions to react or behave.
   c. Traits give rise to behaviors.
   d. A person's traits are easily read from his behavior.

5. Jones and Davis's correspondent inference theory tries to explain
   a. how we reason back from the many effects of an action to the actor's actual disposition.
   b. the logic of mathematical inference.
   c. why personality and styles of inference correspond.
   d. how traits give rise to behavior.

6. According to correspondent inference theory if someone has several reasons, as opposed to just one reason, for his action
   a. an observer will be more confident that she knows the disposition that led to the action.
   b. an observer will be less confident that she knows the disposition that led to the action.
   c. an observer will be neither more nor less confident—it depends on the circumstances.
   d. then that person is confused.

7. Subjects were presented with the story of someone who is applying for a submariner position, which calls for gregarious people; another person is applying to be an astronaut, a position that calls for loners. Which of the following claims were subjects most likely to believe?
   a. The submariner candidate who said that he was gregarious.
   b. The submariner candidate who said that he was a loner.
   c. The astronaut candidate who said that he was gregarious.
   d. b and c

8. Kelley argued that when we perceive behavior we are reasoning much like
   a. poets.
   b. writers.
   c. scientists.
   d. artists.

9. According to Kelley, if we are trying to understand why John is grouchy we are primarily concerned with
   a. whether he has a legitimate reason to be grouchy or not.
   b. seeing if the grouchiness varies with the situation—a flat tire—or whether the cause is internal—John is grouchy in all situations.
   c. our own reactions to John's grouchiness.
   d. whether John had a particularly difficult relationship with his father.

10. According to Kelley, when people try to decide whether a behavior is internally or externally caused they rely on three sources of information
    a. consistency, consensus, and distinctiveness
    b. prurience, dalliance, and prescience
    c. causality, intentionality, and responsibility
    d. gossip, periodicals, and rumor

11. According to Kelley, if Jill laughs only when she sees Professor Smith fall and not when she sees anyone else fall and in fact most students laugh when they see Professor Smith fall, then
    a. Jill's laughter is internally caused.
    b. Professor Smith's fall is not a distinctive stimulus.
    c. there is no consensus about laughing when Professor Smith falls.
    d. Jill's laughter is externally caused.

12. If Claire laughs every time she sees a clown but she laughs at "everything" else also, then Claire's behavior is
    a. high in consistency but low in distinctiveness.
    b. high in consistency and high in distinctiveness.
    c. low in consistency and distinctiveness.
    d. low in consistency but high in distinctiveness.

13. The principle of covariation
    a. can only be used when you can observe multiple instances of a type of behavior.
    b. is supplemented by our general knowledge of the kind of situation we are observing.
    c. is especially supplemented by the model of multiple necessary causes and the model of multiple sufficient causes.
    d. all of the above

14. If we know that Judy falls in love with handsome studs and wonderful cooks and that she is now in love with Marty, what do we know about Marty?
    a. Marty must be a wonderful cook.
    b. Marty must be handsome.
    c. Marty must be both handsome and a good cook.
    d. We can't tell whether Marty is handsome just because Judy loves him because he might be ugly but a good cook. (This is an example of discounting one cause because of the existence of others.)

15. The question of what made Sally burp, would be best handled by
    a. Kelley's model.
    b. Jones and Davis's model.
    c. a model focusing on intentional behavior.
    d. a model that did not focus on the causes of reactions.

16. Which of the following is *true*?
    a. Normative models, such as Kelley's, describe how people *ought* to use information.
    b. Normative models, such as Kelley's, state how people do use information.
    c. Descriptive models, such as Kelley's, state how people ought to use information.
    d. Descriptive models describe the best possible alternative for a person.

17. According to Jones and Nisbett if Henry and John both give money to a charity when they are walking down the street, and Henry is asked to explain why
    a. he is likely to explain that John is generous while he himself gave for very particular reasons.
    b. he is likely to use internal causes for John's behavior but is more likely to use external causes to explain his own behavior.
    c. Henry is likely to describe himself as really generous and John as just trying to impress onlookers.
    d. a and b

18. What is a reason for the actor-observer difference in attribution?
    a. People usually try to make themselves look better than others.
    b. People know a lot more about themselves than they know about observers.
    c. Actors don't sufficiently attend to the properties of their environment.
    d. The actor-observer difference accurately reflects differences in the causes of behavior.

19. Students were asked to explain why they and their best friend chose each of their majors. What was the difference in their explanation of their choices and their friends' choices?
    a. Subjects made more external, situational attributions when describing themselves.
    b. subjects made more internal, dispositional attributions when explaining their friends' choices.
    c. subjects were more likely to use "it depends on the situation" when describing themselves.
    d. all of the above

20. Observers watched people volunteering (or not) to work for a good cause for 50¢ or $1.50. They then were asked to predict whether these people would volunteer to work for free for another charity. What did observers predict and what happened?
    a. Observers predicted that people who volunteered for the first good cause would volunteer for the second. This prediction was correct.
    b. Observers predicted that people who volunteered for the first good cause would *not* volunteer for the second. This prediction was correct.
    c. Observers predicted that people who volunteered for the first good cause would volunteer for the second. This prediction was not correct.
    d. Observers did not believe that anyone would volunteer for the second charity and they were correct.

21. Dormitory resident assistants were rated by students on their floor who did not know them very well and by their friends. Friends used more trait words in describing the assistants then did students on their floor. This finding
    a. supports Jones and Davis's hypothesis of an actor-observer difference.
    b. contradicts Jones and Davis's hypothesis of an actor-observer difference.
    c. shows that people who know you well are less likely to attribute dispositions for your behavior.
    d. shows that friends (as compared to acquaintances) use mainly situational attributions.

22. If subjects are asked to describe themselves and their spouses using a checklist of *desirable and undesirable* traits the actor-observer difference
    a. is much greater than with a checklist of neutral traits.
    b. is about the same as with a checklist of neutral traits.
    c. completely disappears.
    d. reverses.

23. In Storms's experiment actors who saw a videotape of their interaction from the perspective of an observer
    a. responded to a questionnaire in the same way as an observer.
    b. made fewer internal attributions than actors who had not seen the video.
    c. made more internal attributions than actors who had not seen the video.
    d. a and c

24. If a sentence is phrased in the active voice (Mary hit Paul) will readers make fewer or more causal attributions to its subject than if it is phrased in the passive voice (Paul was hit by Mary)?
    a. more
    b. fewer
    c. same number
    d. more if the subject is female and fewer if the subject is male

25. The "fundamental attributional error"
    a. involves not counting the face value of a behavior as being as important as it really is.
    b. involves not properly using distinctiveness and consistency information.
    c. involves taking behavior to be closer to its face value than it really is.
    d. involves reading our own values into an interpretation of someone's behavior.

26. People who read pro-Castro essays that they knew students had been required to write judged that these students were
    a. less pro-Castro than the average student.
    b. more pro-Castro than the average student.
    c. apolitical.
    d. more likely to be conservative than the average student.

27. Students made up difficult questions and other students tried (and usually failed) to answer them. Students who had to answer the questions
    a. saw themselves as significantly less knowledgeable than their peers.
    b. saw the person who made up the questions as more knowledgeable.
    c. did not discount the fact that the person who asked the questions asked questions that they knew.
    d. all of the above

28. People who are informed that most subjects in the Milgram experiments on obedience to malevolent authority go to the end

a. underestimate the likelihood that any particular subject will go to the end.
b. overestimate the likelihood that any particular subject will go to the end.
c. are as likely to apply negative traits to a subject who went to the end as was someone who did not know that most subjects went to the end.
d. a and c

29. Which of the following will *not* decrease the fundamental attributional error in judging the real attitude of a writer required to write an essay supporting a position?
a. The essay writer states that she is writing under constraint.
b. The writer is known to have an ulterior motive for the position she is taking.
c. It is known that the writer is just using arguments supplied by the experimenter.
d. The writer makes clear in the essay that this is not her real position.

30. If 70 personality descriptions of lawyers and 30 descriptions of engineers are placed in a box, then the odds of randomly picking a lawyer are 7 to 3. The 0.7 probability of picking a description of a lawyer if one picks a description blindly from the box is called the
a. diagnostic fact.
b. the fundamental attributional error.
c. the base rate.
d. a and c.

31. Just how much one of the descriptions sounds like a lawyer is called
a. the base rate.
b. the diagnostic fact about the essay.
c. the distinctiveness of the essay.
d. the consistency of the essay.

32. If you pick a description and it sounds like a description of a lawyer you must balance two considerations before deciding on the odds that it is a description of a lawyer:
a. how like a lawyer the description is, the diagnostic fact, and the base rate of lawyers.
b. whether the description appears to be of a lawyer, and how good a description of a lawyer it is.
c. whether the description is primarily of someone with verbal strengths, and whether

the description is one of someone with mathematical strengths.
d. all of the above

33. The diagnostic ratio of how closely the description resembles an engineer, is the ratio of how diagnostic the sketch is of a engineer
a. divided by how diagnostic it is of a lawyer.
b. divided by how diagnostic it is of the average person.
c. divided by seven.
d. divided by the branch of engineering.

34. In order to decide how likely the sketch is of an engineer one would use Bayes's Theorem and multiply
a. the base rate by the diagnostic ratio.
b. the fundamental attributional error by the diagnostic ratio.
c. the diagnostic ratio by itself.
d. all of the above

35. According to Kahneman and Tversky, people pay too much attention to the diagnostic ratio and too little to
a. diagnostic facts.
b. actor-observer differences.
c. base rates.
d. a and c

36. Students were given information about the positive relation between IQ or family income and grades and were asked to predict someone's Grade Point Average.
a. Students did not use any base-rate information.
b. Students used base-rate information on IQ because they saw a causal relation between IQ and grades.
c. Students used both the family income and IQ base-rate information.
d. Students only used the family income base-rate information.

37. Which of the following will make people more likely to use base-rate information?
a. when there is an apparent causal relation between the base rate and the outcome
b. when the base-rate information is presented in a case-by-case form
c. when people are told to think like scientists (as opposed to clinicians)
d. all of the above

38. People drank milk laced with salt and were told how much a sample of others had drunk. They were asked to predict how much future subjects would drink. They predicted that others would do as they did
    a. which correctly takes into account base-rate information.
    b. which correctly assumes that others will do more or less what they did.
    c. which ignores the sample that would provide base rates.
    d. which is an error since they did not calculate a diagnostic ratio.

39. When people overestimate the typicality of their own behavior, they are showing
    a. ethnocentrism.
    b. attributions to internal causes.
    c. emotionally driven thought.
    d. egocentric bias.

40. A cognitive explanation of egocentric bias is that
    a. one's own evaluations are easier to remember and people confuse ease of memory with frequency.
    b. people are emotionally committed to their own evaluations.
    c. people do not trust the accuracy of a sample.
    d. people pay attention only to their own opinions.

41. Self-serving attributions
    a. make a person look better than she really is.
    b. involve external attributions for failure.
    c. involve internal attributions for success.
    d. all of the above

42. Self-serving attributions are
    a. always motivational.
    b. are sometimes cognitive and not motivational.
    c. always derive from people trying to make themselves look good.
    d. always derive from an underlying insecurity.

43. Self-serving attributions
    a. involve actor-observer differences.
    b. involve being more likely to perceive external factors for oneself and internal factors for others.
    c. often involve the fact that people usually expect to succeed and expected outcomes are usually seen as internal.
    d. all of the above

44. According to Hansen when people think about the causes of an event they
    a. find a candidate cause and look no further if they can find evidence for it.
    b. look for the causes of simple actions in the actor's intentions.
    c. look for the causes of an achievement only in the person's situation.
    d. consider evidence for alternative hypotheses.

45. In the study of people trying to determine the rule generating 2-4-6. . . . , what did subjects do wrong?
    a. They never used odd numbers to test their hypothesis.
    b. They never formed a hypothesis about the rule.
    c. They did not try even numbers.
    d. They tried some numbers that they thought would not fit the rule.

46. The tendency to look only for confirming evidence and not to look for disconfirming evidence for a hypothesis is called
    a. confirmation bias.
    b. availability.
    c. wishful thinking.
    d. self-serving attributions.

47. When subjects were asked to test whether someone was an introvert, they asked questions like "do you like intimate get-togethers?" Why is this not a good question?
    a. Introverts don't like intimate get-togethers.
    b. Many extraverts as well introverts like intimate get-togethers.
    c. They were not clear about what the answers to their questions would mean about their hypothesis.
    d. b and c

48. The problem with attributing *the* cause of our crossing the street to get a cup of coffee is
    a. that there might really be a different cause of behavior.
    b. there are no internal causes.
    c. there are likely to be many causes operating simultaneously.
    d. all of the above

49. According to Schank and Abelson, "scripts"
    a. specify what will happen in general terms.
    b. leave out the particulars to be filled in for the specific situation.

c. work in conjunction with plans and goals.
d. all of the above

50. "Actions"
   a. are the same as occurrences.
   b. are explained by goals, what a person is trying to do.
   c. are behaviors that we can't will.
   d. are the same as achievements.

51. What does attribution theory (especially Kelley's) *not* focus on?
   a. occurrences
   b. causes of behavior
   c. covariation (statistical thinking)
   d. actions

52. If you wanted to explain that the cause of your failing the exam was external, you would probably want the teacher to believe
   a. any exam of this sort would be an external cause of failure in poor students.
   b. the test was too hard for a student who did not study.
   c. the test was unfairly hard for an exam of this sort so it wasn't your fault that you failed.
   d. all of the above

53. Compared to attribution theory the critics see the individual as a lay
   a. scientist.
   b. artist.
   c. lawyer.
   d. con artist.

54. According to this alternative view, people may make attributional errors because
   a. they don't have much practice treating people as a scientist might.
   b. people are more interested in judging responsibility than causality.
   c. base rates are not important to moral judgments.
   d. all of the above

55. One criticism of the notion of "egocentric bias" is that
   a. it makes sense to treat evaluations and not just descriptions as the sort of thing that others should see as you see.
   b. it is an error to believe that others will have some of the same evaluations we have.
   c. believing that others will describe the world as we do is an error.

d. all of the above

56. "John came to class today" implies
   a. that John usually comes to class.
   b. that John doesn't usually come to class.
   c. nothing about what John usually does.
   d. that the teacher is having a problem with attendance in this class.

57. The study of what the use of language *implies* is called
   a. histrionics.
   b. egocentric bias.
   c. pragmatics.
   d. attribution theory.

58. According to Grice, speakers attempt to follow certain principles of communication called
   a. attributions.
   b. internal causes.
   c. maxims.
   d. external causes.

59. An acquaintance says "how are you?" and you give him a five-minute account of the state of your health. You are violating the maxim of
   a. quality.
   b. quantity.
   c. relevance.
   d. causality.

60. Maxims are guides to
   a. speaking.
   b. understanding.
   c. finding internal or external causes.
   d. a and b

61. Subjects believed that students who were required to write a pro-Castro essay were more pro-Castro then they indeed were. This has been explained as due to the fundamental attributional error, but it may instead be due to
   a. the subjects believing the experimenter was not being honest.
   b. the subjects believing that the experimenter was following the maxim of relevance in showing them the essay.
   c. the subjects preferring to attribute internal causes.
   d. the subjects being embarrassed to state what they really believed.

62. Subjects' preference for attributing external causes to themselves and internal causes to others may be explained by pragmatics since

a. attributing internal causes to yourself is often seen as bragging.
b. attributing internal causes for positive outcomes to others is a compliment.
c. attributing external causes to oneself is seen as bragging.
d. a and b

63. Schemata
a. control attention.
b. integrate information.
c. guide memory.
d. all of the above

64. When do schemata sensitize people to incongruities and not to similarities?
a. In the beginning stages of forming an impression incongruent behaviors are easier to remember than similarities.
b. In the beginning stages of forming an impression similarities are easiest to remember.
c. When one has a firm impression of someone, then incongruent behaviors are easiest to remember.
d. When one has a firm impression of someone, then it is unlikely that their memory will be sensitive to incongruities or similarities.

65. In the first part of an experiment, subjects saw either the word "adventurous" or "reckless," that is, they were primed with one word or the other. When they were later—in a supposedly unrelated experiment—asked to judge someone's behavior, subjects who had seen "reckless" were more likely to judge the behavior as
a. adventurous.
b. conservative.
c. reckless.
d. nerdlike.

66. It is known that recall cues enhance memory if, and only if, they are in the same terms as the terms in which the subjects originally encoded the material. It has been found that cues giving the name of traits are effective in recalling the associated behavior. This implies that
a. traits are not stored in memory.
b. people must be trained to encode behavior they see in terms of traits.
c. subjects spontaneously encode the behavior they see in terms of traits.

d. traits are rarely used as organizational devices.

67. When subjects were primed with stories stressing internal causes of helpful behavior
a. they are more likely to use trait words relating to helpfulness, but they are no more likely to use "internal cause" words than "external cause" words.
b. they are more likely to use trait words relating to helpfulness, and they are more likely to use words relating to internal causes than external causes.
c. they are more likely to use trait words relating to helpfulness, and they are more likely to use words relating to external causes than internal causes.
d. they are no more likely to use trait words relating to helpfulness than they would have been if they had not been primed with "helpful."

68. Which of the following does *not* affect the impressions we form of people?
a. priming
b. purposes we have in learning information about people
c. whether the information we learn is in terms of internal or external causes
d. the schemata we have activated

69. Someone who believed that he would communicate an impression of a person to someone who disliked him (and is likely to be motivated to be agreeable to and agree with the person he is talking to)
a. remembered more negative traits if he was primed with negative traits.
b. remembered more positive traits.
c. remembered more negative traits whether he was primed with negative traits or positive traits.
d. remembered as many positive as negative traits.

70. Recall for specific traits or behaviors is better when
a. subjects attempt to memorize lists of the traits or behaviors.
b. subjects attempt to form a unified impression.
c. subjects do not attempt to organize or think about the traits.

d. subjects avoid confusion by not attempting to think about possible inconsistencies in their impression of the person given in the trait list.

71. When we form an overall evaluation of someone and remember it we usually
    a. form a dual representation.
    b. both store the specific behavior and our evaluation of it.
    c. store the image of the behavior but not the evaluation.
    d. a and b

72. A behavior even after it has been forgotten may influence our overall impression since
    a. it has affected the starting point of our evaluation.
    b. we never really forget specific behaviors.
    c. we do not store evaluations, just behaviors.
    d. evaluations are only made after behaviors are recalled.

73. According to the dual representation model
    a. early information will have the greatest impact on evaluations.
    b. later information will have the greatest impact on evaluations.
    c. later information will have the greatest impact on the recall of specific behavior
    d. a and c

74. People were given information about someone and told that specific pieces of the information were in error and should be disregarded. Subjects' overall impressions or evaluations after trying to disregard the evidence
    a. were never the same as the impressions of those subjects who had never heard the evidence.
    b. were not the same as the impressions of those subjects who never heard the evidence, except in the case of mock juries where people were able to disregard the inadmissible evidence.
    c. were always the same as the impressions of those subjects who never heard the evidence.
    d. were the same as the impressions of those subjects who never heard the evidence, except in the case of mock juries where the emotions of the cause made subjects unable to disregard the evidence.

Answer Key for Self-Test

1. b (p. 176)	38. c (p. 198)
2. a (p. 177)	39. d (p. 198)
3. d (p. 178)	40. a (p. 199)
4. d (pp. 178-179)	41. d (p. 199)
5. a (p. 179)	42. b (p. 200)
6. b (pp. 179-180)	43. d (p. 200)
7. d (p. 181)	44. a (p. 201)
8. c (p. 181)	45. a (p. 202)
9. b (pp. 182-183)	46. a (p. 202)
10. a (p. 182)	47. d (pp. 202-203)
11. d (p. 182)	48. c (p. 204)
12. a (pp. 182-183)	49. d (p. 205)
13. d (p. 183)	50. b (p. 206)
14. d (p. 183)	51. d (p. 206)
15. a (p. 184)	52. c (p. 207)
16. a (p. 185)	53. c (p. 207)
17. d (p. 186)	54. d (pp. 207-208)
18. b (p. 186)	55. a (p. 208)
19. d (p. 187)	56. b (p. 209)
20. c (p. 188)	57. c (p. 209)
21. b (p. 188)	58. c (p. 209)
22. c (p. 189)	59. b (p. 209)
23. d (p. 190)	60. d (p. 209)
24. a (p. 191)	61. b (p. 210)
25. c (pp. 191-192)	62. d (pp. 211-212)
26. b (p. 191)	63. d (p. 214-215)
27. d (p. 193)	64. a (p. 216)
28. d (p. 194)	65. c (p. 217)
29. c (pp. 194-195)	66. c (p. 219)
30. c (p. 195)	67. a (p. 220)
31. b (pp. 195-196)	68. c (p. 220)
32. a (p. 196)	69. c (p. 221)
33. a (p. 196)	70. b (p. 221)
34. a (p. 196)	71. d (p. 222)
35. c (p. 196)	72. a (p. 222)
36. b (pp. 196-197)	73. d (p. 223)
37. d (p. 197)	74. b (p. 224)

Thought Questions and Exercises

1. It has often been found that people tend to use traits to explain why others do things and tend to be more situationally specific in explaining why they themselves do things. Does this actor-observer difference hold up in your experience? One way to tell is to ask three or four of your friends why they and their best friend came to

college, got the highest mark they (and their best friend) ever got, got the lowest mark, and so on. Did the actor-observer difference hold up?

2. Remember the Ross, Amabile, and Steinmetz experiment where student questioners made up hard general knowledge questions for student contestants. The contestants did not do very well and saw the questioners as a lot more knowledgeable than they were and saw themselves as less knowledgeable than the average student at their school. The contestants failed to discount the fact that the deck was stacked against them. Can you think of any situations in real life where you or someone you know may have made a similar error? Might this argument sometimes apply in the classroom?

3. Because the fundamental attributional error seems to be quite robust, and because many attributional theorists think that it is quite common, it is important to think about when people don't make this error and why. According to the text, when do people *not* make the fundamental attributional error? What does this tell you about cognition in everyday life?

4. The text discusses the notion of "confirmation bias," looking only for supporting evidence for some idea you have. Remember that confirmation bias may not be self-serving. You may desperately want to be liked and yet believe that others don't like you. Because of confirmation bias, you may only notice the times you are rebuffed and not when someone treats you nicely. Can you think of any times that you or people close to you have been guilty of confirmation bias?

5. The broadest difference in outlook in social cognition is between those who see people as "scientists" and those who see them as "lawyers." Explain and illustrate. Imagine that you are trying to explain to your professor why you failed the last exam. Would you be locating causes? Would you be assigning responsibilities and excuses? Discuss.

CHAPTER 6

Gender

Learning Objectives

1. Men are tremendously over-represented in positions of power. There are two general accounts of why this has been the case until now. What are they?

PSYCHOLOGICAL GENDER DIFFERENCES

Differences in Mathematical Ability

2. Do males or females on average do better on standardized tests of mathematical ability? How great is the difference between girls and boys as compared to the differences found among the scores of boys or girls?

Differences in Verbal Ability

3. Do males or females, on average, do better on standardized verbal tests? Are these differences small or large? Have they been decreasing over time or have they remained the same?

GENDER ROLES

4. Describe what Talcott Parsons believes are the two general tasks all groups, including the family, have to perform. Who is the task-oriented leader in the traditional family? Who is the social-emotional leader?

Socialization and Gender Roles

5. Remember socialization does not only mean learning roles, but coming to see the roles as natural. How does this explain stereotypes about male and female traits? Is there serious pressure even in adulthood for us to conform to gender stereotypes? How might these sex-role assumptions be used to justify paying women less?

Changing Gender Concepts

6. In the traditional picture masculinity and femininity are necessarily opposites. This is not the case. Explain.

Measuring Masculinity and Femininity

7. Describe the two questionnaires that have been developed to show the independence of masculine and feminine traits.

The Bem Sex Role Inventory

8. Explain what "normative conceptions" of masculinity and femininity are. In order to develop her scale, Bem started with a list of positive traits that she thought were either masculine or feminine in tone. She gave them to undergraduates to rate how desirable each trait was for a man and for a woman. What was Bem looking for from these ratings?

9. Bem asked male and female undergraduates to rate how descriptive the traits on both masculinity and femininity scales were of them. If masculinity-femininity were a single dimension, what would the results of the ratings be? What were the actual results? Four types of people were actually found. What were they? Were these types evenly divided by gender?

The Personal Attributes Questionnaire

10. Understand the central difference between the way the Personal Attributes Questionnaire (PAQ) was developed and the way the Bem Inventory (BSRI) was developed. Did the PAQ confirm Bem's finding of the independence of masculinity and femininity?

11. Explain what is meant by saying that both the BSRI and the PAQ scales confirm our stereo-

types about men and women, but they disconfirm our belief that masculinity and femininity are somehow "natural."

Masculinity, Femininity, and Adjustment

12. Understand the results of the research on the relations among gender, psychological traits, and adjustment. Are masculine men and feminine women better adjusted than men with feminine and women with masculine traits? Are men and women who are both achievement-oriented and nurturant higher in self-esteem than those who are not?

13. Describe "sex-typed," "androgynous," and "cross-sex-typed" people. Describe the experiment in which people could choose sex-typed or gender "inappropriate" activities to perform and would be paid more for the latter. Have sex-typed men been found to dominate interactions with sex-typed women? What happens when an androgynous male and female share a project—if the male's liberal attitude toward women has been made salient for him?

Gender Schema Theory

14. Understand the difference in the way sex-typed and androgynous people think about the world. According to Bem, how do sex-typed and androgynous people differ in their use of gender schemata?

Effects of Sex Typing

15. Describe how sex-typed people primarily think about themselves. Give an example of how this type of thinking may be harmful. Describe the experiment in which boys and girls were given an identical task either described as about sewing or as about repairing machines. Describe the categorizing experiment that showed that sex-typed subjects were more likely to organize words to be memorized using gender than were androgynous subjects.

GENDER STEREOTYPES

16. Give three views of what "stereotypes" are (one view is in a footnote).

Stereotypes as Base Rates

17. Imagine that there is only one place in a graduate physics program for either a man or a woman. Since men are in general better in math and physics than women, should the man be taken? What is wrong with doing this? What is "base-rate" information? What is "diagnostic"

information? In terms of rationality should you use one of these or both in arriving at a decision?

18. State the ways that people might use gender stereotypes. What is a default option? Describe the experiment in which people read transcripts of a male or female acting passively or actively. Did the subjects ignore diagnostic information? Did they ignore base rates? If no behavioral information is given do subjects apply gender stereotypes?

Gender Stereotypes and Employment Decisions

19. Describe how gender stereotypes may be used to make employment decisions. Basing employment decisions on gender stereotypes is wrong and illegal, but is it irrational? What if we possess no diagnostic information? What if there is sufficient diagnostic information? Résumés were sent to upper-level managers for a gender-neutral, or male or female sex-typed job. The résumés were identical except for a male or female name. The résumés also contained "female" or "male" gender-typed information or gender-neutral information. The managers were asked to infer trait ratings and to decide whether to arrange an interview. What were the results of this study?

Stereotypes and the Assessment of Behavior

20. Buss argues that we evaluate the same behavior differently depending on the gender of the person performing it. Give an example. Buss asked males and females to rate the social desirability of "dominant" acts either when performed by a man or a woman. What did he find? Are all dominant acts rated more severely for a woman than a man? Which sorts are?

21. Understand the relation of gender to dominance and affiliativeness. Shirley Weitz had same-sex and cross-sex pairs interact. Each member of the pair had been measured for dominance and affiliativeness. Raters were given soundless videos of the interaction focused on only one person. What did she find about accommodation in the first minute of a conversation? Does this support the Buss data?

22. Understand how changing gender roles have affected the family. What was Talcott Parsons's view of roles within the family and how this affected the personalities of males and females? How is the modern family different from the family Parsons assumed?

Programmed Exercises

PSYCHOLOGICAL GENDER DIFFERENCES

Differences in Mathematical Ability

1. Males, on the average, do _____ than females on standardized mathematical tests. — better

Differences in Verbal Ability

2. Females, on the average, do _____ than males on standardized verbal tests. — better

3. The difference between the scores of boys and girls is small and _____. — decreasing

GENDER ROLES

4. According to Talcott Parsons all groups, including the family, have to perform two _____ of tasks. — kinds (types)

5. The task-oriented leader accomplishes things such as making _____. — money

6. The social- _____ leader, for instance, keeps the family together as a unit. — emotional

7. In the traditional American family the _____ is the task-oriented leader and the _____ is the social-emotional leader. — father / mother

Socialization and Gender Roles

8. Socialization does not only involve learning sex roles but coming to see the sex role as _____. — natural

9. Traditional stereotypes about male and female _____ serve to justify the sexual division of labor. — traits (roles)

10. In adulthood serious deviation from sex roles is met with pressure to _____ to the roles. — conform

Changing Gender Concepts

11. In the traditional picture masculinity and femininity are _____. — opposites

12. It is now realized that the same person can have both masculine and _____ traits. — feminine

13. It is possible that a person could be both assertive and nurturant or have _____ trait. — neither

Measuring Masculinity and Femininity

14. Bem developed the Sex Role Inventory and Spence and Helmreich developed the _____ _____ _____ in order to show the independence of masculine and feminine traits. — Personal Attributes Questionnaire

15. Bem started from a set of traits that subjects perceived to be more desirable for one _____ than another. — gender

16. Bem formed two _____, one for masculinity and one for femininity. — scales

17. These scales were _____ in the sense that they measured people's ideas about what men and women should be like and not necessarily what they were like.

normative

18. Males and females were asked how descriptive the traits on _____ scales were of them.

both

19. If masculinity and femininity were on a single dimension then the more masculine a subject's score the lower should be the subject's score on the _____ scale. This did not happen.

femininity

20. There was almost no _____ between the two scales.

correlation

21. _____ types were found: people with predominantly masculine traits and few feminine traits; people with predominantly feminine traits and few masculine traits; people with both masculine and feminine traits; and people who did not have many of either type of trait.

Four

22. However it was more likely for _____ to be in the first type, having mainly masculine traits, and _____ to be in the second type, having mainly feminine traits.

men
women

23. The Personal Attributes Questionnaire was developed by directly asking which _____ were more typical of men than women or vice versa.

traits

24. Like the Bem Sex Role Inventory, the Personal Attributes Questionnaire found that there was almost no _____ between a subject's score on the masculinity scale and his or her score on the femininity scale.

correlation

25. If masculine and feminine were tightly linked concepts, then the more masculine a person scored the less _____ the person should score. This is not the case.

feminine

Masculinity, Femininity, and Adjustment

26. Men and women who have both the masculine trait of being achievement oriented and the feminine trait of being nurturant were higher in _____-_____ than men and women who do not.

self-esteem

27. Sex-typed men have mainly _____ traits; androgynous men have both feminine and _____ traits; and cross-sex-typed men have more _____ than masculine traits.

masculine
masculine
feminine

28. Subjects were paid to perform gender "inappropriate" tasks. Sex-typed subjects performed _____ such tasks and felt worse about performing them.

fewer

29. In an interaction between a sex-typed man and a sex-typed woman the man _____ the interaction.

dominates

30. Androgynous people tend to have _____ attitudes toward women.

liberal

31. In an interaction between androgynous males and females, power was _____ if they had filled out a questionnaire on their attitudes just prior to the interaction.

shared

Gender Schema Theory

32. Bem calls the network of associations to the concept of male and female a _____ _____.

gender schema

33. According to Bem, sex-typed people think of themselves primarily in terms of
    _____.   gender

34. This may keep someone from doing something that is seen as gender
    _____.   inappropriate

35. In an experiment boys and girls were given the same task either described as
    one related to sewing or to fixing machinery. Boys made more errors when the
    task was described as related to _____, and girls made more errors   sewing
    when it was described as related to fixing _____.   machinery

36. Sex-typed people have been found to be more likely to categorize on the basis
    of _____ than are androgynous people.   gender

37. Sex-typed subjects are _____ than androgynous subjects at answering faster
    questions about themselves concerning sex-typed traits.

38. Our culture's constant use of gender to categorize people, as in lining up
    students by gender in primary school, leads to people's overuse of
    _____ as a schema.   gender

39. According to Deaux and Spence Bem's concept of gender stereotypes is
    _____.   oversimplified

GENDER STEREOTYPES

40. Stereotypes may mean any view about an entire group, or an unfair view, or a
    _____ view.   false

Stereotypes as Base Rates

41. A woman applies to a physics program and is turned down just because of the
    fact that women are generally worse in math than men. The generalization is
    _____, but what is unfair is that the program did not look at better true
    sources of information about this particular woman.

42. Information about groups of people is _____-_____
    information.   base-rate

43. Information about a particular person is _____ information.
                                                                                diagnostic

44. To maximize one's chance of being right, one should use both _____
    and base-rate information.   diagnostic

45. Gender stereotypes may be used instead of information about a particular
    person, in addition to information about a particular person, or as a
    _____ option, something that is used only when other information   default
    isn't available.

46. Subjects read transcripts of a male or female acting passively or actively.
    Subjects' predictions of future behavior were based on how the people they
    read about behaved, rather than on _____-_____ information base-rate
    about the gender stereotype.

47. In the above situation, if behavioral information is not given, then people use
    _____ _____, that is, _____-_____   gender stereotypes,
    information.   base-rate

Gender Stereotypes and Employment Decisions

48. Upper-level managers had to describe the traits of, and decide whether or not to arrange a job interview for, applicants with identical résumés but male or female names. In addition some résumés contained male sex-typed attributes and others contained female sex-typed information. The managers inferred traits based on _____ information and not gender-based information.   diagnostic

49. But in this study managers were _____ likely to interview a woman for a position than a man.   less

50. In employment situations managers act rationally in inferring traits but _____ in making employment decisions.   irrationally

Stereotypes and the Assessment of Behavior

51. Dominant acts that are self-interested are rated more _____ in a woman than in a man.   negatively

52. Dominant acts that are seen to be in the interest of the group are judged more _____ in a woman than in a man.   positively

53. Shirley Weitz had same-sex and cross-sex pairs interact. Each member of the pair had been measured for dominance and affiliativeness. Raters were given soundless videos of the interaction focused on only one person. Females were _____ dominant with males with higher dominance scores. Females were warmer and _____ assertive with males with higher affiliative scores.   less
more

54. In the above study, male dominance was _____ to female dominance or affiliativeness scores.   uncorrelated
(unrelated to)

55. Parsons assumed a sharp division between the _____ and personalities of males and females in the family.   roles

56. The contemporary family is more egalitarian, but it is an unequal egalitarianism with the female having primary charge of _____.   children

Self-Test

1. On standardized tests
   a. males do better on average on mathematics and females do better on average on verbal tests.
   b. males do better on average on verbal tests and females do better on average on tests of mathematics.
   c. males and females do equally well.
   d. females do better on all standardized tests than males.]

2. The difference between the scores of boys and girls on standardized math tests
   a. is very large.
   b. is about 10 percent of the difference in performance within each gender.

   c. shows that girls score higher than boys.
   d. is almost nonexistent.

3. The task-oriented leader of a group is more concerned with
   a. making members of the group like each other.
   b. keeping the group together.
   c. promoting the desires of the group over his or her own desires.
   d. making money and other practical tasks.

4. The social-emotional leader of a group is more concerned with
   a. promoting group cohesion.
   b. promoting the desires of the group over his or her own desires.
   c. making sure the members of the group like each other.
   d. all of the above

5. According to Talcott Parsons the family must have
   a. a social-emotional leader, the father, and a task-oriented leader, the mother.
   b. a social-emotional leader, the mother, and a task-oriented leader, the father.
   c. a social-emotional leader and a task-oriented leader, but it is irrelevant which role the mother or father takes.
   d. social-emotional and task-oriented functions, but the father might take one role for one task and the mother the same role for a different task.

6. Family socialization involves men and women learning their parts and also learning to feel
   a. that sex roles are parts.
   b. that their sex roles are natural.
   c. coerced into playing their sex roles.
   d. that others who do not play the "appropriate" sex roles are just as normal as they are.

7. Which of the following is (are) a way(s) that people come to stay within their sex roles?
   a. The role feels natural, and they would feel defective if they played the opposite role.
   b. They think that others would see them as being defective if they deviated from their sex role.
   c. They know they would receive pressure from others if they deviated from their sex role.
   d. all of the above

8. In the traditional picture, masculinity and femininity
   a. are opposite—if one has a masculine trait, assertiveness, one couldn't have the "opposite" feminine trait, nurturance.
   b. it was realized that all traits were not natural, but socially assigned.
   c. the same person can have both a masculine and feminine trait at the same time.
   d. referred to a set of traits that most people were not believed to have.

9. Bem's Sex Role Inventory and Spence and Helmreich's Personal Attributes Questionnaire have been used to demonstrate that
   a. the traditional view that masculinity and femininity are necessarily opposite is true.
   b. masculine and feminine traits are independent; people can score high or low on both masculinity and femininity scales.
   c. women are more likely to be conformist than men.
   d. women are no more conformist than men.

10. In order to develop her scale, Bem
    a. started from a set of traits that appeared to be positive in social value and either masculine or feminine in tone.
    b. had subjects select traits that were more desirable for one gender than the other.
    c. measured people's ideas about what men and women should be like and not necessarily what they were like.
    d. all of the above

11. Bem asked males and females how typical both the items on the typical male scale and those on the typical female scale were of them. What was the result?
    a. Males scored very high on the masculinity scale and very low on the femininity scale.
    b. Only females and male homosexuals scored high on the femininity scale.
    c. Males scored higher on the femininity scale, and females scored higher on the masculinity scale.
    d. There was almost no correlation between the scales; some men with high masculinity scores also had high femininity scores.

12. If masculinity and femininity were on a single dimension what would the scores be? Did the data show this to be case?
    a. The higher the subject scores on the masculinity scale the lower he should score on the femininity scale. This was found to be the case.
    b. The lower the subject scores on the masculinity scale the lower he should score on the femininity scale. This was found to be the case.
    c. The higher the subject scores on the masculinity scale the lower he should score on the femininity scale. This was not found to be the case.
    d. The masculinity and femininity scales should be independent. This was not the case.

13. Bem found four types of people using her scale. Which of the following was the *least* common?
    a. males with predominantly masculine traits and a few feminine traits

b. females with predominantly masculine and a few feminine traits

c. females with predominantly feminine traits and a few masculine traits

d. people with both masculine and feminine traits

14. The Personal Attributes Questionnaire also was developed to study masculinity and femininity. It found
   a. that Bem was wrong and that there was a strong negative correlation between scores on the masculinity scale and scores on the femininity scale.
   b. that the more feminine a person scored, the less masculine she was likely to score.
   c. that it was not the case that the more masculine a person scored, the less feminine he or she scored. The masculinity and femininity scales were almost independent (uncorrelated).
   d. that the concepts of masculinity and femininity are subjective concepts.

15. Parsons's view that socialization in the family necessarily produces masculine and feminine people
   a. has been shown to be correct.
   b. is too simple since families produce four types, not two types of people.
   c. is incorrect since families rarely have either social-emotional or task-oriented leaders.
   d. is correct since Parsons assumed four sex-role types.

16. Which of the following are typically best adjusted (have highest self-esteem)?
   a. women high in feminine traits and low in masculine traits
   b. men high in masculine traits and low in feminine traits
   c. both a and b
   d. men and women who are both high on the masculine trait of achievement orientation and the feminine trait of nurturance

17. Which of the following is correct?
   a. Sex-typed men have mainly masculine traits.
   b. Sex-typed women have mainly feminine traits.
   c. Cross-sex-typed women have more masculine than feminine traits and cross-sex-typed men have more feminine than masculine traits.
   d. all of the above

18. Subjects were paid to perform a number of gender "inappropriate" tasks. Sex-typed subjects
   a. performed more of these tasks.
   b. performed these tasks and felt a sense of satisfaction and relief.
   c. performed fewer such tasks and felt bad about performing these actions.
   d. performed the same number of tasks as non-sex-typed subjects.

19. In an interaction between a sex-typed man and a sex-typed woman, the man
   a. dominates the conversation.
   b. courteously allows the woman to dominate the conversation.
   c. shares conversational roles equally with the woman.
   d. rarely speaks to the woman.

20. In an interaction between liberal, androgynous men and women
   a. both always share the conversation.
   b. both share the conversation only if their liberal attitudes have just been made salient.
   c. the woman dominates the conversation.
   d. the male always dominates the conversation.

21. According to Bem, sex-typed people apply gender schemata
   a. too narrowly.
   b. much more broadly than do androgynous people.
   c. not at all.
   d. in an incomplete fashion.

22. According to Bem, sex-typed people
   a. think of themselves primarily in terms of gender.
   b. have a low self-image.
   c. tend to be liberal.
   d. rarely think of themselves in terms of gender.

23. Boys and girls were given the same task, which was either described as related to sewing or to fixing machinery. How did they do?
   a. Boys made more errors when the task was described as related to fixing machines.
   b. The error rate of boys and girls had no

relation to the way the task was described just to how difficult the task was.

c. Boys made more errors when the task was described as related to sewing and girls made more errors when it was described as related to fixing machinery.

d. Girls made more errors when the task was described as related to sewing.

24. Sex-typed subjects are faster than androgynous subjects at
a. answering all questions about themselves.
b. answering questions about themselves that concern sex-typed traits.
c. concealing information about the self.
d. trivia questions.

25. Mary who is very sex-typed and Joan who is androgynous hear a discussion between John, Bill, and Judy. Mary will be more likely than Joan to
a. remember the argument made by Judy.
b. remember the arguments made by the men as opposed to the woman.
c. confuse whether John or Bill made a particular argument.
d. confuse whether John or Judy made a particular argument.

26. In primary school, lining up students by gender
a. might be a source of the tendency to overuse gender as a schema.
b. has no effect on the way that people think about gender.
c. does not concern gender at all—it is just a means of organizing a class.
d. helps clarify students' conceptions of gender-specific abilities.

27. A woman applies to a physics program and is turned down just because women are generally worse in math than men. The generalization is
a. false, and for that reason, unfair.
b. is true, but it is unfair to apply it to an individual if there is a better source of information for this particular woman.
c. true, and hence it is fair not to admit the woman.
d. true, and hence one should not admit a woman unless she is considerably better than males who have been admitted to the program.

28. Which of the following definitions is (are) *correct*?
a. Information about groups of people is "base-rate information," and information about a particular person is "diagnostic" information.
b. Information about groups of people is "diagnostic information," and information about a particular person is "base-rate" information.
c. Information about groups of people is "psychocalisthenic" information.
d. Information about an individual person is "psychodynamic" information.

29. To maximize one's chances of being right one should
a. only use diagnostic information and ignore base-rate information.
b. only use base-rate information and ignore diagnostic information.
c. use neither base-rate nor diagnostic information.
d. use both base-rate and diagnostic information.

30. If a stereotype is used as a default option
a. then it is the first information used.
b. then it is necessary to use this information in order to form a rational judgment.
c. then the stereotype will surely be unfair.
d. then it is used only when other information isn't available.

31. Subjects read transcripts of a male or female acting passively or actively. Subjects' predictions of future behavior were based on
a. what the person in the transcript did (diagnostic information) and not on gender stereotypes.
b. gender stereotypes and not on what the person in the transcript did.
c. both gender stereotypes and diagnostic information.
d. neither gender stereotypes nor diagnostic information.

32. In the above situation if behavioral information is not given then people judge based on
a. diagnostic information.
b. gender stereotypes (base rates).
c. intuition.
d. alphabeticity.

33. Upper-level managers had to describe the traits of, and decide whether or not to arrange a job interview for, applicants with identical résumés but male or female names. In addition, some résumés contained male sex-typed attributes and others female sex-typed information. The managers inferred *traits* based on
    a. diagnostic information and not gender-based information.
    b. gender stereotypes.
    c. base rates.
    d. intuition.

34. In the same study, when the managers were asked whom they would hire they were
    a. equally likely to hire a male or female with the same qualifications.
    b. more likely to hire a female than a male with the same qualifications.
    c. more likely to hire a female even if she had lower qualifications.
    d. more likely to hire a male than a female with the same qualifications.

35. Dominant acts are
    a. always rated more negatively for women than men.
    b. always rated more positively for women than men.
    c. are rated more negatively for women if the act is self-interested, but more positively if it was helpful.
    d. are rated more positively if women are seen as being assertive.

36. Women are generally expected to be
    a. more assertive than men.
    b. more accommodating than men.
    c. neither more assertive nor more accommodating than men.
    d. no more and no less assertive than men.

37. Shirley Weitz had same-sex and cross-sex pairs interact. Each member of the pair had been measured for dominance and affiliativeness. Raters were given soundless videos of the interaction which were focused on only one person. What were the results?
    a. Females were less dominant with males who had higher dominance scores.
    b. Females were warmer and more assertive with males who had higher affiliative scores.

c. In same-sex interactions, the dominance or affiliativeness score of one's partner was unrelated to (uncorrelated with) his or her partner's behavior in the interaction.
d. all of the above

38. For the contemporary American family Talcott Parsons's view of the division of roles in the family
    a. is quite accurate.
    b. completely false.
    c. too narrow.
    d. exaggerates the degree to which sex roles have become more flexible.

Answer Key for Self-Test

1.	a (pp. 228-229)	20.	b (p. 236)
2.	b (p. 228)	21.	b (p. 237)
3.	d (p. 229)	22.	a (p. 237)
4.	d (p. 229)	23.	c (p. 237)
5.	b (p. 229)	24.	b (p. 238)
6.	b (p. 230)	25.	c (p. 238)
7.	d (p. 230)	26.	a (p. 238)
8.	a (p. 231)	27.	b (p. 240)
9.	b (p. 232)	28.	a (p. 240)
10.	d (p. 232)	29.	d (p. 240)
11.	d (p. 233)	30.	d (p. 240)
12.	c (p. 233)	31.	a (p. 241)
13.	b (p. 233)	32.	b (p. 241)
14.	c (p. 233)	33.	a (p. 243)
15.	b (p. 233)	34.	d (p. 243)
16.	d (p. 234)	35.	c (p. 244)
17.	d (p. 235)	36.	b (p. 244)
18.	c (p. 235)	37.	d (p. 245)
19.	a (p. 236)	38.	c (p. 246)

Thought Questions and Exercises

1. Think about informal groups you have been a member of. Was one person a task-oriented leader when something needed to be done or was this role shared? Was one person the social-emotional leader? Was it usually the same person each time this role was called for? If the groups had both males and females, were females more likely to be associated with one role and males with another? How about your

parents? Do your parents play the roles that Talcott Parsons assigns to them?

2. Remember that in devising the Sex Role Inventory Bem started with a list of positive personality traits that struck her as masculine or feminine, i.e., traits that would be more likely for males or females to think that they had. What do you think such traits would be? Make a list of twelve positive traits that you think would differentiate between men and women. After each item place "like me" or "not like me." Give a copy of the list to as many people as you can. It would be best to have at least fifteen males and fifteen females. You may want to collaborate with another student to get enough subjects. Have the subjects fill it out while you wait. It will only take a minute. Note if they are male or female on the sheet. Where were you right and where wrong? Were there items that most females answered "like me" and most males "not like me" and vice versa? Were there items that most males and females responded to similarly? (Answers should be at least 25 percent different between males and females to count as a differentiating answer.) How did your results match with your expectations?

3. (Only if you have done "2") Bem argues that for masculine and feminine traits some people have mainly masculine ones, some feminine, some both, and some neither. Take the traits that discriminated between males and females in general. Now rate each person as to how many "masculine" traits they had and how many "feminine traits." Do you have any females with "masculine" traits or males with "feminine" traits? Do you have anyone who had many of both masculine and feminine traits (as many masculine traits as the average male in your sample and as many feminine traits as the average female in your sample)? Bem believes that androgynous people, those with both higher-than-average "masculinity" and "femininity" scores, are more likely to be flexible and better adjusted than sex-typed males or females. They also are more likely to be liberal than conservative. How might you test this?

4. Bem argues that one comes to think about oneself in terms of gender. Remember that the same mechanical task was presented to children as being related to fixing machines or to sewing. When it was presented as mechanical the boys did better than the girls and when it was presented as sewing-related the girls did better than the boys. In college, males on the average do better than females on standardized math tests. Invent math problems involving cutting patterns for sewing, recipes for baking, etc. Present the same problem relating to baseball or some other male-oriented activity. Give the female form of the problem to ten males and ten females. Do males overall do better than females? Do males do better in the male form? Do females do better in the female form?

5. Remember the text's example of a woman being refused for admission to a physics graduate program just because women on average are worse than men in math and physics. It's true that men are on average better than women in math and physics. Yet it was unfair to refuse the woman only on this basis. Explain why it's unfair in your own words.

6. It has been found that the same *behavior* will be evaluated differently depending on the gender of the person performing it. Is the *person* evaluated differently for the same act depending on sex? Will a woman acting dominantly be judged more harshly than a male doing the same thing? Invent a paragraph-long story involving someone acting assertively, for instance, butting into conversations, interrupting, explaining that someone does not know what they are talking about. Now make up two versions of the story by giving the protagonist a male or a female name. Present the male version to ten male and ten female students and the female version to ten male and ten female students. Ask them to evaluate the protagonist on a seven-point scale: My opinion of this character is: (1) very positive, (2) positive, (3) slightly positive, (4) neutral, (5) slightly negative, (6) negative, (7) very negative. Is there any difference in the evaluation when the protagonist is male or female? Is there any difference when the person doing the evaluation is male or female?

CHAPTER 7

Self-Presentation

Learning Objectives

1. Describe what is meant by self-presentation or impression management. In what sense is being a certain sort of person "an accomplishment" rather then something that we look into our soul and read off?

GOFFMAN'S APPROACH TO SELF-PRESENTATION

Impression Management and Identity

2. One way to think about self-presentation is through the notion that it is to our interest to arrange what conclusions people draw about us; another way develops from the notion of "the definition of a situation." Define and explain how this notion is central to self-presentation. Give several examples of how shared understandings influence behavior. How is the definition of the situation dependent on the social identities of the parties involved? Is it just the formal identity or something more? Give examples.

3. Goffman argues that there is an unstated contract, a working consensus, between, for instance, students and teachers, to treat each other as if each had a certain identity. Give two different reasons why people would want to do this. What happens when the working consensus falls apart?

Impression Management and Embarrassment

4. Explain what Modigliani has to say about the cause of embarrassment. What is the link between losing self-esteem and losing esteem in the eyes of another? Describe Modigliani's experiment demonstrating that people are embarrassed to appear stupid before others, even if they know that what they have done is not stupid.

Embarrassment and Interaction

5. Explain whether embarrassment always leads to loss of self-esteem and whether loss of self-esteem always leads to embarrassment. Give examples. What is the Parrot, Sabini, and Silver account of embarrassment? How does their experiment demonstrate that embarrassment is less concerned with losing esteem than with botching a self-presentation? Did the phony excuse for turning the date down reduce self-esteem or reduce embarrassment as compared to a straightforward refusal?

Empathetic and Secondary Embarrassment

6. Define "empathetic embarrassment." Give an example. Does a person suffer from empathetic embarrassment because of a loss of self-esteem? Define "secondary embarrassment." Does the existence of secondary embarrassment provide evidence for the independence of embarrassment from self-esteem?

Consequences of Embarrassment

7. Describe some of the typical displays of embarrassment. What is "facework"? How does the experiment by Brown illustrate facework? Be sure to include in your answer the effect of the audience's knowing or not knowing the cost of

retaliation. Give some examples of things people are known to do in order to avoid embarrassment.

The How of Self-Presentation: Performances

Sets and Props

8. "While the whole world surely isn't a stage, the whole world does share certain crucial features with stages." What features? Give some examples of everyday set and props. How do they show our audience what sort of person we are?

Teams

9. Playing a character is often a collaborative project. Explain. Having a team is useful in dividing the labor, but it also has informative functions. What are they? One cost of being a team player is that you may be tarnished by the doings of others on your team. Give an example. Team play involves coordination, and even the concealment of that coordination. Why? Give some examples of concealment. Concealed coordination creates a problem for those who have children on their team. Explain.

Appearance and Manner

10. Clothes announce a lot about us, yet we often don't choose our clothes to make an announcement. Explain.

The Dramaturgic Perspective and Faking

11. The dramaturgic perspective has sometimes been mistakenly taken to imply that we all are fakes. This is not true. Use the example of the true friend and the phony friend to show that Goffman would not claim that they are alike but would claim that their "self-presentational" task would have to be alike. How does this example illustrate Goffman's claim that facts that aren't communicated are of no social significance?

12. Goffman rejects the view that only "doing what comes naturally at each moment" (as opposed to self-presentation) makes for authenticity. Why? People wish to present themselves in a favorable light and also to be perceived as they are. Describe the experiment presented to illustrate this point.

STRATEGIES OF SELF-PRESENTATION

Ingratiation and Self-Promotion

13. Define "ingratiation." What are some methods of ingratiation? Why must ingratiators conceal the real aim of their activities—both from their targets and from any audience? How is the "self-promoter" different from the ingratiator? Describe the experiment that compared the relative difficulty of self-promotion and ingratiation. Which was more difficult? What further danger was self-promotion found to have?

Intimidation and Exemplification

14. Define "intimidation." What are some of the dangers of this strategy? What is the strategy of "exemplification"? How is the exemplifier different from the self-promoter? What are some dangers of this strategy? Describe the experiment contrasting the "exemplifier" and the "pragmatist" who have been caught cheating.

Supplication and Self-Handicapping

15. Describe the strategy of "supplication." What are some drawbacks of supplication? Handicaps are not the sort of things we usually wish to have but sometime they are very handy for our self-presentation. Explain and give an example. If we are concerned with our presentation to others then we need an apparent rather than real handicap; if our concern is with what we think of ourselves then acquiring a real handicap may be needed. Explain. Describe the experiment involving choice of performance-enhancing or performance-inhibiting drugs that illustrates this.

Basking and Blasting

16. Describe what Cialdini means by "basking." How did the experiment involving counting the number of students wearing university logos after the college team's football games demonstrate basking? What is the strategy of "blasting"? Describe the experiment that shows basking and blasting after an induced failure. How is blasting related to envy?

Impression Management and Self-Deception

17. Sometimes we engage in impression management not to impress others but in order to enhance our esteem in our own eyes. For this reason we may arrive at a sincere view of ourselves that is really self-deceptive. Explain.

INNER AND OUTER FOCUS OF ATTENTION

18. Describe the two focuses that can be used to distinguish between what people really think and the impression they try to create. Describe which subjects in the Asch and Milgram

experiments can be thought of as "inner directed" and which as "outer directed." Why is "inner and outer focus" a metaphor and not a literal description?

Objective Self-Awareness

19. Explain what George Herbert Mead meant by saying there were two selves, the "I" and the "me." Give examples of different foci of attention involving the I and the me. How does Wicklund develop this distinction? What is "objective self-awareness"? Give several examples of how to put a person in an state of objective self-awareness. According to Wicklund, what is the effect of being in a state of objective self-awareness?

Objective Self-Awareness and Standards

20. Describe an experiment that shows how using a mirror to make a subject objectively self-aware can trigger the subject's concern with her standards of behavior.

Conflicting Standards

21. Explain why the existence of conflicting standards presents a problem for objective self-awareness theory. In an experiment subjects were, or were not, make anxious about their intelligence and then they were given a test that they could solve by cheating. They were also listening, or not listening, to a tape of their own voices. What were the results? Why are the results ambiguous for objective self-awareness theory? What was the result of the experiment with cigarette smokers and why were the results difficult for objective awareness theory?

Self-Consciousness and Motivation

22. Explain how self-focused attention may increase subjects' motivation, or drive. How might this explain the results of the experiment in which cigarette smokers perform a task while facing a mirror? What is the Yerkes-Dodson Law? Why does it suggest that sometimes self-focused attention should interfere with performance? What is Baumeister's explanation for why the home team tends to lose the seventh game of the World Series?

23. Describe some problems of objective self-awareness theory.

Self-Awareness as a Personality Trait

24. Explain what it would mean for self-consciousness to be a personality trait. Give some examples of items on the Self-Consciousness Scale. Conceptually what is "factor analysis"? What are the three distinct factors derived from a factor analysis of the scale? What is "social anxiety"? Give an example of each of these factors.

25. Is there a tendency for someone who is publicly self-conscious to be privately self-conscious or socially anxious? Both the privately and publicly self-conscious are attentive to themselves, but in different ways. Explain.

SELF-MONITORING

26. Describe what Snyder means by a "high self-monitor." What are some of the ways that Snyder thinks that high self-monitors differ from low self-monitors?

27. Explain what it means to say a scale is "reliable." Snyder constructed his Self-Monitoring Scale from questions relating to ways that he thought high self-monitors differ from low self-monitors. How reliable was his scale? What is "validity"? What is "construct validity"? How did the study with the fraternity members help show the validity of the scale?

Self-Monitoring and Conformity

28. Would a high or a low self-monitor conform more if she thought that her behavior was being videotaped? If she thought that others would not be aware of her conformity?

29. What is the difference between high self-monitoring and low self-monitoring women in their willingness to join an affirmative action discussion group. What does this show about self-monitoring? Was the effect the same for men?

30. Are high self-monitors more or less inclined to self-deception? Are low self-monitors liable to be less than tactful?

Self-Monitoring and Relationships

Friendships

31. Describe how high and low self-monitors differ in the pattern of their friendships.

Romantic Relationships

32. Describe the difference between high and low self-monitors in their amount and pattern of dating. Who is more concerned with the physical attractiveness of their dates, high or low self-monitors? Given a choice between a pretty date with a rotten personality or a less-than-pretty

date with a nice personality, what would be the choice of male low and high self-monitors? If they are asked to predict how others would choose, what do the high and low self-monitors predict?

Further Support for the Validity of the Self-Monitoring Approach

33. How is self-monitoring like public self-awareness? In what way do the scales differ?

Criticisms of the Self-Monitoring Scale

Self-Monitoring: A Matter of Social Skills?

34. Might the difference between high and low self-monitors just come down to one of social skill? Explain pro and con.

Empirical Criticisms

35. It has been suggested that the Self-Monitoring Scale contains three factors. What are they? Snyder has revised the scale but it still seems to contain two factors. What are they? Snyder would have preferred that there be only one factor. Why?

Programmed Exercises

1. The study of how people attempt to control the impressions other people form of them is called _____ _____.

impression
management

2. Mead and Cooley believed that knowledge of our selves is a reflection of the opinion of _____.

others

3. They also believed that having a certain sort of self is more involved with _____ actions than private feelings.

public

4. Being a loving friend is an _____ that requires doing certain things, not just having certain feelings.

accomplishment

GOFFMAN'S APPROACH TO SELF-PRESENTATION

Impression Management and Identity

5. Goffman starts from the truism that we know it is to our advantage to influence other people's _____ of us.

impressions

6. The definition of the _____ in which we interact with a person includes the social _____ of the parties involved.

situation
identities

7. A social _____ includes what a person is formally entitled by specific institutions to claim as well as many vague informal expectations.

identity

8. From the point of view of *managing* an interaction, it is _____ very important whether the identity a person claims is true as long as the parties to the interaction act as if it were _____.

not

true

9. A _____ _____ is an implicit contract for all parties to an interaction to treat each other as if they had certain identities.

working consensus

Impression Management and Embarrassment

10. According to Modigliani, we become embarrassed when we perceive that we have suddenly lost _____ in the eyes of others, and because of that lose esteem in own eyes.

esteem

11. In an experiment it was found that subjects were _____ when they publicly failed on a task even though they knew (but they knew their audience didn't know) the task was really quite difficult.

embarrassed

12. According to the Parrot, Sabini, and Silver account of embarrassment, botching the _____ _____ rather than losing self-esteem leads to embarrassment.   working consensus

13. If you are asking someone out for a date and the person turns you down with an excuse you know to be phony, you will be _____ embarrassed than if you had been turned down with a simple refusal.   less

14. The flat turndown, although more embarrassing, might be _____ self-esteem-threatening.   less

15. When we become embarrassed because we are observing someone else's embarrassment we are experiencing _____ embarrassment.   empathetic

16. In an interaction if one person fails in presenting her role, the others in the interaction will feel _____ _____   secondary embarrassment

17. Secondary embarrassment shows that embarrassment is at least sometimes independent of a lowered _____-_____.   self-esteem

18. _____ is an attempt to restore one's fumbled identity.   Facework

19. In Brown's experiment, students were publicly exploited and then allowed to get even with the exploiter but at a cost to themselves. Subjects retaliated _____ when the audience did not know that retaliation was costly. This is an example of _____.   most
facework

20. People will endure great costs to _____ embarrassment.   avoid

The How of Self-Presentation: Performances

21. The _____ perspective sees people as concerned with projecting a character and examines how they do this.   dramaturgic

22. In the theater, and in everyday life, sets and props inform the audience as to the _____ of the actors and the nature of the performance.   character

23. In everyday life we put on joint performances of characters. Goffman calls the people putting on a joint performance a _____.   team

24. By examining how the others on someone's team treat her we have a clue about what sort of person she really is, or at least how she expects to be _____. According to Goffman, for many purposes we don't need to know what a person is really like but only who she is willing to be _____ as.   treated
treated

25. Team play not only involves coordination but sometimes the _____ of that coordination.   concealment

26. Children often do not notice or they _____ tacit coordinating signals.   ignore

The Dramaturgic Perspective and Faking

27. The dramaturgic perspective does _____ hold that we are all fakes.   not

28. A real friend and a phony friend would need to present _____ performances, but when the crunch comes their behavior would be _____.   similar
different

29. Expressing your real feelings at each moment may _____ sincerely acting as a friend.   block (interfere with)

30. In the Swann, Pelham, and Krull experiment, people most preferred someone
who evaluated them _____ on an attribute that they evaluated   positively
themselves positively on. They preferred someone who evaluated them
_____ on something they evaluated themselves negatively on to   negatively
someone who evaluated them positively on something they evaluated
themselves _____ on.   negatively

STRATEGIES OF SELF-PRESENTATION

Ingratiation and Self-Promotion

31. _____ involves illicitly making oneself likeable in another's eyes.   Ingratiation

32. If the ingratiator does not _____ his real aim then the ingratiation will   conceal
backfire.

33. It is often easier to ingratiate oneself with the target of the ingratiation than   observers (an
with _____.   audience)

34. The _____-_____ tries to be seen as competent.   self-promoter

35. In an experiment comparing the relative difficulty of ingratiation and self-
promotion, it was found that _____ was more difficult to achieve.   self-promotion

36. Subjects who failed in their attempts at self-promotion were usually
_____.   disliked

Intimidation and Exemplification

37. The _____ tries to be seen as dangerous.   intimidator

38. The _____ pretends to be morally elevated.   exemplifier

39. If an exemplifier is found out she will be seen as a _____.   hypocrite

Supplication and Self-Handicapping

40. In the strategy of _____ one tries to look helpless in order to be taken   supplication
care of.

41. Sometimes we wish to appear to others as if we had a handicap in order to
_____ failure and enhance _____.   excuse, success

42. To excuse failure before others one only needs to _____ handicapped,   appear (look)
to do it before yourself one needs to _____ handicapped.   be

43. In an experiment subjects who were made confident chose to use a
performance-_____ drug while those who were made unconfident   enhancing
chose to use a performance-_____ drug. This demonstrates   inhibiting
_____-_____.   self-handicapping

Basking and Blasting

44. Students wearing a college logo after the victory of their school team is an
example of _____.   basking

45. When describing defeats of their team students are more likely to use the
pronoun _____, but when describing victories they are more likely to   they
use we.

46. Students who were made unconfident were more likely to _____ a rival university and _____ in their own university than confident students.

blast
bask

Impression Management and Self-Deception

47. Sometimes we engage in impression management not to impress others but to impress _____.

ourselves

48. It is possible to arrive at a _____ view of ourselves that is nonetheless self-deceptive.

sincere

INNER AND OUTER FOCUS OF ATTENTION

49. We use the metaphorical term _____ for what we really think or feel and _____ for what we think other people would prefer we think or feel.

inner
outer

50. Conforming subjects in the Asch experiment would be labeled _____-directed.

outer

51. Inner/outer is a metaphor and not a description since almost all behaviors have both inner and _____ determinants.

outer

Objective Self-Awareness

52. According to Mead, the _____ refers to the active self and the _____ refers to the reflective self.

I
me

53. In embarrassment we focus on the _____, and when we are totally engrossed in a task we are almost all _____.

me
I

54. According to Wicklund, _____ _____-_____ is the state of being focused on the me.

objective
self-awareness

55. Looking in a mirror, and knowing that you are on videotape or audiotape are ways to induce _____ _____-_____.

objective
self-awareness

56. Wicklund proposed that being in a state of objective self-awareness makes a person more likely to think about herself in relation to _____.

standards

57. Subjects given the opportunity to use shock who were strongly in favor of the use of punishment in teaching acted in accordance with their belief in the presence of a _____ but did not do so in its absence.

mirror

58. Dieters who were the objects of the experimenter's attention ate _____ than those who were not made self-aware.

less

59. It is difficult to decide if objective self-awareness theory is correct since there are many different and conflicting _____ and living up to one may conflict with living up to another.

standards

60. Subjects who were made anxious about their intelligence were more likely to _____ if they were listening to a tape of their own voice.

cheat

61. This result is ambiguous for objective self-awareness theory since cheating violates _____ standards but allows the subjects to fulfill self-promoting standards.

moral

Self-Consciousness and Motivation

62. Self-focused attention increases _____ level.

drive (motivation)

63. The Yerkes-Dodson Law states that for complex tasks performance will _____ as motivation (drive) increases.

decrease

64. Since self-focused attention increases motivation, it should interfere with _____ tasks. This might explained why home teams typically _____ the highly charged seventh game of the World Series.

complex
lose

Self-Awareness as a Personality Trait

65. If self-consciousness is a _____ trait then some people are likely to be chronically self-conscious and others chronically unself-conscious.

personality

66. Items on the _____ _____ Scale include questions about concern with one's feelings, one's appearance, and one's regard in the eyes of others.

Self-Consciousness

67. Three factors have been found for the Self-Consciousness Scale. They are _____ _____-_____, _____ _____-_____, and _____ _____.

private self-consciousness, public self-consciousness, social anxiety

68. Public self-consciousness relates to concern with self as a _____ object. Private self-consciousness relates to being attentive to one's real _____. Social anxiety refers to the tendency to get _____ by social attention.

social

feelings, upset

69. The three factors of the Self-Consciousness Scale are related to each other so that someone who is high on one scale is likely to be _____ on the other scales.

high

70. Privately self-conscious people differ from publicly self-conscious people in that they are _____ likely to give in to social pressure.

less

SELF-MONITORING

71. People who pay great attention to the impressions they are giving off are called _____ _____-_____.

high self-monitors

72. Snyder believed that high self-monitors differed from low self-monitors in that they are concerned with the social _____ of their self-presentation, they use others' behavior as a _____, they are able to control and _____ self-presentation, they are willing to modify self-presentation to gain an _____, and they are less _____ in social behavior from situation to situation.

appropriateness
guide
modify
advantage,
consistent

73. Snyder created a _____-_____ _____ using questions reflecting the ways that he thought high self-monitors were different from low self-monitors. It is somewhat _____ in that there is a tendency for items to hang together.

Self-Monitoring
Scale
reliable

Self-Monitoring and Conformity

74. High self-monitors conformed _____ than low self-monitors when they were being videotaped but _____ than low self-monitors when they were not.

less
more

75. High self-monitors who have been induced to endorse an opinion they don't
    have will _____ distort their own beliefs to make themselves look   not
    good in their own eyes; low self-monitors are _____ likely to deceive   more
    themselves.

Self-Monitoring and Relationships

76. Low self-monitors prefer to do many different things with a _____   few
    friends, while high self-monitors prefer _____ friends for different   different
    activities.

77. High self-monitors date _____ partners and have _____   more, shallower
    relationships than low self-monitors.

78. _____ self-monitors are more likely to choose looks over personality   High
    in a date.

Further Support for the Validity of the Self-Monitoring Approach

79. Those _____ in both self-monitoring and public self-awareness are   high
    attentive to the impressions they make on others.

80. Those both _____ in self-monitoring and _____ in private   low, high
    self-awareness are attentive to their internal states.

Criticisms of the Self-Monitoring Scale

81. The Self-Monitoring Scale _____ with measures of social skills.   correlates

82. It is possible that both low and high self-monitoring males prefer shallow
    sexual relationships but only _____ self-monitors are skilled enough   high
    to get them.
                                                                                      other directedness,
83. The Self-Monitoring Scale may contain three factors: _____   acting ability,
    _____, _____, and _____.   sociability
                                                                                      (extraversion)
84. Snyder's revised scale contains two factors: _____ in public and   performing
    _____ _____.   other directedness

Self-Test

1. The study of how people attempt to control the
   impressions people have of them is called
   a. cognitive dissonance.
   b. impression formation.
   c. impression management.
   d. sincerity.

2. Erving Goffman's notion of "the definition of
   the situation" includes
   a. a shared understanding of the situation.
   b. the formal social roles or identities of the
      parties involved.
   c. vague, informal demands deriving from the
      identity of the parties.
   d. all of the above

3. From the point of view of managing an
   interaction
   a. it is important that all the parties to an
      interaction present truthful claims.
   b. it is important that the parties to an
      interaction believe each other's claims.
   c. it is important that the parties to an
      interaction act as if they believed each
      other's claims.
   d. all of the above

4. The working consensus
   a. is an implicit agreement about identities
      necessary for interactions to run smoothly.
   b. is only occasionally needed for an
      interaction to run smoothly.

c. is an agreement about work rules in a factory or office.

d. is only sustained because of fear of punishment from authority.

5. André Modigliani believes that embarrassment occurs when
   a. we realize that we have lost esteem in the eyes of others.
   b. when we believe that we have done something incorrect.
   c. others believe we are wrong but only if we believe they are right.
   d. we have low self-esteem.

6. In an experiment Modigliani found that subjects would be embarrassed before others if they failed in a task
   a. that they realized was an easy one.
   b. that they realized was hard but that they knew other subjects thought was easy.
   c. that was easy or hard.
   d. and they had low self-esteem.

7. On the New York City subway, experimenters asked people for their seats. What happened?
   a. Almost no one gave up their seats.
   b. The experimenters felt very embarrassed.
   c. Most people gave up their seats.
   d. b and c

8. According to the Parrott, Sabini, and Silver theory of embarrassment
   a. embarrassment derives from a loss of self-esteem.
   b. someone might be embarrassed even if they don't lose self-esteem.
   c. the falling apart of the working consensus causes embarrassment.
   d. b and c

9. According to the Parrott, Sabini, and Silver study of embarrassment, people are least embarrassed when they are refused a date if
   a. they are told "no" in an honest straightforward way.
   b. they are given an excuse for the refusal even if they know the excuse is false.
   c. they have strong self-esteem.
   d. a and c

10. When we become embarrassed due to observing someone else's embarrassment we experience
    a. angst.

b. a neurosis.

c. empathetic embarrassment.

d. anger.

11. If we are talking with someone and something embarrassing happens to them and we too feel embarrassed then we are experiencing
    a. secondary embarrassment.
    b. primary embarrassment.
    c. a psychotic fit.
    d. rolfing.

12. In Brown's experiment, students were publicly exploited and then allowed to get even with the exploiter. Brown found that
    a. subjects retaliated against the exploiter only when the audience did not know that retaliation cost them a lot.
    b. subjects would endure considerable costs to look good.
    c. Subjects did not retaliate if the audience realized that the retaliation was costly to them.
    d. all of the above

13. Sets and props
    a. are only used in the theater.
    b. are used by people in everyday life but only if they are pretentious and phony.
    c. are used by ordinary people to display what they are like.
    d. are never used by an audience to make inferences about someone's character.

14. In Goffman's terms, people putting on a joint performance are called a
    a. company.
    b. party.
    c. foxtrot.
    d. team.

15. Team play
    a. involves coordination of roles.
    b. involves concealing the coordination of roles.
    c. involves handling people threatening to the coordination such as children or the tipsy.
    d. all of the above

16. The dramaturgic perspective
    a. sees everyone as basically insincere.
    b. believes that if people do not express their genuine feeling at each moment they are not genuine.
    c. believes that acting as a true friend may

sometimes require you to suppress your actual feelings.

d. believes that only a few people are ever able to pass beyond acting to the expression of genuine feeling.

17. In the Swann, Pelham, and Krull experiment, people preferred someone who evaluated them
   a. positively on an attribute even though they did not evaluate themselves positively on this attribute.
   b. negatively if they themselves evaluated themselves negatively on this attribute.
   c. positively in all circumstances.
   d. positively but only when they did not believe that they really deserved the positive evaluation.

18. The ingratiator
   a. illicitly makes himself likable in another person's eyes in order to gain an advantage.
   b. conceals his real aims—if he does not his ingratiation collapses.
   c. finds it easier to dupe the person he is attempting to ingratiate than to dupe observers.
   d. all of the above

19. The self-promoter
   a. tries by illicit means to make herself appear competent.
   b. has an easier time in achieving her ends than does the ingratiator.
   c. is typically liked even when people realize what she is trying to do.
   d. all of the above

20. Which of the following is *true*?
   a. The intimidator tries to appear dangerous.
   b. The intimidator runs the risk that people will dislike and avoid him.
   c. The exemplifier pretends to be morally elevated and runs the risk of being seen as a hypocrite.
   d. all of the above

21. Sometimes in order to excuse failure or enhance success we try to show that what we have done was done
   a. intentional.
   b. with full concentration.
   c. under a handicap.
   d. with considerable effort.

22. Subjects who did not feel confident were more likely than those who felt confident to choose
   a. a performance-enhancing drug.
   b. a performance-inhibiting drug.
   c. a psychedelic drug.
   d. not to take a drug.

23. Students are more likely to wear a college logo after the victory of their school team. This is an example of
   a. blasting.
   b. ingratiation.
   c. exemplification.
   d. basking.

24. Which of the following is (are) an example(s) of basking?
   a. Students are more likely to use "we" in talking about their team after a success.
   b. People are less likely to bring up the fact that they have the same birthday with someone if that person is successful.
   c. People are more likely to put down a rival university's team after the defeat of their own team.
   d. all of the above

25. Impression management can be used
   a. only to fool other people since we know what is true about ourselves.
   b. to fool others as well as ourselves.
   c. to fool ourselves (as well as others) only when we are insincere.
   d. to fool others only when we are insincere.

26. "Inner" and "outer" in personality theory
   a. are metaphors.
   b. refer to what we really think (inner) and what others want us to think (outer).
   c. cannot exist apart from each other.
   d. all of the above

27. George Herbert Mead calls the reflective part of the self
   a. the I.
   b. the me.
   c. the them.
   d. the it.

28. When we are embarrassed we are focusing almost entirely on
   a. the me.
   b. the it.
   c. the I.
   d. the demands of the task.

29. Which of the following is *not* an example of ways to induce objective self-awareness
    a. looking in a mirror.
    b. seeing yourself in a video.
    c. hearing yourself on an audiotape.
    d. being focused on a task.

30. Subjects given the opportunity to use shock who were strongly in favor of the use of punishment in teaching acted in accordance with their belief
    a. when they were presented with an opportunity to do so.
    b. in the presence of a mirror.
    c. when a mirror was absent.
    b. never.

31. Subjects who were made anxious about their intelligence were more likely to cheat if they were listening to a tape of their own voice. This finding
    a. is clear-cut evidence for objective self-awareness theory.
    b. disproves objective self-awareness theory.
    c. is ambiguous for objective self-awareness theory since cheating maintains standards for self-promotion but violates standards for honesty.
    d. shows that objective self-awareness theory is not applicable to moral situations.

32. In an experiment where smokers who wanted to stop smoking did a task facing a mirror, the smokers smoked
    a. more than smokers who were not facing a mirror.
    b. less than smokers who were not facing a mirror.
    c. the same amount as smokers who were not facing a mirror.
    d. not even one cigarette.

33. How can the results of the cigarette experiment be interpreted in terms of motivation?
    a. Self-focused attention decreases drive level.
    b. Self-focused attention increases drive level, which in turn increases the probability of a well-learned habit.
    c. Self-focused attention has no effect on drive level.
    d. Self-focused attention decreases motivation.

34. The Yerkes-Dodson Law states that
    a. for complex tasks performance will increase as motivation increases.
    b. for complex tasks performance will decrease as motivation increases.
    c. performance is independent of motivation.
    d. performance always decreases.

35. Since self-focused attention increases motivation it will
    a. enhance performance of complex tasks.
    b. decrease performance of complex tasks.
    c. neither increase nor decrease performance of complex tasks.
    d. will increase or decrease performance of complex tasks, depending on the nature of the task.

36. The notion that self-consciousness is a personality trait implies
    a. that some people are likely to be chronically self-conscious and others chronically unself-conscious.
    b. that self-consciousness is a momentary thing.
    c. that all people should be more or less the same on self-consciousness.
    d. that self-consciousness should increase with age.

37. On what scales would you find items about concern over one's appearance, feelings, and how you look in the eyes of others?
    a. Strong's Vocational Interest Blank
    b. Rorschach Test
    c. Sabine Test for Dysfunctional Locutions
    d. Self-Consciousness Scale

38. Three factors have been found for the Self-Consciousness Scale. Which of the following is not a factor?
    a. private self-consciousness
    b. tendency to become absorbed in tasks
    c. public self-consciousness
    d. social anxiety

39. Privately self-conscious people (as compared to publicly self conscious people) are
    a. more likely to give in to social pressure.
    b. more likely to use makeup (if they are women).
    c. less likely to give in to social pressure.
    d. less likely to disclose facts about their private lives.

40. Snyder's term "self-monitors" refers to people
    a. who are very introspective.
    b. who are high in private self-consciousness.
    c. who are unconcerned with the impression they make on others.
    d. who pay great attention to the impressions they are giving off.

41. High self-monitors differ from low self-monitors in that they
    a. are strongly concerned with social appropriateness.
    b. are more likely to use other people's behavior as a guide.
    c. are more willing to modify self-presentation to gain an advantage.
    d. all of the above

42. Which is *true* about a reliable or a valid scale?
    a. In a reliable scale items should hang together.
    b. In a valid scale the items should hang together.
    c. In a valid scale the score on the scale does not necessarily fit with what we would expect given the concept the scale is measuring.
    d. all of the above

43. A high self-monitor will conform
    a. less than a low self-monitor, in general.
    b. more than a low self-monitor, in general.
    c. less than a low self-monitor if she is being videotaped.
    d. more than a low self-monitor if she is being videotaped.

44. Who is more prone to self-deception?
    a. high self-monitors
    b. low self-monitors
    c. neither, it depends on the situation
    d. whoever is more tactful

45. Low self-monitors lack
    a. warmth.
    b. concern with others.
    c. tact.
    d. enthusiasm.

46. Who has a greater variety of friends?
    a. the high self-monitor
    b. the low self-monitor
    c. neither; it depends on the individual
    d. the one who engages in fewer activities

47. Who is more likely to date more, have more sexual relationships, have shallower relationships, and be more concerned with looks?
    a. the high self-monitor
    b. the low self-monitor
    c. neither; it depends on the individual
    d. it depends on who finds the right person first

48. Who is usually better-adjusted?
    a. the high self-monitor
    b. the low self-monitor
    c. the person who is intermediate on self-monitoring
    d. none of the above

49. People who are low in self-monitoring and high in private self-awareness are more likely to be
    a. attentive to their internal states.
    b. attentive to the impression they are making on others.
    c. attentive to the opinions of even people that they disagree with.
    d. none of the above

50. High self-monitors are more likely to have
    a. worse social skills.
    b. better social skills.
    c. intermediate social skills.
    d. better social skills at first, but very soon it becomes apparent that they are insincere.

51. Which factor does the Self-Monitoring Scale not contain?
    a. other directedness
    b. acting ability
    c. sociability
    d. introspection

Answer Key for Self-Test

1. c (pp. 247-248)
2. d (p. 249)
3. c (p. 249)
4. a (p. 249)
5. a (p. 251)
6. b (p. 251)
7. d (p. 251)
8. d (pp. 252-253)
9. b (p. 252)
10. c (p. 253)
11. a (p. 253)
12. d (p. 254)
13. c (p. 255)
14. d (p. 256)
15. d (pp. 257-258)
16. c (pp. 260-261)
17. b (p. 261)
18. d (p. 262)
19. a (pp. 262-263)
20. d (p. 264)

21.	c (p. 265)	37.	d (pp. 274-275)
22.	b (p. 266)	38.	b (p. 275)
23.	d (p. 267)	39.	c (p. 275)
24.	a (p. 267)	40.	d (p. 277)
25.	b (p. 269)	41.	d (p. 277)
26.	d (pp. 269-270)	42.	a (p. 278)
27.	b (p. 270)	43.	c (p. 279)
28.	a (p. 270)	44.	b (p. 280)
29.	d (p. 271)	45.	c (p. 280)
30.	b (p. 271)	46.	a (p. 281)
31.	c (p. 272)	47.	a (p. 281)
32.	a (p. 272)	48.	c (p. 282)
33.	b (p. 273)	49.	a (p. 282)
34.	b (p. 273)	50.	b (p. 282)
35.	b (p. 273)	51.	d (p. 284)
36.	a (p. 274)		

Thought Questions and Exercises

1. The notion of people as actors presented in the dramaturgic perspective sometimes troubles us since it appears to deny sincerity. The text argues that it does not. What was its argument? Do you buy it? Does it leave anything out—spontaneity, for instance?

2. The text discusses Goffman's notion of "teams" and collusion between members of a team. Can you illustrate this from your own experience (for example, your family as a team in front of visitors, or you and your boyfriend or girlfriend in front of your parents)?

3. Goffman points out that we can sometimes get in trouble if we don't keep our teams separate. The performance that a biker puts on in front of his gang may be disrupted by the performance he owes his mother if she happens to bump into him when he is with them. Can you supply examples of such a conflict from your own experience?

4. Think back to a time when you experienced embarrassment or saw someone else being embarrassed. Try to apply the two theories of embarrassment presented in the text. Which one, if either, captures your experience? Where are they lacking?

5. Can you think of a time that you went along with people against your better judgment because you feared being embarrassed if you went against them? Describe.

6. Give examples from your own experience of people trying to get away with the following of Jones's strategies: ingratiation, self-promotion, intimidation, exemplification, supplication, and self-handicapping.

7. Does your school have a team that people, at least occasionally, get passionate about? If so, you can replicate Cialdini's demonstration of basking. Remember Cialdini counted the number of people wearing university logos the Monday after a team victory as well as the Monday after a defeat. You might try to investigate when basking will be strong or weak. Can you think up a hypothesis that will predict which groups will be most likely to bask?

8. The Self-Consciousness Scale clusters into three factors—"private self-consciousness," "public self-consciousness," and "social anxiety." Invent character descriptions of people who would be high or low on various combinations of these factors—for example, high in both public self-consciousness and private self-consciousness, but low in social anxiety; or high in social anxiety and public self-consciousness, but low in private self-consciousness.

9. What does Snyder mean by a high self-monitor? Do you know anyone like that? What are your reactions to him or her? The text describes characteristics of high self-monitors in regard to friendship, sex, self-deception, and likelihood to mope publicly. Does the person you described fit this portrait? To what extent?

CHAPTER 8

Emotion: Experience and Expression

Learning Objectives

THE JAMES-LANGE THEORY

1. William James argued that if you met a hungry bear, you would experience, or do, three things. Which of these three things would be the emotion of fear? Why? How do we know which emotion we are experiencing? Why does James's view make evolutionary sense?

2. Carl Lange, in agreement with James, proposed that we feel an emotion—for instance, fear—when we experience what is now called arousal of the autonomic nervous system. What is evidence for this James-Lange theory? What were Cannon's criticisms of the James-Lange theory?

COGNITIVE AROUSAL THEORY

The Sympathetic Nervous System and Emotion

Necessity of Arousal

3. Understand what is meant by the hypothesis that arousal is *necessary* for the experience of an emotion. Why would the fact that people with severed spinal cords can experience emotion tend to refute the view that sympathetic arousal is necessary for the experience of emotion?

Sufficiency of Autonomic Feedback for Emotion

4. Explain how Marañon demonstrated that sympathetic arousal is not *sufficient* for having an emotion. (You should be able to distinguish between a necessary and a sufficient condition.) Did some of the subjects experience something close to an emotion? What?

The Schachter and Singer Experiment

5. Describe Schachter and Singer's hypothesis about the nature of emotion. How do Schachter and Singer explain why Marañon's subjects did not experience an emotion even though they were physiologically aroused?

Procedure of the Schachter and Singer Experiment

6. Explain how Schachter and Singer tested their hypothesis. What control group did they use? How did they test the cognitive component of their theory? Remember there were several groups testing cognitions—one in which people were told the true effects that the drug would cause them to experience, one in which subjects were not told anything about the effects of the drug, and one in which the subjects were misinformed about the effects of the drugs. What was the purpose of having each of these groups?

7. According to Schachter and Singer's hypothesis, the particular emotion a subject will experience will depend on the subject's beliefs about what caused her arousal. How did the experimenters attempt to manipulate these beliefs?

8. Describe the two ways this experiment measured the dependent variable, the subject's emotional state. According to the Schachter and Singer hypothesis, how should the groups that were accurately informed about the effects of the injection, not informed, and misinformed react to the anger-inducing and euphoria-inducing conditions?

Results of the Schachter and Singer Experiment

9. In the euphoria condition the results from the accurately informed group supported the

experimenters' hypothesis, but the results from the control (placebo) group did not. Describe what happened. How did Schachter and Singer explain the results from the control group? On the self-report measure, was there much difference between placebo, uninformed, and misinformed groups in the anger condition? How did Schachter and Singer explain these results? In the anger condition what were the results of the behavioral measure (made by observing the subjects through a one-way mirror).

Replications of Schachter and Singer
10. Describe the replications of Schachter and Singer's experiment and whether the results supported Schachter and Singer's hypothesis.

Transfer of Arousal
11. Describe Zillmann's transfer of arousal experiments. Do they support Schachter and Singer's concept of emotions? What is misattribution of emotion and what role does it play in Zillmann's experiments?

Complex Nature of Emotions
12. Explain why the sympathetic nervous system is inadequate to account for emotions. Why have "appraisals" been seen as good candidates to fill the gap? William James saw emotions as fundamentally private and personal, while Schachter and Singer see emotions as fundamentally in the person's world, not internal. Explain.

FACIAL EXPRESSION AND EMOTION

13. Darwin had two suggestions about the evolution of facial expressions. The first concerned how facial expressions derived from directly useful facial actions. Explain. The second was the facial feedback hypothesis. What is this hypothesis?

Universality of Emotional Expressions
14. Describe the criterion Darwin proposed to tell if facial expressions are innate. Ekman has attempted to apply this criterion. How? In what way was Ekman's original study limited? How did Ekman repair this limitation? What were the results?
15. Eibl-Eibesfeldt using a side-lens camera has recorded what appears to be a universal gesture —the eyebrow flash. Describe it. What is its apparent function?
16. Do deaf, blind, and handless children show the same nonverbal expressions that sighted and hearing children do? What does this show?

Display Rules
17. Since the facial expressions associated with emotions seem to be universal and innate, does this imply that people in every culture will give off these facial expressions every time they experience the corresponding emotion? Why not? What are "display rules"? Do cultures vary on display rules? How did Ekman demonstrate that the Japanese, a low-display people, display the same emotions we do *when* they display.

Facial Feedback
18. Describe the strong version of the facial feedback hypothesis. Describe the weak version. Since feedback from sympathetic arousal is too diffuse to provide information about *which* emotion you are feeling, what besides cognition about the environment might provide the information?

Physiological Responses and Facial Expressions
19. Describe Buck's method of testing the facial feedback hypothesis. Which people—those with the strongest physiological response or the weakest—were hardest to read? Does this support the facial feedback hypothesis? Subjects who were comparatively the most facially expressive had the least physiological response (compared to the other subjects). On the other hand, for any particular subject the slides that produced the most facial expression produced the most arousal. Does this finding support the facial feedback hypothesis?

Necessity and Sufficiency of Facial Expressions?
20. Tourangeau and Ellsworth attempted to see if facial expressions were necessary or sufficient to the experience of emotion. Describe their experiment. If the strong version of the facial feedback hypothesis were correct, what should the results of this experiment have been? If the weak version were correct, what should the results have been? What were the results of the experiment? How do these results reflect on the feedback hypotheses?

Facial Expressions and Intensity of Emotions
21. The problem with the Tourangeau and Ellsworth experiment was that the subjects might have guessed that they were supposed to be making emotional faces. How did the experiment by

Strack, Martin, and Stepper get around this problem? What were the results of their experiment? Did it support the strong or weak form of the facial feedback hypothesis?

WILLIAM JAMES REVISITED

22. There are two views of how appraisals might be part of the experience of an emotion. The first is one that sees us having direct access to the appraisals we make and the other sees us as making unconscious appraisals and having to infer the appraisals. Explain both positions.
23. If our appraisals are unconscious, then we know our emotions by inference. What are particularly good sources of inferences about the intensity of an emotion, about the quality of an emotion (which emotion it is)? If emotions derive from unconscious appraisals, can we be wrong about which emotion we are experiencing, or have emotions that we don't know we have? What does this position do to the assumption that just by observing internal states more closely we can "get in touch with our feelings"?

EVOLUTION AND FACIAL EXPRESSION

24. Describe the two positions as to why facial expressions evolved—the direct readout view and the social communications view. What is the assumption of the readout view about the relation between emotional state and facial expression? What does the social communications view mean when it says that a facial expression may be a display? According to this view, what kind of function do facial expressions serve?

Readout and Social Communications Views
25. On what point do the readout and social communications views converge?
26. The readout view sees the link between facial expression and emotions as equivalent to the relation between goose bumps and feeling cold. Explain. How is the social communications view different from a "goose bump view"? What are the implications of this difference? What evidence do we have from smiling bowlers for the social communications view of facial expression?

The Detection of Deception

Signaling Systems
27. Assume you are designing an emotion signaling system. What is the disadvantage of giving off a true readout of internal states? Give an example of a human signal system that is under the complete control of the signaler. Give Seyfarth and Cheney's example of a primate signaling system that is under the control of the signaler. How is the problem of "abuse" (a monkey who repeatedly gives false signals) of the system by signalers handled by vervet monkeys? Why can this solution work only with relatively intelligent species with stable social relationships? What is the other solution to this problem?

The Face and Concealing Emotions
28. What evidence do we have that the human face is a leaky system? Is it easy to detect these leaks? Are judges more likely to detect concealment when they focus on the face or on the body? Why? Overall are people good at concealment of emotional state?

Tone of Voice and Concealing Emotions
29. There is evidence that voice tone, apart from what is said, is a good clue to a speaker's feelings. Could subjects detect deception in speech passed through a band-pass filter that preserved pitch, speed, loudness, and rhythm of the speech but made it unintelligible?

Detecting Deception versus Detecting What Is Being Concealed
30. Are people better at detecting *that* deception has occurred than at discovering the person's true feelings? Are people who are particularly good at detecting the presence of concealed feelings especially good at figuring out just what the real feelings were?

Gender and Nonverbal Cues
31. Are women better than men at decoding other people's expressions? Does it matter whether men or women are giving off the messages? Looking only at those studies in which deceptive signaling is involved, is there still a difference between men and women?

Balancing the Interests of Senders and Receivers
32. In the competition between senders controlling their expressions and receivers attempting to decipher the truth beneath, who has the edge?

Programmed Exercises

1. According to William James, a person who met a hungry bear would perceive the bear, have _____ _____, and run.

   bodily reactions

2. James identified _____ _____ with the emotion of fear, since you could run or perceive a bear without feeling afraid.

   bodily reactions

3. It is not the bodily reactions in themselves that make up an emotion, but our _____ of these reactions.

   perception (experience)

4. Lange proposed that the specific bodily states in emotions related to changes in the _____ nervous system.

   autonomic (sympathetic)

5. Some changes caused by the sympathetic nervous system in fear include higher blood pressure, _____ pulse rate, turning off digestion, and increasing the production of a blood clotting vitamin.

   increased

6. Cannon argued against the James-Lange theory by pointing out that sympathetic arousal takes too _____ to respond to an event, and stays activated for too _____.

   long
   long

7. Cannon pointed out that there are a great number of emotions and the sympathetic system is not _____ enough to account for them.

   differentiated

COGNITIVE AROUSAL THEORY

The Sympathetic Nervous System and Emotion

8. If the experience of sympathetic arousal is _____ for having an emotion, then a person who could not experience sympathetic arousal should not have emotions.

   necessary

9. People with severed spinal cords cannot experience sympathetic arousal. But they do have _____, thus disproving the hypothesis that sympathetic arousal is _____ for having emotions.

   emotions
   necessary

10. Adrenaline produces sympathetic arousal. If sympathetic arousal is sufficient for having an emotion, then injecting someone with adrenaline should produce an _____.

    emotion

11. People given an injection of adrenaline did not experience an emotion, although some of them experienced what they described as _____ _____ emotions.

    as
    if

The Schachter and Singer Experiment

12. According to Schachter and Singer both a _____ state and a _____ about the cause of the state are necessary in order to have an emotion.

    physiological
    belief

13. Schachter and Singer attempted to test their hypothesis by manipulating both physiological state and belief about what _____ that state.

    caused

14. Schachter and Singer's experiment included three groups with different views about their physiological state (produced by an injection of epinephrine described as a vitamin): one group was accurately informed about the effects of the drug, one group was told nothing about the effects, and one group was _____.

    misinformed

15. The anger and euphoria manipulations were designed to manipulate the subjects' beliefs about the causes of their _____.

arousal

16. According to Schachter and Singer's theory, both the control group without the injection and the accurately informed group should experience _____ emotion.

no (little)

17. The uninformed and misinformed groups in the euphoria condition should experience _____.

euphoria

18. The dependent variable, the subject's emotional state, was measured by self-report and by _____ through a one-way mirror.

observation

19. In the euphoria condition, the results of the Schachter and Singer experiment supported the hypothesis that informed subjects were _____ emotional than uninformed, misinformed, or control subjects.

less

20. In the euphoria condition, however, the _____ group was as emotional as the misinformed and uninformed groups which does not support the hypothesis.

control (placebo)

21. In the anger condition, the _____ _____ measure supported Schachter and Singer's account less well than did the observational (behavioral) measures.

self-report

22. On the observational (behavioral) measures in the anger condition, the least angry behavior was engaged in by the _____ group, the most angry behavior by the uninformed group, and an intermediate display of anger by the placebo group.

informed

23. In Zillmann's experiments anger at an insult is greater when there is an additional unrelated source of _____.

arousal

24. People who have been riding a bike will retaliate more to an insult than people who have remained _____. This is because people _____ the arousal produced by bike riding to the insult and become angrier. Zillmann calls this _____ of arousal.

inactive, misattribute

transfer

25. Zillmann's work supports Schachter and Singer's view of emotion, since it sees emotion as a mixture of arousal and interpretation as to its _____.

cause

26. Any account of emotions would involve the sympathetic nervous system because the symptoms of strong emotions involve sympathetic _____, which like our experience of the emotions, is _____.

arousal
graded (in degree)

27. Arousal of the sympathetic nervous system is *not* sufficient to account for the variety of emotions since there are _____ emotions and the sympathetic system is not _____ enough to account for them.

many
complex

28. For this reason psychologists assume that _____ also must be part of emotional experience.

appraisals
(cognition)

FACIAL EXPRESSION AND EMOTION

29. Darwin suggested that facial expressions _____ from directly useful facial actions.

evolved

30. The _____ _____ hypothesis suggests that facial expressions _____ the experience of emotion.

facial feedback
intensify

Universality of Emotional Expressions

31. Darwin proposed that if people in every culture express emotions with the same facial expressions, then these expressions must be _____.

innate

32. Ekman tested the recognition of happiness, sadness, disgust, anger, surprise, and fear in five different modern cultures and found there was strong _____ among them. He then tested a primitive New Guinea culture and found there was strong _____ between it and the modern cultures.

agreement
agreement

33. The expression of _____ has also been found to be a universal.

contempt

34. Eibl-Eibesfeldt has found a gesture, the eyebrow flash, a gesture of _____, probably to be universal.

greetings

35. Eibl-Eibesfeldt has provided additional evidence for the universality and innateness of nonverbal expressions in that blind, deaf, and limbless children make the _____ expressions as normal children.

same

Display Rules

36. Although all cultures appear to have the same set of emotional facial expressions, they also have _____ _____ about when and where emotions ought to be expressed.

display rules

37. Japanese students, in private, had the _____ negative facial expressions to a stressful film as American students. In publicly discussing the film the American students' expressions were negative, and the Japanese students' expressions were _____.

same

positive

38. For the Japanese displaying negative emotions such as _____ in public is impolite.

disgust

Facial Feedback

39. According to the strong version of the facial feedback hypothesis, the expression on your face determines _____ emotion you are experiencing, as well as the _____ of the emotion.

which
intensity

40. According to the weak version of the facial feedback hypothesis, the expression on your face affects only the _____ of the emotion you are experiencing.

intensity

41. Since feedback from sympathetic arousal is too diffuse to provide information about which emotion you are feeling, appraisal of the _____ and _____ feedback may supply the additional discrimination.

environment
facial

42. Buck showed that people with strong physiological reactions to emotional slides were more likely to have _____ facial reactions to those slides as compared to other subjects. This result does not support the _____ _____ hypothesis. But these same subjects, if you just compare their own reactions to different slides, did have a _____ facial reaction to a slide that provoked a strong physiological reaction.

weak
facial
feedback
strong

43. In the Tourangeau and Ellsworth experiment, people who were instructed to look sad, neutral, or fearful while looking at emotion-provoking films were emotionally affected by their _____ _____.

facial position

44. An experiment by Strack and his colleagues found that facial expression does not affect _____ emotion is felt but does affect the _____ of the emotion felt.

which, intensity

WILLIAM JAMES REVISITED

45. There are two views of how appraisals might be part of the experience of an emotion: in one we have _____ access to the appraisals and in the other we must _____ the appraisals we have unconsciously made.

direct
infer

46. Facial feedback and visceral changes are good sources of information about the _____ of an emotion, while appraisal of the external circumstances and behavior are good sources for information about _____ emotion we are experiencing.

intensity

which

47. If emotional appraisals are unconscious then we can be _____ about which emotion we are feeling.

wrong (mistaken)

48. We can also have _____ without realizing that we have them.

emotions

EVOLUTION AND FACIAL EXPRESSION

Readout and Social Communications Views

49. There are two positions about why facial expressions evolved; one sees facial expressions as _____, the other as social _____.

readouts, displays
(communications)

50. According to the readout view, facial expression has a _____ connection to emotional state.

mechanical

51. According to the display view, the facial expression of emotions evolved because of their _____ function.

social

52. Both the readout and the social communications views believe that facial expressions are _____.

inherited (innate)

53. The _____ view sees facial expressions as like goose bumps in their linkage to internal states.

readout

54. The _____ _____ view, on the other hand, sees facial expressions as sensitive to social circumstances.

social
communications

55. Bowlers smile in company but not when they are alone. This supports the _____ _____ view.

social
communications

The Detection of Deception

56. One disadvantage of automatically giving off a readout of internal state is that sometimes it is useful to _____ competitors.

mislead

57. A disadvantage of a system that only communicated what the signaler wanted to communicate is that the recipients might not _____ it.

trust

58. _____ is a system under the control of the signaler.

Language

59. Some primates, vervet monkeys, have signals under the control of the _____.

signaler

60. The call of a monkey who frequently signals falsely is _____.

ignored

61. Only intelligent species with _____ social relations can have this solution.

stable

62. A _____ system is one that is neither entirely under the signaler's control nor one that in entirely automatic, a readout. The human face is to an extent a _____ system.

leaky

leaky

63. In the Ekman and Friesen study of nursing students trying to conceal unpleasant emotions it was found that the _____ was more leaky than the _____.

body

face

64. Subjects were _____ able to detect deception in a band-pass-filtered, unintelligible audiotape than they were when seeing a soundless video showing faces.

better

65. People are better at detecting that deception has occurred than in discovering the person's _____ feelings.

true

66. Women are better than men in _____ other people's expressions— whether from men or women. But women are not better than men at detecting _____ affect, concealed messages.

decoding

leaky

67. In cases where senders attempt to control their expressions, and receivers try to get at the truth beneath, _____ have a slight edge over _____.

receivers, senders

Self-Test

1. According to William James, an emotion, say, fear, is the perception of
   a. something in the world—say a threatening object.
   b. a desire to run away.
   c. a bodily reaction.
   d. all of the above

2. Lange developed James's account by identifying the bodily changes in emotions with activity in
   a. the autonomic (sympathetic) nervous system.
   b. the cerebellum.
   c. frontal lobes of the cerebrum.
   d. different systems, depending on the emotion.

3. Which of the following is *not* a change caused by the sympathetic nervous system when a person is afraid?
   a. higher blood pressure
   b. higher pulse
   c. turning off digestive processes
   d. enhanced digestive processing

4. According to Cannon, one major problem with the James-Lange theory is
   a. sympathetic arousal is too fast and disappears too quickly.
   b. there is a greater variety of chemical states in sympathetic arousal than there are discriminable emotions.
   c. sympathetic arousal takes too long to be activated and stays activated too long.
   d. there is no sympathetic arousal for anger.

5. If the experience of sympathetic arousal is *necessary* for having an emotion then
   a. if a person has sympathetic arousal he will experience an emotion.
   b. if there is no sympathetic arousal there will be no emotion.
   c. both a and b
   d. neither a nor b

6. People with severed spinal cords cannot experience sympathetic arousal, but they experience emotions. This
   a. supports the view that arousal is necessary for emotion.
   b. supports the view that arousal is sufficient for experiencing an emotion.
   c. refutes the view that arousal is necessary for emotion.
   d. refutes the view that arousal is sufficient for an emotion.

7. Adrenaline produces sympathetic arousal. If sympathetic arousal is sufficient for having an emotion, then

a. injecting someone with adrenaline should produce an emotion.
b. injecting someone with adrenaline should block her feeling emotion.
c. injecting someone with adrenaline will only produce an emotion with other chemical or psychological factors.
d. injecting someone with adrenaline will have no influence on whether she feels an emotion or not.

8. When Marañon injected people with adrenaline
   a. all experienced an emotion.
   b. most subjects did *not* report experiencing emotions, although some experienced what they described as "as if" emotions.
   c. one-third of the people experienced intense emotions.
   d. people felt incapable of experiencing emotions.

9. According to Schachter and Singer, what is necessary for the experience of an emotion?
   a. only an aroused internal state
   b. a cognitive appraisal alone
   c. an injection of adrenaline
   d. a cognitive appraisal and an aroused internal state

10. Schachter and Singer believed that people will experience fear when
    a. they interpret something threatening as causing their aroused physiological state.
    b. they believe that something is threatening.
    c. they feel aroused.
    d. they have a particularly fearful mental image.

11. In Schachter and Singer's attempted experimental validation of their theory, several groups of subjects were injected with adrenaline. One of these groups was accurately informed about the physiological effects of the adrenaline. If Schachter and Singer are correct, this group
    a. should not experience any particular emotion.
    b. should experience very strong emotions because of the adrenaline.
    c. should fluctuate between having strong emotions and being unable to experience any emotion at all.
    d. would drop out of the experiment.

12. One of the groups was misinformed about the effects of the adrenaline so that it would not attribute the arousal to the drug. It was put in a situation that would encourage feeling an emotion. If Schachter and Singer are correct this group
    a. should not experience a particular emotion.
    b. should fully experience emotion.
    c. should experience less emotion than the group that was accurately informed.
    d. should be very variable in whether individuals in the group would experience emotion or not.

13. Among the results of the euphoria condition of the Schachter and Singer experiment, which result did *not* support the hypothesis?
    a. Informed subjects were less emotional than uninformed or misinformed subjects.
    b. The misinformed group was less emotional than the uninformed and informed group.
    c. The control group (placebo) was as emotional as the misinformed and uninformed groups.
    d. All the results supported the Schachter and Singer hypothesis.

14. On behavioral measures of anger in the Schachter and Singer experiment
    a. the informed group engaged in the least angry behavior.
    b. the uninformed group engaged in the most angry behavior.
    c. the control group (placebo condition) displayed a level of anger between that of the informed and uninformed groups.
    d. all of the above

15. The notion of "transfer of arousal" implies that
    a. anger you feel one day may explode weeks later.
    b. sexual arousal or arousal from exercise will under some circumstances add to anger.
    c. sexual arousal will always decrease the feeling of anger.
    d. all of the above

16. In Zillmann's experiment involving retaliation for an insult
    a. people who have been riding a bike after the insult will retaliate more than people who have remained stationary.

b. people who have been riding a bike will work their feelings off and retaliate less.

c. people who have been riding a bike are neither more nor less likely to retaliate for an insult than those who have remained stationary.

d. people do not retaliate for insults.

17. According to Zillmann, the reason that people who have been riding a bike will retaliate for an insult more than those who have remained stationary is
   a. that people who ride bikes feel more athletic.
   b. that people realize that they have a surge in feeling due to bike riding and decide to "use it."
   c. that people misattribute the arousal produced by the bike riding to the insult and become angrier.
   d. that people who rode a bike were self-selected for the more physical types who would retaliate more.

18. Zillmann's work
   a. refutes Schachter and Singer's hypothesis.
   b. is irrelevant to Schachter and Singer's hypothesis, since it deals with transfer of arousal rather than labeling of emotions.
   c. supports Schachter and Singer's view, since it sees emotion as a mixture of arousal and interpretation as to its cause.
   d. is not on emotion.

19. What is *true* about the role of the sympathetic nervous system in emotion?
   a. Strong emotions involve sympathetic arousal.
   b. Both emotions and sympathetic arousal are graded.
   c. The sympathetic nervous system is not complex enough to account on its own for the variety of emotions.
   d. all of the above

20. If people in every culture express emotions with the same facial gestures, then these gestures are
   a. particular.
   b. not universal.
   c. innate.
   d. learned.

21. Ekman found that a primitive New Guinea tribe judged basic facial emotions
   a. in disagreement with the judgments of Western cultures.
   b. in close agreement with the judgments of Western cultures.
   c. similarly to Western cultures only for happy emotions.
   d. similarly to Western cultures only for negative emotions.

22. Additional evidence for the innateness of nonverbal expression is that
   a. blind children, but not deaf or limbless children, make the same facial expressions as other children.
   b. deaf, but not blind or limbless, children make the same facial expressions as other children.
   c. blind, deaf, and limbless children make different facial expressions than other children.
   d. blind, deaf, and limbless children make the same facial expressions as other children.

23. Display rules
   a. are the same for all cultures.
   b. specify when and where emotions are to be expressed.
   c. cannot inhibit the natural expression of emotion.
   d. are innate.

24. Both Japanese and American students watched a disgusting, stressful film. What were their expressions?
   a. The Japanese and American students had the same expressions both when viewing the film in private and during a public interview.
   b. Both in public and private the Japanese students had a positive expression and the Americans had a negative expression.
   c. In private both the Americans and the Japanese had negative expressions, but in public the Japanese expressions became positive.
   d. The Japanese and Americans both had positive expressions in public.

25. Which of the following is *true* of the facial feedback hypotheses?

a. The strong version holds that facial expressions determine both which emotion you are experiencing and the intensity of the emotion.

b. The weak version holds that facial expressions determine only which emotion you are feeling.

c. The strong version holds that facial expressions determine only which emotion you are feeling.

d. the strong version holds that facial expressions determine only the intensity of the emotion you are feeling.

26. Buck found that if you compare a person's physiological responses to different emotion-provoking slides

a. the slide that produced the most physiological response for the person would produce the most facial reaction.

b. the slide that produced the most physiological response for the person would produce no more intense facial reactions than other slides.

c. the slide that produced the least physiological response would produce the most facial response.

d. there was no relation at all between physiological arousal and facial reaction.

27. Buck also found that subjects who had the strongest physiological reactions (as compared to other subjects) surprisingly

a. had the strongest facial reactions.

b. had weak facial reactions.

c. had comparatively strong but not the strongest facial reactions.

d. had no facial reactions as all.

28. Tourangeau and Ellsworth had subjects adopt facial positions that were either consonant or clashing with the emotional content of a film that they were watching. What did they find?

a. Facial position had no influence on the kind or amount of emotional reaction to the film.

b. Facial position had no influence on which emotion was felt but did have an influence on the intensity of the emotion.

c. Facial position that was consonant with the film watched strengthened the intensity of the emotion felt.

d. Facial position influenced both the kind and intensity of the emotion felt.

29. In an experiment by Strack and his colleagues (that avoided the problem of subjects guessing that the experiment related to facial expression and emotion) it was found that

a. the strong form of the facial expression hypothesis was correct.

b. the weak form of the facial expression hypothesis was correct.

c. there was no relation between facial expression and either which emotion was felt or the intensity of the emotion felt.

d. facial expression only determined which emotion would be felt.

30. Facial feedback and visceral changes are good sources of information about

a. which emotion is felt.

b. the intensity of the emotion.

c. the pleasantness of an emotion.

d. both the intensity and the quality of the emotion.

31. Appraisal of external circumstances and behavior are, according to Schachter and Singer, good sources of information about

a. the intensity of an emotion.

b. the extent of physiological arousal in an emotion.

c. which emotion is felt.

b. both the intensity and quality of an emotion.

32. If emotional appraisals are unconscious then

a. we can have an emotion without realizing it.

b. we can be wrong about which emotion we are experiencing.

c. closely observing our internal states will not guarantee that we will realize which emotion we are feeling.

d. all of the above

33. According to the readout view of facial expressions

a. facial expressions evolved because of social pressure.

b. facial expressions are mechanically, automatically, linked to emotional states.

c. facial expressions evolved in order to express emotional states.

d. facial expressions are always intentional.

34. The social communications view of facial expressions makes sensible why

a. others can directly see our facial expressions but we can't.

b. facial expressions are sensitive to social circumstances.

c. facial expressions may sometimes function to misinform.

d. all of the above

35. Bowlers

a. smile whenever they make a strike; this supports the readout view.

b. smile only when they have audience; this supports the readout view.

c. smile whenever they make a strike; this supports a social communications view.

d. smile only when they have an audience; this supports a social communications view.

36. A system that automatically displays internal states (readouts)

a. is always better than one that communicates only what the sender wishes to communicate.

b. is always worse than one that communicates only what the sender wishes to communicate.

c. will sometimes give out information that will harm it, but it will have the advantage of others trusting the information it does send out.

d. is like our language system.

37. Among vervet monkeys, signals are under the control of the signaler. How do monkeys avoid the disadvantage of this system?

a. They ignore the call of monkeys who have frequently signaled falsely.

b. Vervets are taught never to signal falsely.

c. Vervets calls are readouts.

d. Vervets cannot avoid the disadvantage of this system.

38. The vervet's solution to the problem of deception can only work for

a. a species without a well-developed memory system.

b. a species where the groups rarely stay together.

c. a species with the capacity to recognize individuals and stable social relationships.

d. a species where facial expressions read out emotional states.

39. A system that is neither completely under the signaler's control nor entirely automatic is called

a. defective.

b. a readout.

c. ambivalent.

d. leaky.

40. The human face is

a. a leaky system.

b. a readout system.

c. completely under the control of the sender.

d. an anabolic system.

41. Ekman and Friesen found that student nurses who were trying to conceal unpleasant emotions

a. were better able to control leaky information from their bodies than their faces.

b. were completely unable to control facial leaks.

c. where better able to control leaky information from their faces than from their bodies.

d. were little able to control information leaks from their faces or their bodies.

42. Speech passed through a band-pass filter

a. is understandable but greatly modified in pitch, speed, and loudness.

b. is not understandable because of great changes in pitch, speed, loudness, and rhythm.

c. is unintelligible, but the pitch, speed, loudness, and rhythm of the speech is preserved.

d. just raises the pitch of the speech one octave.

43. Subjects are better able to detect deception if

a. they listen to the band-pass-filtered audiotape than a silent videotape of a face.

b. they look at a silent videotape of a face than a band-pass-filtered audiotape.

c. It is almost impossible to detect deception if the only information is from a band-pass-filtered audiotape or from a silent videotape.

d. none of the above

44. People generally

a. can detect a deception only if they have some idea of the person's true feelings.

b. are very good at spotting information leakage.

c. are better at detecting deception than at discovering what the true feelings are.

d. are always able to detect intentional deception.

45. Women are better than men at
    a. detecting concealed messages.
    b. decoding other people's expressions.
    c. both at detecting concealed messages and at decoding other people's expressions.
    d. detecting happy but not sad emotional states.

46. Questions about "self" are typically about
    a. internal states.
    b. facial expressions.
    c. neurons.
    d. values.

47. We know our self through
    a. self-presentation.
    b. reactions.
    c. emotions.
    d. all of the above

Answer Key for Self-Test

1.	c (p. 288)	25.	a (p. 306)
2.	a (p. 290)	26.	a (p. 308)
3.	d (p. 290)	27.	b (p. 307)
4.	c (p. 291)	28.	a (p. 310)
5.	b (p. 292)	29.	b (p. 312)
6.	c (p. 292)	30.	b (p. 312)
7.	a (p. 292)	31.	c (p. 313)
8.	b (p. 293)	32.	d (pp. 313-314)
9.	d (p. 293)	33.	b (p. 314)
10.	a (p. 293)	34.	d (pp. 314, 316)
11.	a (p. 294)	35.	d (p. 316)
12.	b (pp. 294-295)	36.	c (p. 317)
13.	c (p. 296)	37.	a (p. 318)
14.	d (p. 298)	38.	c (p. 318)
15.	b (p. 299)	39.	d (p. 318)
16.	a (p. 299)	40.	a (p. 319)
17.	c (p. 299)	41.	c (p. 319)
18.	c (p. 299)	42.	c (p. 320)
19.	d (p. 300)	43.	a (p. 320)
20.	c (p. 301)	44.	c (p. 321)
21.	b (p. 302)	45.	b (p. 322)
22.	d (p. 304)	46.	d (p. 323)
23.	b (p. 305)	47.	d (p. 323)
24.	c (p. 306)		

Thought Questions and Exercises

1. It is helpful in considering various theories of emotion to analyze an emotion you have experienced. Have you ever been in love? What was it about the experience and the relationship that makes you want to say you were in love? How was being in love similar to and different from liking someone a lot? Every time you think you have hit upon something essential to your being in love, ask yourself if you could have experienced that same thing even without being in love. Next try the same exercise from a slightly different slant. Someone tells you that he or she is in love. You are dubious. What might make you doubt someone's claim that he or she is really in love? What does this tell you about your concept of "love"?

2. Throughout the text the concept of "necessary" versus "sufficient" conditions is used. It would be helpful if you became comfortable with using this distinction. Oxygen is necessary to life, without it we'd die, but it isn't sufficient to life since we could die in all sorts of ways, for example, starvation with plenty of oxygen. So oxygen is necessary but not sufficient for life. Let's turn to the somewhat easier example of death to look at sufficient, and necessary and sufficient conditions. Can you think of something sufficient but not necessary for death?* How about something that is both necessary and sufficient for death? Think up some other examples of necessary, sufficient, and necessary and sufficient conditions for something. One reason that the concept of necessary and sufficient is important is that it is a way to understand the idea of "causes." For instance, when Schachter and Singer say that arousal and appraisal jointly cause a particular emotion, they are claiming that arousal and appraisal (other things being equal) are both necessary and sufficient for feeling an emotion.

3. You have read of the controversy over the function of facial expressions—social communications or a readout of the personal state. Replicate the Kraut and Johnston field experiment on when bowlers smile (see text, p. 316). Inconspicuously note when or if bowlers

---

* Many other answers will be right, but here is one: Drowning is sufficient for death, but not necessary, since you can die in a lot of other ways. A necessary and sufficient condition for death is trickier, but since we usually identify the ceasing of brain activity with death, stopping brain activity would be both necessary for death and sufficient for death.

smile—how often do they smile when alone, when turning to their group, and so on. Maybe there is something odd about bowling. Can you replicate this experiment using a different game? How about a golfer's solitary driving practice? Have you ever caught yourself smiling when you were alone? Under what circumstances? Most findings have alternative interpretations that must be eliminated. For instance, couldn't smiling to yourself be controlled by a display rule (that is, smiles are readouts, but there are rules against displaying the readout)? Can you think of some way to test this hypothesis? Hint. The lone bowler in the Kraut and Johnston experiment was still in public.

CHAPTER 9

Sex

Learning Objectives

SEXUAL BEHAVIOR IN CULTURAL PERSPECTIVE

Sex on Inis Beag

1. Describe the dominant theme of people's feelings about sex in Inis Beag.

Sex among the Mangaians

2. Explain how adolescents learn about sex in Mangaia. What makes a woman sexually attractive in this culture? How frequent is marital sex in Mangaia? How does this compare with the rate in the U.S.?

Sexual Scripts in Present-Day America

3. Explain how sexual behavior is learned in our culture. Do we have a knowledge of sex independent of our own experience? What is meant by "sexual scripts"?

Sexual Revolution

Sexual Standards

4. Briefly describe both the "official" and actual standard of sexual morality of the 1950s. According to the survey of premarital sexual behavior in a southern university, how did the sexual behavior of males and females change from 1965–1975?

Causes of the Sexual Revolution

5. Explain how the discovery of penicillin after World War II and the removal of the threat of syphilis could have affected sexual attitudes. If this is true what effect will the discovery of

AIDS in the mid-1980s have?

6. Explain how the invention of the IUD and birth control pills in the 1960s could have affected the sexual revolution. How might the subsequent legalization of abortion? How were the IUD and the birth control pill different from previous methods of birth control? What might be the effect on sexual standards of the more recent questioning of the safety of IUD's and contraceptive pills and the attack on abortion rights?

7. Describe what the "female marriage squeeze" is. Why should it have occurred after World War II? How might the female marriage squeeze affect sexual norms? From the 1980s on there has been an oversupply of marriageable men in relation to women. How might this affect sexual attitudes?

8. Explain how the baby boom posed a problem for socialization. How did this contribute to sexual permissiveness? What might be expected with the fall in birth rates?

Counterrevolution?

9. Review the evidence and reasons for a recent sexual counterrevolution. Has the fear of AIDs affected reported college student sexual behavior? Did sexual activity decline even before the risk of AIDS became so prominent (use data for women college students from the early 1970s to the 1980s)?

SEXUAL BEHAVIOR IN EVOLUTIONARY PERSPECTIVE

10. Many scholars claim that evolution not only has shaped the structure of our sexual equipment but

also our sexual desires and behavior. This claim is controversial. Give two reasons why.

Natural Selection

11. Describe what "natural selection" is. What was the function of the British moths' color (before the color of the buildings turned)? What happened to the moths after the Industrial Revolution turned everything sooty? The moths were originally white but some moths were whiter than others. What is the importance of this fact? Why is it important that this variability was genetically based? Did this change in the color of moths over generations involve "purpose," that is, did the moths have to realize their problem and then try to change it? Would the moths' color have evolved if all the moths had originally been of the same color? Would the moths' color have evolved if the moths were of different shades due to differences in diet but all the moths had the identical genetic specifications for color?

Survival of the Fittest

12. The sad case of the male praying mantis shows that "survival" is not what evolution is all about. How? What is evolution about?

The Desire to Pass on One's Genes

13. The text states that we should expect evolution to have acted on our sexual desires and not on our desire to have children. Explain. What is a "proximate mechanism"? Evolution always works on proximate mechanisms. Explain.

14. Evolution works on individuals. If some trait benefits the group but does not cause the individuals who have it to have more viable children than those who don't will the trait evolve?

Adaptation

15. Describe what happened to the moths when the British cleaned up the air. In what sense were the moths adapted to an environment that no longer existed? "Evolution has no foresight." Explain. Over time what happened to the color of the moths? Evolution does not prepare organisms for the future but for the past. Why is this point particularly important in regard to human evolution?

Sexual Reproduction and the Sexes

16. State what is the constant in sexual reproduction. What distinguishes the male contribution from the female's? How do sperm differ from ova? In regard to sperm and ova what is the difference in the male and female reproductive investment?

Asymmetry in Nurturance

17. Female humans biologically have a greater parental investment than male humans do. Why? What is the asymmetry between males and females in the time between one conception and the opportunity for another conception?

Sexual Behavior and Asymmetry in Investment

18. What is the implication of this asymmetry in the investment of males and females for the costs of a genetically bad conception? How does this explain why there would be evolutionary pressure for females and not males to be choosy? Why does the author say that males are competing with each other for the opportunity to mate with females?

Infant Care in K Selected Species and r Selected Species

19. Describe what an r selected species and a K selected species are. Are humans r selected or K selected? What implication does this have for cooperation between males and females in raising the young?

20. Paternity is uncertain, maternity is not. Explain how this gives rise to asymmetric evolutionary pressure on males and females. How should this lead natural selection to favor males who make sure that the young they care for are theirs?

MALE-FEMALE DIFFERENCES

Cross-Cultural Evidence

21. Explain how the two asymmetries between males and females lead to some differences in the desires of male and female humans. Why would the asymmetries cause us to predict a situation in which males would want to have multiple wives but females would not want multiple husbands?

Polygyny and Polyandry Cross-Culturally

22. Are most human cultures monogamous, polygamous, or polyandrous? The single undisputed polyandrous society has a feature that makes it more conformable to evolutionary theory. What is it?

Norms about Virginity

23. Given that paternity is uncertain and maternity certain, men should be concerned that their

wives are virgins but women should not care whether their husbands are or not. What is the evidence from anthropology? Are there any cultures that insist on male but not female virginity?

Age and Status Preferences in Mates

24. From an evolutionary perspective it is clear why males and females would be attracted to sexually mature partners. But why should men prefer younger women and women a bit older men?

Differences in Sexual Behavior

Differences in Premarital and Extramarital Sex

25. What are the data on premarital and extramarital sexual experience of men and women and do they confirm the evolutionary picture? Describe the experiment in which males or females were approached by a confederate and asked for a date or to sleep with them. Was there a difference in acceptance when the confederate was recommended by a friend? Is there evidence that males' greater interest in sexual variety seeking is not just a matter of the double standard? (Use the Mangaian example.)

Sexual Behavior of Gay Men and Lesbians

26. Why does Symons argue that we get a better picture of female and male sexual desire by looking at homosexual men and women (before the AIDS epidemic)? What was the average number of sexual partners of gay men and lesbians in a German sample? Does this support the evolutionary hypothesis? What percent of lesbians and what percent of gay men had had sex with more than ten partners? These data are consistent with the evolutionary hypothesis, but is there an alternate explanation for the findings?

Differences in Sexual Desire and Arousal

27. If evolution has influenced our sexual behavior, has it done so by acting directly on behavior? If not, how does it operate?

Male-Female Differences in Sexual Arousal to Visual Cues

28. According to Kinsey, what percent of men and women were aroused by erotic stories? What other non-experimental evidence is there that men are more easily aroused by sexual stimuli? What have experimental studies of reactions to erotica found—in regard to arousability, likeli-

hood to increase later sexual behavior, guilt? Does this support or go against the evolutionary hypothesis? The women involved in studies of erotica may not be typical of women in general and this may account for the lack of difference in response to erotica. Explain.

Male-Female Differences in Masturbation

29. Why is masturbation likely to be the "purist" indicator of an individual's sexual arousability? What differences did Kinsey find in the rate of masturbation in men and women? How about the frequency of masturbation among men and women who do masturbate?

Perspectives on Genetic Influences

30. Is it true that if something has a genetic base then it is unchangeable? Give the example of innately aversive tastes. Are genes destiny?

Evolution and Morality

31. If something is "natural," shaped by evolution, does it mean that it is moral? What is the "naturalistic fallacy"? Does evolution dictate the proper relationship between the sexes?

Evolution and Happiness

32. Evolution does not tell us how we must live or how we should live, but does it tell us how we will be happiest? Is there any reason to believe that the happiest creatures are those with the greatest reproductive success?

EVOLUTIONARY MYSTERIES

Homosexuality

33. What percent of the males in Kinsey's sample considered themselves exclusively homosexual? What percentage of females? Why is homosexuality a mystery from the evolutionary perspective? It would appear that there could not be a gene for homosexuality since it would not lead to having children, yet this is an oversimplification. Use the model of sickle cell anemia to explain how a gene for homosexuality might confer reproductive advantage on its possessor.

34. If homosexuality is inherited, then the siblings of homosexuals should be more likely to be homosexual than would be expected from the base rate of homosexuality in the population. Is this true? What would be another explanation for this finding?

Intrauterine Influences

35. How many chromosomes do the human sperm and egg have? What are the X and the Y chromosomes? Is there any observable difference between XX and XY fetuses until the third month? What happens in the third month? What is the importance of the secretion of testosterone? What is the effect on XX fetuses of an accidental exposure to testosterone? As children what behavioral effects were observed? Is there any evidence of an effect on subsequent sexual choice?

Puberty and Sexual Preference

36. Describe Storms's hypothesis for why males have a higher rate of homosexuality than females. According to this hypothesis, which girls and which boys will be more likely to become homosexual? Is this prediction correct?

Reanalysis of Kinsey's Data

37. Describe which facts about gay men and lesbians found in a reanalysis of the Kinsey data are consistent with the Storms position and which are consistent with the intrauterine hypothesis.

Human Hypersexuality

38. Explain why a highly K selected species might not be expected to be so sexual.

The Classical Solution

39. Describe Desmond Morris's account as to why noncyclical female sexual receptivity evolved in humans. (Explain the importance of "bonding" in this hypothesis.) For what other reason would it be likely that bonding would evolve? What other unique features of humans would contribute to bonding?

Monogamous Gibbons

40. What information about the gibbon has cast doubt on Desmond Morris's hypothesis?

Female Selective Advantage

41. The classical view is that males compete for partners while females select. What is Hrdy's challenge to the classical view? How does the fact of primate infanticide enter into Hrdy's account? How does coupling with dominant male candidates and concealing estrus work to the advantage of a female's genes?

42. "Genes place our behavior on a leash." Explain. Should the leash be equally long for all behaviors? Which types of behavior should have the shortest leash?

Programmed Exercises

SEXUAL BEHAVIOR IN CULTURAL PERSPECTIVE

Sex on Inis Beag

1. The dominant theme of people's feelings about sex in Inis Beag is anxiety and _____.

   guilt

Sex among the Mangaians

2. In Mangaia _____ males are instructed in detail on sexual techniques such as bringing one's partner to multiple orgasms before ejaculation and are then initiated into sexuality by an older woman.

   adolescent

Sexual Scripts in Present-Day America

3. A sexual script is an ordered sequence of _____ that we know to enact in a sexual encounter.

   behaviors

4. Individuals have sexual scripts _____ of their individual sexual experiences.

   independent

Sexual Revolution

5. In the 1950s the official standard of morality was that both sexes should be
_____ until marriage, but in actuality _____ were allowed to
have sexual experience.   virgins, males

6. In a survey of premarital sexual behavior in a southern university it was shown
that between 1965 and 1975 the rate of premarital intercourse doubled for
_____. And the male and female rates were tending to _____.   women, converge

7. In the same survey there was a tendency to _____ permissiveness in
attitudes toward sex.   greater

8. In the same survey both males and females shifted toward a _____
standard of sexual morality, at least in judging people with many sexual
partners.   single

9. In the 1970s a collection of _____ standards took the place of the
single "1950s standard."   different

10. The trend toward greater sexual permissiveness began in the generation
coming of age in the _____ and accelerated in the 1960s.   1920s

11. One cause of the change in sexual attitudes was the discovery at the end of
World War II of penicillin, which almost removed the threat of _____   venereal (syphilis)
disease as a reason to refrain from sex.

12. The _____ _____ and the _____ invented in the   contraceptive pill,
1960s were both more effective than previous means of birth control and   IUD
intercourse independent.

13. The _____ _____ _____ causes an oversupply of   female marriage
marriageable women in relation to marriageable men.   squeeze

14. The oversupply of women has been seen as related to greater sexual
permissiveness, especially for _____.   women

15. Since the 1980s there has been an oversupply of men of marriagable age; this
should lead to a decrease in sexual _____.   permissiveness

16. The baby boom made social control of the new generation more
_____, thus making it easier for the generation to challenge the   difficult
culture's norms.

17. There is evidence that there has been something of a counterrevolution in
sexual attitudes and behavior since the _____.   1980s

18. In a study of sexual behavior of college _____ in the year 1983–1984   women
the number of those who were sexually active declined from 50 percent to 35
percent (which it had been in the late seventies).

19. In the survey of the southern university previously mentioned, belief in the
double standard decreased in the 1960s and 1970s and _____ in a   increased
survey conducted in 1980.

SEXUAL BEHAVIOR IN EVOLUTIONARY PERSPECTIVE

20. Many scholars claim that evolution not only has shaped the structure of our
sexual equipment but also our sexual desires and _____.   behavior

21. This claim is controversial since it is hard to verify historical claims about ancient _____ and because such claims have been used to justify the subjugation of _____.

behavior
women

Natural Selection

22. _____ _____ is the mechanism by which evolution is propelled.

Natural selection

23. White British moths were _____ against the background of white trees and white buildings and therefore avoided predators. When the trees and buildings darkened, the moths were not camouflaged but rather _____ _____ and were more likely to be eaten.

camouflaged

stood
out

24. Some moths were _____ than others. The difference in whiteness among the moths was due to differences in their _____. _____ moths stood out more and were eaten more frequently and hence were less likely to reproduce. Darker moths more frequently _____ and were thus more likely to reproduce. The next generation of moths was likely to be _____.

whiter
genes
Lighter

escaped
darker

25. The difference in color between one generation and another is _____, but over many generations the moths evolved from white to black.

small

26. The moths did not _____ to change color. There was no purposiveness or intelligence in this instance of _____.

try
evolution

27. If the difference in color between the moths had been due to diet and not to genes then the moths would not have _____ to a new color.

evolved

28. The female praying mantis kills the male during sex. A male that had a genetic mutation causing it to avoid sex would live _____. This male, on the other hand, would not pass his _____ on to his offspring since he wouldn't have any. This shows that a mutation that promotes _____ will not necessarily be passed on. Evolution is not about survival, rather evolution of the fittest means fittest to _____.

longer
genes
survival

reproduce

29. This shows that natural selection has to do with competition among members of one's own species to produce _____.

offspring

30. Evolution makes people want to do things that have the _____ that their genes will be passed on.

effect

31. Before the invention of contraceptives, sex led to babies whether people wanted them or not. If evolution increased _____ _____, this would have the effect of increasing the number of babies even if people gave no thought to babies or did not want babies.

sexual desire

32. Evolution works through _____ _____, which include anything that is involved in reproduction.

proximate
mechanisms

33. If some trait benefits the group but does not cause individuals to have more viable children (than those without the trait) then the trait will _____ evolve.

not

34. When the British cleaned their environment and the trees and buildings were no longer sooty the moths no longer were _____. The moths were adapted to an environment that no longer _____ and not to the present

camouflaged
existed

environment. Natural selection prepares a species for the environment that its _____ faced and not necessarily the one it will have to face.

ancestors

35. Modern culture is very different from the culture of our hunter-gatherer ancestors yet since evolution is slow and cultural change is fast we are probably adapted to a _____-_____ way of life.

hunter-gatherer

Sexual Reproduction and the Sexes

36. The constant in all sexual reproduction is that there is a _____ of the genetic material of two parents.

combination

37. One thing that distinguishes the sperm from the ovum is that the _____ is much larger since it must contain nutrition for the zygote formed by the union of sperm and egg. Ova are more "expensive to make" and the female produces far fewer _____ than the male produces sperm.

ovum

ova

38. In animals that fertilize outside the body, such as fish, either the male or the female can _____ for the offspring from the moment of conception. In animals that fertilize inside the body, only the _____ can nurture the offspring until delivery.

care

female

39. Among mammals the mother both carries the fetus and produces milk for the newborn, thus having a _____ biological investment in the newborn than does the male.

larger

40. A female human once she conceives must wait more than _____ _____ until the next conception; a man could wait less than a _____ _____. Thus a female ties up much more of her _____ life with each conception than a male does.

nine

months

one day

reproductive

41. A male who conceives with a female who has genes that will lead to the death of their offspring will be able to conceive again the same _____. A female who conceives with a male who has genes that will lead to the death of their offspring will be able to conceive again after _____. This leads to evolutionary pressure for females to be _____ in their choice of mates. Even the worst mating for a male will give a greater chance of an offspring than no _____. There should be evolutionary pressure for males not to be very _____.

day

months

selective (choosy)

mating

selective

42. Fish, who produce many young that do not survive to sexual maturity, are examples of _____ selected species. Parents of these species give little or no care to their _____.

r

offspring

43. K selected species, such as primates, produce few offspring; these offspring are _____ likely to survive to maturity than the offspring of r selected species.

more

44. Primate offspring demand more _____ than r selected offspring.

care

45. Humans, at least in their original hunter-gatherer habitat, faced evolutionary pressure for mothers and fathers to _____ to raise young. This pressure goes against and lessens the asymmetry between the sexes in parental _____.

cooperate

investment

46. Paternity is _____; maternity is certain. A male who invests in the care of *his* children will have an advantage (in passing on his genes) over one who doesn't but a male who invests in another male's young will suffer a

uncertain

genetic _____. Natural selection should favor males who make sure   disadvantage
that the _____ they take care of are their genetic offspring.   young

MALE-FEMALE DIFFERENCES

Cross-Cultural Evidence

47. According to this evolutionary argument, females should be _____   less
concerned than males if their partner is having sex with someone else.

48. Males should be attracted to multiple wives, _____ while females   polygyny
should *not* be attracted to multiple husbands, _____.   polyandry

49. _____ should be more jealous than _____.   Males, females

50. In the Ford and Beach survey, most societies were _____, less than a   polygynous
quarter were _____, and only one was (certainly) _____.   monogamous,
    polyandrous

51. Since paternity is uncertain and maternity certain, men should be concerned
that their wives are virgins and women should be _____ about   unconcerned
whether their husbands are virgins or not.

52. In the Ford and Beach survey, there were some cultures that insisted on both
partners being virgins, some that insisted on neither being a virgin, some that
required female but not male virginity, but there are no cultures that required
_____ but not female virginity.   male

53. Both men and women are attracted to secondary sexual characteristics since
these signal _____.   fertility

54. From an evolutionary point of view men should be attracted to _____,   young
fertile women since they will be able to care for offspring longer.

55. Females should select males who can provide maximum resources for the
offspring; this is likely to be males older than _____.   adolescence

56. David Buss investigated age preferences for ideal mates in many cultures. He
found that men preferred _____ women, and women preferred men   younger
who were slightly _____ than they were.   older

Differences in Sexual Behavior

57. According to Kinsey _____ of women in the early 1950s but a much   50%
higher percent of men had premarital intercourse. By age forty _____   50%
of men and _____ of women had had an extramarital affair.   25%

58. In a study of college students roughly half of the males and females accepted a
date when approached by a stranger of the opposite sex; _____ of the   none
females, but _____ of the males accepted an offer to go to bed with   69%
the stranger.

59. The difference in willingness of males and females to engage in casual sex
may be due to the double _____.   standard

60. However, among the Mangaians, a culture supposedly without a double
standard for adolescents, the boys still have _____ sexual partners   more
than the girls do.

61. Symons argues that we can get a better picture of male and female sexual desire by studying _____, since the behavior of heterosexuals represents a compromise between the desire of males and females.

homosexuals

62. In a German survey, the typical lesbian has had sexual relations with _____ partners; the typical gay male has had sexual relations with _____ partners. The data are _____ with the evolutionary hypothesis but there are alternate explanations.

2
16, consistent

Differences in Sexual Desire and Arousal

63. According to Kinsey a much larger percent of _____ than _____ report being aroused by erotic stories.

men
women

64. Recent experiments have found equal responsivity of men and women to sexual stimuli; this is _____ with evolutionary arguments. It is possible, however, that _____ who volunteer for experiments involving erotica are not typical.

inconsistent
women

65. Rates of masturbation may be the "purist" measure of _____ since masturbation requires no partner and is done in private.

arousability

66. Most, but not all studies, show that for males and females who masturbate males masturbate considerably _____ frequently.

more

Perspectives on Genetic Influences

67. It is _____ that if something has a genetic base then it is unchangeable. Human infants find caffeine, alcohol, and chile innately _____, yet they are among the favorite foods of most adults.

false

aversive
(unpleasant)

68. If something is "natural," shaped by evolution, then it may or may _____ be moral. The confusion between facts about nature and moral facts is known as the _____ _____.

not
naturalistic fallacy

69. What is evolutionarily natural may not be what makes us _____. The motor of evolution is _____ _____ and not happiness.

happiest
reproductive success

EVOLUTIONARY MYSTERIES

Homosexuality

70. On the face of it an evolutionary perspective does not predict the existence of _____.

homosexuality

71. A gene for homosexuality might in some way confer reproductive _____ that was more important than the loss of reproduction caused by homosexuality.

advantage

72. There is no observable difference between XX and XY fetuses until the _____ month. Then the XY fetus begins to form _____, which produce _____, the male sex hormone. This _____ the developing genitalia.

third, testicles
testosterone
masculinizes

73. XX fetuses that have been accidentally exposed to testosterone develop more boy-like _____, and as children they behave like _____. The evidence is _____ as to whether they are more likely than the average female to become lesbians at puberty.

genitalia, tomboys
mixed

74. Girls experience puberty earlier than boys but boys feel the first stirring of sexual _____ earlier than girls.

arousal

75. Storms believes that the reason that males are more likely to be homosexual than females are is that when males first experience arousal they are likely to be in an all-_____ group. But when females first experience arousal they are likely to be in mixed-sex groups.

male

76. According to the Storms hypothesis males and females who mature earlier and hence experience arousal earlier are more likely than late maturers to be _____; this correlation has been found. Contrary to the Storms hypothesis gay men had _____ boy companions and more girl companions at age ten than the average male.

homosexual
fewer

Human Hypersexuality

77. Humans are more sexual than other highly _____ selected species such as the gibbon. By human "hypersexuality" it is meant that humans engage in sexual behavior much more than is needed for _____.

K

reproduction

78. Desmond Morris argues that human female noncyclical receptivity and human hypersexuality have the evolutionary function of _____ bonding. He claims that males were more likely to stay around a continuously _____ receptive female.

increasing

sexually

79. Gibbons, a monogamous primate species, _____ have sex. This fact goes against Desmond Morris's hypothesis since male and female gibbons _____ together without the enticement of frequent sex.

rarely

stay

80. The classical evolutionary view is that males compete and females _____. Hrdy argues that females also _____.

select, compete

81. In primates, infanticide of the offspring of the previous dominant male is in the interest of the genes of the new _____ male but not in the genetic interest of the mothers of the offspring.

dominant

82. Having sex with males of the troop that may some day become dominant and concealing estrus is in the _____ interest of the female. This is because the newly dominant male will not be certain that the offspring aren't _____.

genetic

his

83. Hrdy does *not* claim that females are _____ seeking in the way that males are, but only sexually interested in those males likely to become dominant.

variety

84. Genes can be seen as placing the possible behaviors that occur in an environment on a _____, the length of which depends on the relevance to reproductive _____ of the behavior.

leash
advantage

85. Cultural and historical differences in even sexual behavior suggest that the leash is fairly _____.

long

Self-Test

1. The dominant feeling(s) about sex in Inis Beag is
   a. anticipation.
   b. pleasure.
   c. anxiety and guilt.
   d. boredom and disinterest.

2. Sexual attitudes and practices in Mangaia
   a. are at the opposite extreme from Inis Beag.
   b. are more free and demonstrate more knowledge of sexual technique than those of the U.S.
   c. derive from explicit training and approved premarital practice.
   d. all of the above

3. A "sexual script"
   a. is used in the theater for love scenes.
   b. can only be derived from actual experiences.
   c. is an ordered sequence of behaviors that we know to enact in a sexual encounter even if we have not experienced all of the behaviors.
   d. always produces guilt.

4. According to a survey of premarital sexual behavior in a southern university between 1965 and 1975
   a. there had been a great increase in the rate of premarital intercourse for males but not females.
   b. the rate of premarital intercourse of females doubled, almost converging with that of males.
   c. there was no change in the rate of premarital intercourse for either males or females.
   d. there was a decrease in the rate of premarital intercourse in females.

5. In the same sample there was evidence that between 1965 and 1975 male and female attitudes toward sex
   a. became more permissive and tended toward a single standard.
   b. became more rigid; the double standard became stronger.
   c. did not change even though behavior changed.
   d. became more permissive for men but not for women.

6. The trend toward greater sexual permissiveness began
   a. in the generation coming of age in the 1960s.
   b. in the generation coming of age in the 1950s.
   c. in the generation coming of age in the 1920s and accelerated in the 1960s.
   d. in the generation coming of age in the 1980s.

7. One reason for the acceleration in attitudes toward sexual permissiveness in the generation coming of age in the 1960s was medical. It was
   a. the polio vaccine.
   b. better nutrition causing increased sexual stamina.
   c. the discovery of penicillin, greatly reducing the threat of syphilis.
   d. a cure for yellow fever.

8. Another reason for the acceleration of attitudes toward sexual permissiveness in the generation coming of age in the 1960s had to do with contraception. It was
   a. the invention of contraceptive pills and the IUD, which were both more effective than previous methods and intercourse independent.
   b. the discovery of the first contraceptives.
   c. the invention of a marketing strategy that caused men to like using prophylactics.
   d. all of the above

9. Another reason for the acceleration of permissiveness of sexual attitudes and toward a single standard in the generation coming of age in the 1960s had to do with the ratio of marriageable men to women:
   a. In the 1960s generation there were more marriageable men than women, and the surplus of men caused a liberalizing of sexual standards.
   b. In the 1960s generation there were more marriageable women than men, and the surplus of women caused a liberalizing of sexual standards.
   c. In the 1960s there was an almost perfect balance between marriageable women and men, thus causing a liberalizing of sexual standards.
   d. The 1960s saw a 33 percent decrease in marriages, thus causing a liberalizing of sexual standards.

10. The large number of children conceived after the war and called the "baby boom" made the 1960s generation
    a. desperate for affection.
    b. work oriented.
    c. more difficult to control, including in sexual matters.
    d. all of the above

11. There is evidence of a counterrevolution in both sexual behavior and attitudes in the 1980s. This is because of
    a. oversupply of marriageable men in the 1980s as opposed to women in the 1960s.
    b. the appearance of the AIDS epidemic.
    c. the end of the baby boom.
    d. all of the above

12. Sociobiological evolutionary theory claims that evolution has shaped
    a. our sexual anatomy but not our desires or behavior.
    b. our sexual behaviors but not our desires.
    c. our sexual anatomy, behavior, and desires.
    d. only our sexual desires.

13. "Natural selection" is the mechanism
    a. of learning in natural environments.
    b. by which evolution is propelled.
    c. by which a culture socializes its young.
    d. used by stock raisers to improve a breed.

14. White British moths when they rested on white trees or buildings were
    a. more difficult to see by birds that would eat them and is an example of "camouflage."
    b. more difficult to see by birds that would eat them and is an example of light adaptation.
    c. easier to see by birds that would eat them.
    d. none of the above

15. When the soot of the Industrial Revolution caused the buildings and trees to darken
    a. the moths were still camouflaged.
    b. the moths now stood out and were more likely to be eaten by birds.
    c. the moths were still hidden from the birds.
    d. the moths were no more likely to be eaten by the birds than before.

16. Darker moths escaped birds more often and hence survived to reproduce. The next generation of moths will have proportionally more dark moths

a. if the darkness of the moths is due to environmental influences such as diet.
b. if the darkness of the moths is due to genes rather than some environmental influences such as diet.
c. if the moths try hard to make use of the advantage of darkness.
d. if the darkness of the moths is not genetically caused.

17. The difference in color between one generation of moth and another is
    a. large.
    b. too small to cause a change from white to black even over many generations.
    c. very small but over many generations the moths evolve from white to black.
    d. moderate but in two or three generations the moths completely change color.

18. If the difference in color between the moths had been due to diet and not to genes then the moths would
    a. have evolved more slowly.
    b. have evolved more rapidly.
    c. not have evolved.
    d. have evolved along a different path.

19. When the female praying mantis kills the male during sex, this demonstrates that
    a. evolution is about survival of the fittest.
    b. evolution does not always work.
    c. males that avoid females will be more likely to pass on their genes.
    d. evolution is not about survival but about success in passing on one's genes.

20. A mutation in the genes of a male praying mantis that caused him to avoid females and survive longer
    a. would not be passed on.
    b. would be passed on since it caused the mantis to survive longer.
    c. would make the mantis more fit and guarantee the passing on of the mutated gene.
    d. would sometimes be passed on and sometimes not, depending on other factors.

21. Natural selection has to do with competition
    a. with members of other species, predators, in order to survive.
    b. with members of one's own species to

reproduce and not a struggle against other species, predators, to survive.

c. with members of one's own species to survive.

d. with both the members of one's own and other species in order to survive.

22. Evolution works through success in passing on one's genes. One does not have to have heard of a gene or even want to reproduce in order to pass on one's genes. A mutation that increased sexual desire in people (before the invention of contraception)

a. would increase the passing on of genes whether people desired to pass them on or not.

b. would increase the passing on of genes only if people wanted to pass them on.

c. would increase the passing on of genes because sexual desire always includes a desire to have children.

d. would decrease the passing on of genes.

23. Let us say that having more offspring in certain circumstances confers reproductive advantage. Evolution might shape having more offspring not by selecting for a "desire to have more offspring" but rather by increasing sex drive independent of a desire for children. This would work indirectly to increase the number of children. The mechanism—increased sex drive—by which evolution works to increase the number of children is called a(n)

a. involute mechanism.

b. convolute inversion.

c. proximate mechanism.

d. distal hypertrophy.

24. If some trait benefits the group but does not cause individuals to have more viable children than those who do not have the trait, then the trait will

a. not evolve.

b. evolve more slowly.

c. only evolve in those that desire to help the group.

d. evolve more quickly.

25. After the moths had changed from white to black over many generations the British cleaned up their environment. What happened?

a. The moths lost their camouflage and were being eaten more frequently once again.

b. The moths were adapted to an environment that no longer existed.

c. The moths would start evolving from black to white.

d. all of the above

26. Natural selection prepares a species for the environment that

a. its ancestors faced and not necessarily the one it will have to face.

b. it must face in the future.

c. that it is facing at the current moment.

d. it needs to face.

27. Modern culture is very different from the culture of our hunter-gatherer ancestors, yet since evolution is slow and cultural change fast we are probably adapted for

a. an urban way of life.

b. an agricultural way of life.

c. a way of life similar to that of the ancient Babylonians.

d. a hunter-gatherer way of life.

28. The ovum is

a. much smaller than the sperm since the sperm must contain sufficient food for traveling to the ovum.

b. much larger than the sperm since it must contain nutrition for the zygote formed by the union of the sperm and ovum.

c. the same size as the sperm.

d. of variable size, sometimes larger and sometimes smaller than the sperm.

29. There is an asymmetry of "cost" in male and female mammals because

a. fertilization and fetal development occur inside the body, unlike for instance for fish or for birds (after the egg is hatched).

b. ova are more expensive to make than sperm, and females have far fewer ova than males have sperm.

c. human males can conceive with more than one mate on the same day; females must wait over nine months to conceive with a different mate.

d. all of the above

30. Biologically does the male or female mammal lose the most opportunity for passing on genes by a "bad" conception?

a. male

b. female

c. both equally

d. It completely depends on circumstances.

31. Because the female mammal has the greater investment in reproduction
    a. there is evolutionary pressure for females to be choosy.
    b. there is evolutionary pressure for females to have sex only for love.
    c. there is evolutionary pressure for females sexually to experiment widely.
    d. there is no consistent evolutionary pressure; each individual confronts pressure to decide for herself.

32. There is evolutionary pressure for males not to be choosy. Why?
    a. Males can reproduce again the same day, so even a bad mating will give a greater chance of viable offspring than a missed opportunity.
    b. There is pressure for females to be choosy, so that males must compete with other males for access to females.
    c. The cost for a bad conception is low for a male.
    d. all of the above

33. Fish, who do not care for their young and who produce many young (most of whom do not survive although a few do), are an example of
    a. an r selected species.
    b. the type of species that will not survive long.
    c. a K selected species.
    d. an inferior species.

34. K selected species
    a. have many fewer offspring than r selected species.
    b. have offspring that are much more likely to survive than are offspring in r selected species.
    c. have offspring that need more care to survive than do those of r selected species.
    d. all of the above

35. The asymmetry in investment between human males and females
    a. is lessened by the necessity to cooperate in raising the young.
    b. is increased by the necessity to cooperate in raising the young since the female has the highest investment in the young.
    c. is increased by the necessity to cooperate in raising the young since the male rarely cooperates with the female in the raising of the young.
    d. is not changed by the necessity of raising the young.

36. Maternity is certain; paternity is not. This fact should produce evolutionary pressure
    a. toward male jealousy.
    b. toward an egalitarian relationship.
    c. toward females being more jealous than males.
    d. toward males and females being equally jealous.

37. Which of the following would *not* be a consequence of male variety seeking and jealousy?
    a. Males should be attracted to multiple wives (polygyny).
    b. Males should favor monogamy.
    c. Males should be more jealous than females.
    d. Males should not favor polyandry (one wife, several husbands).

38. The cross-cultural evidence demonstrates that
    a. monogamy is the most common form of marital arrangement.
    b. polygyny (one man, several wives) is the most common form of marital arrangement.
    c. polyandry (one woman, several husbands) is the most common form of marital arrangement.
    d. monogamy and polygyny are equally common.

39. In the Ford and Beach sample, in the only undisputed polyandrous society, the Toda,
    a. a woman marries a man and his brother.
    b. a man marries a woman and her sisters.
    c. there is genetic advantage for taking care of the offspring of one's neighbor's children if he is killed.
    d. all of the above

40. According to evolutionary theory since paternity is uncertain men should be more concerned with their mate's virginity than women are. What is the cross-cultural evidence?
    a. There are no cultures that insist on male virginity.
    b. All cultures insist on female virginity.

c. There are no cultures that require male virginity but not female virginity.

d. There are no cultures that require both the male and the female to be virgins.

41. According to evolutionary theory what ages of women should be most attractive to men?
a. young girls right before reaching sexual maturity
b. young, fertile women since they will be able to care for offspring longer
c. older, more sexually experienced women
d. There is no one age that should be most attractive to all men.

42. Buss in a cross-cultural study found that in most cultures
a. men prefer slightly older women.
b. men prefer younger women, and women prefer men who are the same age or slightly younger than they are.
c. men prefer younger women, and women prefer men who are slightly older than they are.
d. women prefer younger men.

43. In rating the desirability of a marriage partner, American female college students emphasized
a. only looks.
b. only status.
c. both looks and status.
d. neither looks nor status.

44. According to Kinsey's study (conducted in the forties and fifties), what percent of women had premarital sexual intercourse? How does this compare with the rates for males?
a. 10 percent of all women; much lower than the male rate
b. 60 percent of all women; the same as the male rate
c. 50 percent; the same as the male rate
d. 50 percent; considerably lower than the male rate

45. According to the Kinsey survey, by age forty what percent of men and what percent of women have had extramarital affairs?
a. 10 percent of all men and 5 percent of all women
b. 90 percent of all men and 10 percent of all women
c. 50 percent of all men and 25 percent of all women

d. 50 percent of all men and 55 percent of all women

46. In a study of male and female college students an opposite-sex stranger (confederate) asked for a date or sex for that evening. What percent of men and women accepted?
a. All of the men accepted the proposal for the date and for sex; no women accepted either.
b. About 40 percent of the women accepted the date, but none accepted the date and the sexual proposition.
c. Twenty percent of the men and women accepted the date, and 10 percent accepted the sex.
d. Fifty percent of the men and women accepted the date; 30 percent of the men and 40 percent of the women accepted the sexual proposition.

47. The difference in sexual behavior between men and women may be due to the double standard that women are punished more severely for casual sex than men. What happens in Mangaia where everyone is supposed to have sex?
a. Boys and girls have about the same number of sexual partners.
b. Girls have more sexual partners than boys.
c. Boys have more sexual partners than girls.
d. Number of partners is an individual decision and not related to gender.

48. Symons argues that we can get a better picture of male and female sexual desire using homosexual couples since heterosexual couples
a. have to compromise on sexual desires.
b. quarrel frequently, which interferes with sexual desire.
c. are sexually inhibited.
d. are not honest about sexual relations.

49. What is the comparison in number of sexual partners between gay men and lesbians (pre-AIDS) in the German sample?
a. The typical lesbian had had sexual relations with ten partners; the typical gay male had had sexual relations with fifteen partners.
b. The typical lesbian had had sexual relations with two partners; the typical gay male had had sexual relations with sixteen partners.
c. The typical lesbian had had sexual relations with sixteen partners; the typical gay male had had sexual relations with two partners.

d. The typical lesbian had had sexual relations with twenty partners; the typical gay male had had sexual relations with 20 partners.

50. In terms of interest in erotic pictures and stories
    a. according to Kinsey a much larger percent of men than women reported being aroused by erotic stories.
    b. pornographic magazines and movies almost entirely cater to men.
    c. recent experiments on sexual responsivity show that women are as responsive as men but more likely to feel quilt when watching pornography.
    d. all of the above

51. Differences in masturbation, since masturbation is solitary and private, are a good measure of sexual arousability, especially for people once they learn how to masturbate. Most studies have found that for people who masturbate,
    a. females and males masturbate with the same frequency.
    b. females masturbate more than males.
    c. males masturbate more than females.
    d. amount of masturbation is individual and cannot be divided by gender.

52. If a trait has a genetic base than
    a. it is unchangeable.
    b. it is changeable only with very great effort.
    c. it may (or may not) be easily changed.
    d. it is always easily changed.

53. Caffeine, alcohol, and chile are
    a. innately aversive to infants yet liked by most adults.
    b. innately attractive to infants and liked by most adults.
    c. innately neutral to infants.
    d. innately aversive to infants and disliked by adults.

54. If something is "natural," that is, shaped by evolution then
    a. it is certainly moral.
    b. it may or may not be moral.
    c. it must be moral.
    d. it is immoral.

55. When one commits the "naturalistic fallacy"
    a. one confuses facts about nature with moral facts.
    b. one does not realize that facts about nature are the same as moral facts.

c. one tries to get back to nature.
d. one avoids biological facts.

56. What is evolutionarily natural
    a. is also what will make us happiest.
    b. might make us happy or unhappy.
    c. cannot be resisted.
    d. will always make us unhappy.

57. Homosexuality is
    a. a puzzle for evolution since genes for homosexuality would not appear to be passed on.
    b. is expected by evolutionary theory.
    c. is not treated in evolutionary theory.
    d. none of the above

58. According to Kinsey's survey (1940s and 1950s)
    a. 10 percent of American men and 5 percent of American women are exclusively homosexual.
    b. 2 percent of American men and 1 percent of American women are exclusively homosexual.
    c. 1 percent of American men and .5 percent of American women are homosexual.
    d. 22 percent of American men and 25 percent of American women are homosexual.

59. Sickle cell anemia is a life-threatening genetic disorder. If both parents have the gene for sickle cell anemia the child will have the disease. Why should the gene for this disease have been passed on?
    a. The gene will be passed on by chance.
    b. Sickle cell anemia is not that serious a disease.
    c. If only one parent has the gene for the anemia, then the combination of an anemia and a non-anemia gene will make the child resistant to malaria.
    d. It will be passed on because a cure for the disease has not yet been discovered.

60. The genes for homosexuality might operate in a similar way to the sickle cell anemia gene and
    a. confer some heterosexual advantage for those with one gene and homosexuality for those with two.
    b. only make people homosexual in rare cases.
    c. make people homosexual whether they have one or two genes for the trait.
    d. confer some other advantages on those who are homosexual.

61. Which of the following are correct?
    a. The sperm contains an X or a Y chromosome.
    b. The egg contains only an X chromosome.
    c. If the fertilized egg has an X and a Y chromosome then the child will be a boy and if it has XX the child will be a girl.
    d. all of the above

62. What happens at the third fetal month?
    a. By the third fetal month the sexes are distinguishable.
    b. Until the third fetal month there is no observable difference between XX and XY, but at this point in the male testicles begin to form and secrete testosterone.
    c. In the third fetal month the XX fetus begins to secrete testosterone.
    d. By the third fetal month the brain has already largely developed.

63. The presence of testosterone will masculinize the fetal genitalia of
    a. only the XX fetus.
    b. only the XY fetus.
    c. both the XX and the XY fetus.
    d. neither the XX nor the XY fetus.

64. An XX fetus has accidentally been exposed to testosterone in the third fetal month. What sort of effect will this have on the postnatal development of the little girl?
    a. The girl's physical development will be stunted.
    b. She will most likely be a tomboy.
    c. She will develop a speech impediment.
    d. all of the above

65. Which of the following is *true*?
    a. Boys experience both puberty and sexual stirring before girls.
    b. Boys experience both puberty and sexual stirring after girls.
    c. Boys experience puberty after girls but have their first sexual stirring before girls.
    d. Boys experience puberty before girls but have their first sexual stirring after girls.

66. Michael Storms believes that the reason why more males are homosexual than females is that males experience the stirring of sexual arousal
    a. at a younger age than girls, when they are likely to be in all-male groups.
    b. at a younger age than girls, when they are in mixed-sex groups.
    c. at an older age than girls, when sexual experience is more likely to have a lasting effect.
    d. at an older age than girls, when they are more likely to be in mixed-sex groups.

67. According to the Storms hypothesis, both females and males who mature early are more likely to be
    a. heterosexual.
    b. shy.
    c. indifferent to sex.
    d. homosexual.

68. In a reanalysis of the Kinsey data it was found that both gay men and lesbians at the age of ten had fewer same-sex companions than did heterosexuals. If sexual stirrings start this early, then
    a. this information supports the Storms hypothesis.
    b. this neither supports nor goes against the Storms hypothesis.
    c. this goes against the Storms hypothesis.
    d. a conditioning view is supported.

69. Human "hypersexuality" means
    a. humans have too much sex for their own good.
    b. humans engage in sexual behavior much more than is needed for reproduction.
    c. that sex makes humans "hyper."
    d. all of the above

70. Desmond Morris argues that the function of hypersexuality
    a. is bonding, long-term couples.
    b. is happiness of the species.
    c. is reproduction since humans are relatively infertile.
    d. has no function.

71. The fact that gibbons are highly monogamous but rarely have sex
    a. supports Desmond Morris's hypothesis.
    b. goes against Desmond Morris's hypothesis.
    c. shows that gibbons must have a much higher rate of reproduction than humans.
    d. is irrelevant to the Morris hypothesis.

72. Sarah Hrdy has proposed a view that modifies the classical position that males sexually compete and females select. She argues
    a. that females compete.
    b. that female primates are interested in having sex with dominant males, not only the leader.
    c. that females are not interested in indiscriminate sex in the way that males are.
    d. all of the above

73. Primate males when taking over a troop often kill the offspring of the previous dominant male. Why does this occur?
    a. This demonstrates a pathology in the troop.
    b. This is in the interest of passing on the leader's genes.
    c. This only occurs when there is an embittered fight for leadership.
    d. This almost never occurs.

74. It is in the female primate's sexual interest to have her offspring survive. One behavior that would promote this is
    a. to have sex with members of the troop who may become dominant, hence making it unclear whose genes her progeny carries.
    b. to become variety seeking.
    c. to become more bonded to the leader.
    d. to abstain from sex.

75. Humans are a product of both genes and environment. Genes place what you can become on a leash. The leash should be shortest with
    a. intellectual behaviors.
    b. hunting behaviors.
    c. sexual behavior.
    d. emotions.

Answer Key for Self-Test

1.	c (p. 328)	11.	d (pp. 335-336)
2.	d (pp. 328-329)	12.	c (p. 337)
3.	c (p. 330)	13.	b (p. 338)
4.	b (p. 331)	14.	a (p. 338)
5.	a (p. 332)	15.	b (p. 338)
6.	c (p. 334)	16.	b (pp. 338-339)
7.	c (p. 334)	17.	c (p. 338)
8.	a (p. 334)	18.	c (p. 339)
9.	b (p. 335)	19.	d (p. 340)
10.	c (p. 335)	20.	a (p. 340)

21.	b (p. 340)	49.	b (p. 351)
22.	a (p. 340)	50.	d (pp. 351-352)
23.	c (p. 340)	51.	c (p. 353)
24.	a (p. 341)	52.	c (p. 354)
25.	d (p. 341)	53.	a (p. 354)
26.	a (p. 341)	54.	b (p. 354)
27.	d (p. 341)	55.	a (p. 354)
28.	b (p. 342)	56.	b (p. 355)
29.	d (pp. 342-343)	57.	a (p. 356)
30.	b (p. 343)	58.	a (p. 356)
31.	a (p. 343)	59.	c (p. 356)
32.	d (p. 343)	60.	a (p. 357)
33.	a (p. 343)	61.	d (p. 357)
34.	d (p. 343)	62.	b (p. 357)
35.	a (p. 344)	63.	c (p. 358)
36.	a (p. 344)	64.	b (p. 358)
37.	b (pp. 344-345)	65.	c (p. 359)
38.	b (p. 345)	66.	a (p. 359)
39.	a (p. 345)	67.	d (p. 359)
40.	c (p. 346)	68.	c (p. 360)
41.	b (p. 346)	69.	b (p. 361)
42.	c (p. 347)	70.	a (p. 361)
43.	c (p. 347)	71.	b (p. 362)
44.	d (p. 349)	72.	d (pp. 362-363)
45.	c (p. 349)	73.	b (p. 363)
46.	b (p. 349)	74.	a (p. 363)
47.	c (p. 350)	75.	c (p. 363)
48.	a (p. 350)		

Thought Questions and Exercises

1. When is it right to have sex? Is there now one standard for both sexes or a double standard? Make up a list of questions about people's sexual standards. Try to include questions about both the most and least restrictive standards. Give the list to two friends and see if they agree with you about the ordering from most to least restrictive. Here are some examples of questions to ask, but you should think of a lot more: "Is it alright to have sex with someone if you like and respect each other but are not in love?" "Is it alright to have sex with someone if you both agree to have sex?" "Should you have sex with someone only if you are engaged?" "Should you have sex only if your are married?" "Should you have sex only if everyone in your crowd is doing it?" "Should you have sex only if the other person wants to?" "Should you have sex if the other doesn't say no?" Now that you have a list of questions about what would be acceptable and unacceptable sexual

behavior, you can use these questions to see if there is still a difference in what people think is permissible for males and females. Present the questionnaire using a female name when giving it to a female, and a male name when giving it to a male: Your friend Jill (John) is younger than you are and is not sure about the rights and wrongs about sex. She (He) asks you your advice. In general, which of the following alternatives would correspond most closely to your advice? You may also want to ask your subjects which of the standards correspond to their actual behavior (as opposed to what they think is right), and which of the standards correspond to the sexual behavior of some of their male and female friends. Is there a difference in standards for males and females? Does it matter whether a male or a female is doing the judging? Are there different groups of standards?

2. Another way to investigate double standards is just to tell people that "John is quite sexually active and has slept with six women this year" or "Jill is quite sexually active and has slept with six men this year." Please write several lines describing what you think John (Jill) is like. Is there a difference in the descriptions of John and Jill? Does it make a difference whether males or females are describing them?

3. Supposedly since the 1980s a new sexual conservatism has set in. If you are able to give the questionnaire in #1 to people who are ten to fifteen years older than you are, you will probably have a rough indication of changes in attitude. (If you find a difference, is it necessarily a generational difference? What other causes might there be for different answers?)

4. One of the difficulties that students have in understanding the theory of evolution is that organisms need not try to evolve, want to evolve, or have any idea that they are evolving. The text points out, for instance, that if evolution increased lust, then in the absence of birth control it would increase having children. It is possible that people would not want to have more children, or that they would be trying to have more children, or that they would not even be thinking about children while they are engaged in sex; yet lust leads to sex, and sex in the absence of birth control leads to children. Lust, in this example, is the "proximate mechanism," and increased number of children is the effect. Think of two or three other examples where the evolutionary effect would be very different from the proximate mechanism.

5. The text points out that evolution shapes us for the world of our ancestors. Cultural change is relatively rapid, and the adaptations needed for a hunter-gatherer society may not be advantageous for a technological, literate society. Think of things that you believe would be adaptive in a hunter-gatherer society. List them. Which are adaptive now and which are not? What features do you think are particularly adaptive for a technological society? Would they be adaptive in a hunter-gatherer society?

6. The evolution of sexual behavior presents a striking contrast between what "is," what "should be," and what "leads to happiness." The author argues that what "is" is not necessarily what "has to be" and that humans often can choose. Explain his argument. What do you think of it?

CHAPTER 10

Altruism

Learning Objectives

THE CONCEPT OF ALTRUISM

1. Describe what altruism is. What are some of the reasons to doubt whether altruism really exists? What is "vulgar cynicism"? Is vulgar cynicism plausible as an account of all altruism?

Altruism and Evolution: Selfish Genes and Altruistic Individuals

2. Explain the difference in the definition of altruism when it is applied to animals. What is the *evolutionary* puzzle about altruism? Natural selection mainly works via competition between members of the same species. Why does this make it appear that evolution must lead to selfish individuals?

Altruism and Inclusive Fitness

3. Describe how evolution can account for altruism. Hamilton argues that natural selection works on the level of the gene and not on the level of the individual. Let us assume that selfish X and unselfish Y have genes determining their selfishness or unselfishness. Each has a child who also has their selfish or unselfish gene. Now a predator is going to eat the child. Given that X is selfish, X will lose the child but save herself. How many copies of the selfish gene will be left? Y is unselfish and will try to save the child. She may save the child and sacrifice herself or save both of them. At worst how many of her genes will be saved? At best? On these simplifying assumptions, whose genes will gradually take over? How does the fact that a child inherits one-

half of each parent's genes affect the probability of the selfish or non-selfish gene taking over? How can you extend this argument to relatives who share less than 50 percent of one's genes.

4. Explain what "inclusive fitness" means. Describe some of the oversimplifications of the model: unselfish Y's genetic cost in foregoing the future opportunity to have other children; the possibility of saving more than one child. How does belonging to an r or K species affect the likelihood of altruism developing?

Reciprocal Altruism

5. Describe what "reciprocal altruism" is. Under which conditions is it likely to develop? Explain the problem of "cheater genes." What is meant by an "evolutionarily stable strategy"? Trivers suggests a way that reciprocal altruism may be a stable strategy. What is it? Why would a gene with the double effect of disposing an organism to reciprocal altruism *and* to punishing those who don't reciprocate, lead to a stable strategy?

6. Does what we know about evolution support the notion of "vulgar cynicism"?

Subtle Cynicism

7. Describe what "subtle cynicism" is. According to this view, what motivates altruistic acts?

Altruism and Distress at Another's Distress

8. Describe the evidence that proves that babies as young as three days are distressed by the crying of other infants. Describe the evidence that shows that people will learn things quickly in order to terminate the pain of another person. What part of the subtle cynic's claim does this confirm?

Empathy and Reducing Distress

9. Describe how the text defines "empathy." Is distress at another's pain the same as empathy? How did Batson attempt experimentally to distinguish empathy from distress? In what condition did Batson's distress group and his empathy group offer to trade places with the victim? In what condition did the empathy group, but not the distress group, offer to trade places with the victim? The results of this experiment argue against one form of "subtle cynicism." Explain.

10. Cialdini has a way to rescue the "subtle cynics's" position. According to Cialdini what is the empathic subject's selfish payoff when he helps the sufferer? Describe Cialdini's experimental attempt to demonstrate his point. How did Batson attempt experimentally to rebut Cialdini?

11. The text argues argues that even if subtle cynicism is true, it isn't that cynical. Explain. The text argues that there is at least one extrinsic reward, acting for the reward of knowing that one has done the right thing, that is very different from acting for mood elevation. A person is still an altruist if he helps another for the extrinsic reward of "doing the right thing." Explain.

THE DEVELOPMENT OF EMPATHY

12. Describe the difference between empathy and being distressed at another's distress. Hoffman argues that feeling distress at another's distress is a necessary precondition of empathy. Why?

Overcoming Egocentrism

13. Before one feels empathy one must be able to see the world as others see it. According to Piaget when does this ability develop? Describe how Piaget attempted to demonstrate this point in the three-mountain experiment. What does Piaget assume about the relation between perceptual and other types of egocentrism? Is he right? For young children, if they have sufficiently overcome egocentrism are they necessarily altruistic? If they have not sufficiently overcome egocentrism can they be altruistic?

Socializing Altruistic Behavior

14. Describe factors that lead a child to learn to care about others. Present an experiment that shows that it is not enough for parents to get children to act generously but that they must also lead the child to believe that the generosity derived from their own impulses.

MOODS AND GENEROSITY

Good Moods and Altruism

15. Adults were led to believe they had succeeded or failed on a measure of general creativity. They were then asked to contribute to a charity. Who contributed more? Give examples of various things that put people in a good mood that have been found to lead to generosity.

16. Describe the studies that conclude that subjects in a good mood are not directly altruistic, rather they are more likely to do things, including altruism, that sustain their good moods and less willing to do things that would wreck their good moods. What is the evidence that self-gratification and generosity go together in a good mood?

Bad Moods and Altruism

17. Describe the evidence that bad moods sometimes *increase* altruism (include the studies on guilt and altruism). What happens to subsequent altruism when something good happens to the guilty person?

ALTRUISM AND DOING THE RIGHT THING

18. In addition to altruism, doing the right thing by following social norms is a reason why people help. What problem arises from the fact that norms are abstract?

Bystander Intervention in Emergencies

19. Present Latané and Darley's five-step model of how people come to intervene in an emergency. How did Latané and Darley explain why people did not intervene in the Kitty Genovese murder?

Failure to Pay Attention to the Victim

20. Describe the study of seminary students by Darley and Batson. Describe the essentials of the Milgram experiments on obedience to malevolent authority. The author argues that both in the Darley and Batson and the Milgram experiments the subjects had tunnel vision. Explain.

Deciding an Event is an Emergency

21. What is it about the nature of emergencies that makes it difficult to decide whether something is an emergency or not?

Pluralistic Ignorance

22. Describe how pluralistic ignorance develops. Describe Latané and Darley's study demonstrating how being with others can inhibit inter-

vening in an emergency. How does this experiment show that it is not apathy that prevents people from intervening?

23. Describe what can be done to make bystanders more likely to intervene. Describe the Shotland experiment on the most effective way to get bystander intervention in a rape.

Diffusion of Responsibility

24. Aside from pluralistic ignorance what other major factor involving the presence of other people has a role in inhibiting people from helping? Describe in detail the "epileptic fit" experiment. The cause of nonintervention in this experiment *must be* different from the cause of nonintervention in the "where is fire" experiment. Explain why. Show how the set-up of this experiment does not allow for the development of pluralistic ignorance.

Altruism and Focusing Responsibility

25. "If diffusion of responsibility inhibits helping, then focusing responsibility should increase it." Explain. Present the Jones Beach and the Manhattan automat experiments. How did the experimental manipulation in these experiments "focus responsibility"?

26. Although the effect of number of people present on helping in an emergency is well confirmed there are several studies that have not found the effect. Describe the "helping in the subway" experiment that failed to find this effect. What are some possible reasons for why it didn't show the effect.

WHO IS LIKELY TO HELP?

Helping in Emergencies and Personality

27. Describe what has been found about the relation between helping and personality.

Urban-Rural Differences in Helping

28. Is there evidence that people in rural areas are more likely to be helpful than people in urban areas? Milgram argues that this is an effect of coping with cognitive overload. Explain.

Reactions of the Person in Need of Help

29. Receiving help is a mixed blessing. Explain. Are there situations in which people would prefer muddling through a problem to receiving help? Present an experiment showing that fear of loss of esteem can mediate someone's asking or not asking for help.

Programmed Exercises

THE CONCEPT OF ALTRUISM

1. Altruism is behavior motivated by the _____ to help others.

    desire

2. Altruism is related to our ability to consider _____ interests as well as our own.

    others'

3. "Vulgar cynicism" is the position that seemingly altruistic acts are really motivated by material _____-_____ in disguise.

    self-interest

Altruism and Evolution: Selfish Games and Altruistic Individuals

4. A gene for altruism would not appear to benefit the possessor of that _____ but to benefit others.

    gene

5. For the above reason there is an evolutionary _____ about altruism.

    puzzle

6. When we talk about altruism in animals we talk about behavior that need not be _____ to help as long as it does.

    intended

7. If X and Y are in the same group and S is genetically geared to act altruistically and Y is not, then _____ will get the benefit of X's help along with its own efforts and X will not. For this reason _____ will be more likely than X to have offspring.

    Y
    Y

8. For this reason over the generations there should be _____ altruism genes and more _____ individuals.

    fewer
    selfish

9. Yet there are numerous documented cases of _____ in animals.   altruism

10. Y and her child have an altruistic gene; X and her child have a non-altruistic gene. A predator is about to eat the children. Y will try to _____ her child and X will not.   save

11. If the predator eats the child, X will still have her non-altruistic gene but not that of her ex-child. If Y dies while saving her child then there will still be _____ altruistic gene, the child's, and if both survive there will be _____ altruistic genes. Over generations altruistic genes should become _____ common.   one
two
more

12. In species like ours, the child has 50 percent of the genes of the _____.   parent

13. In reality if a parent with an altruism gene sacrifices himself there is only a _____ percent chance that the surviving offspring will have an altruism gene. This means that the altruism gene will be likely to pass on only if the odds are better than 50 percent chance that the parent (as well as the child) will _____.   50

survive

14. The altruism gene will be likely to be passed on in the case of nieces or nephews, who have a relatedness of 25 percent, only if the risk to the aunt or uncle is less than _____ percent.   25

15. Hamilton's notion of _____ _____ involves judging the fitness of a gene by how the gene affects its organism and also how the gene affects relatives (according to the degree of relatedness).   inclusive fitness

16. This model also takes into account the cost of foregoing having other _____ with the gene by sacrificing for a present offspring.   children

17. Fish, an r selected species, have few of a large number of offspring surviving, hence _____ is unlikely to evolve in fish.   altruism

18. According to the account of evolution developed so far, genes for altruism to _____ people would be unlikely to evolve.   unrelated

19. _____ altruism involves the tendency to reciprocate altruism done to you.   Reciprocal

20. Reciprocal altruism would be likely to evolve if the cost of helping the other was sufficiently low and the value of being helped was sufficiently _____.   high

21. The evolutionary strategy of reciprocal altruism runs into the problem of _____ genes.   cheater

22. A cheater gene would dispose someone to take advantage of altruism but not to be _____.   altruistic

23. The possibility of cheater genes appears to make altruism not an evolutionarily _____ strategy.   stable

24. Trivers has suggested that genes that lead us to act altruistically but also to _____ those who do not reciprocate, lead to an evolutionarily stable strategy.   punish

25. Neither vulgar cynicism nor _____ theory provide reason to disbelieve in altruism.   evolutionary

Subtle Cynicism

26. While the "vulgar cynic" believes that people appear to act altruistically for material gain, the "subtle cynic" believes that people appear to act altruistically for _____ gain.   psychological

27. The subtle cynic believes that people help only to get pleasure or avoid _____.   pain

28. Very young infants respond with distress to the _____ of another infant.   cries

29. People become _____ physiologically aroused at another's pain.   unpleasantly

30. This confirms part of the subtle cynic's claim: relieving another's pain can relieve our _____ (and motivate learning).   own

31. What these studies do not show is that people try to reduce another's suffering _____ to reduce their own.   only

32. _____ involves understanding another's distress and being motivated to relieve it.   Empathy

33. Distress at another's pain involves being _____ by it.   upset (pained, distressed)

34. In an experiment by Batson, subjects who saw someone receiving shocks were divided into the _____ and the _____.   distressed, empathetic

35. When the subjects were told that the person would continue to be given shocks but that they would not see it the _____ subjects, but not the _____ subjects, offered to exchange places with her.   empathetic distressed

36. Insofar as "subtle cynicism" argues that people help others only to relieve their own distress, this experiment _____ this position.   refutes (disproves)

37. Cialdini has a different "subtle cynic" interpretation of the Batson results. He argues that empathetic subjects relieve distress to improve their own _____.   mood

38. Cialdini using an experimental scenario similar to Batson's showed that subjects instructed to be empathetic were no more likely to help the sufferer than subjects not so instructed, if they had a _____ experience in between seeing the suffering and having the opportunity to switch places.   pleasant

39. Cialdini takes his results to show that empathetic subjects only help to improve their own _____ and not out of genuine concern with the sufferer.   mood

40. Batson attempted to rebut Cialdini in an experiment in which people were exposed to an empathetic help appeal and told (or not told) that before they could help they would see a mood-elevating film. If subjects only helped as a means to improve their mood they would _____ have helped the sufferer when they expected to be in a good mood regardless of whether they helped. Yet subjects helped in both conditions.   not

41. The world that "subtle cynicism" portrays is not as horrible as that of "vulgar cynicism" since people at least do get genuine _____ out of helping others.   pleasure

42. Sometimes people may act in order to receive a reward and yet still be altruistic; this is the case when the reward is the knowledge that one has done the _____ thing.   right

THE DEVELOPMENT OF EMPATHY

43. Hoffman argues that feeling distress at another's distress is a necessary precondition of _____.

empathy

44. If a child is _____ then she cannot see the world from someone else's perspective.

egocentric

45. The performance of young children between ages three and six on various egocentrism tasks correlates with _____. For children older than six there is no correlation between _____ and egocentrism.

altruism
altruism

46. Overcoming egocentrism is _____ but not sufficient for the development of altruism.

necessary

SOCIALIZING ALTRUISTIC BEHAVIOR

47. In addition to overcoming egocentrism there are five factors that go into a child's developing altruism: how _____ the parents are with the children, whether parents explain how the child's behavior affects the _____ of others, the _____ the parents show that they place on altruism, the _____ of altruistic behavior by adults, how the parents _____ to the child when she is generous.

affectionate
feelings
value
modeling, respond

48. It is not only important that parents induce their children to be generous, but they also must lead the children to believe that they were generous from their own _____.

impulses

MOODS AND GENEROSITY

Good Moods and Altruism

49. Adults were led to believe they had succeeded or failed on a measure of general creativity. They were then asked to contribute to a charity. The successful gave _____ than the unsuccessful.

more

50. Being given a cookie, finding a dime, and sunny weather all put people in a good mood and made them more _____.

generous

51. Subjects in a good mood are not directly altruistic, rather they are more likely to do something, including an altruistic act, if it sustains their _____ _____ and less willing to do something that would wreck it.

good
mood

52. A good mood enhances self-gratification and _____, while a bad mood just enhances self-gratification.

generosity

53. Being in a good mood _____ attention, being in a bad mood restricts attention.

enhances (increases, focuses)

54. Good moods have opposing effects on helpfulness. Good deeds that are pleasant will be _____ likely, but those that involve unpleasantness will be _____ likely.

more
less

Bad Moods and Altruism

55. Bad moods often make people _____ altruistic.

more

56. Subjects were made to feel guilty and then solicited for a favor. They were _____ likely to do the favor than subjects who had not been made to feel guilty.

more

57. If these subjects were complimented or unexpectedly paid after the guilt induction but before being asked for the favor they were _____ more likely (than those who had not been made to feel guilty) to do the favor.

not

58. To a person in a bad mood being _____, being _____, and doing someone a _____ are substitutable ways to improve the mood.

paid, complimented favor

ALTRUISM AND DOING THE RIGHT THING

59. _____ _____ are necessarily abstract, leaving particular applications undecided. For this reason it is difficult to predict behavior in a specific case from knowledge of the _____ a person holds.

Social norms

norms

Bystander Intervention in Emergencies

60. Latané and Darley have a five-step model of how people come to help in emergencies: people must _____ that something is happening; they must come to believe that it is an _____; they must decide that it is their _____ to act; they must _____ what to do; they must know _____ to do it.

notice
emergency
responsibility, know
how

61. In an experiment seminary students memorized the parable of the Good Samaritan and then had to cross campus to present the parable. They were told that they had plenty of time or that they were in a rush. Across their path lay someone needing aid. _____ percent of the seminarians in a rush aided the person while _____ percent having plenty of time helped him.

10
63

62. Being rushed seemed to produce _____ vision so that the subject did not think of the relevance of the situation to the norms she believed in.

tunnel

63. Emergencies are by their nature _____.

ambiguous

64. The screams of Kitty Genovese, at first, may have sounded like part of a husband and wife conflict. We have norms _____ to intervene in such a conflict.

not

Pluralistic Ignorance

65. Latané and Darley claim that in the presence of others, people look to the others for guidance, and the others look to them. Since everyone is waiting for someone else to act and define the situation, no one _____ and everyone decides that it is a situation not needing action. _____ _____ develops.

acts
Pluralistic ignorance

66. In an experiment subjects waiting in a room alone or with two nonresponsive confederates (or with two other naive subjects) perceived smoke coming from under a door. The subjects who waited _____ were most likely to report smoke.

alone

67. Subjects who did not intervene invented many _____ interpretations of the smoke, apparently to justify their inaction.

nonthreatening

68. In this experiment the subjects themselves were in danger, hence an explanation that people do not intervene because of _____ is inapplicable to this study.

apathy

69. The presence of nonreactive others in this experiment both _____ the subjects and inhibits them because they fear embarrassment from seeming to _____.

confuses

overreact

70. When subjects are sitting back to back they are much less likely to intervene at

the sound of a crash than if they are _____ each other. This is because · facing
subjects can use the other's startle response as information that there is an
_____. · emergency

71. Subjects who do not intervene in the first thirty seconds typically do not intervene at all, but they do not _____ not to intervene, rather they feel that · decide
they are still waiting to decide.

72. In a study it was found that the best way to recruit aid if one is being raped is
to yell help _____, rather than yelling "fire" or blowing a police whistle. · rape
It was found that about _____ percent of the subjects, both men and · 40
women, helped. The help was mainly _____; it was in the form of · indirect
going for aid.

Diffusion of Responsibility

73. People are inhibited from helping others because of pluralistic ignorance. They
are also inhibited from helping because of _____ _____ · diffusion of
_____. · responsibility

74. In the epileptic fit experiment, when the subjects believed that only they and
the person having the fit were in the group _____ percent tried to help. · 100
When the subjects believed that four other people could hear the person in
distress, then about _____ percent tried to help. · 60

75. The subjects could not see nor, at the moment, communicate with other subjects;
hence, _____ ignorance could not account for their behavior. The · pluralistic
reason subjects did not help was because of _____ _____ · diffusion of
_____; each subject believed that someone should help but not · responsibility
necessarily her.

Altruism and Focusing Responsibility

76. If diffusion of responsibility inhibits helping, focusing of responsibility should
_____ helping. · increase

77. At the beach it was found that just asking someone to "watch my things"
caused _____ percent of the people asked to intervene with a "thief." · 95
If the request had been "do you have a light" only _____ percent · 20
intervened.

78. If the main reason that people did not intervene with possible thieves was fear
of danger then people would not have almost unanimously _____. · intervened (helped)

79. In a study of a man falling on the subway, almost _____ percent of the · 90
cases people came to his aid. This was independent of the _____ of · number
people present.

80. The reason why the number of people did not inhibit helping may have been
because of the clear norms in the situation, such as the closest male to the
incident should be the one to _____. · help

81. Even the most trivial relationship between people will undo the effects of
diffusion of _____. When the people in a "diffusion experiment" are · responsibility
supposed to meet after the experiment _____ of responsibility does · diffusion
not occur. Diffusion of responsibility is characteristic of _____ with · interactions
strangers who we expect to remain strangers.

WHO IS LIKELY TO HELP?

Helping in Emergencies and Personality

82. Latané and Darley administered personality questionnaires to their subjects but did not find any personality measure that predicted _____.

helping

83. Recent research has found one personality trait, _____, that predicts _____ helping in both males and females. This may be because seeing oneself as poised and cool gets in the way of _____ in an emergency where there is always the risk of looking foolish.

masculinity
less
helping

84. It has been found that people in _____ settings are more likely to help than people in _____ settings.

rural
urban

85. According to Milgram, people in cities in attempting to cope with _____ turn a deaf ear to constant appeals.

overload

Reactions of the Person in Need of Help

86. One drawback of receiving help is that by doing so you admit you need it, which may reduce _____-_____.

self-esteem

87. Males are _____ likely to ask an attractive female for help than an unattractive one. Females are _____ likely to ask an attractive male for help than an unattractive one. This may be because of sex-role stereotypes. Men feel that a dependent male will be seen as less attractive to a woman, while women feel that a dependent women will not be seen as less _____ to men.

less
more

unattractive

Self-Test

1. Altruism is behavior motivated by
   a. the desire to look good.
   b. the desire for gain.
   c. the desire to help others.
   d. thoughtlessness.

2. In order to be altruistic
   a. one must be able to understand the interests of others.
   b. one must want to suffer.
   c. one must be able to find a way to gain from the situation.
   d. one need not understand the interests of others.

3. "Vulgar cynicism" is the position that seemingly altruistic acts
   a. are material self-interest in disguise.
   b. are really selfless.
   c. are quite frequent.
   d. are vulgarly inappropriate in the modern age.

4. When we talk of altruism in animals we mean that
   a. they intend to help.
   b. their behavior consistently helps another in a particular situation whether the behavior is intended or not.
   c. they really want to help other animals.
   d. all of the above

5. Which of the following statements are consistent with the notion that altruism, common in nature, is a puzzle for the theory of evolution?
   a. By sacrificing itself an animal with an altruistic gene is less likely to survive and pass its genes on.
   b. Non-altruistic animals will get the benefit of the altruistic act and be more likely to pass on their "non-altruistic gene."
   c. Over the generations there should be fewer and fewer altruistic genes and altruism should die out.
   d. all of the above

6. One way out of the evolutionary puzzle is to realize that animals
   a. want to be altruistic despite the negative genetic effect.
   b. learn altruism; it is not inherited.
   c. share genes with their offspring (and relatives).
   d. are never altruistic.

7. The altruism gene would be successfully passed on when a parent sacrificed himself for his offspring if
   a. the altruistic acts would still leave the parent with a better than 40 percent chance of survival, since a parent shares 40 percent of his genes with his offspring.
   b. the altruistic acts would still leave the parent with a better than 50 percent chance of survival, since a parent shares 50 percent of his genes with his offspring.
   c. the altruistic acts would still leave the parent with a better than 70 percent chance of survival, since a parent shares 70 percent of his genes with his offspring.
   d. the altruistic acts would still leave the parent with a better than 90 percent chance of survival, since a parent shares 90 percent of his genes with his offspring.

8. More distant relatives share genes with the potential altruist, but they share fewer genes than the altruist does with his or her offspring. How should this affect altruism?
   a. Relatives should also be the object of altruism but only when the chances of survival for the altruist are better than the odds of surviving an altruistic act for offspring.
   b. Relatives should never be the object of altruism.
   c. Relatives should be the object of altruism only if the altruism is taught to the animal.
   d. Relatives should be more likely to receive altruistic acts than offspring.

9. Hamilton's notion of "inclusive fitness" involves judging the fitness of an organism that has a certain gene. It does this by calculating how the gene affects its organism and also how the gene affects
   a. relatives according to the degree of relatedness.
   b. strangers according to their degree of likability.
   c. members of the same group according to the extent the animals have been reared together.
   d. members of the group according to how important the particular group is to all its members.

10. In species in which animals have very many young, for instance, fish
    a. altruism always evolves.
    b. altruism occurs in 50 percent of the organisms.
    c. altruism is unlikely to evolve.
    d. altruism occurs as a learned, not as an inherited behavior.

11. The evolution of altruism to unrelated people
    a. cannot be explained in the same way as the evolution of altruism to relatives.
    b. is explained in the same way as the evolution of altruism to relatives.
    c. is impossible according to evolutionary theory.
    d. depends on the fact that an individual's sacrifice can greatly benefit an entire group.

12. Reciprocal altruism is
    a. altruism toward relatives.
    b. altruism that gets progressively smaller as the need for the altruism gets larger.
    c. nonexistent.
    d. the tendency to reciprocate the altruism done to one.

13. Reciprocal altruism
    a. cannot evolve.
    b. could evolve if the cost of helping others were low and the benefits of reciprocating were high.
    c. could evolve only if genes were shared between the altruist and those doing the reciprocation.
    d. would tend to evolve in nonsocial species.

14. The evolutionary strategy of reciprocal altruism runs into the problem of
    a. the low intelligence of most nonhuman animals.
    b. the low number of genes that nonrelatives have in common.
    c. cheater genes that dispose animals to act as if they would reciprocate even though they will not do so.
    d. all of the above

15. Trivers has suggested that
    a. cheater genes make the evolution of altruism impossible.
    b. cheater genes could not have evolved.
    c. if the altruism gene also made animals more likely to punish those who did not reciprocate, then reciprocal altruism could evolve.
    d. if the "altruism gene" also made punishment of non-reciprocation possible then altruism would not evolve.

16. On the face of it "the evolutionary puzzle of altruism" makes it appear that altruism could never develop (just as the "vulgar cynic" would maintain). Yet altruism is compatible with evolution. Which of the following show(s) that

altruism is compatible with evolution?
a. the evolutionary possibility of altruism toward relatives
b. the evolutionary possibility of reciprocal altruism
c. the fact that our relatives share genes with us
d. all of the above

17. While the "vulgar cynic" believes that people just appear to act altruistically for material gain, "subtle cynics" believe that people appear to act altruistically
a. for career advancement.
b. for psychological gain.
c. for no reason at all.
d. because they had an unhappy childhood.

18. Which of the following is *true* of young infants?
a. Infants feel distress at another's distress; they will cry if another infant cries.
b. Infants do not feel distress at another's distress; they will cry as much at a loud noise as at another infant's cry.
c. Infants only react to their own distress.
d. Infants are altruistic.

19. Which of the following are experimentally demonstrated examples of adults feeling distress at another's distress?
a. Subjects learn more quickly when they perceive that a correct response will end someone's pain.
b. People become physiologically aroused at another's pain.
c. Subjects solved problems more quickly when told that the solution will end someone's pain.
d. all of the above

20. The above studies support one element of the subtle cynic's claim that discomfort at another's pain can motivate us. It does not touch on the second and more important part of the claim, which is that
a. people only appear to act altruistically to gain material advantage.
b. people only appear to act altruistically in order to gain sex or career advancement.
c. people try to reduce another's suffering only to reduce their own (because seeing suffering makes them feel uncomfortable).
d. people try to reduce suffering only in order to brag.

21. Empathy (in humans)
a. is the same as distress at another's distress.
b. involves not only distress at another's distress but the motivation to relieve the other's pain for the other's sake.
c. involves doing something helpful for others whether we intend to do so or not.
d. does not exist.

22. In an experiment Batson had subjects watch someone receive nonpainful shocks that were for personal reasons very upsetting to her. How did the subjects react?
a. Subjects classified as "distressed at distress" volunteered to switch places only if they knew they would continue to see the person suffer.
b. Subjects classified as "empathetic" volunteered to switch places even if they knew they would not continue to see the person's suffering.
c. The "distressed at distress" subjects volunteered to switch places even when they would no longer be seeing the person suffer.
d. a and b

23. In the Batson experiment the difference between the "empathetic" and the "distressed at distress" subjects was that
a. the empathetic subjects helped even though they knew that their own distress would be relieved whether they helped or not.
b. the empathetic subjects were more upset at the pain than the distressed subjects.
c. the empathetic subjects were less upset at the pain than the distressed subjects.
d. the empathetic subjects only helped if they knew that helping would relieve their own discomfort.

24. Cialdini attempted to rescue the subtle cynic position from Batson's evidence by arguing that empathetic subjects were just trying to relieve their own mood. In an experiment similar to Batson's he showed that
a. empathetic subjects were less likely to help than other subjects.
b. empathetic subjects were no more likely than nonempathetic subjects to switch places with the sufferer if they had a pleasant experience between seeing the suffering and being given a chance to switch places.
c. empathetic subjects only volunteered to switch places with the sufferer if everyone knew that they were doing this.

d. empathetic subjects only offered to switch places after making sure that their good deed would be reciprocated.

25. In another experiment Cialdini showed that if empathetic subjects were given a placebo and told they would not be able to change their mood during the experiment then
   a. they helped much more than a control group that believed their mood was very changeable.
   b. they helped less than subjects who believed that their mood was very easily changed.
   c. their helping was not affected by the belief that their mood was easy or difficult to change.
   d. they did not help at all.

26. The Cialdini studies contradict Batson's by presenting evidence that
   a. empathetic subjects are just trying to reduce their own discomfort or better their mood.
   b. empathetic subjects in certain circumstances do not help.
   c. vulgar cynicism is correct.
   d. empathetic subjects will not help if they know they will not witness a person's suffering.

27. In response to Cialdini, Batson conducted an experiment in which people were exposed to an empathetic help appeal and told that before they would have a chance to help they would see a mood-elevating film. What were the results?
   a. According to Cialdini's account, people should be less altruistic if they anticipated a pleasant film than if they did not, yet they acted equally altruistically in both situations.
   b. According to Cialdini's account, people should be less altruistic in this situation than when they did not anticipate the film, and in fact they acted less altruistically.
   c. According to Cialdini's account people should be more altruistic in this situation than when they did not anticipate the film, yet they acted equally altruistically in both situations.
   d. According to Cialdini's account people should act more altruistically in this situation than when they did not anticipate the film, and they acted more altruistically.

28. One "external" motive, "doing the right thing,"
   a. does not show that a person acting because of this motive is not altruistic.
   b. is unlike mood elevation that can be gotten from many very different experiences.

c. is a reward.
   d. all of the above

29. Hoffman argues that developmentally, feeling distress at another's distress is a precondition for
   a. being able to manipulate others.
   b. the preoperational period of development.
   c. the development of empathy.
   d. formal reasoning.

30. For children the ability to perceive things from another's perspective
   a. correlates with empathy for children between three and six.
   b. correlates with empathy for all children up until age twelve.
   c. does not correlate with empathy in young children but does correlate with empathy in older children.
   d. does not develop until adolescence.

31. Egocentrism, the inability to see things from another's perspective,
   a. enhances altruism.
   b. makes altruism impossible.
   c. is the only block to being altruistic.
   d. develops later than empathy.

32. In addition to overcoming egocentrism, what other factors go into a child's developing altruism?
   a. how affectionate the parents are with the children
   b. whether parents explain to the child how the child's behavior affects the feelings of others
   c. the value the parents show that they place on altruism and the model of altruistic behavior adults provide
   d. all of the above

33. Which of the following tend to make people more generous?
   a. being told that they are creative
   b. being in a good mood
   c. sunny weather
   d. all of the above

34. Subjects who are put in a good mood
   a. are always more generous.
   b. are more generous only if it sustains their good mood.
   c. are less generous if the generosity will interfere with their good mood.
   d. b and c

35. Children were put in good, bad, or neutral moods. They were then allowed to help themselves to cookies and to give to charity. In what way were children in a good or bad mood different from children in a neutral mood?
    a. Children in a good or bad mood took more cookies and gave more to charity.
    b. Children in a good mood took more cookies and children in a bad mood took fewer cookies; both gave more to charity.
    c. Children in a good or bad mood took more cookies, but the children in a good mood gave the most to charity.
    d. Children in a bad mood took fewer cookies, but they gave more to charity.

36. The above experiment demonstrates that at least in children
    a. a good mood enhances both self-gratification and generosity, while a bad mood only enhances self-gratification.
    b. a bad mood enhances both self-gratification and generosity.
    c. a good mood diminishes generosity.
    d. a bad mood increases generosity but decreases self-gratification.

37. Bad moods often have what effect on altruism?
    a. They make people more altruistic.
    b. They make people less altruistic.
    c. They have no effect on altruism.
    d. They make men more altruistic and women less altruistic.

38. Guilt
    a. increases helping the victim, but does not increase helping others.
    b. increases helping the victim and others.
    c. increases helping people in general but does not increase helping the victim.
    d. does not increase helping.

39. Catholics are more likely to give to a charity
    a. on their way to Mass.
    b. on their way from Mass.
    c. coming or going to Mass.
    d. on days when they are not going to Mass.

40. Subjects who were made to feel guilty and then solicited for a favor were more likely to do the favor than subjects who hadn't been made to feel guilty. This was true except in one circumstance. In which of the following would the guilty be no more likely to give than the non-guilty?
    a. if asked to give to charities that they aren't

very familiar with
    b. if put in a good mood and then asked the favor
    c. if they are only moderately guilty
    d. all of the above

41. Adults are more likely to help in a bad mood and children are not. This may be because
    a. children are more spontaneous than adults.
    b. both adults and children focus inward in a bad mood, inhibiting helping, but adults realize that helping will improve their mood so they overcome this tendency; children do not know the connection between mood and helping so they don't help.
    c. adults are more selfish than children.
    d. both adults and children focus inward in a bad mood, and thus are inhibited from helping, but children want to stay in a bad mood once they are in it and adults do not.

42. Social norms are necessarily
    a. rigid, in that they cannot take into account new experiences.
    b. inconsistent.
    c. abstract, in that they leave the specific applications of the norms undecided.
    d. incoherent.

43. Latané and Darley believe there are several steps by which people come to help in emergencies. People
    a. must notice that something is happening.
    b. must come to believe that it is an emergency.
    c. must decide that it is their responsibility to act and must know what to do and how to do it.
    d. all of the above

44. Latané and Darley argue that people failed to intervene in the Kitty Genovese murder because
    a. they did not notice that anything was happening.
    b. they were not sure it was an emergency and that it was their responsibility to act.
    c. they did not know what to do to help.
    d. they derived secret gratification from the crime.

45. In an experiment seminary students memorized the parable of the Good Samaritan and then had to cross campus to present the parable. They were told that they had plenty of time or that they were in a rush. Across their path lay someone needing aid.
    a. Sixty-three percent of the seminarians who

were in a rush aided the person, while 10 percent of those having plenty of time failed to help.

b. Almost all of the seminarians helped in both conditions.

c. Ten percent of the seminarians who were in a rush aided the person while 63 percent of the seminarians who had plenty of time helped.

d. Half the seminarians in both conditions helped.

46. Being rushed in the Good Samaritan experiment and being pressured by the experimenter in the obedience experiments
   a. produced tunnel vision so that the subject did not think of the relevance of the situation to the norms she believed in.
   b. decreased people's desire to help.
   c. brought out authoritarian tendencies in people.
   d. only affected motivation.

47. Emergencies are by their nature
   a. very clear-cut.
   b. challenging in terms of courage but not in terms of intellect.
   c. ambiguous, confusing, unclear.
   d. uninteresting.

48. Latané and Darley claim that when we are among others we look to them for guidance and they look to us. They are waiting for us to react, and we are waiting for them to react, so no one reacts and because of this everyone decides it is not an emergency. This has been called
   a. indifference.
   b. pluralistic ignorance.
   c. multiple perspectives.
   d. apathy.

49. One reason that pluralistic ignorance develops is that
   a. people believe that emergencies are things that anyone can perceive, like rocks, and if others aren't perceiving it then there must not be an emergency.
   b. people don't really care about what happens in an emergency and hence they rely on what others are doing from indifference.
   c. everyone in an emergency is equally ignorant. They don't really look to each other for guidance it's just that when everyone's ignorance is added together the result is pluralistic ignorance.
   d. all of the above

50. Subjects waiting in a room alone, with two confederates, or with two other naive subjects, noticed smoke coming from under a door.
   a. The subjects who waited with other naive subjects were most likely to report the smoke.
   b. The subjects who waited with the nonresponsive confederates were most likely to report the smoke.
   c. The subjects who waited alone were most likely to report the smoke.
   d. There were no differences between waiting alone and waiting with others in likelihood to report the smoke.

51. In this experiment the subjects themselves were in danger, hence an explanation that people do not intervene because of apathy
   a. is inapplicable to this study and thus cannot be a complete explanation of why people do not act in emergencies.
   b. is confirmed.
   c. is shown to be true in this instance but not in other instances.
   d. is shown never to be applicable to emergencies.

52. The presence of nonreactive others in the above experiment
   a. both makes the subjects apathetic and increases their concern with their own well-being.
   b. makes the subjects more reactive to external cues.
   c. both confuses the subjects and inhibits them since they are afraid of being embarrassed in front of others by over-reacting.
   d. all of the above

53. When subjects are sitting back to back they are much less likely to intervene at the sound of a crash than if they are
   a. facing each other.
   b. in a group of nonreacting people.
   c. far away.
   d. blindfolded.

54. The results in the above experiment are due to the fact that when subjects face each other
   a. conformity pressures are much lower.
   b. they can use the other's startle response as information that there is an emergency.
   c. it is easier to disregard the other's reactions.
   d. they will almost always ask the others for their opinion.

55. In the intervention experiments what has been found about timing?

a. Subjects who wait several minutes are most likely to help since they have most maturely considered the issue.

b. Subjects who do not intervene in the first thirty seconds typically do not intervene.

c. Subjects who jump up very quickly in the first thirty seconds usually sit down again and don't intervene.

d. There is no relation between timing and intervention.

56. An experimenter dropped a dollar before bystanders in the college library and a thief scooped it up. If the experimenter did not appear to know that he had lost the money

a. he was more likely to be helped than if he fumbled in his pocket and gave other evidence that he knew he had lost the money.

b. he was much less likely to be helped than if he fumbled in his pocket and gave other evidence that he knew he had lost the money.

c. people helped whether he showed he realized he had lost the money or whether he appeared ignorant of the fact.

d. people did not help whether he showed he realized he had lost the money or whether he appeared ignorant of the fact.

57. The best way to recruit aid if one is being raped is

a. to yell fire.

b. blow a police whistle.

c. yell "help rape."

d. any of the above

58. In the above study what percent of men and women helped?

a. 2 percent

b. 10 percent

c. 20 percent

d. 40 percent

59. In the epileptic fit experiment subjects interacted with people in nearby booths (using mikes so that they could communicate but not see each other). A confederate apparently had an epileptic fit while speaking to the group. Under what conditions were subjects most likely to respond?

a. If the subjects believed that the group was made up of just them and the person having the fit, then everyone responded.

b. If the subjects believed that the group was made up of just them and the person having the fit, then 60 percent responded.

c. If subjects believed that there were five other people in addition to the person having a fit

and themselves, they were more likely to respond than when they thought they were alone.

d. Subjects were equally likely to help no matter how many other people they thought were present.

60. In the epileptic fit experiment the subjects could not see each other nor communicate with other subjects at the moment the confederate was having a fit. Which of the following is *true*?

a. Pluralistic ignorance accounts for their behavior.

b. Pluralistic ignorance cannot account for their behavior.

c. The effects of "apathy" can be demonstrated or ruled out in a particularly straightforward manner in this experiment.

d. A desire to act like the other subjects and imitate their behavior is a probable cause of not intervening.

61. Latané and Darley believed that subjects were inhibited from helping by their knowledge of the presence of others in the epileptic fit experiment because of

a. pluralistic ignorance.

b. diffusion of responsibility—subjects felt that there were others who could help instead of them.

c. apathy.

d. imitation of the behavior of others.

62. At the beach the mere request "please watch my things"

a. caused no one to intervene with a thief since intervention was dangerous.

b. focused responsibility and caused 95 percent to intervene with a thief.

c. caused 50 percent to intervene with a thief.

d. diffused responsibility and caused everyone to whom the request was made to refuse.

63. In the same study the request "do you have a light" caused

a. 95 percent to intervene.

b. 50 percent to intervene.

c. 20 percent to intervene.

d. no one to intervene on account of the danger.

64. What does this study show about fear of danger as a cause of not helping?

a. focusing responsibility is enables people to overcome fear of danger.

b. fear of danger is the primary reason why people do not get involved.

c. fear of danger is never a cause of someone's refraining from intervening.

d. if there is fear of danger in a situation, this fear overrides all other considerations.

65. In the study of people coming to the aid of a man falling on the subway
a. no one helped.
b. 90 percent helped, and the help was independent of the number of people present.
c. only men helped.
d. only whites helped when the person needing aid was white and only blacks helped when the person needing aid was black.

66. The results of this experiment contradicted Latané and Darley's finding that the more people present the less the help. Why may this have been the case?
a. It was very clear that someone was in trouble—the situation was not ambiguous.
b. The norms for who should help were clear.
c. There was no possibility of danger or misunderstanding in the situation.
d. a and b

67. Diffusion of responsibility will inhibit helping
a. except when the people have a relationship.
b. in all situations.
c. except when the emergency is serious.
d. except when the victim is old.

68. When people in the diffusion experiment are supposed to meet after the experiment
a. diffusion of responsibility is intensified.
b. diffusion of responsibility does not occur.
c. diffusion of responsibility is as strong as if people were not supposed to meet.
d. the diffusion of responsibility effect turns into a conformity effect.

69. One of the only personality characteristics that has been found to be related to helping in emergencies is that "maleness" (dominance and aggression), whether found in men or women, leads to less helping. This seems to because
a. people with these traits care less.
b. people with these traits wish to appear in charge, cool, and in helping they risk looking foolish.
c. people who have these traits are sadistic.
d. people who have these traits are helpful in other ways.

70. People in a rural setting are

a. more likely to help than people in an urban setting.
b. less likely to help than people in an urban setting.
c. as likely to help as people in an urban setting.
d. likely to be suspicious and not helpful to strangers.

71. According to Milgram the reasons why people in cities are less helpful is that
a. they are less friendly.
b. they are liable to look down on people needing help.
c. they are attempting to cope with cognitive overload.
d. fewer people ask for help in the city.

72. Needing help
a. may make someone feel more secure.
b. may enhance self-esteem.
c. may threaten self-esteem.
d. does not affect self-esteem.

73. If one knows that one will be able to reciprocate in the future, one is
a. more likely to ask for help.
b. less likely to ask for help.
c. unlikely to ask for help from fear of being taken advantage of in the future.
d. more likely to demand, than to ask, for help.

74. If males or females need help and can ask an attractive or unattractive member of the opposite sex, which will they ask?
a. Males will ask the attractive female, and females will ask the attractive male.
b. Males will ask the unattractive female, and females will ask the attractive male.
c. Males and females will ask the unattractive person.
d. Males will ask the attractive female, and females will ask the unattractive male.

75. What accounts for the results of this experiment?
a. Males fear being dependent before females they wish to attract, while females do not fear being dependent before males they wish to attract.
b. Males are less interested in attractive women than women are in attractive men.
c. Males are shy with attractive women.
d. College women are dominant and intimidating.

76. Rejecting someone's offer of help when you obviously need help is seen as
    a. polite.
    b. insulting.
    c. a neutral personality characteristic.
    d. normal.

Answer Key for Self-Test

1.	c (p. 366)	39.	a (p. 386)
2.	a (p. 366)	40.	b (p. 386)
3.	a (p. 367)	41.	b (p. 387)
4.	b (p. 368)	42.	c (p. 388)
5.	d (p. 368)	43.	d (p. 389)
6.	c (p. 369)	44.	b (p. 390)
7.	b (p. 369)	45.	c (p. 390)
8.	a (p. 369)	46.	a (p. 390)
9.	a (p. 369)	47.	c (pp. 390–391)
10.	c (p. 370)	48.	b (p. 391)
11.	a (p. 371)	49.	a (p. 391)
12.	d (p. 371)	50.	c (p. 391)
13.	b (p. 371)	51.	a (p. 392)
14.	c (p. 372)	52.	c (p. 392)
15.	c (p. 372)	53.	a (p. 392)
16.	d (pp. 368–373)	54.	b (p. 392)
17.	b (p. 373)	55.	b (p. 392)
18.	a (p. 374)	56.	b (p. 393)
19.	d (p. 375)	57.	c (p. 393)
20.	c (p. 376)	58.	d (p. 393)
21.	b (p. 376)	59.	a (p. 394)
22.	d (p. 376)	60.	b (p. 394)
23.	a (p. 376)	61.	b (p. 394)
24.	b (p. 377)	62.	b (p. 395)
25.	b (p. 377)	63.	c (p. 395)
26.	a (pp. 377–378)	64.	a (p. 395)
27.	a (p. 378)	65.	b (p. 396)
28.	d (p. 379)	66.	d (p. 396)
29.	c (p. 380)	67.	a (p. 396)
30.	a (p. 381)	68.	b (p. 396)
31.	b (p. 381)	69.	b (p. 397)
32.	d (p. 382)	70.	a (p. 397)
33.	d (p. 383)	71.	c (p. 397)
34.	d (p. 384)	72.	c (p. 397)
35.	c (p. 384)	73.	a (p. 398)
36.	a (p. 384)	74.	b (p. 399)
37.	a (p. 386)	75.	a (p. 399)
38.	b (p. 386)	76.	b (p. 399)

Thought Questions and Exercises

1. Think of something you have done that you would call altruistic. How would a vulgar cynic (who knows you well) explain your deed? How would a subtle cynic (who knows you well) explain your good deed? Are they right? If you don't agree with one or both of them, how might you show that your act was genuinely altruistic?

2. The notion that "selfish genes" could produce genuine altruism appears on the surface to be paradoxical. How is it possible? (It will help if you remember that genes really can't be selfish or unselfish.)

3. The text conceptually and experimentally distinguished between distress at another's distress and altruism. Can you think of examples from your own observations that would distinguish them? Have you ever seen, or read about, cases in which distress at another's distress actually led to not helping or even mistreating someone?

4. The Cialdini-Batson controversy between the subtle cynic and the believer in altruism is a good example of the way that psychologists use experiments to conduct an argument and thereby refine their positions. Briefly retrace the steps of the argument. Who do you think has made a better case? What should be the next step? What sort of experiment is needed next?

5. The "mood and altruism" type of experiments are easy for students to replicate. Decide on a charity you wish to collect for. Try to make the targets of your collection as similar as possible. Now collect during a sunny day or during a cloudy day; collect before and after lunch, etc. Think up situations where people should be in slightly better or worse moods and then compare how much they donate to your charity.

6. The text says that people are less willing to gamble when they are in a good mood. Is this always true? In your neighborhood are there church bazaars that allow gambling roulette wheels and the like? Give out free cookies to every third person going to play the wheel. Compare how much they gamble with the other two cookieless gamblers. You will need a fair number of potential gamblers to do this, say, fifteen.

7. Catholics going to Mass have been found to give more to charity than Catholics coming from Mass. What should be the case in terms of religious obligations? Why did the experimenters believe that people going to Mass would be more generous than people coming from Mass? You can rather easily replicate this experiment.

8. Review the text's discussion of the Kitty Genovese murder. Latané and Darley showed that, psychologically, apathy was not a necessary cause of not helping (since people don't always act even to save themselves). Even if this is true, is it still fair to call the people who did not help apathetic—from a moral point of view? Why or why not?

9. Have you ever been a bystander at an emergency? Did you act? What factors do you think made you more likely to act? Were there bystanders who did not act? What aspects of Latané and Darley's model apply to this situation?

10. Diffusion of responsibility and pluralistic ignorance are quite different factors. You can experimentally tease them apart. For instance, the epileptic fit experiment measures diffusion of responsibility without pluralistic ignorance. Since the subjects couldn't see each other, they couldn't check what the others were doing, try to conform to the others, and so forth. Most emergency situations involve both factors. Take an emergency and try to disentangle aspects of the emergency that you think led to pluralistic ignorance and aspects that led to diffusion of responsibility.

CHAPTER 11

Justice

Learning Objectives

1. Explain the difference between being "altruistic" and being "just."
2. Define "substantive (or distributive) justice" and explain how it differs from procedural justice.

EQUITY THEORY

3. Describe "equity" in terms of inputs and outputs. Give an example of a work relation that would involve equity and one that would not. What is the difference between equity and equality?
4. Describe Adams's two basic assumptions about people's motivations in regard to equity. Describe Adams's experiment with "overpaid" workers and how they reestablish equity.

Problems for Equity Theory

5. Describe the two distinct claims of equity theory. What is the status of these two claims?

Gender Differences in the Allocation of Rewards

6. Explain what Leventhal discovered about women's and men's preference for the division of rewards (in same-sex groups).
7. Describe Stake's evidence that the males and females in Leventhal's study had different goals in the interaction. How did males and females act in distributing rewards when they were told that their goal was (1) to maximize productivity, (2) to reward fairly, or (3) to make the workers'

relationships to each other as pleasant as possible? Describe how the gender difference relates to traditional sex roles. Describe some circumstances that will alter these allocation strategies.

Ability and Equity

8. Do people count ability as well as effort in deciding what a person's "inputs" are? Can innate ability sometimes make people see someone as less deserving of a reward?

Relative Deprivation

9. Describe the findings of "relative deprivation theory." According to Stouffer why were the airmen more discontented with their chances at promotion than were the military police? What is a "reference group"?According to Faye Crosby there are four conditions required for people to feel resentment at their being unable to possess something. What are the conditions? In experimentally testing her hypothesis Crosby found that one of her conditions actually had the reverse of the expected effect. Which one?
10. Kahneman and Tversky point out that we are much more disappointed at what we consider near misses than at far misses. Why is this the case? What happens when subjects' performance on one procedure will not get them a bonus but if they had participated in an alternative procedure their performance would have gotten them the bonus? What if they realize that there is a

justification for the procedure? What bearing do these results have on relative deprivation"?

Equity Theory and the Problem of Need

11. Sometimes we take need into account when we allocate goods and believe we should do so; sometimes we believe it would be unfair to take need into account. Give an example of each sort of circumstance.

Equity Theory and the Problem of Allocating Losses

12. Subjects had to allocate profits to five partners who worked equal amounts of time at a booth at a flea market. Due to an accident one subject suffered a major loss; the others made differing amounts of money. How did a substantial number of subjects assign the profits? When the subjects were asked to allocate expenses what did they do? If people allocated expenses equally would they thereby be allocating profits equally? What does this experiment demonstrate?

Equity Theory and Culture

13. Equity theory assumes that people try to equalize outcomes relative to inputs. As we have seen, however, it has run into a variety of problems. Review the problems relating to "ability," "relative deprivation," "needs," and "inconsistency." What is the role of cultural understandings in applying the notion of equity? What is the role of "common law" in deciding difficult cases of equity?

PROCEDURAL JUSTICE

14. Explain the difference between the "adversarial" and the "inquisitorial" models of justice. Describe Thibaut's experiment to determine whether subjects believed the adversarial or inquisitorial procedure was more fair. How did the knowledge of their side's innocence or guilt affect the judgment of fairness?

15. Do Europeans, whose countries' legal systems are inquisitorial, have the same or different assessments of fairness as do Americans, whose legal system is adversarial? Was the reaction of ethnically Chinese students from Hong Kong the same as that of Americans?

BELIEF IN A JUST WORLD

Victim Derogation

16. Describe the Lerner and Simmons's experiment. What was the difference in the evaluation of the "victim" between people who were able to help the victim and those who knew they would not be able to stop the shocks for ten more minutes?

17. According to Lerner and Simmons, the subjects' desire for a just world explains their derogation of the victim that they cannot help. How? The text offers another explanation. What is it? How does the difference between the ratings of subjects who thought they would see the suffering for ten minutes more and those who thought that the experiment would be ended after the ratings, support the text's explanation?

Limitations of the Just World Hypothesis

Responsibility for the Injustice

18. It has been argued that subjects derogated the victim, not from a belief in a just world in general, but because they felt somehow responsible for her pain. How did experimenters modify the Lerner experiment to demonstrate this? Show how this explanation is a form of a cognitive dissonance explanation.

Shared Fate

19. Lerner now argues that derogation only occurs when the subject perceives a possible "shared fate" with the victim. Explain. The text calls this new version not a just world account but a "just neighborhood" account. Explain.

Victim Derogation and Rape

20. Explain how the tendency to hold a women who has been raped partly responsible for her fate might be attributable to a belief in a just world. What happened when subjects were given a description of a rape in which there was no evidence that the victim was at all at fault and asked to indicate the degree to which they believed the victim was at fault and to assign a prison sentence to the rapist? What was the difference if the victim was described as a divorcée, a married woman, or a virgin?

Programmed Exercises

1. Altruism has to do with being _____ while justice has to do with being _____.

   kind (generous)
   fair

2. Both altruism and empathy are _____ sentiments equally opposed to selfishness.

   moral

3. Substantive or distributive justice concerns the fair _____ of goods.

   distribution

4. Procedural justice concerns which sets of procedures are _____ to use in making a decision.

   fair

EQUITY THEORY

5. Equity is one type of _____ justice.

   distributive (substantive)

6. If a group has equity, then the _____ of what one gets relative to what one puts in are the same for everyone.

   outputs

7. An equal distribution of pay would not necessarily be _____.

   equitable

Experimental Evidence

8. Adams assumes that people will work to reestablish _____.

   equity

9. In an experiment, student proofreaders believed that they were overpaid, or paid according to their ability. Those who believed they were overpaid made _____ errors; thus reestablishing equity.

   fewer

Problems for Equity Theory

10. There are two distinct claims in equity theory, one is that people are at least sometimes _____ to produce equity; the other is that the equity formula accurately describes the way that we think about equity.

    motivated

11. The first claim is well-_____ the second is problematic.

    supported

12. In an experiment using same-sex pairs, Leventhal found that men adhered to _____, but successful women adhered to _____.

    equity, equality

13. It it possible that males and females had different _____ in allocating rewards.

    goals

14. If males and females are asked to distribute a reward *fairly*, then both will tend to distribute according to _____.

    equity

15. If males and females are asked to make workers' relationships to each other as pleasant as possible, they will both tend to distribute according to _____.

    equality

16. If they are asked to maximize productivity, they will both tend to reward on the basis of _____.

    ability

17. These results suggest that women in the Leventhal experiment had the goal of maintaining pleasant _____ rather than equity.

    relationships

18. The male and female behavior in the Leventhal experiment fits traditional _____ _____.

    sex roles

19. One study found that when the allocations were made private the gender difference _____.

reversed

20. When males or females cooperate on a stereotypically sexually appropriate task they are more likely to divide the reward _____.

equitably

21. When males or females cooperate on a stereotypically sexually inappropriate task they are more likely to divide the task _____.

equally

22. The research suggests that women's preferences for equal versus equitable allocations do _____ reflect fundamental differences in the way men and women construe fairness.

not

23. People count _____ as well as effort in deciding what a person's inputs are.

ability

24. The relationship between ability and payoff is complex; sometimes more ability increases what is seen as the appropriate payoff and sometimes it _____ it.

decreases

25. In World War II, the Air Corps had a rapid rate of promotion and the Military Police a slow rate. The Air Corps men were _____ satisfied with their chances to advance than were the Military Police; this is an example of relative _____.

less

deprivation

26. Each soldier decided on how well he was doing in comparison with people in his unit. A soldier who did not advance in a unit with rapid advancement would feel more _____ than a soldier in a unit with slow advancement.

deprived

27. The feeling of deprivation is relative to the group one compares oneself to. This group is called a _____ group.

reference

28. According to Faye Crosby, four conditions must be fulfilled for people to feel resentment: someone _____ to get something they want, someone feels _____ to possess it, someone thinks it is _____ to possess it, and someone does not _____ himself for his failure to possess it.

fails
entitled, feasible
blame

29. In an experimental test of Crosby's conditions it was found that contrary to expectations people felt _____ resentment when they blamed themselves for failure to attain something.

more

30. Kahneman and Tversky have studied _____ factors in the experience of disappointment. They found that people feel more disappointment for a _____ miss than for a far miss. They explain this by claiming that such misses are more _____ imaginable.

cognitive

near
easily

31. Some subjects miss out on a bonus for good performance and learn that they might have been in a variant where their performance would have earned the bonus. Other subjects do not learn of the variant. Subjects who believed that they might have earned the bonus in the variant were _____ discontented than subjects who did not know of a variant.

more

32. In the above statement, if subjects knew of a justification for their being in the more difficult experiment, then the discontent effect did _____ occur.

not

33. It would be unfair if a doctor did not devote more attention to a sicker than a less sick patient. This is an example of taking _____ into account in deciding on the right thing to do.

need

34. We usually feel it would be unfair to pay two workers a different wage just because one _____ money more.

needed

35. Subjects had to allocate profits to five partners who worked equal amounts of time at a booth at a flea market. Due to an accident one subject suffered a major loss, while the others made differing amounts of money. A substantial number of subjects assigned _____ *profits* to all the partners. When the subjects were asked to allocate *expenses* a sizable number assigned expenses _____ even though this would involve an unequal distribution of _____.

equal

equally
outcomes (profits)

Equity Theory and Culture

36. Equity theory has not been able to specify when needs and abilities qualify as "inputs," nor how to determine which group an individual compares herself to in deciding what are appropriate _____. _____ understandings specify what counts as equity in many specific circumstances as does _____ law.

outcomes, Cultural

common

PROCEDURAL JUSTICE

37. Procedural justice concerns the fairness of the _____ by which a decision is reached.

procedure

38. In an _____ legal system two sides of a dispute compete in finding and presenting evidence to support their cases.

adversarial

39. In an _____ legal system the judge investigates the matter under dispute and presents the evidence.

inquisitorial

40. America has an _____ legal system, while France has an _____ legal system.

adversarial,
inquisitorial

41. In an experiment comparing inquisitorial and adversarial procedures, both participants and observers believed that the _____ procedures were more fair and preserved greater dignity for the participants.

adversarial

42. Groups who thought that their side was guilty believed in the greater fairness of the _____ system as much as those who thought their side was innocent.

adversarial

43. French and German students, whose legal systems are inquisitorial, saw the _____ system as fairer.

adversarial

44. Chinese students from Hong Kong saw the inquisitorial system as _____ fair as compared to the adversarial system.

equally

45. For observers an adversarial system that allows both sides to present evidence is seen as fair, but for the losing team the ability to _____ one's lawyers is also important.

pick (choose)

46. The unpopularity of an inquisitorial system can be relieved if both sides are allowed to _____ in their own behalf and appeal a _____.

testify, verdict

47. Chinese culture stresses harmony and the benefit of the group as opposed to competition. This is one determinant of why Chinese subjects did not prefer the _____ to the _____ systems.

adversarial, inquisitorial

48. Interviews about people's experience with the police revealed that procedures were seen as fair only if the officer they dealt with was neutral, trustworthy, and treated them with _____.

respect

49. People believe that a procedure is fair, even if they believe the outcome was incorrect, if they were able to get their side of the story presented and if the decision maker is _____.

unbiased

BELIEF IN A JUST WORLD

Victim Derogation

50. Subjects believed that they were studying the emotional cues of someone being shocked during a learning experiment. After seeing the "victim's" distress for ten minutes some subjects were told that they could end the shocks if they wished to. _____ did.

All

51. Other subjects believed that the "victim" would be shocked for ten more minutes. Both groups were asked to evaluate the victim. The group who thought the victim would continue to be shocked evaluated her more _____ than did the group that had been able to help her.

negatively

52. According to Lerner and Simmons people wish to see the world as _____. As such, they _____ the victim if they cannot help her, but do not do so if they are able to help her.

just
derogate

53. In another condition subjects who believed the experiment was over after the ten-minute period derogated the victim _____ than did subjects who believed that they would continue to see the victim suffer.

less

54. The results of the above conditions suggest that subjects may have also been blaming the victim for their own (the subjects') _____.

distress

Limitations of the Just World Hypothesis

55. It has been argued that subjects derogate the victim because they feel somehow responsible for her _____.

suffering

56. An additional condition was added to the Lerner and Simmons experiment. In this variant it was very clear that the subject had nothing to do with the suffering of the victim. In the standard version subjects _____ the victim, but in this variant they did not.

derogated

Victim Derogation and Rape

57. According to the just world hypothesis people would tend to hold rape victims partly to blame for their fate. The more "respectable" a woman is, on this hypothesis, the _____ she will be blamed for her fate.

more

58. Subjects were asked both to assign degree of responsibility to a rape victim and an appropriate prison sentence to her rapist. Subjects held "virgins" _____ responsible than "married women" or "divorcées," and gave the rapist of virgins the _____ sentence.

more
longest

Self-Test

1. What is the difference between "altruism" and "justice"?
   a. Altruism has to do with being fair while justice has to do with being kind.
   b. Altruism has to do with being kind and justice has to do with being fair.
   c. Altruism has only to do with giving away money while justice has to do with being fair.
   d. Altruism has been proven to be phony while justice is a real phenomena.

2. Substantive justice
   a. is the same as procedural justice.
   b. is the same as distributive justice.
   c. does not concern fairness.
   d. has been shown not to exist.

3. Substantive justice
   a. concerns the fair distribution of goods.
   b. concerns substance abuse.
   c. concerns which sets of procedures are fair to use in making a decision.
   d. is different from distributive justice.

4. Procedural justice
   a. concerns the fair distribution of goods.
   b. concerns ways to beat red tape.
   c. concerns which sets of procedures are fair to use in making a decision.
   d. is the same as distributive justice.

5. Equity is
   a. a type of procedural justice.
   b. a type of distributive justice.
   c. a term only used in relation to the stock market.
   d. a way to decide on the appropriate procedures to use in a decision.

6. If a group has equity then everyone's input in relation to their output
   a. is equal.
   b. is determined by seniority.
   c. is determined by sex.
   d. is random.

7. If a group has equity then if a person puts more in than anyone else
   a. she will get the same amount as anyone else.
   b. she will get more than anyone except if they have seniority.
   c. she will get more than anyone else in the group.
   d. she will get less than some members of the group.

8. Student proofreaders in an experiment believed that they were overpaid or paid according to their ability. Those who believed they were overpaid made
   a. more errors than those who were paid according to ability, thus restoring equity.
   b. the same number of errors as those who were paid according to ability.
   c. sometimes more and sometimes fewer errors than those who were paid according to ability.
   d. fewer errors than those who were paid according to ability, thus restoring equity.

9. In an experiment using same-sex pairs, Leventhal found that
   a. men adhered to strict equality while women were variable.
   b. men and women adhered to equity.
   c. men and women adhered to equality.
   d. men adhered to equity and women adhered to equality.

10. If males and females are asked to make workers' relationships to each other as pleasant as possible then how will they divide up rewards?
    a. Males will tend toward equity, and females will tend toward equality.
    b. Males will tend toward equality, and females will tend toward equity.
    c. Both males and females will tend toward equality.
    d. Both males and females will tend toward equity.

11. If males and females are asked to distribute a reward fairly then
    a. males will tend toward equity, and females will tend toward equality.
    b. males will tend toward equality, and females will tend toward equity.
    c. both males and females will tend toward equality.
    d. both males and females will tend toward equity.

12. If males and females are asked to distribute a reward so as to maximize productivity then
    a. males will tend toward equity, and females will tend toward equality.

b. males will tend toward equality, and females will tend toward equity.

c. both males and females will tend toward equality.

d. both males and females will reward on the basis of capability.

13. The results of the Leventhal experiment in which males and females rewarded on the basis of different principles shows

a. males and females were pursuing different goals.

b. males always pursue equity.

c. males never pursue equality.

d. females never pursue equity.

14. In most experiments it has been found that males pursue equity while females pursue maintaining pleasant relationships. When has this *not* been found to be the case?

a. when the reward is large or it is a same-sex group

b. when the allocations are made in private

c. when the task is stereotypically inappropriate for the female sex role

d. b and c

15. The research suggests that women's preference for equal versus equitable allocations

a. does not reflect fundamental differences in the way men and women understand fairness.

b. shows that men and women have very different notions of fairness.

c. shows that women see equity as a matter of equality.

d. shows that men do not understand the concept of fairness.

16. The relationship we perceive between ability and deserved payoff is

a. simple—the greater the ability the greater the deserved payoff.

b. complex—sometimes more ability increases what is seen as the appropriate payoff and sometimes it decreases it.

c. never considered when rewards are allocated.

d. simple—the greater the effort the greater the reward no matter what the ability.

17. During World War II the Air Corps had a rapid rate of promotion and the Military Police a slow rate. It was found that

a. the Air Corps men were less satisfied with their chances to advance than were the Military Police; this is an example of relative deprivation.

b. the Air Corps men were more satisfied with their chances to advance than were the Military Police; this is an example of relative deprivation.

c. the Air Corps men were as satisfied with their chances to advance as were the Military Police; this is an example of relative equality.

d. both the Air Corps men and the Military Police were dissatisfied with their chances to advance; this is an example of Newtonian relativity.

18. The feeling of deprivation

a. is independent of the group that you compare yourself to, your reference group.

b. is relative to the group you compare yourself to, your reference group.

c. is purely internal and independent of any reference group.

d. is a sign of neurosis.

19. According to Faye Crosby which of the following are necessary for people to feel resentment?

a. They must fail to get something they want.

b. They must feel entitled to get it and not blame themselves for not having it.

c. They think that it is possible to get it.

d. all of the above

20. Kahneman and Tversky explain why people are more disappointed at a near miss than at a far miss by arguing that

a. in a near miss the lost success is easier to imagine.

b. in a near miss the lost success is less easy to imagine.

c. in a far miss it is easy to imagine the lost success.

d. people are naturally sore losers.

21. The relation between need and our perception of deserved payoff

a. is essentially the same in all cases.

b. is never taken into account.

c. overwhelms all other considerations.

d. is similar to the relation of ability to our perception of deserved payoff—it is complex.

22. Subjects had to allocate profits to five partners who worked equal amounts of time at a booth at a flea market. Due to an accident one subject suffered a major loss, while the others made

differing amounts of money. Substantial numbers of subjects assigned
a. equal profits to all the partners.
b. equal expenses to all the partners.
c. both equal profits and equal expenses even though one can't do both at the same time.
d. unequal profits and expenses to the partner.

23. A legal system in which two sides of a dispute compete in finding and presenting evidence to support their cases is called
a. procedural.
b. adversarial.
c. inquisitorial.
d. implosion therapy.

24. A legal system in which the judge investigates the matter under dispute and presents the evidence is called
a. procedural.
b. adversarial.
c. inquisitorial.
d. implosion therapy.

25. In an experiment two teams each with a "president" and "creative director" competed in making up creative names; the winner was eligible for a $5 prize. In the middle of the experiment the subjects were told that there had been an accusation of plagiarism and that there would be a trial. The prize would go to the winner of the trial. The "presidents" were led to believe either that their creative director was innocent, guilty, or that the issue was uncertain. In one condition each side could select their "attorneys" (adversarial system), in another a single investigator was appointed by the court to present the evidence on both sides (inquisitorial system). In both cases a mock judge delivered the verdict. Both participants and observers of the trial believed that
a. the inquisitorial procedure was the most fair.
b. both procedures were equally fair.
c. the adversarial procedure was more fair, but the inquisitorial preserved the dignity of the participants better.
d. the adversarial procedure was more fair and better able to preserve the dignity of the participants.

26. Groups who thought that their side was guilty believed in the greater fairness of the adversarial system (as compared to the inquisitorial system)

a. as much as those who thought their side was innocent.
b. much less than those who thought that their side was innocent.
c. more than those who thought their side was innocent.
d. not at all

27. In the above experiment French and German students, whose legal systems are inquisitorial, saw the
a. inquisitorial system as slightly fairer than the adversarial system.
b. inquisitorial system as much fairer than the adversarial system.
c. inquisitorial system as less fair than the adversarial system.
d. inquisitorial system as the only possible fair system.

28. Chinese students from Hong Kong
a. did not see the adversarial system as fairer than the inquisitorial system since Chinese culture stresses group harmony as more important than competition.
b. saw the adversarial system as fairer than the inquisitorial system, just as the French students did.
c. saw the adversarial system as fairer since their culture stresses competition.
d. b and c

29. Do people ever believe that a procedure is fair, even if they believe the outcome was incorrect?
a. no, never
b. yes, if they were able to get their side of the story presented
c. yes, if the decision maker is unbiased
d. b and c

30. Subjects believed that they were studying the emotional cues of someone being shocked during a learning experiment. After seeing the "victim's" distress for ten minutes some subjects were told that they could end the shocks. Other subjects believed that the "victim" would continue to be shocked after the ten-minute break. Both groups were asked to evaluate the victim. The group who thought the victim would continue to be shocked
a. evaluated her more negatively than the group that had been able to help her.
b. evaluated her more positively than the group that had been able to help her.

c. neither evaluated her more positively nor more negatively than the group that had been able to help her.

d. refused to evaluate her.

31. Lerner and Simmons believe that the above results may be explained by people wanting to believe that they are living in a just world. This explains the experimental results because

a. subjects who were not able to save the distressed person derogated her since it is not as unjust for a bad person to be in distress.

b. the subjects who were able to save the "victim" from distress were able to perceive the world as just without derogating the victim.

c. in a just world the bad will suffer and the good will be saved.

d. all of the above

32. In another condition of the above experiment subjects who believed the experiment was over after the ten-minute period derogated the victim less than victims who believed that they would continue to see the victim suffer. In this condition subjects appear to be

a. trying to help the victim.

b. blaming the victim.

c. acting according to the just world hypothesis.

d. acting, or at least fantasizing, in a sadistic vein.

33. An additional condition was added to the Lerner and Simmons experiment. In this variant it was very clear that the subject had nothing to do with the suffering of the victim. In this version of the experiment the subject

a. derogated the victim much more than in the original experiment.

b. derogated the victim as much as in the original experiment.

c. derogated the victim slightly less than in the original experiment.

d. did not derogate the victim.

34. Subjects were given an account of a rape and asked to assign degree of responsibility to the victim and to decide on what would be an appropriate sentence for the rapist. The victim was described as a virgin, a married women, or a divorcée. Subjects

a. assigned the most "responsibility" to the divorcée and the longest sentence to the rapist of the divorcée.

b. subjects assigned the least "responsibility"

to the virgin and the longest sentence to her rapist.

c. subjects assigned the most "responsibility" to the virgin and the longest sentence to her rapist.

d. subjects assigned the least responsibility to the married woman and assigned her rapist the longest sentence.

Answer Key for Self-Test

1.	b (p. 402)	18.	b (p. 410)
2.	b (p. 403)	19.	d (p. 410)
3.	a (p. 403)	20.	a (p. 412)
4.	c (p. 403)	21.	d (p. 414)
5.	b (p. 403)	22.	c (p. 414)
6.	a (p. 404)	23.	b (p. 416)
7.	c (p. 404)	24.	c (p. 416)
8.	d (p. 405)	25.	d (p. 416)
9.	d (pp. 405–406)	26.	a (pp. 416–417)
10.	c (p. 406)	27.	c (p. 417)
11.	d (p. 406)	28.	a (pp. 417–419)
12.	d (p. 406)	29.	d (p. 418)
13.	a (p. 406)	30.	a (p. 420)
14.	d (p. 407)	31.	d (p. 420)
15.	a (p. 407)	32.	b (p. 421)
16.	b (p. 408)	33.	d (p. 422)
17.	a (pp. 409–410)	34.	c (pp. 423–424)

Thought Questions and Exercises

1. Altruism and justice are both moral virtues, but sometimes they pull in opposite directions. Can you think of some examples of conflicts between altruism and justice (being kind and being fair) that you have faced? How did you resolve the conflict?

2. The "equity" part of this chapter discusses various ways to allocate rewards to a group effort— equity, equality, according to the greatest competence. It was found that different instructions (see text, p. 406) led to different ways of allocating rewards. Invent a story about a group effort and use it to see if you can replicate these findings. Without any instructions men and women supposedly decide on different ways to allocate rewards. With the same story you can replicate this finding and if you compare a condition in

which the person answers publicly before a group or privately you can check to see if the male/female difference holds up when people judge in private (one study found that it did not).

3. Sometimes we think it appropriate to count need or to count ability when we decide on a fair allocation of a reward and sometimes we do not. The text says that the only way to know that is appropriate is to look at what our culture tells us to do in specific circumstances. Are there any principles that you can think of that would decide when it was proper and when it was improper to take need (or ability) into account?

4. What is "relative deprivation"? Give four examples of relative deprivation from your own experience.

5. The "just world hypothesis" predicts that we should be more likely to attribute responsibility, carelessness, stupidity, or the like, to the victim of a crime the more serious the crime—the more pain and damage to the victim. Make up several versions of a story about a mugging. Let each version be identical except for the severity of the damages, for instance, length of time in the hospital or the amount of permanent damage. Now, using a five-point scale, ask subjects about the extent that the victim's carelessness, and so on, contributed to the disaster. Do people see the more injured person as more responsible? (You may also want to ask about what would be an appropriate sentence for the mugger if he were caught.)

CHAPTER 12

Strategic Interaction

Learning Objectives

1. Describe what "strategic interaction" is. What are the two features of strategic interactions? Give some examples of everyday strategic interactions.
2. Describe what "experimental games" and "simulations" are. How do psychologists justify using games and simulations in order to make claims about real-world conflict? (Use the comparison with physics.) What is the argument against this justification?

BARGAINING

3. Give some examples of perfectly competitive bargaining. How does reasoning about the *fair* price affect the selling or buying of a house? Purely competitive bargaining typically takes place between what people?

Duopoly Bargaining

4. Describe what "duopoly bargaining" is. At the start of a duopoly bargaining situation what does each party know? What is the "resistance point" or "limit"? What happens when the seller's lower limit is higher than the buyer's upper limit? What happens when the seller's lower limit is lower than the buyer's upper limit?

Level of Aspiration

5. Siegel and Fouraker studied pairs of students bargaining over the price of a product. Explain what a person's "level of aspiration" is and how it affects her profit. How does tough bargaining— the seller starting high and going down slowly and the buyer starting low and going up slowly— affect one's opponent's level of aspiration?

Reciprocity

6. Describe the "norm of reciprocity." What did Komorita demonstrate about matching concessions in his series of bargaining experiments? What happens, especially with very competitive subjects, when concessions are not reciprocated? Is it better to reward one's opponents' concessions with bigger concessions on your own part? How is the strategy of "matching concessions" (especially when coupled with a tough initial offer) perceived?

Doors in the Face

7. Cialdini had experimenters approach people and ask them to volunteer to work with kids for two hours a week for two years. How many people volunteered? The experimenters then asked them to take the kids to the zoo once. How many people volunteered? Another group of people was just asked the second request. What were the results? There are two possible interpretations for the difference between the two groups in regard to the zoo request. What are they? How did Cialdini experimentally distinguish between the two?

Information about One's Opponent's Profits

8. What is Schelling's hypothesis about what happens in a bargaining situation when one person knows the costs and potential profits of her opponent but the opponent is ignorant of her costs? Is there some evidence for this?

Integrative Bargaining

9. Contrast bargaining situations in which the gain of one is the loss of another and situations in which there is the possibility of jointly beneficial

solutions. From your own experience give an example of each type of bargaining situation.

10. Describe Pruitt's experiment involving a bargaining situation in which the buyer cared more about the price of iron, while the seller cared more about the price of coal, and where at the beginning of the sessions the partners knew about their own profits but not about that of the others. What were Pruitt's hypothesized three factors that would facilitate finding the optimal solution?

11. Describe what is meant by an "integrative" solution. To reach an integrative solution is it helpful for bargainers to have specific bargaining goals in mind? How does time pressure affect finding integrative solutions? What is "logrolling" and why is it helpful when negotiations concern several issues? How does expectation of future cooperative interaction interact with aspirations and motivation?

Oligopoly Bargaining

Opening Strategies

12. Explain how a "free market" is different from a "duopoly." What happened when subjects could negotiate with four different sellers over the price of a car? Was a "soft" or a "tough" bargaining strategy most effective?

Framing Effects

13. Describe how framing possible outcomes of a bargaining situation in a positive or negative way can have an effect on the outcome of negotiations. How can framing affect union-management negotiations? These findings dovetail with Kahneman and Tversky's findings that people treat gains and losses in quite different ways. Explain.

Negotiations among Representatives

14. Give some examples in which people bargain as representatives of a side rather than for themselves. What is a "mediator" to a dispute? What is an "arbitrator"?

Bargaining as a Representative of a Constituency

15. When someone bargains for a constituency, is she likely to bargain tougher or easier than when she bargains for herself? Why are negotiators typically under conflicting pressures? What happens to the manner of bargaining and the likelihood of reaching a favorable outcome when the negotiator bargains in front of her constituents?

Third-Party Intervention

16. Describe what "binding arbitration" is. Describe what "final offer arbitration" is. The trial of Socrates is an example of final offer arbitration and a demonstration of what happens when the final offer of one party is not reasonable. Explain.

17. In addition to helping each side to form a realistic picture of the other, proposing new integrative solutions, and pressuring both sides to be reasonable, the mediator allows the opposing parties in the negotiation to save face. Explain.

18. Describe when third-party intervention is most likely to be helpful. What form of third-party intervention is most likely to be effective?

NON-ZERO SUM CONFLICTS

19. Describe "zero sum" or "constant sum" conflict. Describe non-zero sum situations.

Decision Theory

20. Describe what "decision theory" is.

The Prisoners' Dilemma Situation

21. Describe the prisoners' dilemma situation. What does the D.A. offer the first prisoner if he confesses and his partner does not? In this case what will happen to his partner? What will happen if the first prisoner confesses and his partner also confesses? What will happen if the two prisoners both refuse to testify? What is by far the best outcome for each prisoner? Notice that the best outcome for each prisoner is the worst outcome for his partner. What would happen if both tried to get the best outcome and thus both confessed? Is this a good outcome? What if neither confessed? How does this compare to the other outcomes? Why is it rational for each prisoner to confess? Show that what is individually rational leads both prisoners to a collectively and individually worse payoff.

What People Do in a Prisoners' Dilemma

22. Describe what laboratory examples of the prisoners' dilemma are like. What is the typical result in these studies? Do people become more or less cooperative over time?

23. Describe the problem of the "pacifist strategy" of always cooperating no matter what your partner does.

24. Describe the "Tit for Tat" strategy. Does it induce cooperation? What is better—a strategy that is contingently cooperative or one that is completely cooperative or one that is completely

uncooperative? Axelrod computer-modeled various strategies, including some very complex ones submitted by professionals. Which strategy won the competition? Does the Tit for Tat strategy win in a single head-on competition? What is the best that it can do in a head-on competition? If the Tit for Tat strategy loses or draws in each round, how does it wind up winning (amassing the most points overall)?

25. Explain whether the findings of the prisoners' dilemma research are compatible with those of bargaining. How are people who play Tit for Tat (concession for concession) perceived? Notice that in a purely competitive context without moral strictures the equitable solution turns out to be the most effective one.

Decomposed Prisoners' Dilemmas

26. The typical behavior of subjects in the prisoners' dilemma with their high rates of defections and less-than-optimal joint payoffs appears self-defeating. But the subjects might not be trying to amass points as they have been instructed to do. What may they be trying to do that would explain their behavior?

27. McClintock and McNeel created a game that would "decompose" two motives—amassing the most points and maximizing the difference between the opponents' scores. Explain. What happened when subjects played a decomposed game? What happened when the amount of money for amassing points was increased? What happened when both opponents were shown each other's cumulative scores?

28. Explain how games have been used to assess subjects' dominant motives. People who were found to have predominantly competitive (maximizing differences), predominantly cooperative (attempting to maximize joint outcome), or predominantly individualistic (attempting to get the largest number of points for themselves) motives on a decomposed game played the prisoners' dilemma against someone who was using a 100 percent cooperation, 100 percent defection, or Tit for Tat strategy. What happened? This experiment suggests that the benefit of the Tit for Tat strategy is primarily due to its effect on one type of opponent. Who?

29. Pruitt invented a set of different decompositions of a prisoners' dilemma game. The payoffs for each variant are the same. Is behavior the same on each? It appears that the decompositions reveal to the subjects the nature of their dependence on each other, something that is more difficult to

grasp in the standard form of the prisoners' dilemma. What is the evidence for this?

Tragedy of the Commons

30. Present the story of the tragedy of the commons. Why wouldn't people reduce the number of cattle once they perceived that the commons was being overgrazed? Explain what the problems of overpopulation and pollution have in common with the tragedy of the commons. How is the problem of the commons similar to a n-person prisoners' dilemma?

Communication and the N-Person Prisoners' Dilemma

31. It has been found in two-person prisoners' dilemma games that having a chance to talk to the other player increases cooperation. What did Dawes find when he examined the role of communication in an n-person prisoners' dilemma? Was it communication per se that was important in fostering cooperation or was it task-relevant communication?

Identifiability and Choice

32. Most important social dilemmas have repeated trials. Give some examples. Is there any experimental support for the notion that in dilemmas with repeated trials the identifiability (as opposed to anonymity) of the person making the decision increases cooperative decisions?

Structural Solutions

33. Hardin believed that "individual restraint" was not a solution to the problem of the commons. To illustrate this, the text gives the example of two companies: one installs expensive equipment to combat air pollution and the other does not. Which company will make a greater profit? Will people in both companies equally share the benefit of cleaner air? What are Hardin's solutions?

34. In experimental games in which subjects are all drawing from a common resource will subjects accept controls on their use of the resource if they perceive that it is being depleted? Why don't subjects adopt a Tit for Tat solution to the n-dimensional prisoners' dilemma?

The Public Goods Problem

35. Another version of the commons dilemma concerns whether people will provide a public good (something that all members of a community can use) at their own cost. What is the problem with public goods (the "free-rider" problem)? Remember the experiments that compared the amounts that people would invest in public goods that paid off to the community as a whole versus private goods that would pay off to the

investor alone. What were the results? Are the findings from this sort of problem similar to what has been found for cooperative groups in general?

36. One can sometimes frame the same problem as a "commons" dilemma (will people restrain themselves from taking too much of a common resource?) or as a "public goods" problem (will people contribute to a common good that they will use?). Frame the problem of pollution as a commons dilemma and as a public goods problem. Do people manage better when the management of resources involves taking less or giving more?

Motivation and Social Dilemmas

37. What are the two basic motivations for a person to defect in both two-person and n-person prisoners' dilemma type situations? A public goods experiment in Japan attempted to manipulate whether people whose dominant motivation was greed or fear of exploitation would react differently than others in conditions designed to tap these motivations. What were the results of this experiment when run with strangers and with groups of friends?

Education and Social Traps

38. Describe Rapaport's experiment designed to study the effect of explicit instruction on choices in social traps. Which group followed the optimal group strategy? Did it make a difference whether the experimenter emphasized or just mentioned the optimal strategy? What did Rapaport find out about education and organization in his "largest number" experiments?

Coalitions

39. Describe the problem of coalition formation. Simmel was interested in triads. What did he say sometimes happens in triads? How does his point relate to students' satisfaction with three-person dormitory rooms?

40. Explain what "tertius gaudens" means. Why is it ironical? Review the text's example showing this with three candidates.

41. Minimum resource theory makes two claims. What are they? What is Kelley's criticism of minimum resource theory? What does minimum power theory (an application of Kelley's views to more than three people) maintain?

42. Both minimum resource theory and minimum power theory see the distribution of power and rewards in a coalition as equitable, but they see what constitutes equity differently. Explain.

43. Bargaining theory agrees with minimum resource theory and minimum power theory in claiming that in the *initial* coalitions that people form people maximize their payoff within the constraints of equity. In comparison to the two other theories, what does bargaining theory claim is an equitable initial distribution? After the initial coalitions, as individuals become more experienced, equity will matter less and bargaining in the strictly competitive sense will matter more. Why? According to bargaining theory, will equity characterize the stable coalitions that develop? If not, what will characterize them?

Programmed Exercises

1. In a _____ _____ each party aims to influence the other to behave in a way that is favorable to her own interest.

   strategic interaction

2. Strategic interactions involve both a _____ of interests and an attempt by each party to _____ the future behavior of the other.

   conflict
   influence

3. Experimental _____ involve artificial strategic interactions where the conflict is about winning points or trivial sums of money.

   games

4. In _____ people pretend to bargain for large sums of money.

   simulations

BARGAINING

5. In perfectly competitive bargaining every dollar gained by one side is a dollar _____ by the other side.

   lost

6. In bargaining for a house, a perfectly competitive bargaining situation, concern

about fairness enters into issues of concealing or disclosing defects but not into issues of _____.

price

7. Purely competitive bargaining is most likely to occur between _____ (except in the cases of games and sports).

strangers

Duopoly Bargaining

8. In _____ bargaining there is only one potential buyer and one potential seller.

duopoly

9. The _____ _____, or limit, is the most that the buyer will pay.

resistance point

10. If the seller's lower limit is higher than the buyer's upper limit then a sale is _____. If the seller's lower limit is lower than the buyer's upper limit then a sale is _____.

impossible
possible

11. In bargaining the level of _____ of a bargainer is the profit she thinks is just adequate. This is _____ the limit but _____ the initial offer.

aspiration
above, below

12. According to Siegel and Fouraker the best strategy in bargaining is for the _____ to start low and go up slowly and for the _____ to start high and go down slowly.

buyer, seller

13. In a set of bargaining experiments by Komorita it was found that _____ concessions was a better strategy than not _____ them. It was also found that making a bigger concession than one's opponent, in order to reward him, leads to a _____ outcome than making an equal or smaller concession; the bigger concession leads to one's opponent's having a _____ level of aspiration.

reciprocating
reciprocating

worse

higher

14. According to Komorita the strategy of "matching concessions" (especially when coupled with a tough initial offer) is perceived by one's opponents as tough but _____ and is the best bargaining strategy.

fair

15. Cialdini had experimenters approach people and ask them to volunteer to take kids out for two hours a week for two years. _____ volunteered. The experimenters then made a smaller request, for the subjects to take the kids to the zoo once. _____ volunteered. The experimenters asked another group of people to take the kids to the zoo but without having made the prior larger request. About _____ percent volunteered.

None

Half

25

16. One interpretation of this result is _____ contrast, the second request seems smaller after hearing the first. Another interpretation of this result is that the people treated the requests as a bargaining situation, the smaller request as a concession, and their agreeing to do the small request as a _____ _____.

perceptual

counter-concession

17. If the perceptual interpretation is true, then whether the large and small requests are made by the same person should _____ matter; if the bargaining interpretation is true, then only if the large and small request are made by the same person will there be the high rate of agreement. The prediction of the _____ interpretation was correct.

not

bargaining

18. A(n) _____ information condition is one in which one competitor but not the other knows his opponent's costs. Schelling argued that not having the knowledge in such a condition may be _____ since the knowledge-

asymmetric

beneficial

able competitor is constrained by her knowledge of her opponent's costs and the ignorant competitor is not.

Integrative Bargaining

19. Pruitt devised a bargaining situation in which the seller and buyer could _____ joint profit if the buyer made concessions on coal and the seller on iron, so as to come up with the _____ _____ .

maximize
optimal solution

20. Pruitt found that three factors helped in the discovery of the optimal solution; a _____ -_____ orientation, _____ , and _____ about one's own profits.

problem-solving,
motivation,
truthfulness

21. Dividing each unpleasant domestic chore in half is typical of a contentious, _____ orientation. A _____ -_____ approach would discover different distastes and preferences, which are unlikely to be identical, and thus it would provide a basis to optimize joint satisfaction.

individualistic,
problem-solving

22. Attaining the maximal joint outcome in both the Pruitt and the domestic example are instances of _____ solutions.

integrative

23. Time pressure interferes with finding integrative solutions and tends to lead to _____ .

compromises

24. Working on all issues at once allows for _____, in which each party concedes on the issues more important to the other.

logrolling

25. A cooperative orientation only leads to a high joint benefit if there are high _____ and the partners are _____.

aspirations
motivated

Oligopoly Bargaining

26. In free market conditions buyers and sellers are _____ to trade with any other buyer or seller. When subjects could negotiate with four different sellers over the price of a car, the sellers who used _____ strategies did less well than those who used soft strategies. Hence, the most effective strategy in a duopoly is least effective in a free _____ .

free

tough

market

27. In an experiment involving multiple buyers and sellers and the possibility of an integrative solution, framing costs and payoffs positively in terms of profits to be made, made an integrative solution _____ likely than framing costs and payoffs negatively in terms of expenses.

more

28. Kahneman and Tversky found that people treat gains and _____ in very different ways.

losses

29. People prefer sure things to gambles when they can _____ money, but prefer gambles to sure things when they stand to _____ money.

make
lose

30. According to Kahneman and Tversky people are risk _____ for profit and risk _____ in order to avoid loss.

averse
seeking

Negotiations among Representatives

31. Sometimes people do not negotiate for themselves but as a _____ of a side.

representative

32. A(n) _____ is a third party to a negotiation who consults with both parties to facilitate an agreement.

mediator

33. A(n) _____ is a third party to a negotiation who is by mutual agreement of the parties empowered to impose a settlement.

arbitrator

34. Someone who is bargaining for a constituency is likely to bargain _____ for her group than she would if she were bargaining for herself.

harder

35. Negotiators bargaining in front of their constituents are more likely to bargain in a _____ way and to reach a less favorable outcome than if they had bargained in isolation.

rigid

36. When male constituents are observing the bargaining, the negotiator is likely to be _____ hostile than when female constituents are observing. Males or females negotiating on behalf of _____ negotiate less cooperatively than if they were negotiating on behalf of _____.

more
females
males

37. One study has shown that _____ to a constituency only increases aggressiveness when negotiators do not expect future negotiations with their counterparts.

accountability

38. In final offer arbitration each side submits its _____ offer to an arbitrator who must pick between them (she cannot compromise). This is intended to force both sides to be _____ in their final offer.

final

reasonable

39. Mediators can facilitate agreements between opposing parties as long as they are seen as _____.

impartial

40. Mediators help in a variety of ways: they help both sides form a _____ picture of the other; they can think up new _____ solutions; they pressure both sides to be _____ by threatening to expose them to the public; they help both sides to save _____; they help each side to reduce _____ disagreements.

realistic
integrative
reasonable
face
internal

41. In experimental bargaining situations an opponent who gives in at the request of a mediator is seen (by herself and by the opponent) as less _____ than one who gives in without the request of a mediator.

weak

42. Third-party intervention is _____ likely to be helpful when the parties in the conflict are fairly close in their positions, and _____ likely to be helpful when they are far apart.

most
least

43. The threat of _____ is more likely to induce concessions from the rival groups than is _____.

arbitration
mediation

NON-ZERO SUM CONFLICTS

44. A zero-sum situation is one in which the _____ of one party is the gain of the other.

loss

45. Integrative solutions involve _____-_____ sum situations.

non-zero

Decision Theory

46. A "nontrivial decision" either involves conflict between positive and negative aspects of a situation or _____.

uncertainty

47. Decision theory concerns the _____ of long-run satisfaction with a decision.

maximization

48. The D.A. tells each prisoner that if he confesses and his partner doesn't he will get _____ months and the partner will get _____ years. If the prisoner refuses to defect to the D.A. but his friend succumbs to temptation then he has gotten the sucker's payoff and will get _____ years. If both prisoners confess in the hope of suckering the other, they will get the

3, 20

20

punishment payoff for mutual defection of _____ years. On the other
hand, if both prisoners hold fast, they are rewarded for their mutual
cooperation and each gets only _____ year.

10

1

49. Being the only one to defect is the _____ a prisoner can do, but
refusing to cooperate when your partner does is the worst.

best

50. Mutual cooperation in silence is a _____ outcome than mutual
defection.

better

51. Each prisoner faces only two decisions, to _____ or to _____;
but whether a decision is a good or bad one depends on what the other prisoner
does.

cooperate, defect

52. Each prisoner realizes that he does not know what the other will do. Each realizes that if the other stays pat then he will do better to confess and if the other
confesses he will do better to confess since if he were to stand pat he'd get
twenty years. Confessing then is the most _____ solution for each.

conservative
(sensible, rational)

53. But if both follow this sensible conservative strategy then they will each get
_____ years, and if they had cooperated and stood pat they would
only have gotten _____ year.

10

1

54. In the "pacifist" strategy a player _____ no matter what her partner
does. The problem with the pacifist strategy is that the partner will
_____ it.

cooperates

exploit

55. In the "Tit for Tat" strategy a player does to her partner exactly what her
_____ did to her on the last round; it is _____ cooperative.

partner, contingently

56. A strategy that is contingently cooperative elicits _____ cooperation
than one that is completely cooperative or uncooperative.

more

57. Axelrod computer-modeled various strategies, including some very complex ones,
submitted by professionals. The _____ _____ _____
strategy (in which the player cooperated on the first move) won.

Tit for Tat

58. Using "Tit for Tat," a strategy that exemplifies the "don't be envious rule," a
player can never _____ against another player although she will
ultimately win the competition by amassing the most points.

win

59. In both the prisoners' dilemma and the bargaining situation, a strategy of
matching concession for concession has been found to be _____ in the
context of repeated rounds with the same competitor. People who play in this
way are perceived to be tough but _____.

best

fair

60. In both the prisoners' dilemma and bargaining situation, people search for the
most practically effective solution, yet in the context of repeated play with a
single partner the best strategy is a moral one, _____.

equity

61. The actual behavior of subjects in the prisoners' dilemma involves a high rate
of mutual _____ and less than optimal joint return.

defection

62. If subjects are not trying to amass the most points (as they have been instructed
to do) but rather trying to win or at least not to _____ to (get fewer
points than) their opponent, then their strategy is _____.

lose
rational

63. Decomposed games have been used to assess subjects' predominant motives:
_____ (maximizing differences), _____ (maximizing joint
outcomes), _____ (maximizing the individual's outcome).

competitive,
cooperative
individualistic

64. Subjects who showed themselves to be in each of the three motivational categories on a decomposed game played the prisoners' dilemma against someone who was using a completely cooperative, completely defecting, or a Tit for Tat strategy. The cooperators (in the decomposed game) cooperated with both the Tit for Tat and cooperative opponent; the competitors (in the decomposed game) defected against _____ strategies; the individualists (in the decomposed game) cooperated only with the _____ _____ _____ strategy.

all
Tit for Tat

Tragedy of the Commons

65. The tragedy of the commons involves a scenario wherein a medical discovery allows more cattle to flourish and individuals add more cattle to the commons, which benefits them as individuals but leads to overgrazing on the commonly held commons, which hurts the community. This is an example of a _____ _____.

social trap (social dilemma)

66. But the advantage of adding a cow to the pasture for any particular herder is _____ as compared to the disadvantage caused by hurting the commons.

great

67. The problem of the commons occurs also in the world crises of _____ and _____.

pollution
overpopulation

68. Dawes found that in an n-person dilemma _____ communication increases cooperation over no communication.

relevant

69. According to Dawes, what is important about communicating is that it allows one to make _____, which leads to trust.

promises

70. There is some experimental support for the notion that groups playing repeated trial prisoners' dilemma games _____ more if the decision makers are identifiable (not anonymous).

cooperate

71. Hardin suggests that individual restraint is an _____ solution of "tragedy of the commons" type problems. In the example of the polluting companies with equal access to the common air, the company that installs expensive pollution-controlling equipment will make _____ profit than the one that does not; it will not be likely to survive.

unlikely

less

72. Hardin suggests three solutions to this problem: government-imposed _____ for pollution; a _____ on pollution greater than the profit to be made from polluting; allowing people to _____ for damages.

penalties, tax
sue

73. The Tit for Tat solution _____ be used in the n-person prisoners' dilemma since the damage that an individual can do to punish a defector is spread among all members.

cannot

74. _____ _____ allow the collectivity as a whole to punish a defector in an n-person version of the prisoners' dilemma.

Structural solutions

75. _____ _____ are those that every member of the community can use, and they involve a conflict between the individual and the _____ good. This is because _____ can use a public good such as a park or road and not just those who _____ for it.

Public goods
collective (group)
anyone
paid

76. If everyone makes the convenient free-rider decision then there will be no _____ _____.

public goods

77. People invest substantially _____ in public goods than is optimal to maximize the profit of the group as a whole.

less

78. One can sometimes frame the same problem as a _____ dilemma (will people restrain themselves from taking too much of a common resource?) or as a _____ _____ problem (will people contribute to a common good that they will use?).

commons

public goods

79. There is evidence that people manage resources better when they have to take _____ than when they have to give more. Hence if a problem can be phrased either as a commons dilemma or a public goods problem, then it is best to phrase it as a _____ _____.

less

commons dilemma

80. Rapaport found that when the optimal group strategy was emphasized, as opposed to just mentioned, subjects were _____ likely to approximate the optimal strategy.

more

81. Rapaport found that even when groups could win very large amounts of (real) money and are educated as to how the "social trap" works, _____ is of the greatest importance.

organization

COALITIONS

82. The problems of coalition formation arises when there is a prize that no one person has the resources to win. A group must form, pool _____, and decide how to split the payoff.

resources

83. "Tertius gaudens" means "the third who enjoys." A more ironic way to put this point is "weakness is _____." The point of this is that if there are three parties and two are needed to form a coalition, then each of the strongest will seek out the _____ and not each other.

strength

weakest

84. Given the above reasoning, if three candidates had 48 percent, 30 percent and 22 percent of the delegates, then it is the candidate with _____ percent who is likely to be excluded from the coalition.

48

85. Minimum resource theory claims that of all possible coalitions the coalition with the _____ amount of resources needed to win will be formed. It also claims that once a coalition is formed then the rewards will be divided in _____ to the resources that the members have brought to the coalition.

minimum (least)

proportion

86. Kelley argues that with repeated exposure to this sort of coalition subjects will realize they have equal _____ and demand equal _____.

power, rewards

87. Minimum power theory, an application of Kelley's views to more than three people, claims that the power (and the spoils) a coalition member is entitled to depends on the number of coalitions that could win _____ with her (divided by the total number of possible coalitions).

only

88. Both minimum resource theory and minimum power theory assume that a coalition's earnings will be divided _____.

equitably

89. While both theories agree that which coalition a person joins is in part determined by equity, minimum resource theory sees equity as involving distribution in proportion to _____ and minimum power theory sees equity as involving distribution in proportion to _____ _____.

resources

pivotal power

90. Bargaining theory claims that initial coalitions are governed by people's attempts to maximize their payoff within the constraints of _____. In the

equity

initial coalitions, bargaining theory assumes that people will choose a point
_____ between a distribution in terms of resources and one in terms of   midway
power. With experience, _____ will matter less to coalition formation,   equity
and bargaining in the strictly _____ sense will matter more. This is   competitive
because people who have been _____ from a coalition will be willing   excluded
to accept a less-than-equitable settlement to get back in.

91. Bargaining theory predicts that the stable formations of coalitions will be
determined by what maximizes outcome independent of considerations of
_____.   equity

Self-Test

1. Strategic interactions
    a. involve conflict of interests.
    b. involve an attempt by each party to influence the future behavior of the other party.
    c. always involve military aggressive behaviors.
    d. a and b

2. Perfectly competitive bargaining
    a. implies that each dollar won by one side is lost by the other.
    b. is exemplified by bargaining for a house with a stranger.
    c. is rarely concerned with issues of *fair* price.
    d. all of the above

3. In *duopoly* bargaining
    a. there is only one potential buyer but many sellers.
    b. there is only one potential buyer and one potential seller.
    c. there is an open market.
    d. a and b

4. The "resistance point" or "limit"
    a. is the most that the buyer will pay.
    b. is the least that the buyer will pay.
    c. is the lowest amount that the seller will sell at.
    d. a and c

5. If the seller's lower limit is higher than the buyer's resistance point (limit) then
    a. a sale can be made.
    b. a sale will be made quickly.
    c. a sale will be difficult but possible.
    d. a sale will be impossible.

6. The "level of aspiration"
    a. is the same as the resistance point.
    b. is the profit that a bargainer believes is just adequate.

    c. is the lowest price that someone will sell for.
    d. all of the above

7. According to Siegel and Fouraker the best strategy in bargaining is
    a. for the buyer to start at some intermediate point and go up slowly and for the seller to start at an intermediate point and go down slowly; this strategy will tend to lower the opponent's level of aspiration.
    b. for the buyer to be honest with the seller and tell him what he is really prepared to pay.
    c. for the seller to be honest with the buyer and tell him or her what is the lowest acceptable price.
    d. for the buyer to start low and go up slowly and for the seller to start high and go down slowly; this strategy will tend to lower the opponent's level of aspiration.

8. In a set of bargaining experiments by Komorita it was found that reciprocating concessions (matching concessions) was
    a. a worse strategy than intransigence (not reciprocating them).
    b. better than making a bigger concession than one's opponent in order to reward him since making a bigger concession leads one's opponent to have a higher level of aspiration.
    c. about as good as intransigence but not as good as making bigger concessions in response to one's opponent's concessions.
    d. not consistent from trial to trial; the best strategy was entirely determined by the personalities of the two players.

9. Cialdini had experimenters approach people and ask them to volunteer to take youths out for two hours a week for two years. None volunteered. The experimenters then asked the people for a smaller request, to take the youths to the zoo once.

a. Half the subjects volunteered for the second request as compared to only one-quarter of the subjects who hadn't been asked the first request.
b. None of the subjects volunteered for the second request.
c. Three-quarters of the subjects volunteered for the second request as compared to only one in ten of the subjects who hadn't been asked the first request.
d. All the subjects volunteered for the second request as did all the subjects who hadn't been asked the first request.

10. An asymmetric information condition is one in which
a. person X knows Y's cost, but person Y does not know X's cost.
b. Both X and Y know each other's costs.
c. X has an advantage over Y.
d. b and c

11. Schelling argued that *not* having knowledge in an asymmetric information condition may be
a. very damaging.
b. beneficial.
c. neutral.
d. constraining.

12. Pruitt devised a bargaining situation in which the seller and buyer maximize joint profit if the buyer made concessions on coal and the seller on iron. Each person knew only about his own payoffs. In order to maximize their profits the subjects had to discover the optimal solution. Which of the following is *not* a factor that was found to be helpful in finding the optimal solution?
a. a problem-solving orientation
b. motivation to do as well as one can
c. a belief that one's loss was one's opponent's gain, and one's gain the other's loss
d. truthfulness about one's own profits

13. A problem-solving approach to the dividing up of housework between two housemates
a. would involve each housemate's doing half of each chore.
b. would involve taking an individualistic orientation to the problem.
c. would involve discovering the different dis-tastes and preferences of each housemate and allocating chores according to interest (or least distaste) to optimize joint satisfaction.
d. would involve one housemate browbeating the other into doing all of the work.

14. If there are many issues to be settled then what is likely to be the best way to handle the problem?
a. Work on all issues at the same time.
b. Use logrolling, where each party concedes on the issues more important to the other.
c. All members of the negotiations should be oriented to an integrative solution.
d. all of the above

15. Free market conditions
a. are the same as duopoly conditions.
b. involve buyers and sellers being free to trade with any other buyer or seller.
c. have the same advantageous strategies as duopoly competitive conditions.
d. involve monopolies.

16. When subjects could negotiate with four different sellers over the price of a car the sellers who used
a. tough opening strategies did better than those who used soft opening strategies.
b. the same strategies as those that had been most effective in duopoly bargaining were most effective.
c. soft opening strategies did better than those who used tough opening strategies.
d. tough opening strategies did as well as those who used soft opening strategies.

17. An experiment involved multiple buyers and sellers and the possibility of an integrative solution. Positively framing costs and payoffs in terms of profits to be made as opposed to costs
a. made an integrative solution less likely.
b. made an integrative solution more likely even though economically framing something in terms of profits or costs amounts to the same thing.
c. made impractical any successful bargain.
d. hardened positions.

18. Kahneman and Tversky found that people treat gains and losses in different ways even though the difference may be just a matter of phrasing (for instance, if it is 50:50 that you will win it is 50:50 that you will lose). Which of the following does *not* support this contention?
a. People prefer sure things to gambles when they can win money, but they prefer gambles to sure things when they are liable to lose money.
b. People are risk *averse* for profit and risk *seeking* for loss.

c. People sometimes make high bets even though the odds are against them.

d. Bargainers are more conservative and less likely to reach an integrative solution when they are dealing with losses than when they are dealing with gains.

19. Which of the following is *correct*?

a. A mediator is a third party to a negotiation who consults with both parties to facilitate an agreement.

b. An arbitrator is a third party to a negotiation who is by mutual agreement of the parties empowered to impose a settlement.

c. A mediator is a third party who is empowered to impose a settlement.

d. a and b

20. Someone who is bargaining as a representative for others

a. is likely to bargain less hard than if she were bargaining for herself.

b. is likely to be uninterested in the bargaining.

c. is likely to bargain harder than she would for herself.

d. is likely to take bribes.

21. Accountability to a group increases aggressiveness when

a. negotiators do not expect future negotiations with their bargaining counterparts.

h. negotiators expect future negotiations with their bargaining counterparts.

c. negotiators are negotiating in front of women.

d. negotiators are negotiating on behalf of men.

22. In final offer arbitration

a. each side submits its best offer to an arbitrator who must pick between them (she cannot compromise).

b. the arbitrator is not allowed to propose a third (compromise) solution.

c. both sides are forced to be reasonable in their final offer from fear that an unreasonable offer will cause the arbitrator to pick their opponent's offer.

d. all of the above

23. Mediators help in a variety of ways. Which of the following is a way that mediators do *not* help?

a. They help both sides form a realistic picture of the other.

b. They can think up new integrative solutions.

c. They pressure both sides to be reasonable by threatening to expose them to the public.

d. They pick between alternatives submitted to them by the parties.

24. In experimental bargaining situations an opponent who gives in at the request of a mediator is seen (by herself and by the opponent) as

a. more indecisive than one who gives in without the request of a mediator.

b. the sort of person who will bend to pressure.

c. weaker than one who gives in without the request of a mediator.

d. less weak than one who gives in without the request of a mediator.

25. The D.A. tells each prisoner that if he confesses and defects from his partner and his partner doesn't do the same he will get three months and his partner will get twenty years. If the prisoner refuses to defect to the D.A. but his friend defects he will get twenty years and his friend three months. If both prisoners confess they will each get ten years. On the other hand if both prisoners hold fast they only get a year each. This is an example of

a. the prisoners' dilemma.

b. vice cops.

c. the hangman's pride.

d. crime not paying.

26. Each prisoner faces only two alternatives—to cooperate or to defect—but whether a decision is a good one or not depends on

a. whether the prisoner has thought through his options.

b. whether the prisoner basically likes his partner in crime or not.

c. whether the prisoner has chosen cooperation or defection.

d. what the other prisoner does.

27. Let us say the Prisoner 1 would like both of them to refuse to confess. What is his problem?

a. His partner might choose to defect, which would give Prisoner 1 the worst option of twenty years.

b. His partner might also choose refusal.

c. His only problem is a psychological one.

d. He has none.

28. By confessing, Prisoner 1 avoids the risk that he will not confess but his partner will (thereby getting the worst sentence of twenty years). What is the advantage and disadvantage of this strategy?

a. The advantage is that he gets the best outcome; there is no disadvantage.

b. The advantage is he gets ten years if his partner confesses and only three months if he
doesn't; the disadvantage is that since his partner will probably reason like he does he will
get ten years and if they had both not squealed
they could have gotten only one year each.

c. The advantage is that he is sure to get only
three months; the disadvantage is that his
partner is sure to get twenty years.

d. There are no advantages to this strategy.

29. In the prisoners' dilemma individual rationality
leads both prisoners to a collectively and
individually
a. better payoff.
b. maximized payoff.
c. worse payoff than they could have achieved.
d. higher state of rationality and benevolence.

30. If you are making a series of prisoners' dilemma
decisions with the same person and another
element is added (in comparison with a single
trial), you can use your response on one trial to
affect your partner's response on future trials.
Repeated trials
a. give no strategic possibilities not contained
in a single trial.
b. are rarely taken advantage of when people
actually play a prisoners' dilemma game;
cooperation declines over repeated play.
c. cause people to be more cooperative over time.
d. cause a level of cooperation in the 60–80
percent range.

31. One may use various strategies in repeated play
of the prisoners' dilemma. In the Tit for Tat
strategy
a. a player chooses to cooperate no matter
what her opponent does.
b. a player chooses to defect no matter what
her opponent does.
c. a player does to her partner exactly what her
partner did to her on the previous round.
d. a player chooses to defect or cooperate by
using a random device (a die).

32. Axelrod computer-modeled various strategies,
including some very complex ones, submitted by
professionals. The Tit for Tat strategy (in which
the player cooperated on the first move) was
a. worse than the pacifist strategy of always
cooperating.
b. worse than the tough guy strategy of always
defecting.

c. the best strategy.
d. the worst strategy submitted.

33. Using the Tit for Tat strategy a player
a. always wins in any individual round.
b. never defeats an opponent over trials, but
across opponents will gain the most points
while the tough guy opponents will keep
each other's points down.
c. wins about half the individual rounds.
d. loses on overall points as well as on most of
the individual rounds.

34. In both the prisoners' dilemma research and bargaining research a strategy of matching concession
for concession has been found to be
a. unstable.
b. the best strategy even if you are only playing
one round.
c. the best strategy in the context of repeated
rounds with the same competitor.
d. sometimes a good strategy but usually a
mediocre one.

35. In both the prisoners' dilemma and bargaining
situations people search for the most practically
effective solution independent of what is moral
or not. In the context of repeated play with a
single partner the best strategy is
a. a moral one—equity.
b. a moral one—turn the other cheek.
c. an immoral one—Tit for Tat.
d. an immoral one—always defect.

36. The actual behavior of subjects in the prisoners'
dilemma involves a high rate of mutual defection
and a less-than-optimal joint return. McClintock
found that this was because
a. subjects are trying to amass the most points
no matter what's good for their opponents.
b. subjects are irrationally hostile and prefer
aggression to winning.
c. subjects are trying to win, or at least not to
lose, relative to their opponent.
d. subjects have no consistent goals when they
play the prisoners' dilemma game.

37. The advantage of the Tit for Tat strategy is that
it can reach
a. individualistic opponents, that is, those who
are trying to maximize their own outcome.
b. competitive opponents, that is, those who are
attempting to win relative to their opponent.
c. cooperative opponents, that is, those who
are trying to maximize joint outcomes.

d. opponents who are serious about their strategy.

38. The commons is owned by all and can be used for grazing by everyone's cattle. A discovery allows more cattle to flourish, which causes overgrazing. It would be in everyone's benefit if fewer cattle were grazing, since overgrazing will ultimately kill the commons. Yet this is unlikely to happen since
    a. the petty feuds that occur in a small town make many people spiteful.
    b. people are not worried, at the moment, about the danger of overgrazing.
    c. the advantage of adding a cow to the pasture for any particular herder is large compared to his disadvantage in hurting the commons.
    d. some herders are not injured by the overgrazing of the commons.

39. Although it is to everyone's advantage not to have overgrazing, it is not to anyone's advantage not to add cows until
    a. the point that an additional cow would kill the entire pasture (at this point it would be too late to save the pasture).
    b. the point that an additional cow would make a noticeable decrease in the quality of the pasture.
    c. people become conscience stricken.
    d. other people notice that you are adding cows.

40. What other important world problems are like the problem of the commons?
    a. peace negotiations
    b. racial tensions and ethnic unrest
    c. pollution and overpopulation
    d. all of the above

41. There is experimental support for the notion that groups playing repeated trial prisoners' dilemma games cooperate more if the decision makers are
    a. college students.
    b. identifiable (not anonymous).
    c. anonymous (not identifiable).
    d. in a hurry.

42. Hardin suggests that individual restraint is an unlikely solution of "tragedy of the commons" type problems. Consider two polluting companies with equal access to the common air. The company that installs expensive pollution-controlling equipment will
    a. make less profit than the one that does not and be at a competitive disadvantage.

b. make more profit since people prefer to buy from nonpolluting companies.
    c. will make the same amount of profit.
    d. will by its example convince the other company to stop polluting.

43. Hardin suggests three solutions to the problem of the polluting and nonpolluting companies. They are government-imposed penalties for pollution, a tax on pollution greater than the profit to be made from polluting, and
    a. making moral appeals to polluters.
    b. trying to buy from nonpolluting companies.
    c. explaining to the polluters the real damage they are inflicting on the community.
    d. allowing people to sue for damages.

44. The Tit for Tat solution cannot be used in the n-person prisoners' dilemma since the damage that an individual can do to punish a defector
    a. just applies to the defector and is not a lesson for anyone else.
    b. is not effective because only a cooperative strategy is effective.
    c. is spread among all members including the cooperators.
    d. does not spread sufficiently among the other opponents.

45. A public good is
    a. one that only representatives of the public can use.
    b. one that works only because of publicity.
    c. identical to an individual good.
    d. one that every member of the community can use.

46. The problem with public goods is that
    a. anyone can use a public good such as a park, not only those who pay for it; but if no one pays for it there will be no public good.
    b. not enough people use public goods.
    c. people often don't appreciate public goods.
    d. too many people want to pay for public goods to get the prestige involved with being a supporter.

47. In experiments in which people can choose either to invest in public goods that will contribute to the whole community or to invest in private goods that will only benefit the investors, people invest in
    a. both at an approximately equal level.
    b. only private goods.
    c. mainly public goods.

d. both, but substantially less in public goods than is optimal to maximize the profit of the group as a whole.

48. Do people manage resources better when they have to take less (a commons dilemma) or when they have to give more (a public goods problem)?
   a. They manage resources better when they have to take less (commons dilemma).
   b. They manage resources better when they have to give more (public goods problem).
   c. There is no difference between them.
   d. It depends on the temperament of the individuals involved.

49. In the various dilemmas and games, what are the two basic reasons a person might defect?
   a. greed and fear of being exploited
   b. anger and pride
   c. greed and cynicism
   d. sloth and fear of strangers

50. Rapaport found that even when groups could win very large amounts of (real) money and were educated as to how "social traps" work, they will not be able to win unless they are
   a. organized.
   b. intelligent.
   c. friendly with each other.
   d. know each other to a minimal extent.

51. The problem of coalition formation arises when there is a prize that no one person has the resources to win. What is necessary for a coalition to form?
   a. Individuals must form a group.
   b. Resources must be pooled.
   c. How the payoff is to be divided must be agreed upon.
   d. all of the above

52. If there are three parties and two are needed to form a coalition, then according to Simmel each of the strongest parties
   a. will seek out the party stronger than they are.
   b. will seek out the next strongest party.
   c. will seek out the weakest party and not each other.
   d. will not decide on the basis of strength or weakness.

53. Minimum resource theory claims
   a. that the coalition with the fewest resources needed to win will be formed and that rewards will be divided in proportion to the resources

each member brings to the coalition.
   b. that the coalition with the greatest resources needed to win will be formed and that rewards will be divided in proportion to the resources each member brings to the coalition.
   c. that the coalition with the greatest resources needed to win will be formed and that rewards will be divided according to priority of entry into the coalition.
   d. that there really are sufficient resources available to make it worthwhile to form a coalition.

54. Kelley claims that resources do not determine the allocation of rewards in a coalition. What does?
   a. goodness
   b. charm
   c. power
   d. temporal priority

55. Minimum power theory claims that the power and the spoils a coalition member is entitled to depend on
   a. the number of coalitions that could win only with her (divided by the total number of possible coalitions).
   b. the number of coalitions that could divide up their resources most efficiently (divided by the total number of possible coalitions).
   c. how little power the member has in relation to the group—the less power the more likely that other members will protect her.
   d. all of the above

56. In the initial coalitions bargaining theory assumes that people will choose a point midway between an equitable distribution in terms of resources and an equitable distribution in terms of power. In the later coalitions
   a. equity will matter more.
   b. equity will matter less.
   c. strict competition will matter less.
   d. a and c

57. Equity will matter less over time because people who have been excluded from a coalition will
   a. be resentful and refuse to come into the coalition unless they get more than their share.
   b. join other coalitions and start divisive wars with the coalition that originally rejected them.
   c. be willing to accept a less-than-equitable settlement to get back in.
   d. will refuse to join any coalition ever again.

Answer Key for Self-Test

1.	d (pp. 425–426)	30.	b (p. 447)
2.	d (pp. 427–428)	31.	c (p. 448)
3.	b (p. 429)	32.	c (p. 449)
4.	d (p. 429)	33.	b (p. 449)
5.	d (p. 429)	34.	c (pp. 450–451)
6.	b (p. 431)	35.	a (pp. 450–451)
7.	d (p. 431)	36.	c (p. 451)
8.	b (p. 432)	37.	a (p. 453)
9.	a (p. 433)	38.	c (p. 457)
10.	a (p. 434)	39.	a (p. 457)
11.	b (p. 434)	40.	c (p. 457)
12.	c (pp. 435–436)	41.	b (p. 459)
13.	c (p. 437)	42.	a (p. 460)
14.	d (p. 437)	43.	d (p. 460)
15.	b (pp. 437–438)	44.	c (p. 461)
16.	c (p. 438)	45.	d (p. 461)
17.	b (p. 439)	46.	a (pp. 461–462)
18.	c (p. 439)	47.	d (p. 462)
19.	d (p. 441)	48.	a (p. 462)
20.	c (p. 440)	49.	a (p. 462)
21.	a (p. 441)	50.	a (p. 466)
22.	d (p. 441)	51.	d (p. 466)
23.	d (p. 443)	52.	c (p. 467)
24.	d (p. 443)	53.	a (p. 467)
25.	a (p. 445)	54.	c (p. 468)
26.	d (p. 446)	55.	a (p. 468)
27.	a (p. 446)	56.	b (p. 469)
28.	b (p. 446)	57.	a (p. 468)
29.	c (p. 447)		

Thought Questions and Exercises

1. The text contrasts two sorts of bargaining situations. One is of complete conflict, A's loss is B's gain and B's loss is A's gain. The other is one in which there are elements of conflict and elements of cooperation needed to maximize profit. Think up examples not presented in the text of each type of bargaining situation.

2. Replicate the Cialdini door-in-the-face experiment. Remember Cialdini asked people to work with juveniles two days a week for two years (all refused), and then he asked them to take some kids to the zoo just once. Twice as many people who had just refused the two-year request volunteered to take the kids to the zoo as did people who were just asked to take the kids to the zoo without the prior request. Cialdini showed that this effect works only when the same person makes both requests. He uses this to argue that people are more likely to volunteer on the second request because they see themselves as being in a bargaining situation and needing to respond to a lowered bid. How else might you test whether people saw themselves in a bargaining situation? (For instance, if the second offer was about something else—a completely different charity, a personal favor, for example, do you think compliance on the second request would be as high?) If Cialdini is right in his "bargaining interpretation," then in a real bargaining situation an offer that has been preceded by a quite unacceptably high offer should get more takers than the same offer without the preceding unacceptable bid. If you or someone you know are having a garage sale, work in a flea market, or something of the sort, then you should be able to test this out. If it works for the seller does it also work for the buyer?

3. When a joint optimal solution is possible, it may not be reached because the opponents do not come to realize what it is. Pruitt has presented evidence (see text, pp. 435–436) that a problem-solving orientation, motivation, and truthfulness between the players are essential for reaching the optimal solution. The text applies Pruitt's analysis to people dividing up housework. If there are three people sharing an apartment would everyone doing exactly one-third of each chore be the joint optimal solution? Why? Why not? How would a problem-solving orientation facilitate an optimal solution? Why would contentiousness and suspicion between the partners not allow for such a solution? Apply Pruitt's notions to relationships other than housemates—for instance, people sharing a vacation trip, or the sorts of nonhousehold "chores" that friends and lovers wind up doing for each other.

4. The text discusses mediators in the context of union-business negotiations. When are mediators likely to be effective? Does the text's discussion of mediators have any application to "personal mediators"? Have you ever tried to mediate in a dispute between two friends? When is this sort of mediation likely to be successful? What are the dangers in this sort of mediation? Are any of these dangers different from the dangers you would expect in union-business negotiations? Why?

5. In the prisoners' dilemma, the tragedy of the commons, and the public goods problem the most straightforwardly rational choice for individuals leads to collective disaster and ultimately to a less-than-optimal outcome for the individual. Why? Why is it argued that the solution for the commons problem and for the public goods problem cannot be on the individual level but must be on the collective level? Why is it argued that if the prisoners' dilemma is played for only one round there is no way out of the dilemma? Why does playing many rounds of the prisoners' dilemma with the same opponent allow a different solution? What common public problems are captured by the analysis of each of these three problems?

6. Simmel thought that there was something unstable about the relationships of triads: that a triad sometimes invited coalition formation, with two ganging up on one. Think back to situations in which you have been a member of a triad. When did the triad lead to coalition formation? Was it always the same coalition, the same scapegoat, or did the coalition vary? Have you ever been in a stable triad? What made the triad stable?

CHAPTER 13

Aggression

Learning Objectives

WHAT IS AGGRESSION?

1. Explain what aggression is. Is accidentally hurting someone aggression? Distinguish between impulsive (emotional) aggression and instrumental aggression.

ANIMAL AGGRESSION

2. Name the different types of animal aggression. Describe how the different forms of animal aggression can be distinguished.

Predatory Aggression

3. Describe what "predatory aggression" is. Consider the example of the aggression of the hunting cat and the threatened cat. Do each of these instances of aggression look the same? What is the evidence that different neural systems are involved in these two types of aggression?

Inter-Male Aggression

4. Describe what "inter-male aggreession" is, and why males tend to fight each other more often than females fight each other. Is there a relation between testosterone, male fighting, and male rough-and-tumble play? Is there an evolutionary reason for a distinct form of inter-male aggression? Is inter-male aggression more or less likely to be lethal than other forms of aggression?

5. Name three common forms that inter-male aggression takes.

Dominance Hierarchies

6. Describe how roosters establish a "peck order" between them. In what sense is this a "hierarchy"?

When is such a hierarchy a "dominance hierarchy"? What qualifications must we add to the notion of a pure dominance hierarchy so that it will be reflective of actual behavior?

7. Human behavior sometimes follows a peck order. Does this imply that we have inherited genes that lead us to act like chickens? Why not?

Territoriality

8. Explain what "territoriality" is. Illustrate two major elements of territoriality using the example of the finch.

9. Explain how human wars and territorial inter-male aggression are similar. Is this similarity sufficient to conclude that human warfare is a result of territorial instincts? The argument that we go to war because we have territorial instincts assumes that we each have a gene disposing us to defend some territory of our own. Is this what soldiers in modern war are trying to do?

10. Explain what inter-male aggression and sports have in common. Explain what the major difference between them is.

Sex-related Aggression

11. Explain what "sex-related aggression" is. How is it different from territorial inter-male aggression whose ultimate goal is the ability to breed?

Maternal Aggression

12. Describe what "maternal aggression" is. What are the necessary conditions for maternal aggression to occur? What are the genetic benefits and risks to defending a child?

Danger-induced Aggression

13. Describe the most common reaction of animals to

danger. What are some other reactions? What is an animal likely to do if its path to escape is blocked?

14. Review the distinction between predatory aggression and danger-induced aggression. What is one way that danger-induced aggression is different from inter-male, sex-related, and maternal aggression?

Irritable Aggression

15. Explain what causes "irritable aggression." If rats are shocked what will they do?

16. Self-defensive (danger-induced) aggression and irritable aggression are very similar. How? In what way are they different?

RESEARCH ON HUMAN AGGRESSION

Motives for Human Aggression

17. Describe what "impulsive aggression" is. What are the two broad opposing views about the nature of human anger?

Aggression as Response to Transgression: The Aristotelian Account

18. Explain what Aristotle believed was the source of human anger. What is anger directed at? In what sense is this a social account of anger? In what sense is anger pro-social?

Aggression as Response to Frustration: The Freud-Yale Account

19. Explain what "frustration" is. According to Freud, what is the relation between the frustrations inherent in socialization and aggression? What was the claim that Dollard and his colleagues made about the relation between frustration and aggression?

20. Contrast the Aristotelian and Freud-Yale positions. Is all aggression caused by frustration?

Does Frustration Always Lead to Aggression?

21. Subjects were asked to imagine frustrating situations including one in which a bus driver passed people by at a bus stop, thus frustrating them. How did the subjects report that they would feel in these situations? Does this appear to support or refute the frustration-aggression hypothesis?

Justified and Unjustified Frustration

22. Describe Pastore's hypothesis relating illegitimate frustrations to anger? How did he test his hypothesis?

23. Describe the effect of "mitigating information" on the likelihood of responding with aggression

to a frustration. What are some examples of mitigating exchanges?

24. A more moderate version of the frustration-aggression hypothesis would be that frustration did not lead to aggression but to the *desire* or *impulse* to hurt someone. Explain.

Aversive States and Anger

25. Describe Berkowitz's experiment in which subjects, while keeping their hands in annoyingly cold water or tepid water, had to assign rewards and punishments to a confederate. Do his results support the frustration-aggression hypothesis? Was the confederate in any way responsible for the subject's hands being in cold water? Explain how Aristotelians handle Berkowitz's results. What is the difference between the Berkowitz and the Aristotelian positions? (Remember to include their different views of the causal relations between thoughts of transgression and aggression.)

The Modulation of Anger

Frustration and Degree of Anger

26. Understand different conditions that may increase or decrease the amount of anger felt. Describe an experiment that studied frustration by varying the amount of the possible reward, the prior expectation of success, and the manner of frustration (unjustified, justified, personal). What were the results of the "manner of frustration" manipulation? Did subjects who lost $1 get angrier than those who thought they had only lost 10¢? What was the result of the "expectation of success" manipulation?

Cues Associated with Aggression and Anger

27. Understand how cues associated with aggression can affect the expression of aggression. Subjects who had seen either an aggressive film or a peaceful one were able to retaliate against a confederate who had insulted them. Which group of subjects retaliated more? If the confederate had the same name as the brutally beaten boxer in the movie did subjects retaliate more in the experiment than if the confederate had a neutral name? Describe Berkowitz's experiment supposedly demonstrating a "weapons effect." Berkowitz believes that the above cues affect aggression in an immediate, unreasoned way, but there is another explanation. What is it? What is Carlson's evidence on this point?

Aggression and the Transfer of Arousal

28. Explain how Zillmann accounts for the increased aggression after seeing the *Champion* film. What is the role of transfer of arousal in his account? Describe Zillmann's experiment in which he compared a sexually arousing film with *Champion* to determine which would produce more subsequent aggression against the confederate. What happened when the experiment was replicated with arousal produced by riding an exercycle?

29. Describe how Zillmann experimentally verified that the Schachter and Singer view of the role of arousal was a correct interpretation of how arousal affects aggression.

30. Baron had a confederate insult subjects and then had the subjects see one of five progressively more sexually arousing slides. What would Zillmann predict about the effect of increasing sexual arousal on aggression? What happened?

31. Zillmann argued that there is a difference between how sexual films (his original experiment) and slides affect subjects. Explain. Describe Zillmann's experimental verification of his point. Was his account supported? The new transfer of arousal view calls attention not only to how arousing an intervening activity is but also to how distracting, how cognitively engaging the intervening activity is. Explain.

Aversive States and Aggression

32. Describe what has been found about the relation between high temperatures and violent crime. Is there a relation between air pollution and aggression? What are two hunches about the cause of the relation between temperature and other aversive stimuli and aggression?

SEXUAL AGGRESSION

Date Rape

33. Describe what "date rape" is. Describe the study in which undergraduate men who had admitted to date rape were interviewed and their responses compared to undergraduates who were not rapists. What is the role of sexual arousal in date rape? What are the date rapists' attitudes toward women and sex?

34. Investigators gave male and female subjects invented newspaper accounts of rapes in which the rapist and victim were either strangers, dating, or dating and previously having had consensual sexual intercourse. Who judged the rapes as more serious? Did the subjects believe the crime to be less serious if the victim and the rapist knew each other than if they didn't? How about if they had been dating and sexually intimate?

35. Describe the position of the law on date rape. Are men who hold very stereotypical views of women's roles more likely to see date rape as a different matter from stranger rape?

Pornography and Rape

36. Describe the two main effects of nonviolent pornography on people. Is there any relation between amount of time spent looking at pornography and negative attitudes toward women in undergraduate males?

The Effects on Men of Pornography with Aggressive Themes

37. Male subjects were angered by either a male or female confederate. They then were shown a neutral, erotic, or erotic-aggressive film clip before being allowed to retaliate. The erotic and aggressive-erotic films produced greater retaliation, as would be expected by what is known about transfer of arousal. But what was the relation between the retaliation to the female confederate after the erotic film and after the erotic-aggressive film? Can this be explained by transfer of arousal?

38. The sexual responses to audiotapes of rape and consenting sex of self-confessed rapists versus other men were compared. Was there a difference? What is the relation between becoming aroused by depictions of rape and having used sexual coercion against women? What are the more general attitudes toward women and sex of men who become aroused by the depiction of rape?

39. A study varied both the actual amount of alcohol male subjects drank and the amount they *thought* they drank. The subjects had heard audiotapes of mutually pleasurable sex, rape, and a nonsexual aggression of a man against a woman. What effect did drinking alcohol have on the reaction to all of the tapes? How did the subjects who *thought* they had been drinking a soft drink behave (whether they had had any alcohol or not)? How about those who thought they were drinking alcohol?

Rape Myths and Aggression against Women

40. Male and female students saw either a film that depicted a woman falling for someone who had

abused or raped her, or a tender, romantic film. What happened several days later when the students filled out questionnaires about rape and violence toward women? Do the results of this study imply that there is a danger posed by pornography that shows women as attracted to rape?

Male Jealousy and Aggression

41. In the United States roughly equal numbers of husbands and wives kill each other, but the motive in both cases seems to relate to the husband's suspicion of his wife's infidelity. Explain.

42. Explain Daly and Wilson's evolutionary account of the difference in male and female toleration of infidelity.

LEARNING AND AGGRESSION

Learning How to Aggress

43. Describe the Bobo doll experiment that attempted to show how children learn aggression from models.

Learning Not to Express Aggression

Modeling

44. Children saw a bully pick on another child and either be punished for his behavior or get away with it. A control group saw a child in vigorous but not aggressive play. How did they react to this in their own play?

Punishment and Aggression

45. Punishing a child inhibits the behavior for which the child was punished, but it also may have another, unintended effect. Describe this effect.

46. Parents were interviewed to assess the techniques they used to control their children, and then their children were observed in nursery school play. What sort of discipline was related to the degree that the child displayed hostility in school? Describe some of the effects of parents' use of arbitrary power to discipline their children.

Television and Responses to Aggression

47. Describe the relation between the amount of violent TV watched at home and arousal to the sight of other childrren fighting.

Modeling and Justified Aggression

48. Subjects who had been insulted by a confederate watched either a TV program depicting justified or unjustified aggression. They retaliated more in which condition?

Does Viewing Violence on Television Cause Aggression?

49. There is a well-established relation between the amount of aggressive TV that children watch and the degree to which they are hostile. Does this prove that the TV watching causes hostility?

Aggression and Popularity of Television Shows

50. Are aggressive shows more popular? What has been found to be the correlation between violence and the popularity of a television show?

Television and Covetousness

51. Did the crime rate in the United States go up because of the introduction of TV? If TV had been introduced in all of the United States at the same moment and crime rates had then risen would it be possible to conclude that TV had caused the rise? Why not? How was TV introduced and why did this make an analysis possible? Was the introduction of TV associated with an increase in violent crime? With an increase in theft? Why?

DISINHIBITION OF AGGRESSION

Deindividuation and Aggression

52. Explain how deindividuation, or anonymity, is one factor that may lead to disinhibition, or the breakdown of restraint. What factors other than anonymity lead to disinhibition through deindividuation? Describe the study in which undergraduate women were dressed in lab coats and hoods or wore large name tags and then were told to administer shock to someone. Who shocked more? Why?

Aggression and Institutions

The Zimbardo Prison Study

53. Describe Zimbardo's prison study. How were guards and prisoners selected? What was done to make the prisoners feel like real prisoners? How were they made to feel "depersonalized"? How were they made to feel and look to the guards like children? How were the guards absorbed into their prison role? How did the institutional setting encourage brutality?

Aggression and Dehumanization

54. How did the dehumanization of the prisoners make it easier to be brutal to them? What is the evidence that Franz Stangl, the commandant of the Treblinka death camp, provided about dehumanization and the disinhibition of brutality?

Obedience and Aggression

55. Describe how the power of authority can affect aggression. Was the tacit approval of the experimenter in Zimbardo's study one reason for the brutality of the guards? How did the power of authority affect aggression in the Milgram obedience experiment?

Programmed Exercises

WHAT IS AGGRESSION?

1. Aggression is _____ harm doing. Accidentally hurting someone is _____ aggression.

    intentional
    not

2. Punching someone because she has insulted you is an example of _____ aggression.

    impulsive
    (emotional)

3. Punching someone in order to steal their wallet is an example of _____ aggression.

    instrumental

4. _____ aggression has as its goals hurting someone, while with _____ aggression the violence is a byproduct of some other goal.

    Impulsive
    instrumental

ANIMAL AGGRESSION

5. Different types of aggression in animals are marked off by: different _____ manifestations, different triggering _____, and different _____ and _____ underpinnings.

    behavioral, stimuli
    neural, hormonal

Predatory Aggression

6. Predatory aggression is the aggression of the hunter killing her _____.

    prey

7. One example of predatory aggression is that of a cat hunting a mouse. The cat quietly _____ the mouse, and quickly bites through the mouse's neck. This is unlike _____ aggression, wherein the cat aggresses out of pain; it hisses, lashes out with its paws, and its fur stands on end.

    stalks
    emotional

8. Emotional and predatory aggression are different in form, and each type involves a different _____ center.

    neural (brain)

Inter-Male Aggression

9. In most species males fight each other _____ than females fight each other. Typically the male young in these species engage in rough-and-tumble _____. Both of these are related to the presence of _____, the male sex hormone.

    more
    play, testosterone

10. In most species males compete for access to females more often than females compete for access to males; this may be the evolutionary basis for _____ aggression.

    inter-male

11. There are specific forms of behavior associated with inter-male aggression. For example, male deer fight each other by lowering their antlers and charging; they fight anything other than a male deer by using their _____.

    hooves

12. In many species inter-male aggression is _____ lethal than other forms of aggression.

    less

13. In some species inter-male aggression is continual; in others it is limited by _____ _____ and _____.

    dominance hierarchies
    territoriality

14. When two roosters are brought together for the first time they will furiously peck at each other. Eventually one will still peck the other, briefly, but the other will not peck back. These two roosters now have a _____ _____ between them. The dominant member of the pair will have _____ access to food and hens; the nondominant member will avoid repeated losing fights.

    peck order

    greater

15. A stable hierarchy in which each organism dominates those below and is dominated by those above is called a _____ _____.

dominance hierarchy

16. The notion of a peck order can be seen in many human _____. When resources are limited there are just a few ways of dividing it up; a peck order is one of those ways. Human peck orders may just be _____ to chicken social structures.

organizations

analogous

17. In territorial species most inter-male aggression occurs on the _____ of territories.

boundaries

18. _____ involves space defended by one member of a mating unit, typically male, against intruders and in which the unit breeds and cares for the young.

Territoriality

19. Human wars and territorial inter-male aggression are similar in that they both involve the _____ of a region against the invasion of others, but aggressive motives are transient while the enduring motive of an individual in a war is _____. Just because the goal of a war might be aggression does not mean that the goal of the individual soldier is _____. The goal might be love of religion, a regular salary, seeing the world, ideology, and so forth.

defense

obedience
aggression

Sex-related Aggression

20. Sex-related aggression is aggression elicited by _____ stimuli.

sexual

21. Testosterone, the male sex hormone, leads both to increased _____ desire and to an increase in various forms of _____. Sex-related aggression is different from inter-male aggression in that it depends on sexual arousal and the presence of sexual _____.

sexual

aggression

stimuli

Maternal Aggression

22. _____ _____ is released only when the mother is in the hormonal state associated with having given birth and if she is in sight of her young.

Maternal aggression

Danger-induced Aggression

23. The most common reaction of an animal facing danger is to _____. Other responses include freezing or feigning _____. As a last resort animals will _____ the threat.

flee
death
attack

24. In cats danger-induced aggression is different from _____ aggression in that it is less precise, involves arousal hissing and the use of claws instead of teeth. Danger-induced aggression unlike sex-related, inter-male, or maternal aggression is _____ common in males and females.

predatory

equally

Irritable Aggression

25. Irritable aggression is caused by a variety of _____. Irritable aggression and danger-induced aggression are similar in that they both involve sympathetic nervous system _____, occur in both sexes, and in some senses are responses to a(n) _____. The major difference is that danger-induced aggression is usually preceded by attempts to _____, while irritable aggression is not.

annoyances

arousal
attack
flee

RESEARCH ON HUMAN AGGRESSION

Motives for Human Aggression

26. Impulsive aggression is aggression born of _____.   anger

27. According to Aristotle the source of human anger is the perception of an _____, or more broadly a _____.   insult, transgression

28. Anger is a social phenomena since it is sensitive to social _____; "transgression" implies social standards. Aristotle saw anger as a _____ emotion, serving to maintain the social order by punishing those who transgress against it.   norms / pro-social

29. "Frustration" means the blocking or inhibition of a _____.   response

30. According to Freud the frustration inherent in _____ leads to a reservoir of aggression to be released by future frustration.   socialization

31. Dollard and his colleagues claimed that all impulsive aggression presupposed _____, which leads to aggression.   frustration

32. Aggression, anger, is a blind, _____ response to frustration. According to this view we respond to frustration with aggression even if the aggression will _____ remove the frustration or even if the frustration is morally legitimate. Therefore anger is a _____ to the social order.   irrational / not / threat

33. The essential difference between the Yale and the Aristotelian views of anger is whether frustration is a _____ cause of anger.   sufficient

Does Frustration Always Lead to Aggression?

34. Subjects were asked to imagine frustrating situations including one in which a bus driver passed people by at a bus stop, thus frustrating them. The subjects reported that they would feel angry in _____ of the situations.   all

35. Pastore noticed that in the "imagining frustrating situations" experiments the frustrations were also _____, that is, they were transgressions.   illegitimate (unjustified)

36. Pastore matched a justified version of the frustrating situation to each previous version. He found that people reported _____ anger to justified frustrations.   less

37. Some experimenters have found that contrary to the Yale hypothesis, people become aggressive only if the aggression relieves that _____.   frustration

38. _____ information is information that the person who committed a transgression is not as bad as he might seem. It has been found that this information sometimes _____ retaliation.   Mitigating / reduces

39. A more moderate form of the frustration-aggression hypothesis claims that frustration just leads to the _____ to hurt someone.   desire (impulse)

40. In an experiment by Berkowitz, subjects while keeping their hands in annoyingly cold water or in tepid water had to assign rewards and punishments to a confederate. They were either told that punishment would help or hurt the subject. In the punishment hurts condition the subjects with their hands in _____ water punished the confederate more than those with hands in   cold

_____ water. This finding _____ the frustration-aggression hypothesis since the confederate was in no way _____ for the subject's hands being in cold water.

warm, supports
responsible

41. One way for an Aristotelian to handle these results is to claim that _____ _____ lower the threshold for the perception of a transgression.

aversive states

The Modulation of Anger

42. An experiment studied frustration by varying the amount of the posible reward, the prior expectation of success, and the manner of frustration (unjustified, justified, personal). Subjects who were unjustifiably frustrated were _____ angry; most subjects who were made to feel that the frustration was their fault were _____ angry; and subjects who were justifiably frustrated experienced anger _____ the two conditions.

most
least
between

43. When the missed reward was greater subjects became _____ than when the missed reward was smaller.

angrier

44. When subjects believed that success was likely they became _____ frustrated than when they believed that success was unlikely.

more

45. Subjects who had seen either an aggressive film or a peaceful one were able to retaliate against a confederate who had insulted them. The subjects who saw the _____ film retaliated more. If the conferderate had the same name as the brutally beaten boxer in the movie subjects retaliated _____ than if the confederate had a neutral name.

aggressive
more

46. Zillmann claims that aggressive cues are _____.

arousing

47. Zillmann believes that there is increased retaliation against the confederate after the subject sees *Champion* because *Champion* is more _____ than the control film. This _____ to the subject's anger.

arousing
tranfers

48. To demonstrate that it is arousal and not aggressive cues that cause the aggression a very _____ arousing, nonaggressive film was shown instead of *Champion*. This film produced a _____ level of aggression than did *Champion*.

sexually
higher

49. Even arousal produced by riding an exercycle produced more _____ against the confederate than did a nonarousing activity.

retaliation
(aggression)

50. Schachter and Singer and Zillmann claim that arousal affects emotion and behavior _____. According to this account, when people are aroused they try to figure out the _____ of the arousal and act according to their interpretation. If someone thinks the arousal is due to an insult she will _____, if she thinks it is due to the attractiveness of the confederate she will become _____, and if she thinks that the arousal is just a byproduct of a drug she _____ experience an emotion.

indirectly
cause
retaliate
romantic
won't

51. Zillmann reasoned that immediately after exercising insulted subjects should realize that their arousal comes from exercise but after a while this should be less clear; hence he predicted that immediately after exercising subjects _____ even though drive is highest then.

under-retaliate

52. Physically fit people experience a very rapid decrease of arousal while unfit people experience a slow decrease of arousal, hence a while after exercise

_____ subjects should retaliate more than _____ subjects.   unfit, fit
This effect occurred.

53. Baron had a confederate insult subjects and then had the subjects see one of
five progressively more sexually arousing slides. Zillmann would predict that
the more the arousal the _____ the retaliation against the confederate.   more
In fact, all but one of the erotic slides _____ retaliation.   reduced

54. Zillmann argued that these results were because slides produce fantasies, and
the fantasies will _____ subjects from thinking about the source of the   distract
anger. But if the insult is intense enough subjects will not fantasize to the
slides, and _____ won't be reduced.   retaliation

55. In an experiment some subjects were mildly provoked and others severely
provoked by the experimenter. These subjects either saw an erotic movie or
erotic slides. As Zillmann predicted subjects who saw the _____ over-   movie
retaliated even to the mild provocation; subjects who saw the _____   slides
only over-retaliated to the severe provocation.

SEXUAL AGGRESSION

Date Rape

56. "Date rape" is _____ in the context of a dating relationship.   rape

57. Undergraduate men who admitted to rape had a history of deceit and _____   fraud
in getting women to have sex with them, and believed that their _____   friends
approved of or encouraged their activities.

58. Investigators gave male and female subjects invented newspaper accounts of
rapes in which the rapist and victim were either strangers, dating, or dating and
previously had had consensual intercourse _____ judged the rapes in   Women
all three situations to be more serious than _____ did. Subjects of both   men
sexes believed the crime to be _____ serious if the victims and the   less
rapist knew each other. If the rapist and victim had been dating and sexually
intimate, subjects found the crime to be _____ serious.   least

59. Men who hold very stereotypical views of women's roles are _____   more
likely to see date rape as a different matter from stranger rape.

Pornography and Rape

60. Nonviolent pornography has been shown to have two effects on men and
women, one is a transient sexual _____, the other is an increase in   arousal
their typical sexual _____.   behavior

61. Undergraduate men were asked about the amount of time they spent with
erotic material and their attitudes toward women. There was no _____   correlation
between the two.

62. Male subjects were angered by either a male or female confederate. They then
were shown a neutral, erotic, or aggressive-erotic film clip before being allowed
to retaliate. The erotic and aggressive-erotic films produced _____   greater
retaliation. This result is as would be expected by what is known about
_____ of arousal. But the retaliation against the _____   transfer, female
confederate after the aggressive-erotic film was twice as great as after the
aggressive film. This cannot be explained by transfer of arousal.

63. Men who are aroused by depictions of rape are more likely to accept
_____ against and dominance over women.   violence

64. A study varied both the actual amount of alcohol male subjects drank and the
amount that they thought they drank. The subjects then heard audiotapes of
mutually pleasurable sex, rape, and nonsexual aggression of a man against a
woman. Drinking alcohol lowered arousal to _____ of the tapes.   all
Subjects who *thought* they had been drinking a soft drink (whether they had
had alcohol or a soft drink) showed _____ arousal to the tape of the   less
rape than to the tape of consenting sex. Those who thought they were drinking
alcohol (whether they had had alcohol or not) were _____ aroused to   equally
the tape of the rape as to the tape of consenting sex.

65. Male and female students saw films that depicted a woman falling for someone
who had abused or raped her, or tender romantic films. Several days later the
students filled out questionnaires about rape and violence toward women.
Women who had seen the "women love rape" film were even _____   more
anti-rape than they had been while men were _____ anti-rape.   less

Male Jealousy and Aggression

66. Roughly _____ numbers of husbands and wives kill each other in   equal
disputes relating to jealousy. Most disputes focus on the _____   husband's
jealousy since wives often kill husbands in self-defense in a jealous feud.

LEARNING AND AGGRESSION

Learning How to Aggress

67. Children are _____ likely to beat, kick, or fling a Bobo doll if they see   more
an adult do so first.

Learning Not to Express Aggression

68. One reason not to harm others is moral; another is that we will be _____   punished
for aggression. Children saw a bully pick on another child and either be
punished for his behavior or get away with it. A control group saw a child in
vigorous but not aggressive play. Children who watched the unpunished
aggression played _____ aggressively with a Bobo doll; children who   most
saw vigorous nonviolent play were _____ aggressive with the doll.   least

69. Parents were interviewed to assess the techniques they used to control their
children and then their children were observed in nursery school play. The
degree to which the parents used _____ power, that is, disciplined the   arbitrary
child while not explaining why, was related to the degree the child showed
_____ in school.   hostility

70. Parents using arbitrary power at home teach their child two things:
(1) not to _____ at home, and (2) acting in a hostile way is an   aggress
_____ way to get what you want.   appropriate (useful)

Television and Responses to Aggression

71. Eight- to ten-year-old children who had seen a violent TV program became
_____ aroused at a "real" fight than did children who had seen a   less
peaceable TV program. The emotional response to another child being hurt
presumably inhibits _____ against others.   aggression

72. Subjects who had been insulted by a confederate watched either a TV program depicting justified or unjustified aggression. They retaliated more after the program of _____ violence.

justified

73. There is a well-supported relation between the amount of aggressive TV that children watch and the degree to which they are _____. This does not show that TV watching _____ hostility.

hostile
causes

74. TV was introduced into the United States area by area over years. Comparing the crime rates in areas before and after the introduction of TV showed _____ increase in violent cirme, but an _____ in the rate of thefts.

no, increase

75. The effect of TV was to expose people to the lifestyles of the _____ class and increase _____.

upper
covetousness

DISINHIBITION OF AGGRESSION

Deindividuation and Aggression

76. Deindividuation is related to _____ and the feeling of being submerged in a group.

anonymity

77. Zimbardo claimed that several factors in addition to anonymity lead to deindividuation. They include: loss of a sense of _____, physiological _____, intense _____ stimulation, and being in a _____ situation.

responsibility
arousal, sensory,
novel

78. Zimbardo had undergraduate women dress in lab coats and hoods or wear name plates. They had to administer shock to someone. The deindividuated subjects (in the hoods) were told that the experimenter could not tell who gave what level of shock. The _____ subjects gave more shocks than did those with _____ plates.

hooded
name

79. The subjects who were not deindividuated shocked an _____ confederate more than an agreeable confederate. Deindividuated subjects shocked the obnoxious and the agreeable confedcrates _____.

obnoxious

equally

80. On Halloween children who were trick-or-treating were studied. Before the door was a bowl of candy and a bowl of money. The householder (experimenter) told them to take one piece of candy and then left them alone. Children in groups took _____ than children alone; children who had given their names took _____ than children who hadn't given their names; children in groups in which the smallest child had been appointed to make sure they just took one candy took _____ than groups in which no one was appointed.

more
less

more

81. Mann has investigated newspaper accounts of cases in which onlookers have baited people threatening suicide (encouraged them to jump). People are likely to bait under conditions that heighten _____, for instance, darkness or being part of a large crowd.

anonymity

Aggression and Institutions

82. In Zimbardo's prison experiment college men were _____ assigned to be either prisoners or guards.

randomly

83. Prisoners had to wear smocks and stocking caps and were assigned numbers instead of being able to use their names; this was to destroy the prisoners' sense of _____ and dignity. Guards were made to _____ with their role and feel distanced from their everyday roles by being made to wear uniforms and being addressed as "Mr. Corrections Officer" instead of by name.   individuality, identify

84. The experiment had to be _____ after six days instead of the planned twenty since the level of brutality of the guards was higher than expected.   ended (terminated)

85. One institutional factor that encouraged brutality was that the setting provided ideological _____ for the guards' treatment of the prisoners.   justification

86. Degradation, by stripping away dignity, and the reminders of humanity, makes _____ against a person easier.   brutality

Obedience and Aggression

87. The tacit _____ of the experimenter was one reason for the brutality of the guards.   approval

88. In the Milgram experiment subjects were ordered by an authority to deliver increasingly _____ shocks to a protesting victim. Contrary to expectations _____ subjects obeyed the orders of the experimenters. In the immediate presence of a(n) _____ people were not able to bring their common, moral sense to bear on their immediate situation.   dangerous (painful) most authority

89. Our willingness to evade our common, moral sense and obey authorities is a factor in the disinhibition of _____.   aggression

Self-Test

1. Aggression is
   a. any harm doing.
   b. intentional harm doing.
   c. accidental harm doing.
   d. nasty feelings toward someone.

2. Punching someone
   a. as a way to steal their wallet is instrumental aggression.
   b. as a way to steal their wallet is impulsive aggression.
   c. because they have insulted you is instrumental aggression.
   d. as a way to steal their wallet is emotional aggression.

3. The violence in instrumental aggression
   a. has as its direct object hurting someone.
   b. is a byproduct of some other goal.
   c. is an emotional over-reaction.
   d. all of the above

4. The violence in impulsive aggression
   a. is a byproduct of some other goal.
   b. is a byproduct of instrumental aggression.
   c. has as its direct object hurting someone.
   d. all of the above

5. There is (are)
   a. only one type of aggression in animals.
   b. several types, but they are all triggered by the same stimuli.
   c. several types, but the behavioral manifestations of aggression in animals are always the same.
   d. several types that vary by having different triggering stimuli, different behavioral manifestations, and different neural and hormonal underpinnings.

6. A cat exhibiting predatory aggression
   a. is a hunter.
   b. will silently stalk a mouse.
   c. will quickly bite through the mouse's neck.
   d. all of the above

7. If a cat aggresses when it is threatened or in pain
   a. it does so silently.
   b. it uses its teeth.
   c. it lashes out with its paws, hisses, and its hair stands on end.
   d. all of the above

8. Inter-male aggression
   a. is related to the presence of testosterone.
   b. is related to the competition of males for females.
   c. in male deer involves fighting with antlers instead of the more typical fighting with hooves yet is usually less lethal than other forms of aggression.
   d. all of the above

9. When two roosters are brought together for the first time they will furiously peck at each other. Eventually one will still peck the other, briefly, but the other will not peck back. This is called
   a. a peck order.
   b. being hen pecked.
   c. rolfing.
   d. courtship.

10. The advantage of a peck order to both of its members is
    a. the dominant member gets a feeling of satisfaction, and the subordinate member gets its masochistic cravings indulged.
    b. the dominant member gets greater access to food and hens, and the nondominant member avoids repeated losing fights.
    c. the dominant member gets greater access to food, but the nondominant member gets the sympathy of the hens.
    d. the dominant member gets food and hens, but the nondominant member gets an immediate opportunity to start the pecking battle over again.

11. A dominance hierarchy
    a. is a stable, hierarchically arranged peck order.
    b. is an intentional creation of dominant roosters.
    c. has no place for subordinate roosters.
    d. all of the above

12. Roosters may not always have a stable dominance hierarchy because
    a. who pecks who is entirely random.
    b. one individual may be dominant in regard to one resource, and another individual dominant in regard to another resource.
    c. A may peck B, and B peck C, but C may then peck A.
    d. b and c

13. A "peck order" can be seen in many human organizations. Does this mean that we are determined by some of the same genes as roosters?

a. Yes, form follows function.
b. No, when resources are limited there are just a few ways of dividing them up; the peck order in humans is *analogous* to the peck order in roosters.
c. No, it is impossible to have an instinct in lower animals that is also in humans.
d. Yes, humans have a close phyletic relationship with chickens.

14. In territorial species inter-male aggression
    a. occurs on the border of territories.
    b. occurs throughout the year.
    c. occurs as frequently in females as males, but in females the aggression is called inter-female aggression.
    d. occurs against all but dominant males.

15. Territoriality involves
    a. space defended by one member of a mating unit, typically the male.
    b. space defended against intruders.
    c. space containing the unit that breeds and cares for the young.
    d. all of the above

16. Human wars and territorial inter-male aggression are similar in that
    a. they both involve the defense of a region against the invasion of others.
    b. they both involve dominance hierarchies.
    c. they both demonstrate a general desire to dominate.
    d. all of the above

17. Human wars and territorial inter-male aggression, among birds are different in that
    a. individual birds guard their own particular territory; humans in a war are not just defending their own plot of land.
    b. individual people are embedded in a social structure during a war; birds are not.
    c. the motive of the individual human is obedience to authority; the motive of the bird is aggression against an invader of his territory.
    d. all of the above

18. Which of the following is *not* true of *sex-related* aggression?
    a. It is elicited by sexual stimuli.
    b. It is intensified by testosterone.
    c. It is dependent on sexual arousal.
    d. It is the same as inter-male aggression but is as common in females as in males.

19. Maternal aggression
    a. is released when the mother is in the hormonal state associated with having given birth and occurs only if she is in sight of her young.
    b. is misnamed since it is almost as common in fathers as in mothers.
    c. occurs even when the child is out of sight of the mother if she senses that it is in danger.
    d. is independent of any hormonal state the mother happens to be in.

20. Danger-induced aggression
    a. is the first resort of animals faced with danger.
    b. occurs when the animal can't flee, freeze, or feign death.
    c. is very similar in form to predatory aggression.
    d. is more common in males than females.

21. Irritable aggression
    a. is caused by territorial rivalry.
    b. is very different from danger-induced aggression.
    c. is caused by a variety of pains and annoyances.
    d. all of the above

22. In what way is irritable aggression and danger-induced aggression different?
    a. Only one involves sympathetic nervous system arousal.
    b. Only irritable aggression occurs in both males and females.
    c. Danger-induced aggression is usually preceded by attempts to flee, while irritable aggression is not.
    d. Irritable aggression mobilizes the parasympathetic nervous system, and danger-induced aggression does not.

23. According to Aristotle the source of human anger is
    a. the perception that one has not gotten what one wanted.
    b. the perception of an insult, or more broadly, a transgression.
    c. private and irrational.
    d. all of the above

24. Anger (in Aristotle's account)
    a. is a social matter since it is sensitive to social norms and the perceived transgression in anger implies social standards.
    b. is irrational.
    c. is not social but rather is private, personal, and unrelated to social norms.
    d. is inherently disruptive of the social order.

25. "Frustration" means
    a. a feeling of annoyance.
    b. sexual deprivation.
    c. the blocking or inhibition of a response.
    d. never having to say "I love you."

26. Dollard and his colleagues claimed that all
    a. aggression was caused by frustration.
    b. aggression was produced by low self-esteem.
    c. frustration produced aggression.
    d. a and c

27. According to this view aggression is
    a. rational.
    b. planned.
    c. an irrational lashing out to frustration even when the lashing out will do no good.
    d. an intelligent response to frustration that will usually correct the situation.

28. Since it is widely recognized that instrumental aggression is *not* caused by frustration, the frustration-aggression view now contends that
    a. frustration is sufficient for aggression.
    b. frustration is necessary for aggression.
    c. frustration is irrelevant to aggression.
    d. aggression produces frustration.

29. In an experiment in which subjects had to imagine frustrating situations, the subjects claimed that all sixteen frustrating circumstances would anger them. Pastore replicated this experiment, but added to each frustrating situation a condition in which the frustration was clearly legitimate. He found
    a. that legitimate frustrations produced more anger than illegitimate frustrations.
    b. that there was no difference in the anger produced by legitimate and illegitimate frustrations since they were all frustrating anyway.
    c. that illegitimate frustrations produced considerably more anger than legtitimate frustrations.
    d. that people did not get angry when imagining any of the frustrating scenes.

30. Some experimenters have found that in a circumstance in which aggression could not change the frustrating conditions
    a. people did not become frustrated.
    b. people became more frustrated.
    c. people did not become aggressive.
    d. people became more aggressive.

31. Mitigating information
    a. is information that the person who committed a transgression is not as bad as the transgression made it seem.
    b. reduces retaliation as compared to when there is no mitigating information.
    c. increases retaliation in most circumstances.
    d. a and b

32. In an experiment by Berkowitz subjects, while keeping their hands in annoyingly cold water or tepid water, had to assign rewards and punishments to a confederate. They were either told that punishment would help or hurt the subject's performance. In the "punishment hurts" condition
    a. subjects with their hands in warm water shocked more.
    b. subjects with their hands in cold water kept forgetting to shock because they were distracted by the annoyingly cold water.
    c. subjects with their hands in cold water shocked more.
    d. subjects in both groups hardly shocked at all.

33. The finding of the Berkowitz experiment
    a. supports the frustration-aggression hypothesis.
    b. goes against Aristotle's account since the confederate did not commit any transgression.
    c. can be handled by a modified Aristotelian account that claims that aversive states lower the threshold for the perception of transgression, and that people irrationally perceive transgressions.
    d. all of the above

34. An experiment studied frustration by varying the amount of possible reward, the prior expectation of success, and the manner of frustration (unjustified, justified, personal). How did manner of frustration affect anger?
    a. Subjects who were unjustifiably frustrated were least angry, subjects who were made to feel that the frustration was their fault were most angry, and subjects who were justifiably frustrated experienced anger between the two conditions.
    b. Subjects who were unjustifiably frustrated were most angry, subjects who were made to feel that the frustation was their fault were least angry, and subjects who were justifiably frustrated experienced anger intermediate between the two conditions.
    c. Subjects who were unjustifiably frustrated were least angry, subjects who were made to

feel that the frustration was their fault were only slightly more angry than subjects who were unjustifiably frustrated, and subjects who were justifiably frustrated experienced intense anger intermediate between the two conditions.
    d. There was no difference in the amount of anger experienced.

35. In the above experiment
    a. when the missed reward was greater, the subjects became angrier than when the reward was smaller.
    b. the size of the reward caused no difference in the amount of anger experienced.
    c. if the subjects believed that the reward was quite likely and they didn't get it, they were more frustrated than if they believed the award was unlikely.
    d. a and c

36. Subjects who had seen either an aggressive film, *Champion,* or a peaceful one were able to retaliate against a confederate who had insulted them.
    a. The subjects who saw the peaceful film retaliated more.
    b. The subjects who saw the aggressive film retaliated more, especially if the confederate had the same name as the bruised character in the film.
    c. The subjects who saw the aggressive film retaliated more *except* when the confederate had the same name as the bruised character in the film.
    d. There was no difference in retaliation that depended on which film the subjects saw.

37. The aggressive cues in the movie could have directly influenced the aggression or the subjects could have caught on to the experimenter's intent and gone along. What did Carlson find about the relation between suspecting the experimenter's intent and being aggressive?
    a. Aggressive cues only facilitate aggression with unsuspicious subjects.
    b. Aggressive cues only facilitate aggression with suspicious subjects.
    c. Aggressive cues reduced aggression in unsuspicious subjects.
    d. On reanalysis there was no relation between aggressive cues and violence for any subjects.

38. Zillmann claims that aggressive cues are
    a. inhibiting.
    b. frightening.
    c. delicious.
    d. arousing.

39. Zillmann interprets the subject's increased retaliation against the confederate after seeing the film *Champion* as being because *Champion*
    a. has more aggressive cues than the peaceful film.
    b. is sillier than the peaceful film.
    c. is more arousing than the control film.
    d. all of the above

40. According to Zillmann, the arousal in the *Champion* experiment
    a. transfers to the anger of the subject and the aggression against the confederate.
    b. inhibits aggression.
    c. distracts the subject.
    d. has no noticeable effect.

41. To demonstrate that it is arousal and not aggressive cues that cause the aggression a very sexually arousing nonaggressive film was shown in addition to *Champion* and the peaceful control film. What effect did seeing the films have?
    a. The subjects shocked the confederate most after seeing the sexual film even though there were no violent cues.
    b. The subjects shocked the confederate most after seeing the peaceful film.
    c. There was no difference in how much the subjects shocked the confederate after seeing the sexual film and the peaceful control, but the subjects shocked the confederate the most after seeing *Champion*.
    d. The subjects left the experiment in the middle of the sexual film.

42. What sorts of arousal allow for transfer of arousal to aggression?
    a. sexual arousal
    b. arousal caused by watching violent movies
    c. arousal produced by riding an exercycle
    d. all of the above

43. According to Zillmann, people try to figure out the causes of their arousal. If they think that the arousal is due to
    a. an insult, they will retaliate.
    b. someone's attractiveness, then they will feel romantic.

    c. the side effect of a drug, then they will not experience an emotion.
    d. all of the above

44. If there are two sources of arousal, exercise and being insulted,
    a. people will realize which arousal is due to the exercise and which is due to the anger at being insulted.
    b. people may mistakenly attribute some arousal caused by exercise to the arousal produced by the insult and thus over-retaliate.
    c. people will not really feel either, although they will be generally more energetic.
    d. exercise will automatically produce arousal that enhances exercise and insult will automatically produce anger.

45. Immediately after exercise the fact that the exercise is due to arousal should be quite clear, but after a while the arousal and the source of arousal should be less obvious. For this reason transfer of arousal from exercise to retaliation
    a. should be least likely immediately after exercise.
    b. should be more likely immediately after exercise.
    c. should never occur.
    d. should be moderately likely immediately after exercise.

46. Physically fit people experience a very rapid decrease of arousal while unfit people experience a slow decrease of arousal; hence according to Zillmann's transfer of arousal account, a while after exercise
    a. fit subjects should retaliate more than unfit subjects; this is what occurred.
    b. fit subjects should retaliate less than unfit subjects; this is what occurred.
    c. fit and unfit subjects should retaliate equally; this is what occurred.
    d. unfit subjects should retaliate more than fit subjects; this effect was not found.

47. Baron had a confederate insult subjects and then had the subjects see one of five progressively more sexually arousing slides. Zillmann would predict that the more the arousal the more the retaliation against the confederate. What in fact happened?
    a. The more the arousal the less the retaliation against the confederate.

b. There was no retaliation at all against the confederate after any of the sexually arousing slides.

c. All but one of the erotic slides reduced retaliation.

d. The more the arousal the more the retaliation against the confederate.

48. Zillmann explained the results of the Baron experiment by saying that sexual films produce arousal directly while slides
a. do not really produce arousal.
b. produce arousal only if the subject fantasizes to them and the fantasies distract the subject from thinking about the source of anger.
c. produce arousal only if the subject fantasizes to them and the fantasies add to the subject's anger at the confederate.
d. produce so much sexual arousal that the subject only thinks about sex.

49. In an experiment some subjects were mildly provoked and others so severely provoked that Zillmann argued that they would not be distracted by sexual slides. These subjects either saw an erotic movie or erotic slides. What did Zillmann predict and what, in fact, happened?
a. Zillmann predicted that subjects who saw the film would over-retaliate even to the mild provocation; he predicted that subjects who saw the slides would over-retaliate only to the severe provocation. This is what happened.
b. Zillmann predicted that subjects who saw the film would over-retaliate even to the mild provocation; he predicted that subjects who saw the slides would over-retaliate only to the severe provocation; this did not happen. The subjects who saw the slides shocked to both provocations.
c. Zillmann predicted that subjects would only retaliate after seeing the film. This is what happened.
d. Zillmann predicted that subjects would only retaliate after seeing the slides. This is what happened.

50. Violent crimes are more common
a. on spring days.
b. in the summer and on days with heavy pollution.

c. on the more exhilarating days that are not too hot and not polluted.
d. in the winter.

51. Date rape is rape in the context of a dating relationship. College men who commit date rape
a. are also more likely than other undergraduate males to have used deceit—such as falsely promising an engagement or marriage or falsely professing love in order to get sex.
b. believed that their activities are approved of by their friends.
c. are also more likely than other undergraduates to have tried to intoxicate a woman to get sex.
d. all of the above

52. Investigators gave male and female subjects invented newspaper accounts of rapes in which the rapist and victim were either strangers, dating, or dating and having previously voluntarily had intercourse. How did the subjects view the crime?
a. Women judged the rapes in all three situations to be more serious than men did.
b. Subjects of both sexes believed the crime to be less serious if the victim and the rapist knew each other.
c. If the rapist and victim had been dating and sexually intimate, subjects found the crime to be the least serious, even though the law does not take prior acquaintance into account when determining whether an incident is a rape or not.
d. all of the above

53. Nonviolent pornography has what effects?
a. It increases the likelihood of rape.
b. It causes transient sexual arousal and increases typical sexual behavior in both men and women.
c. It increases men's negative sex-role stereotypes toward women.
d. all of the above

54. In one study undergraduate men were asked about the amount of time they spent with erotic material and their attitudes toward women. In another experiment male volunteers were exposed to four hours of psychology films or four hours of erotica. What were the effects of the erotica on the men in these studies?

a. In the first study there was a correlation between time spent with erotica and negative attitudes toward women, but in the second there was no difference between the two groups in attitudes toward women.
b. In neither group was there any relation between time spent with nonviolent erotica and attitudes toward women.
c. In the first study there was a correlation between time spent with erotica and positive attitudes toward women; in the second group there was a more negative attitude toward women that was associated with seeing the erotic films.
d. In both groups exposure to erotica was associated with negative attitudes toward women.

55. Male and female students saw films that depicted a woman falling for someone who had abused or raped her or saw a tender, romantic film. Several days later the students filled out questionnaires about rape and violence toward women. What were the results of the study?
a. Women who had seen the "women love rape" film were even more anti-rape than they had previously been, while men were less anti-rape.
b. Both men and women who had seen the "women love rape" film were less anti-rape than they had previously been.
c. Both men and women who had seen the "women love rape" movie were more anti-rape than they had previously been.
d. There was no change in attitudes caused by seeing either the romantic or the pro-rape movie.

56. Although roughly equal numbers of husbands and wives kill each other in disputes over jealousy, the focus of these disputes is usually
a. the wife's suspicions about the husband's infidelity.
b. the husband's suspicions about the wife's infidelity.
c. infidelity, no matter if it is the husband's or the wife's.
d. over money matters even though the cause of the dispute is really sexual jealousy.

57. Children saw a bully pick on another child and either be punished for his behavior or get away with it. A control group saw a child in vigorous but not aggressive play. How did the children subsequently play with the Bobo doll?
a. Children who watched the unpunished aggression played most aggressively with a Bobo doll.

b. Children who saw vigorous, nonviolent play were most aggressive with the doll.
c. Children who saw vigorous, nonviolent play were least aggressive with the doll.
d. a and c

58. Parents were interviewed to assess the technqiues they used to control their children and then their children were observed in nursery school play. The degree to which the parents used arbitrary power, that is, disciplined the child while not explaining why,
a. was unrelated to the degree the child showed hostility in school.
b. was positively related to how cooperative the child was in school.
c. was positively related to how well the child obeyed the teacher.
d. was positively related to the degree the child showed hostility in school.

59. Parents who use arbitrary power with their children
a. teach their children not to aggress at home.
b. teach their children that aggressing is an appropriate way to get what you want.
c. model the use of arbitrary power.
d. all of the above

60. Children who had seen a violent TV program
a. became more aroused at a "real" fight than did children who had seen a peaccable TV program; this was particularly true of children whose TV diet contained a high proportion of violence.
b. became less aroused at a "real" fight than did children who had seen a peaceable TV program; the only exception to this were children whose TV diet contained a high proportion of violence.
c. became less aroused at a "real" fight than did children who had seen a peaceable TV program; this was particularly true of children whose TV diet contained a high proportion of violence.
d. were not affected by the program; there was no relation between watching a violent TV program and arousal at the sight of "real" violence.

61. Subjects who had been insulted by a confederate watched either a TV program depicting justified or unjustified aggression. They retaliated more after the program of
a. unjustified violence.
b. justified violence.

c. justified violence for female subjects but unjustified violence for male subjects.

d. unjustified violence for female subjects but justified violence for male subjects.

62. There is a well-supported relation between amount of aggressive TV that children watch and the degree to which they are hostile. This
a. shows that TV watching causes hostility.
b. shows that hostile children watch more aggressive TV.
c. shows that either TV watching causes hostility, hostility causes TV watching, or that there is some third factor that causes both the hostility and the TV watching.
d. shows that TV watching could not be the cause of hostility in children.

63. What is the correlation between the amount of violence shown on a TV episode and the popularity of that episode?
a. a very high positive correlation
b. a moderate positive correlation
c. a small but significant correlation
d. an almost zero correlation

64. TV was introduced into the United States area by area over years. Comparing the crime rates in areas before and after the introduction of TV showed
a. a moderate increase in violent crime.
b. an increase in larceny, that is, thefts.
c. an increase in both violent crimes and larceny.
d. no increase in any sort of crime.

65. "Deindividuation" is caused by
a. anonymity, including a feeling of being submerged in a crowd.
b. standing out.
c. a feeling of being the center of attention for the people who matter to you most.
d. eating too many carrots.

66. According to Zimbardo, which factors in addition to anonymity lead to deindividuation?
a. loss of a sense of responsibility
b. physiological arousal
c. intense sensory stimulation
d. all of the above

67. Zimbardo had undergraduate women dress in lab coats and hoods or wear name plates. They had to administer shock to someone. The deindividuated subjects (in the hoods) were told that the experimenter could not tell who gave

what level of shock. What were the results of the experiments?
a. The deindividuated subjects gave fewer shocks than did those for whom personal responsibility was stressed (had name plates and believed that the experimenter could tell who gave what level of shock).
b. The deindividuated subjects gave more shocks than did those for whom personal responsibility was stressed (had name plates and believed that the experimenter could tell who gave what level of shock), but only when the person to be shocked acted in an obnoxious manner.
c. "Responsible" subjects shocked less than did the deindividuated subjects, but to the extent they shocked they shocked the obnoxious confederate and the agreeable confederate equally.
d. Deindividuated subjects shocked more than responsible subjects did, and they shocked the obnoxious and the agreeable confederates equally.

68. Children who were trick-or-treating on Halloween were studied. In front of the door was a bowl of candy and a bowl of money. The householder (experimenter) told them to take one piece of candy and then left them alone. What were the results of the experiment?
a. Children in groups took more candy than children alone.
b. Children who had given their names took less than children who hadn't been asked their names.
c. Children in groups in which the smallest child had been appointed to make sure they just took one piece of candy took more than those in groups in which no one was appointed.
d. all of the above

69. Mann has investigated newspaper accounts of cases in which onlookers have baited people threatening suicide (encouraged them to jump). People are likely to bait under conditions that heighten
a. visibility.
b. the victim's ability to see an individual yelling for him to jump.
c. anonymity, such as darkness or being part of a large crowd.
d. empathy.

70. In Zimbardo's prison experiment college men were randomly assigned to be either prisoners

or guards. The prisoners were made to feel a loss of personal identifying features by being made to wear smocks and stocking caps, and to use assigned numbers instead of being able to use their names. The purpose of this was

a. to introduce uniformity to allow efficient processing.
b. to reduce the prisoners' sense of dignity and individuality and make it easier for the guards to aggress against them.
c. to make it easier for the guards to remember which prisoner was which.
d. to make adjustment to prison life easier for the prisoners.

71. In the Zimbardo experiment the guards wore uniforms and were addressed as "Mr. Corrections Officer" instead of by name. The purpose of this was

a. to make the experiment more fun for the guards and prisoners.
b. to make it easier for a prisoner to address a guard without having to remember his name.
c. to distance the guards from their everyday identity and heighten the salience of their role as "guard."
d. all of the above

72. The Zimbardo experiment was planned to last twenty days. Instead

a. it lasted ten days because funding ran out.
b. it lasted thirty days because the guards and prisoners voted to extend it.
c. it lasted twenty days but with only half of the guards and prisoners that started the experiment.
d. it lasted only six days since the level of brutality of the guards was much higher than anticipated and the experiment had to be ended.

73. One factor that encouraged brutality in the Zimbardo experiment was that

a. the setting, including the "warden" who did not intervene, provided an ideological justification for the treatment of the prisoners.
b. the guards were all sadists before they entered the experiment.
c. only mentally unstable people volunteered for the experiment.
d. all of the above

74. In the Milgram experiment subjects were ordered by an authority to deliver increasingly painful and dangerous shocks to a protesting victim. What were the results of the experiment?

a. Subjects disobeyed the orders of the experi-

menter, except for 2 percent who were sadists.
b. A majority of subjects obeyed the order, showing that in the immediate presence of an authority people were not able to bring their common, moral sense to bear on their immediate situation.
c. A majority of subjects obeyed the order, showing that people are just waiting to have a "legitimate" opportunity to aggress against others.
d. No one shocked the victim once he started to protest.

Answer Key for Self-Test

1.	b (p. 473)	38.	d (p. 492)
2.	a (p. 474)	39.	c (p. 492)
3.	b (p. 474)	40.	a (p. 492)
4.	c (p. 474)	41.	a (p. 492)
5.	d (p. 474)	42.	d (p. 492–493)
6.	d (pp. 474–475)	43.	d (p. 493)
7.	c (p. 475)	44.	b (p. 493)
8.	d (p. 476)	45.	a (p. 493)
9.	a (p. 477)	46.	b (p. 494)
10.	b (p. 477)	47.	c (p. 494)
11.	a (p. 477)	48.	b (p. 494)
12.	d (p. 477)	49.	a (p. 495)
13.	b (p. 478)	50.	b (pp. 495–496)
14.	a (p. 478)	51.	d (pp. 497–498)
15.	d (p. 478)	52.	d (p. 498)
16.	a (p. 479)	53.	b (p. 499)
17.	d (p. 479)	54.	b (p. 499)
18.	d (pp. 480–481)	55.	a (pp. 502–503)
19.	a (p. 481)	56.	b (p. 504)
20.	b (p. 482)	57.	d (p. 506)
21.	c (p. 482)	58.	d (p. 506)
22.	c (p. 482)	59.	d (p. 506)
23.	b (p. 483)	60.	c (p. 507)
24.	a (p. 484)	61.	b (p. 508)
25.	c (p. 484)	62.	c (p. 509)
26.	d (p. 484)	63.	d (p. 510)
27.	c (p. 484)	64.	b (p. 511)
28.	a (p. 484)	65.	a (p. 512)
29.	c (p. 485)	66.	d (p. 513)
30.	c (p. 486)	67.	d (p. 513)
31.	d (p. 486)	68.	d (p. 514)
32.	c (pp. 487–488)	69.	c (p. 514)
33.	d (p. 488)	70.	b (p. 514)
34.	b (p. 489)	71.	c (pp. 514–515)
35.	d (p. 489)	72.	d (p. 515)
36.	b (p. 490)	73.	a (pp. 515–516)
37.	a (p. 491)	74.	b (p. 516)

Thought Questions and Exercises

1. What are the six forms of animal aggression? What types of human aggression are like each of these? The text claims that similarity may be due to an analogy (a similar sort of solution independently arrived at to a similar sort of problem). What might the analogy be for each parallel? (Hint: The text discusses the analogy between territorial aggression and war in humans. You might use this as a model.)

2. The Aristotelian account of anger makes anger quite rational; the frustration-aggression account makes it totally irrational. Think back to times that you have been made angry. What was the object or trigger of the anger? Did you just feel frustrated, or did you feel that something wrong, mean, unfair had happened to you? Collect ten incidents of anger and see which model seems to apply better. Can you apply the view that anger is due to a perceived unfairness, transgression, but that frustration and arousal intensify the anger (and even cause people to misperceive innocent mishaps as transgressions)?

3. You can replicate Pastore's experiment comparing people's reactions to justified and unjustified frustration. Remember Pastore took common frustrations such as missing a bus and asked people how angry they would become. In one version the bus said "out of service"; in the other the bus had riders and it was obvious the driver had noticed the people waiting. Think of ten situations with justified and unjustified variants, for example, your date doesn't meet you— because she couldn't tear herself away from a soap opera, or because she had to accompany a sick relative to the hospital. Measure anger by asking people to rate how angry they would feel from 1 (not angry at all) to 10 (furious).

4. You can use the procedure described in #3 to study the effect of excuses, justifications, and mitigations on how angry people become at a transgression. One version of the scene should contain the bald transgression and the other should contain the same transgression but with a mitigation, excuse, or justification.

5. The problem of date rape is just beginning to get attention as a serious policy issue. Male undergraduates may want to interview other male undergraduates as to what sort of pressure they feel is fair to apply to women to have sex— e.g., would they have sex with a woman who has passed out from drinking at a party? Also ask questions about women's rights, women's intelligence, and whether the men have close nonsexual female friends. It will be interesting to explore attitudes on your campus toward the use of deceit, fraud, and force to have sex, and then to relate these attitudes toward women in general. (Think up a list of "pressuring" situations, from the most mild—one that you think would meet approval from even women—to the most severe—forcible rape—and ask which your interviewee has done, which he thinks that he might do if in certain situations. I'd suggest collaborating with some of your female classmates when making the list of pressuring situations.)

6. The research up to this point shows that nonviolent pornography or erotica does not have a negative effect on attitudes toward women, toward rape, and toward violence against women. On the other hand, violent pornography or depictions of women enjoying rape do appear to have a negative effect on male attitudes toward women. Do people's attitudes toward pornography reflect this distinction or are attitudes polarized, so that some people believe that all pornography or erotica leads to derogation of women and some believe that no pornography or erotica does?

7. Remember the experiment that compared arousal to a tape of a rape both when the subject drinks alcohol and when he thinks he has been drinking (even though he wasn't). What does this say about the dangers of drinking that aren't due to the pharmacological effects of alcohol?

8. The most important difference between animal and human aggression is that most human aggression is in an institutional context. What do the Milgram obedience and the Zimbardo prison studies have to tell us about the dangers of aggression from people who may be, initially at least, quite friendly, mild, and unfrustrated?

CHAPTER 14

Interpersonal Attraction

Learning Objectives

PROPINQUITY

Westgate

1. Describe why the Westgate project was an ideal real-life laboratory for studying the development of friendships. What was found to be the most important determinant of friendship choice?

Functional Distance and Liking

2. Explain the difference between "physical distance" and "functional distance." Does the distance effect make a difference only for relatively large distances—e.g., between Baltimore and Philadelphia—or does it have an effect over small (even very small) distances? Does distance also come into play when people are choosing spouses? What is the evidence?

MERE EXPOSURE

3. Give Zajonc's evidence that the more one sees a nonsense word (or picture) the more likely one is to believe that it has a pleasant meaning (refer to a laboratory study and a field study).
4. Describe the experiment in which Zajonc showed that mere exposure predicts our liking for strangers.
5. Amount of exposure doesn't always predict liking. Zajonc believes that the relation between liking and exposure is shaped like an inverse U. What does this mean? Give an example of something that you first liked to a greater extent the more you heard (or saw) it and then began to like less the more you heard (or saw) it.

SIMILARITY

6. Heider proposed another explanation for attraction, saying that it is related to the human tendency to prefer cognitive balance to imbalance. What does this mean? Give an example.

Research on Similarity of Attitudes and Attraction

7. According to balance theory, we should prefer that people we already like share our attitudes, and we should prefer that people we become attracted to also share our attitudes. Describe Newcomb's attempt to test this hypothesis. Did Newcomb's subjects initially perceive the people they were attracted to as having similar attitudes? Did they have similar attitudes? Were subjects' perceptions more accurate toward the end of the study?
8. Describe Byrne's "bogus stranger" technique. How was it used to show that perceived similarity is a key determinant in liking?

Explanations for Relation of Similarity and Attraction

9. Describe Byrne's explanation for why similarity is attractive. What is his evidence? (Include physiological effects of perceived attractiveness.)
10. Elliot Aronson has proposed another reason why we like similar people: We believe that they will like us. Describe a study in which Aronson shows that it is perceived liking and not similarity alone that causes attraction.
11. Explain what it is about a shared attitude that makes the people sharing it attractive to each other. What is it for Heider, for Byrne, for Aronson?
12. For Heider, Byrne, and Aronson the more important a shared attitude the more the liking. Deborah Davis has evidence that liking is not influenced

by the importance of the attitude but by how the attitude affects interaction. Explain. Make up an illustration contrasting importance with effect on interaction. What did Davis do to test her hypothesis?

Similarity and Discrediting Traits
13. Describe when similarity doesn't breed liking. In the experiment in which subjects interact with an obnoxious confederate, did they like the subject more when they found that they shared many traits in common or few traits in common? Show how this finding doesn't contradict the proposed explanations for why similarity leads to liking.

EVALUATION

Patterning of Evaluation and Attraction
14. Aronson proposes that we not only react to the content of another's evaluation but also to its pattern. What does he mean by this? Whom would we like more, someone who initially had a negative view of us that turned positive or someone who has had a positive view of us all along? Briefly describe Aronson's experimental demonstration of this point.

Ingratiation and Attraction
15. It might seem that the easiest way to get someone to like you is to pretend to like them. How might this backfire? Describe what "ingratiation" is. In an experiment by Jones and others, confederates were instructed either to act very aggreeably or "respectful but autonomous" to a subject. Subjects were told either that the confederate had been instructed to act the way he acted or that he was acting spontaneously. Describe the results of the experiment. In what condition did the autonomous confederate get "extra credit"? In what ways does this experiment demonstrate the importance of perceived sincerity as a determinant of liking?

Competence and Attraction
16. Competence isn't always attractive. According to Aronson, what we like is "competence in a human package." Describe his experiment demonstrating this. Who did subjects like more, the graceful, competent student or the competent student who spilled coffee on himself? Did clumsiness improve the popularity of the mediocre student? A later study showed that high, medium, and low self-esteem people react differently to this scene. Explain.

PHYSICAL ATTRACTIVENESS

Attractiveness and Culture
17. Give some examples of standards of beauty that are universal. Are there evolutionary reasons why this might be the case?
18. Cunningham argues that neoteny is a universal determinant of female beauty. What is "neoteny"? What is his evidence that neotenous features are likely to be seen as more attractive?

Physical Attractiveness and Dating
19. Compare the importance of physical attractiveness with shared interests, extroversion, and intelligence for the success of an initial date. Give the "computer dance" experiment as evidence. Is the relation between liking and physical attractiveness true for both males and females? In this study what other variables, if any, contributed to liking for one's date?

The Matching Hypothesis
20. If people are attempting to get the most attractive partner that they can, then couples should wind up being roughly matched on attractiveness. Why should this be the case? How is this a simple consequence of "market forces"? What is the evidence for this hypothesis?
21. Describe the relation between attractiveness of their spouses and satisfaction with their marriage for both men and women. What is the relation between marital satisfaction and the perception of how attractive their spouses find them for both men and women?

Physical Attractiveness and Same-Gender Relationships
22. Describe the relation between physical attractiveness and popularity for people of the same gender. Are the most attractive people the most popular?

Physical Attractiveness and Task Evaluation
23. Give an experimental example showing how a person's physical attractiveness can influence how well we think of that person's work.
24. Give the evidence showing that physically attractive people are believed to have more positive qualities than unattractive people.
25. Describe the evidence as to whether physically attractive people are in fact more socially skilled than others. Does this fact modify your interpretation of why attractive people in the "computer dance study" did so well? Explain.

26. Describe the experiment that demonstrates that merely being *thought to be* attractive makes a person more self-confident, warmer, and outgoing. Is this effect true of both sexes or just one?

ANXIETY AND AFFILIATION

27. Describe Schachter's experimental demonstration that people who are scared or anxious prefer to wait with others rather than wait alone. What was Schachter's control group? Why was this control group necessary?
28. What sort of company did Schachter's subjects want to wait with? Was any company as good as any other? Did they want only company they could talk to about what was worrying them? How did Schachter show this? Show how the results of these experiments support Schachter's hypothesis that it was the desire for social comparison that made the subjects want to wait with others.
29. Affiliation under stressful conditions is not desired by all people. Who desires it?

Anxiety and Affiliation: Follow-up Research

30. Do people who are worried that they will be embarrassed wish to wait with others who face the same embarrassment? How does this finding affect Schachter's hypothesis?

Affiliation in Real-Life Anxiety-producing Situations

31. Did women who were about to give birth prefer to be with other women also about to give birth? If they were placed with other women also about to give birth, what did they discuss? How does this finding affect Schachter's hypothesis?
32. Give evidence for the conclusion that comparing one's emotional state to other people's is sometimes a reason to affiliate when anxious, but so is desire for reassurance. Describe the study of men facing life-threatening surgery and who they preferred to have as roommates.

Being with Others and Anxiety

33. Describe Wrightsman's experiment and whether he found that waiting with other people reduced anxiety more than did waiting alone. Did his results vary for first-borns as opposed to people in general?
34. Compare Schachter's findings about whether people prefer to wait with others to Wrightsman's findings about the effects on anxiety of waiting with others. What is the "homogenization" of anxiety? How does the fact that anxiety homogenizes in groups support the claim that anxious people compare their emotional states?

Programmed Exercises

PROPINQUITY

Westgate

1. The Westgate project showed the powerful effect of _____ on friendship choice.

propinquity

Functional Distance and Liking

2. The type of distance that most determined friendship choice was _____ rather than physical.

functional

3. Marriage choice is also strongly influenced by _____.

propinquity

Mere Exposure

4. According to Zajonc, mere exposure to something leads to increased _____ for it.

liking

5. The more subjects saw made-up "Turkish" words the more they thought the words had a _____ meaning.

pleasant (good)

6. The more often subjects bumped into another subject in Zajonc's experiment the more _____ they rated her.

positively

7. Beyond a certain point more exposure may _____ liking. The relationship between exposure and liking is shaped like an inverse _____.

decrease
U

SIMILARITY

8. If Al likes Bill and Bill likes Al and both dislike Ninja Turtles, they are in a _____ state.

balanced

9. If both Al and Bill like each other, but Al likes baseball and Bill is bored by it then they are in an _____ state.

unbalanced

10. According to Heider, people are psychologically drawn toward _____ states and away from _____ states.

balanced
unbalanced

11. According to Heider, we prefer that people we like _____ our attitudes.

share

12. Newcomb found that when people are first attracted to each other they are likely to believe that they are _____ similar in belief than they really are.

more

13. After people got to know each other _____ depended on real agreement.

attraction

14. Byrne's _____ _____ technique falsely makes people think that others are very similar or dissimilar to them.

bogus stranger

Explanations for Relation of Similarity and Attraction

15. Byrne believes that similarity produces attraction because similarity is _____.

reinforcing

16. For this reason similarity should produce a bodily _____, and if it doesn't then similarity should _____ produce attraction.

reaction (arousal)
not

17. Aronson suggests that the reason we like similar people is that we like people who _____ us and believe that similar people are _____ likely to like us.

like, more

18. In Aronson's experiment confederates who _____ with the subject but liked him were liked as much as those who agreed with the subject.

disagreed

19. Byrne believes that the more _____ an issue is to you the more similarity on that issue will produce liking.

important

20. Davis, on the other hand, believes that liking is not proportional to the importance of agreed-on issues but rather depends on how much the agreement or disagreement on the issues will affect _____.

interaction

Similarity and Discrediting Traits

21. If someone has undesirable traits we will dislike him or her more if he is _____ us.

like (similar to)

EVALUATION

Patterning of Evaluation and Attraction

22. In Aronson's experiment, subjects liked most the partner who first evaluated them _____ and then later evaluated them _____.

negatively, positively

23. According to Aronson's "law of infidelity," the constant loving spouse is at a _____ compared to someone demonstrating a new attraction.

disadvantage

24. Berscheid in contrast showed that when subjects were exposed to continuous regard and new regard *at the same time* they preferred _____ regard.

continuous

Ingratiation and Attraction

25. An ingratiator's praise is not _____.

sincere

26. In Jones's experiment subjects liked a confederate who they thought had praised them _____ more than one who they believed was instructed to praise them.

spontaneously

27. The confederate who withheld praise, in a respectful manner, was liked more if she was seen as going _____ instructions to be agreeable.

against

Competence and Attraction

28. In Aronson's "College Bowl" experiment a very competent fellow who spilled coffee on himself was liked _____ than one who did not. This held most strongly with people who have _____ self-esteem.

more
moderate

29. A mediocre fellow who spilled coffee on himself was liked _____ than one who did not.

less

PHYSICAL ATTRACTIVENESS

Attractiveness and Culture

30. Cleanliness, a good complexion, and perhaps plumpness are near _____ standards of female beauty.

universal

31. _____ features are features that the young of many species share.

Neotenous

32. Female faces judged to be more attractive by males were also found to be more _____.

neotenous

Physical Attractiveness and Dating

33. In the computer dance study, _____ _____ was more important than intelligence, similarity of attitudes, or extroversion when measuring satisfaction with one's partner on the first date. This result was true of _____ sex(es).

physical attractiveness

both

The Matching Hypothesis

34. The "matching hypothesis" predicts that couples will be roughly _____ on physical attractiveness. This is a consequence of _____ forces, the same forces that determine the price of shoes.

matched
market

Physical Attractiveness and Same-Gender Relationships

35. The most attractive men and women in a same-sex dorm were most likely to be
_____ by their dorm-mates.   rejected

Physical Attractiveness and Task Evaluation

36. Male students were asked to evaluate an essay. Attached to it was a picture of
an attractive or unattractive woman. The males' rating of the essay was
_____ by the appearance of the author.   affected

37. When subjects were asked to rate people's traits just on the basis of their
pictures they rated attractive people more _____.   favorably

38. It has been found that physically attractive men and women are to some extent
_____ socially skilled than others.   more

39. In the computer dance study, attractive people may have been so popular not
only because of attractiveness but because they are more likely to be

_____ _____.   socially skilled

40. Men had a ten-minute phone talk with a woman they thought to be attractive or
unattractive. Women who the men thought were attractive were _____   more
self-confident and warm than those who the men thought were unattractive.

ANXIETY AND AFFILIATION

41. In Schachter's experiment on anxiety and affiliation, a group of subjects waiting
to be shocked preferred to wait _____.   together

42. Schachter proposed that anxious people wished to wait with others so that they   reactions,
can compare their _____. This is called _____ _____.   social comparison

43. _____-_____ children experience more anxiety than   First-born
_____-_____ and wish to affiliate when anxious.   later-borns

Anxiety and Affiliation: Follow-up Research

44. People who are worried that they will be embarrassed _____ company.   avoid

Affiliation in Real-Life Anxiety-producing Situations

45. In studies of anxiety and affiliation in hospitals, women waiting to give birth
prefer to wait _____. When waiting with others in the same situation,   alone
they do not want to talk about the _____.   delivery

46. Patients waiting for life-threatening surgery wanted _____ rather than   reassurance
_____ _____.   social comparison

Being with Others and Anxiety

47. Waiting with others in a stressful situation reduces anxiety in _____-   first-borns
_____.

48. Waiting with others while stressed produces a _____ of anxiety, in   homogenization
that the anxiety levels of the group members are more similar to each other
than they were before they waited together.

Self-Test

1. In the Westgate study the most powerful determinant of who would be friends was
   a. religion.
   b. physical or functional distance.
   c. where people were born.
   d. money.

2. Which of the following have been found to be effects of propinquity?
   a. In the Westgate study it was found that a family living two doors down from another was only one-half as likely to socialize with them than with a family living next door.
   b. Functional distance, the way that spatial layout affects the likelihood that people will casually bump into each other, is a more important determinant of liking than physical distance.
   c. The nearer the neighbor, the greater the likelihood for disliking as well as liking.
   d. all of the above

3. According to Zajonc's studies, mere exposure to something leads to
   a. indifference.
   b. hostility.
   c. curiosity.
   d. liking.

4. If Mary and Fran like each other and also like baseball but neither can stand Bill then
   a. their relationship is "balanced."
   b. their relationship is "unbalanced."
   c. their relationship is probably unstable.
   d. they probably will stop being friends.

5. Newcomb found that when two people are first attracted to each other they are likely to think that their beliefs
   a. are quite different from each other.
   b. are irrelevant to their relationship.
   c. are more similar than they really are.
   d. are quite similar since they really are.

6. Byrne argues that similarity produces attraction because
   a. it is a sign of future compatibility.
   b. it is reinforcing.
   c. it is a balanced state.
   d. it is desirable.

7. Aronson believes that similarity produces attraction because similarity is a sign that something else is probably the case. What?

   a. Similarity is a sign of mutual strengths and weaknesses.
   b. Similarity is a sign that the other will like you.
   c. Similarity is a sign of reinforcement.
   d. Similarity is a sign that you are not too different.

8. In Aronson's experiment confederates who disagreed with the subject but liked him were
   a. liked less than those who had similar attitudes.
   b. liked less than those with similar attitudes who disliked him.
   c. liked as much as those who had similar attitudes and liked him.
   d. Liking for the confederate was not influenced by whether the confederate liked the subject or not.

9. Davis believes that similarity produces liking because
   a. it is reinforcing.
   b. it is a sign of probable liking.
   c. it is a balanced state.
   d. it makes interaction easier.

10. According to Davis which of the following pairs will like each other most?
    a. two people who share religious and political beliefs that they consider important but that do not come up much in everyday life
    b. two people who share an interest in listening to rock music and going to concerts as frequently as they can
    c. a partisan Republican and a partisan Democrat since opposites attract
    d. any of the above depending on individual temperament

11. If someone has undesirable traits
    a. we will dislike her more if she is unlike us.
    b. we will dislike her less if she is unlike us.
    c. we will dislike her equally whether she is like us or unlike us.
    d. we will tend to like her out of sympathy for her.

12. In an experiment by Aronson on the effect of the pattern of another's evaluation of us upon our liking for them it was found that subjects liked a partner most who
    a. consistently evaluated them positively.
    b. first evaluated them negatively and later evaluated them positively.
    c. consistently evaluated them negatively.
    d. first evaluated them positively and later evaluated them negatively.

13. In Jones's experiment, subjects liked a confederate more if they thought that he praised them
    a. under orders.
    b. spontaneously.
    c. because they were similar.
    d. because he wanted to ingratiate.

14. In Aronson's College Bowl experiment, a very competent contestant who spilled coffee on himself
    a. was liked more than one who didn't.
    b. was liked less than one who didn't.
    c. was liked the same amount as one who didn't.
    d. Only incompetent contestants are liked more if they spill coffee.

15. Cross-cultural universals for attractiveness (in women)
    a. do not exist.
    b. include cleanliness, a good complexion, and "neotenous features."
    c. include thinness.
    d. include athletic ability.

16. What trait was most important for men and women for a successful first date in the computer dance study?
    a. intelligence
    b. similarity of attitudes
    c. extroversion
    d. physical attractiveness

17. The matching hypothesis
    a. predicts that couples will be roughly matched on attractiveness.
    b. predicts that in a couple the female will be more attractive (compared to other females) than the male will be (compared to other males).
    c. works on a different principle than economic studies of supply and demand.
    d. predicts that male attractiveness is not important.

18. The most attractive men and women in a same-sex dorm were most likely to be
    a. sought out.
    b. treated like everyone else.
    c. rejected.
    d. admired.

19. Males were asked to evaluate an essay supposedly written by either an attractive or unattractive female. The essays
    a. by the attractive and unattractive female were judged to be equal.
    b. by the attractive female were judged to be better.
    c. by the unattractive female were judged to be better.
    d. by the unattractive female were judged to be better only if the essay was quite good.

20. Investigators rated high school photos of college dorm-mates for attractiveness. They found that
    a. the students they had rated most attractive were the most popular with their dorm-mates.
    b. the students they had rated as slightly less attractive were the most likely to be accepted by their dorm-mates.
    c. the students they had rated most attractive were the most likely to be rejected by their dorm-mates.
    d. b and c

21. Attractive people are judged more favorably because
    a. we have favorable stereotypes about them.
    b. they in fact are to some extent more socially skilled than unattractive people.
    c. they are responded to more favorably and hence respond more warmly and self-confidently.
    d. all of the above

22. Knowing one is thought attractive
    a. does not affect behavior or attitudes.
    b. has been found to affect self-confidence, warmth, and outgoingness.
    c. causes people to panic.
    d. only influences behavior if the person is genuinely attractive.

23. In Schachter's experiment on anxiety and affiliation, subjects who thought they would be shocked wanted
    a. to wait alone.
    b. to wait with other people but not those who also would be shocked.
    c. to wait with other people who were also going to be shocked.
    d. to wait with others or alone; it didn't matter.

24. Schachter believes that these subjects wanted to wait together
    a. because they wanted to be distracted.
    b. because they just wanted someone to talk to.
    c. to compare notes.
    d. to see if their reactions are similar to the others—social comparison.

25. Joe, Bill, Mary, and Tanya are about to take an exam in an hour. Joe is most anxious and Tanya is least anxious. Waiting as a group would
    a. help Joe but make Tanya more upset.
    b. help all the students.
    c. make all the students more upset.
    d. help Mary and Tanya but not Joe and Bill.

26. People who are facing embarrassment
    a. seek out others facing embarrassment.
    b. avoid company, but if they have to have company most prefer people facing the same embarrassment.
    c. avoid company, but if they have to have company prefer not to be with people facing the same embarrassment.
    d. are comfortable with company or alone.

27. Patients waiting for life-threatening surgery prefer to wait with someone who
    a. has just been through the surgery.
    b. is awaiting the same surgery.
    c. has not and will not undergo surgery.
    d. They would prefer to wait alone.

28. The studies on anxiety, embarrassment, and affiliation show
    a. that social comparison is one reason why we affiliate with others when "stressed" but not the only reason.
    b. that social comparison is the only reason we affiliate with others when stressed.
    c. that we always want to affiliate with others when stressed.
    d. that reassurance is always a less important motive than social comparison.

29. Waiting with others in stressful situations really reduces anxiety
    a. for everyone.
    b. for no one.
    c. for first-borns.
    d. for last-borns.

30. After waiting with others in a stressful situation the levels of anxiety of the group members are
    a. more similar to each other than before they waited with the group.
    b. more different from each other than before they waited with the group.
    c. the same as when they went in.
    d. unchanged.

Answer Key for Self-Test

1.	b (p. 524)	16.	d (p. 541)
2.	d (p. 524)	17.	a (p. 542)
3.	d (p. 526)	18.	c (p. 543)
4.	a (p. 528)	19.	b (p. 543)
5.	c (p. 529)	20.	d (p. 543)
6.	b (p. 531)	21.	d (pp. 543–544)
7.	b (p. 532)	22.	b (p. 544)
8.	c (p. 532)	23.	c (pp. 546–547)
9.	d (p. 533)	24.	d (p. 547)
10.	b (p. 533)	25.	a (p. 547)
11.	b (p. 534)	26.	c (p. 548)
12.	b (p. 535)	27.	a (p. 549)
13.	b (p. 536)	28.	a (p. 549)
14.	a (p. 538)	29.	c (p. 550)
15.	b (p. 539)	30.	a (p. 550)

Thought Questions and Exercises

1. Various studies have shown the very powerful effect of nearness on one's choice of friends and lovers. Is this true for you? Make a list of your best friend and boyfriends or girlfriends over the last five years. How did you meet them? Where did they live, attend class, exercise, and so on, in relation to you?

2. According to Zajonc mere exposure leads to increased liking. Will this be true of tastes people initially dislike? Sample sodas, drinks, snack foods, vegetables, and so on, and find some that you think people will dislike. Perhaps one is sickeningly sweet or another has an odd flavor. Recruit four or five of your friends. Have them rate the taste of the soda from 1 (the most awful taste ever) to 10 (the best taste). Over a period of a week have them taste and rate the drink six or seven times. Do they like it more by the end? Did the people who most disliked the initial taste change the most? Did they change the least? If you have any food or drink you really dislike you might want to try it seven or eight times and see if the Zajonc principle will work for you.

3. According to Newcomb when we first become friendly with someone we think that their beliefs are more similar to our own than they really are. With friends of long standing there is also a

perceived attitude congruence, but it is based on real similarity. Do you have any relatively new friends? Make a list of issues and attitudes that are important to you and guess your friend's positions. Have your friend do the same. Did you believe that his or her attitudes were very like yours? Were you right? Where you disagreed, did your friend think that you were more similar to him or her than you were and vice versa? Do the same with a friend of long standing.

4. Aronson argues that the reason why we tend to like people who are similar to us is that we like people who like us and believe that similar people are more likely to like us. Think back over the close friends that you have had over the years. Were any of them really different than you were in beliefs and temperament? How did you handle these differences? Have you ever found yourself liking someone who was really different when you discovered that they thought you were really nice?

5. Many studies seem to show that attractive people are in general evaluated more favorably even for tasks that have nothing to do with physical beauty. You might want to do a simplified replication of the Landy and Sigall (1974) study reported on page 543 of your text. Have subjects grade an essay. Attach to the essay a picture of a quite attractive man, an unattractive man, a quite attractive woman, or an unattractive woman. Will the person's looks affect how the essay is graded? If yes, does this happen for the opposite sex, for the same sex, or for both? Does it happen for male subjects, female subjects, or both?

CHAPTER 15

Relationships

Learning Objectives

FRIENDSHIP

What Is a Friend?

1. Explain what "voluntary interdependence" is. In what sense might friendship be related to voluntary interdependence? What aspect of friendship does "voluntary interdependence" leave out?

2. Wright proposes that friends provide each other with three sorts of goods. What are they? Why is friendship and other social support associated with better physical and psychological well-being?

Self-Disclosure

3. Explain what "self-disclosure" is. What is the relationship between lack of self-disclosure and loneliness?

Self-Disclosure and Reciprocity

4. In Jourard's study describe the relation between disclosing intimate information to someone and receiving intimate information from that person. What was the relation between the degree of mutual self-disclosure and liking?

5. In an experiment on the relation between self-disclosure and liking, after a ten-minute conversation female subjects privately rated how much they liked each other. They then chose to ask the other person one of seven questions varying in intimacy. What was the relation between initial liking and the intimacy of the question asked? Did disclosure increase liking? Did it increase return disclosure?

6. Explain how both Jourard's position and this experiment can both be seen as examples of exchange

theory. How do they illustrate the "norm of reciprocity"?

Gender Differences in Self-Disclosure

7. Understand that there are gender differences in self-disclosure. How do men differ from women in self-disclosure? What, in general, is the difference between men's and women's friendships? How does this difference relate to norms of self-disclosure for men and women?

8. Use the "intimate disclosure on the airplane" experiment to show that both males and females find disclosing males and nondisclosing females maladjusted. What are the limits—concerning appropriate amounts of self-disclosure—to this finding? What is the evidence that both men and women understand self-disclosure to be a "good"?

Reciprocity and Expressions of Concern

9. Describe ways to meet the demands of reciprocity in response to a self-disclosure other than by making another self-disclosure. In Berg and Archer's study was self-disclosure in response to a self-disclosure the most attractive response?

The Drawbacks of Friendship

10. Describe some negative aspects of friendship. What is "envy"? In at least one context distinguish between envy and jealousy. Describe some things that determine people's reactions to the success of a friend. How can a person choose friends to avoid situations that lead to envy?

Loneliness

11. Describe some of the experiences included on the UCLA Loneliness Scale that are indicative of being lonely. What are the two fundamental

aspects of loneliness (as found by the scale)? What are some traits that have been found to be correlated with loneliness? What percent of the population is experiencing intense loneliness at any moment?

ROMANTIC LOVE

What Is Romantic Love?

Features of Romantic Love

12. Describe the necessary features of romantic love. According to Zick Rubin's work what else is there besides sexual attraction that distinguishes romantic love from mere liking?
13. Describe what Sternberg believes are the three elements of love. How are "romantic love," "companionate love," and "consummate love" made up of different blends of these three elements?

Romantic Love as an Adventure

14. Explain how the interruption of routines, living for the moment, and a sense of "internal continuity" contribute to the sense of romantic love as an adventure, as something apart from our drab everyday world. In what sense is love like gambling? Why is it that the very specialness of love as an adventure means that romantic love will wane?
15. Describe some of the virtues of post-romantic long-term relationships.

The Enhancement of Romantic Love

16. According to Schachter and Singer the experience of emotion consists of two parts. What are they? How do Berscheid and Walster apply Schachter and Singer's theory to romantic love?

Physiological Arousal and Romantic Love

17. Dutton and Aron conducted an experiment using two bridges, one scary and one boring, to test Berscheid and Walster's conception of romantic love. Describe the experiment. Crossing over which bridge aroused more interest in the pretty research assistant? Why? How did Dutton and Aron rule out alternative interpretations?
18. What is Kenrick and Cialdini's alternative explanation of this experiment? Why is this "calming" interpretation not tenable? Kenrick now believes that arousal itself facilitates any reaction, positive or negative. How can this explain the original Dutton and Aron results?

Jealousy

19. Describe what provokes jealousy. Explain why evolutionary theory would predict on average a difference between male and female jealousy. Describe some of the features of jealousy in our culture.

PREMARITAL ROMANTIC RELATIONSHIPS

Relationship Stability

20. Describe the factors that predicted whether the couples in the Boston study of premarital relationships would be together in two years. Which partner was more likely to determine whether the couple would be sexually intimate? Did sexual intimacy contribute to or distract from the couples overall satisfaction with the relationship or the odds that they would be together after two years?

Exchange and Equity in Premarital Relationships

21. Describe exchange theory's central proposition concerning relationships. In what way are the rewards and costs in a particular relationship relative to our comparison level for such a relationship?
22. Describe how relationships differ in the kinds of things exchanged. In what way(s) is the exchange of "goods" in a relationship different than the exchange of money and goods at the grocery store? How do "love" and "money" differ on the particularism dimension? How do "love" and "cars" differ on the concreteness-symbolic dimension?
23. Describe how equity theory differs from exchange theory. Describe the relation between equitableness of a relationship and the likelihood that a relationship is sexual. Does equity affect satisfaction with and stability of a relationship?
24. Describe the evidence that although equity matters the absolute level of rewards matters even more.

Investment in a Relationship and Stability

25. Discuss the role that having other alternatives and the amount of investment in a relationship play in determining commitment to a relationship.
26. Explain how investment in a relationship can lead to commitment. What is the fallacy of sunk costs? Why is it a fallacy? Is staying in a relationship because of your investment in it necessarily an example of sunk costs? Why should investment in a relationship genuinely count for something?

Communal Relationships and Exchange

27. Describe what communal relationships are. How are they different from exchange relationships? Describe the "joint payment" experiment, which

attempts to illustrate the influence of communal relationships on behavior.

The Desire for Intimacy

28. Describe McAdams's evidence that there is a type of person who seeks out "communal" relationships.
29. Fiske argues that there are four different types of personal relationships. What are they? Give an example of each. Can the same person experience all four types of relationships? What is the evidence that parental and romantic relationships aren't only exchange relationships?

Cohabitation

30. Describe what "cohabitation" is. Give two possible causes for the increase in cohabitation since the 1970s. Is cohabitation typically a stage on the path to marriage or a long-term alternative to marriage?
31. Describe how the cohabiting couples in the Boston study were similar to and different from the dating couples—in satisfaction with the relationship, in intention to marry, in likelihood to be married or split up by the end of the study, and in marital satisfaction if they did marry each other. The Gainsville, Florida, study had a different result. What was it?

Who Chooses Whom?

Homogamy

32. Define "homogamy." What is Burgess and Wallin's evidence that we marry people similar to ourselves (similar as compared to a randomly selected couple)?

Complementarity of Needs

33. Explain what is meant by "complementarity of needs." What is the evidence that people select mates on the basis of complementarity as well as similarity?

MARRIAGE

Love and Marriage in Sixteenth-Century England

34. Stone points out that our culture has three interrelated beliefs about marriage. What are they? Were these beliefs also common in the sixteenth century? Did the notion of romantic love exist in the sixteenth century? Was it seen as an appropriate basis for marriage?

Changing Conceptions of Marriage and the Family

35. Describe how the institution of marriage has changed historically. What has contributed to this change? What is the "marriage squeeze"? How has it contributed to this change?

Marital Satisfaction

Marital Satisfaction and Self-Disclosure

36. Describe the relation between marital satisfaction and self-disclosure.

Sex-Role Attitudes and Marital Satisfaction

37. Until the mid-1960s it was found that marriages were happiest if the partners fulfilled their assigned sex roles. What has been found more recently? Which marriages are the least satisfying?

Children and Satisfaction in Marriage

38. Describe the relation between having children and marital satisfaction. How does the division of household labor change after the birth of a child? What happens to the amount of time that husbands and wives are able to devote to their careers? What is the relationship between wives' marital satisfaction and the extent that the division of labor becomes a traditional division after the birth of a child?

Marital Satisfaction and Power

39. Explain what is meant by "power" in a relationship. What are strong power tactics and weak power tactics? Do dependent partners use weak tactics regardless of sex? Do wives use weak tactics more than husbands, leaving aside degree of dependence? Does the likelihood of using weak tactics depend more on the gender of the person using it or on the gender of the target? How does the division of power affect marital satisfaction?

Marital Satisfaction and Behavioral Exchange

40. Describe the differences in everyday interaction between distressed and happy couples. Distressed couples are more "reactive" to the events of the day in judging how satisfied they are with their relationship than are happy couples. Explain.
41. Explain how distressed and nondistressed couples differ in interpreting their partner's messages. What is the "communication deficit" model? Is a distressed couple or a nondistressed couple more accurate in detecting the partners' emotional reactions?
42. Describe what is meant by "negative affect reciprocity." How do distressed couples particularly demonstrate this? What is meant by "greater physiological linkage" in distressed as opposed to nondistressed couples? How might this be a result of and a cause of their problems?

Attributions and Marital Discord

43. Describe and illustrate the different attributional patterns of distressed and nondistressed couples. The text states that "in happy marriages couples worry less about why their partners do what they do; in unhappy marriages there is simply a greater desire, and perhaps need, to analyze each others' behavior." Illustrate this point.

DIVORCE

Social Factors: Recent Trends in the Divorce Rate

44. Describe some factors that might account for the increase in the divorce rate between 1867 and 1979. Has our attitude toward divorce changed especially in the last forty years?

Individual Factors: Who Divorces?

45. Race, age at first marriage, religion, educational level, and whether the partners complete whatever educational program they have begun are all related to the likelihood of divorce. How?

46. Levinger reviewed the literature on marital stability circa 1965 and organized a list of "rewards," "barrier strengths," and "potential satisfactions outside of marriage." Give examples of rewards in marriage. What are "barrier strengths"? What are "disjunctive social relations"? How are the income of the husband and the wife differently related to marital stability?

Divorce and the Institution of Marriage

47. Give reasons why the increase in divorce does not mean that marriage is a dying institution.

Programmed Exercises

FRIENDSHIP

What Is a Friend?

1. Wright suggest that the stronger the friendship the _____ the voluntary interdependence.

   more

2. Wright suggests that friends provide each other with three sorts of goods: _____, _____ _____, and _____ _____.

   stimulation, material benefits, ego support

Self-Disclosure

3. Self-disclosure is the revealing of _____ aspects of your self to others.

   private

4. Lonely people are _____ likely (than people in general) to disclose themselves to others.

   less

5. In Jourard's study the more you disclosed to someone the _____ they disclosed to you and the _____ they liked you.

   more
   more

6. Jourard's study illustrates the norm of _____ since people are likely to return disclosure with disclosure.

   reciprocity

7. Men like women _____ intimate disclosures, but being disclosed to is not as _____ to men as it is to women.

   return (reciprocate)
   rewarding

8. In general, friendship for men consists of _____ things together and for women friendship consists of sharing _____ matters.

   doing
   intimate

9. In the plane study male and female subjects believed that the male who disclosed his mother's breakdown was _____ and that the female who didn't disclose it was _____.

   maladjusted
   maladjusted

10. Undergraduate women liked a high self-discloser _____ than a moderate self-discloser.

    less

11. The norm of reciprocity does not necessarily require a disclosure to a disclosure; the expression of _____ may be enough.

    sympathy

The Drawbacks of Friendship

12. The envious person reacts to a friend's accomplishments that point up his own lacks by _____ the friend.

undercutting

13. The further away your friend's accomplishments are from your own interests the _____ likely you will feel envy.

less

14. Tesser has found that children choose as their friends those who are as accomplished as they are but in _____ domains.

different

Loneliness

15. The two fundamental aspects of loneliness are _____ loneliness and _____ loneliness.

social
emotional

16. Lonely people are more likely to _____ social skills and to be _____ toward others.

lack
negative

ROMANTIC LOVE

What Is Romantic Love?

17. Rubin found that there were three features aside from sexual attraction that distinguish romantic love from friendship: a more intense _____ need, a greater predisposition to _____, and a sense of _____.

dependence
help, exclusiveness

18. Sternberg argues that all kinds of love have three elements: _____, _____, and _____.

passion
intimacy,
commitment

19. According to Simmel, the interruption of routines, living for the moment, and a sense of "internal continuity" make romantic love like a(n) _____.

adventure

20. What passion is for romantic love, _____ is for long-term love.

loyalty

The Enhancement of Romantic Love

21. Berscheid and Walster have proposed that romantic love will grow when people become _____ in each other's presence and _____ this as being due to attraction.

aroused, interpret

22. In Dutton and Aron's experiment crossing over the scary bridge aroused more interest in the pretty research assistant than crossing over the boring one. This was because the male subjects misinterpreted _____ as _____.

fear, arousal

Jealousy

23. Jealousy is provoked by a _____ to an important relationship. Evolutionary theory predicts that males should be _____ sexually jealous than females. This prediction is about _____ and not about every man or woman.

threat
more
averages

PREMARITAL ROMANTIC RELATIONSHIPS

Relationship Stability

24. The Boston study of premarital relationships found that being sexually intimate neither influenced nor detracted from _____ with the relationship, nor did it predict whether the relationship would _____ two years.

satisfaction
last

25. According to exchange theory, we stay in a relationship because the rewards

are greater than the _____. A person's comparison level includes the affection she is used to and the _____ she thinks she can get.

costs
affection

26. Intimate relationships depend on the exchange of _____ and _____ goods.

particular
symbolic

27. _____ theory holds that people are happiest when rewards (minus costs) are highest, but _____ theory holds that they are happiest when the rewards of the individual and her partner (relative to costs) are equal.

Exchange
equity

28. In a study of dating couples _____ relationships were more likely to be sexual and also more likely to last.

equitable

29. Although equity matters the _____ level of rewards is more important.

absolute

30. While rewards and costs contribute to how satisfied people are with a relationship, the availability of alternatives contributes to how _____ people are to the relationship.

committed

31. When people commit the fallacy of _____ _____ they continue investing in something just because they have been investing in it instead of investing in what now looks to be the greatest future return.

sunk costs

32. One reason that the fact that people stay in a less satisfying relationship is not necessarily an example of sunk costs but that _____ itself is a value.

continuity

33. Unlike in exchange relationships, in _____ relationships people are given what they need.

communal

34. Fiske found that there are four bases for relationships: _____, _____, _____, and _____.

exchange
communal,
authority, equality

35. Cohabitation has increased greatly since the 1970s, in part because the average age of marriage and having a first child has _____.

increased

36. In the Boston study of dating couples almost all the men and women cohabiting expected to _____ someone eventually.

marry

37. Cohabiting couples and non-cohabiting couples were _____ likely to be married by the end of the study.

equally

Who Chooses Whom?

38. The tendency to marry people like oneself is called _____. Burgess found that engaged couples are more similar in traits than are _____ paired couples.

homogamy
randomly

39. In addition to selecting mates who are similar to them, Winch argues that couples want their mates to be _____ to them on some traits.

complementary

MARRIAGE

Changing Conceptions of Marriage and the Family

40. Historically there has been a progressive change in the nature of marriage to marriages based on _____.

companionship

41. Since about 1957 there has been a _____ _____. This means that there have been more marriageable women then men, leading to greater resentment at _____ marriage arrangements and to pressure for greater _____ in marriage.

marriage squeeze

traditional
equality

Marital Satisfaction

42. The _____ marriages through the mid-1960s were those in which the   happiest
    mates fulfilled their assigned sex roles. This is no longer the case. Presently the
    least happiest couple is one in which the woman is modern and the man is
    _____.   traditional

43. The more that a couple self-discloses the _____ their marital satisfac-   greater
    tion. Couples who are _____ in their styles of self-disclosure are less   discrepant
    satisfied than couples who are _____ in their styles.   similar

44. Marital satisfaction begins to _____ sharply with the birth of the first   decline
    child. Marital satisfaction begins to _____ when the last child leaves   increase (rise)
    home. On the other hand children are a source of _____ in their own   satisfaction
    right.

45. Before the birth of a child dual-career couples spend _____ time on   equal
    their careers. After the birth the husband spends approximately the same amount
    of time but the wife spends ten hours _____. The more traditional the   less
    division of labor in child-rearing the _____ satisfied wives are.   less

46. The more something detracts from the amount of companionship in a marriage
    the _____ the marital satisfaction.   less

47. Bullying is an example of a _____ power tactic, while manipulation is   strong
    a _____ power tactic.   weak

48. Being financially less attractive or having less money than one's partner makes
    it more likely that _____ power tactics will be used. Independent of these   weak
    factors women are more likely to use _____ power tactics then men.   weak

49. Egalitarian marriages, where power is divided equally, are happiest; but if
    power is unequal marriages with the male having _____ power are   more
    happiest.

50. _____ couples are more likely to use aversive control than positive   Distressed
    control.

51. Given the same message from their partner, members of a distressed couple
    are more likely to interpret the message as _____ than nondistressed   negative
    couples.

52. Distressed couples are more likely to experience greater _____   negative
    _____ _____, that is, if one partner begins to have negative   affect reciprocity
    feelings in an interchange then the other will shortly also. They are also more
    likely to have _____ _____, that is, if one partner gets   physiological
    aroused then the other will also.   linkage

53. Nondistressed couples see their partners' _____ behaviors as charac-   positive
    teristic of them and _____ behaviors as accidental, while distressed   negative
    couples perceive their partners' _____ behaviors as characteristic of   negative
    them and _____ behaviors as accidental.   positive

DIVORCE

Social Factors: Recent Trends in the Divorce Rate

54. Increased _____, and the ability of women to _____ outside   urbanization, work
    the home, and more accepting _____ about divorce are factors in a   attitudes
    greatly increased divorce rate.

55. _____ people who divorce will marry again.   Most

Individual Factors: Who Divorces?

56. Those married before twenty have a substantially _____ divorce rate   higher
    than those married older.

57. The more socially integrated a person is the _____ likely she will   less
    divorce.

58. Levinger found that similarity leads to _____ in marriages.   stability

59. Greater earnings by the husband lead to greater marital stability; greater
    earnings by the wife lead to greater _____.   instability

60. Lowell Kelly in his forty-five-year follow-up of couples married in the 1930s
    found _____ predicted marital instability.   neuroticism

Self-Test

1. Wright holds that friends
   a. are voluntarily interdependent.
   b. provide stimulation and material benefits for
      each other.
   c. provide ego support for each other.
   d. all of the above

2. Self-disclosure
   a. is the revealing of information such as
      height and weight.
   b. is the revealing of private information about
      yourself.
   c. is done less often by people who are sociable.
   d. is done more often by people who are lonely.

3. In Jourard's study of self-disclosure
   a. disclosing to someone made it more likely
      that they would disclose to you.
   b. a norm of reciprocity was involved.
   c. disclosure can be seen as an exchanged
      reward.
   d. all of the above

4. Men unlike women
   a. reciprocate disclosed intimate information
      but don't like the discloser more for it.
   b. don't reciprocate intimate information.
   c. reciprocate intimate information and like the
      discloser more for it.
   d. reciprocate intimate information but dislike
      the discloser for it.

5. Generally males value different things in
   friendships than do females. For males

a. friendship consists of doing things together.
b. friendship consists of sharing intimate
   information.
c. friendships consists of talking about problems.
d. friendship consists of being able to show
   real feelings.

6. In the plane study both males and females
   believed that
   a. a male who disclosed his mother's break-
      down or a female who didn't disclose it
      were adjusted.
   b. a male who disclosed his mother's break-
      down or a female who didn't disclose it
      were not adjusted.
   c. both a male who disclosed his mother's
      breakdown or a female who didn't disclose
      it were both adjusted.
   d. no one should talk about a mother's
      breakdown.

7. For females if a disclosure is a rarity
   a. it will be valued even if it is not very
      intimate.
   b. it will be valued only if it is intimate.
   c. it will not be valued.
   d. it will be valued only if it is not intimate.

8. If someone is envious of a friend then he
   a. will attempt to support his friend although
      he may feel depressed.
   b. will attempt to undercut his friend's
      accomplishments.
   c. will attempt to compete fairly with his
      friend.
   d. will immediately break up the relationship.

9. Which of these is not an aspect or feature of loneliness?
   a. a lack of social skills
   b. a lack of friends
   c. unsatisfying, superficial relationships
   d. a willingness to disclose oneself to others

10. Rubin argues that three features in addition to sexual attraction distinguish romantic love from friendship. They include all but the following:
    a. a more intense dependence need
    b. a greater interest in the other's life and work
    c. a greater predisposition to help
    d. a sense of exclusiveness

11. Sternberg argues that
    a. romantic love includes passion, intimacy, and commitment.
    b. romantic love includes passion and intimacy but lacks commitment.
    c. companionate love includes intimacy, commitment, and passion.
    d. companionate love includes intimacy and passion but not commitment.

12. The interruption of routines, living for the moment, and a sense of "internal continuity" make romantic love like a(n)
    a. intimate experience.
    b. disruption.
    c. adventure.
    d. pleasure.

13. Just as passion is the governing sentiment of romantic love, what is the governing sentiment of long-term love?
    a. loyalty
    b. exchange
    c. overvaluing of the object
    d. boredom

14. In Dutton and Aron's experiment males crossing over the scary bridge were more attracted to the female research assistant who stopped them as they were crossing than were those who were crossing the safe bridge because
    a. they looked heroic and hence thought they would be more romantically successful.
    b. they misinterpreted fear as sexual attraction.
    c. they thought that the research assistant would be interested in them.
    d. the bridge made them dizzy.

15. The best way to be romantically alluring is

    a. to play hard to get for everyone.
    b. to play easy to get.
    c. to play hard to get yet to make it appear that you would really like to be easy for the one you wish to attract.
    d. to play neither hard nor easy to get.

16. Jealousy
    a. is provoked by a threat to an important relationship.
    b. is seen by sociobiology as not universal.
    c. is seen by sociobiology as no more common in the male than the female.
    d. is always irrational.

17. The Boston study of premarital relationships found that being sexually intimate
    a. detracted from overall satisfaction with the relationship.
    b. increased satisfaction with the relationship and made it more likely that the relationship would last two years.
    c. made it less likely that the relationship would last two years.
    d. did not increase or decrease the satisfaction with the relationship nor the likelihood that the couple would be together in two years.

18. According to exchange theory, relationships consist of an exchange of
    a. rewards and costs.
    b. information.
    c. money.
    d. affection.

19. The value of rewards and costs of affection in a relationship
    a. depends on the affection that could be gotten elsewhere.
    b. depends on the difference in sincerity of each member of the relationship.
    c. depends on the comparison between reality and what you think your partner is capable of.
    d. is not relevant for serious relationships.

20. Intimate relationships depend on the exchange of
    a. general and concrete goods.
    b. particular and concrete goods.
    c. particular and symbolic goods.
    d. concrete and symbolic goods.

21. According to equity theory people are happiest when
    a. the rewards minus costs for an individual in a relationship are highest.

b. the rewards (in relation to costs) for each individual in the relationship are equal.
c. everyone gets what he or she needs.
d. the level of rewards is sufficient given his or her background.

22. Studies of equity have found that
a. equity is more important than the absolute level of reward.
b. equitable relationships are more likely to be sexual and to last.
c. equitable relationships are less likely to be sexual and more likely to break up.
d. equity is generally unimportant in relationships.

23. In a study of undergraduate relationships Rusbult found that
a. the more rewards in a relationship the more satisfaction and commitment, and the more costs the less satisfaction and commitment.
b. the more rewards in a relationship the more satisfaction and commitment, but costs had little relation to satisfaction and commitment.
c. neither rewards nor costs had a strong relationship with satisfaction or commitment.
d. the more the rewards in the relationship the more the satisfaction but the less the commitment.

24. The fallacy of sunk costs involves
a. investing in the South Sea bubble.
b. continuing to invest in something with lower returns just because you have sunk money into it.
c. prematurely deciding that your investment is sunk and jumping to something else.
d. sinking investments into things that are not readily recoverable.

25. A dating couple staying in a relationship in part because of a shared history
a. is an example of sunk costs if they could get better deals elsewhere.
b. is not necessarily committing the fallacy of sunk costs because continuity itself is a value.
c. is an example of sunk costs if the rewards at present are less than the costs.
d. is an example of sunk costs except in the case where they are married and attempting to live up to their marriage vows.

26. In communal relationships, unlike in exchange relationships, each member

a. is given what he or she earns.
b. is given an equal amount.
c. is given what he or she needs.
d. is given what he or she has the power to demand.

27. Fiske found that there are four types of relationships. These include communal, exchange, equality (equity), and
a. authority.
b. antagonistic.
c. protagonistic.
d. orderly.

28. Which of the following is *not* a reason why cohabitation has greatly increased during this century?
a. The average age of marriage has increased.
b. Attitudes toward cohabitation are less negative.
c. The age that people have children has decreased.
d. The age that people have children has increased.

29. In the Boston study of dating, cohabiting couples
a. were equally likely to be married by the end of the study as were non-cohabiting couples.
b. were less likely to expect to marry someone eventually than were non-cohabiting couples.
c. were less likely to be married by the end of the study than were non-cohabiting couples.
d. were more likely to have broken up by the end of the study than were non-cohabiting couples.

30. Couples tend to be:
a. homogamous.
b. complementary to each other on some traits.
c. both a and b
d. neither a nor b

31. Stone shows that romantic love
a. has always been considered a suitable basis for marriage.
b. is universal in all historical periods.
c. is universal in all cultures.
d. did not exist before the twelfth century in Europe and existed but was not considered a suitable basis for marriage in the sixteenth century.

32. Historically there has been a progressive change in the nature of marriage to
a. marriage based on economic considerations.
b. marriage based on companionship.

c. marriage where the woman handles the emotional tasks and the man handles the economic tasks.

d. marriages with less intense feeling of the partners for each other.

33. Through the mid-sixties the happiest marriages were those in which the mates fulfilled their traditional sex roles. Since then
a. this is still the case.
b. the unhappiest couple has a traditional man and a "modern" woman.
c. there is no relationship between being traditional and being modern and marital happiness.
d. only "modern," equal relationships are happy.

34. Marital satisfaction is likely to
a. decrease with the birth of the first child.
b. increase with the birth of the first child.
c. be only briefly affected by the birth of a child.
d. decrease when the last child leaves home.

35. In two-career couples the birth of a child significantly affects
a. the amount of time spent by the husband and wife at work.
b. the amount of time spent by the husband at work but not the amount of time spent by the wife.
c. the amount of time spent by the wife at work but not the amount of time spent by the husband at work.
d. neither the husband's nor the wife's time spent at work (after the first eleven months).

36. What is the evidence that anything that detracts from the companionship of husbands and wives is likely to decrease marital satisfaction?
a. The birth of children decreases time of the couple alone with each other and also decreases marital satisfaction.
b. The more the division of labor turns traditional after the birth of a child the less satisfied wives are (presumably this leads to more separate role-related behaviors and less joint activity).

c. When the last child leaves home marital satisfaction increases.
d. all of the above

37. Strong power tactics are more likely to be used by
a. those making less money.
b. those trying to get their way with a man.
c. those trying to get their way with a woman.
d. women.

38. Distressed couples are more likely (than nondistressed couples)
a. to interpret messages from their partner accurately.
b. to start to feel negative or aroused if their partner was feeling negative.
c. to be afraid to use aversive controls.
d. to see their partner's occasional positive behavior as characteristic of their "real" self.

39. Which of the following groups do not have a higher rate of divorce?
a. couples who marry before twenty
b. blacks
c. those without religion
d. people who finish a level of education (high school, college)

40. For marriages started before 1965 Levinger found that greater earnings
a. by the husband led to greater marital stability.
b. by the wife led to greater marital stability.
c. no matter by whom led to greater marital stability.
d. did not relate to marital stability.

41. Marriage
a. is a dying institution given the huge increase in divorce in the last century.
b. is not a dying institution since those who divorce almost always remarry.
c. is not a dying institution since the increase in the rate of divorce in the last century has not been that great.
d. is a dying institution because of the large increase in the number of couples cohabiting.

Answer Key for Self-Test

1.	d (p. 554)	22.	b (p. 576)
2.	b (p. 555)	23.	b (p. 577)
3.	d (pp. 555–556)	24.	b (p. 578)
4.	a (p. 557)	25.	b (pp. 578–579)
5.	a (p. 557)	26.	c (p. 579)
6.	b (p. 558)	27.	a (p. 581)
7.	a (pp. 558–559)	28.	c (p. 583)
8.	b (p. 560)	29.	a (p. 583)
9.	d (pp. 561–562)	30.	c (pp. 584, 588)
10.	b (p. 563)	31.	d (pp. 589–590)
11.	b (p. 564)	32.	b (p. 590)
12.	c (p. 566)	33.	b (p. 592)
13.	a (p. 566)	34.	a (p. 592)
14.	b (p. 569)	35.	c (p. 593)
15.	c (p. 571)	36.	d (p. 594)
16.	a (p. 572)	37.	c (p. 595)
17.	d (p. 574)	38.	b (p. 598)
18.	a (p. 574)	39.	d (p. 601)
19.	a (p. 574)	40.	a (p. 603)
20.	c (p. 575)	41.	b (p. 604)
21.	b (p. 575)		

Thought Questions and Exercises

1. In general it has been found that men's friendships are a matter of doing things together while women's friendships are a matter of talking to one another about intimate matters. Is this sex difference true of your friendships and the friendships of the people you know? Are some of your friendships of one sort and some of the other? What are your nonromantic friendships with members of the opposite sex like? You may want to get together with someone of the opposite sex and prepare a list of things that people typically do in friendships, and then have males and females rate the items from most to least important. Is there a difference?

2. Some experimenters have found a double standard relating to self-disclosure. Males who disclose intimate information to acquaintances are looked down upon while females who *don't* disclose are looked down upon. Is this true in your own experience? Why do you think that this is the case? Do you think that this should be the case?

3. Have you ever felt really lonely? When? What brought about and what ended this feeling? According to Russell et al. there are two aspects of loneliness: social loneliness and emotional loneliness (see text p. 562). When you felt lonely did you experience both emotional and social loneliness?

4. Wright describes the sort of things we get out of friendship (p. 554) and Rubin describes the ways, other than sexual attraction, that romantic love differs from friendship (p. 563). Do you agree with Wright's and Rubin's analyses? Can you apply them to your friendships and romances? What do they leave out that you think is important? Does Sternberg's analysis fit your thinking better than Rubin's?

5. Simmel compares romantic love to an adventure. In what ways? Does this fit your experience or observations? Do you think that this is a useful way to think of romance?

6. What is jealousy? Have you ever experienced jealousy or been the object of jealousy? Sometimes jealousy is rational. If you are committed to a relationship, then you should be upset by a threat to that relationship. But when people talk about jealousy they most often talk about its less than rational aspects. When is jealousy rational? When is it irrational? What are the different ways that jealousy can be irrational?

7. Reread the section on relationships and exchange theory (pp. 574–580). What is your gut reaction to this picture of human relationships? How much do you think it applies to relationships you have been involved in?

8. Fiske found that there are four bases for relationships: exchange, communal, authority, and equality (see p. 581). All four can occur at different times with the very same people. Give examples of how each could be represented in five different relationships.

9. The text talks of changes in expectations in the roles of husband and wife. Quickly review this. What are your expectations? If you have a boyfriend or girlfriend what are his or her expectations? It seems that the relationship most at danger is the one in which the male and female have incompatible expectations about sex roles. Use the text and discussion with your friends to construct a list of questions about sex roles. Give it to each member of a seriously dating couple as early in the term as possible. Then check to see if there is any relation between agreement or disagreement about sex roles and whether they have stayed together or not. Part of a term may be too short a time interval to test this hypothesis. You may instead want to give them a questionnaire aimed at finding out how much they argue and then relate the results of this questionnaire to congruence in expectations about sex roles.

10. The text presents data that although married couples may be happier because they have children their happiness with each other and with the relationship is lower for the whole period that there are children in the home. From your observations do you think that this is the case?

CHAPTER 16

Attitudes and Attitude Change

Learning Objectives

WHAT ARE ATTITUDES?

1. Define "attitudes." What do we mean when we say that someone has a positive or negative evaluation of something?

The Psychological Functions of Attitudes

2. Attitudes have three functions. What are they? Give an example of each function. Attitudes are both social and individual. Explain.

Attitudes as Social Elements: The Bennington Study

Attitude Change in Students at Bennington

3. Describe the puzzle that Newcomb set out to solve at Bennington. In what ways was Bennington a "community"? What evidence did Newcomb find that attitude change was a function of integration in (including leadership in) the community? To what degree was the shift in attitude of the Bennington students genuine and to what extent was it self-deception (use evidence of stability of attitudes)?

Long-Term Effects of Being at Bennington

4. Almost thirty years after the original study did the Bennington women still hold to their college-produced attitudes? Describe some of the specific forces that sustained their liberalism. Discuss the effects of both mate and friend selection.

Intra-Individual Mechanisms of Attitude Change

Attitudes and Associationism

5. In the 1930s associationism drawn from learning theory was used to explain attitudes. How? Is associationism compatible with the view that attitudes derive from examining evidence and reasoning? Does it see our attitudes as rational?

The Lorge Experiment

6. Lorge attempted to show the irrationality of attitudes by attributing the same statement to different political figures. What were the results of his study? In what way, according to Lorge, do these results show our attitudes to be irrational?

Asch's Reanalysis

7. Asch argued that although the words in the statement Lorge used were the same, their meaning was not. Explain. Asch used Lorge's statements but asked subjects not only to indicate degree of agreement but also to write down what they thought the statements meant. What did he find? Were the subjects being rational in using authorship to interpret the meaning of the statements?

8. Explain whether you can infer that someone's reasoning has not been rational if he comes to the wrong conclusion. Why or why not? What can be learned from the Lorge-Asch controversy?

COGNITIVE CONSISTENCY

Balance Theory

9. Describe Fritz Heider's notion of cognitive consistency. What is meant by "balance"? If you like Mary and hate psychology and Mary likes psychology, are your attitudes in balance? Will you feel pressure to change one of the attitudes? Are balanced structures easier or more difficult to learn than unbalanced structures?

Cognitive Dissonance Theory

10. Describe the claims of cognitive dissonance theory. What happens when people have in mind two or more inconsistent cognitions? What will they do when they experience this? In what way does Festinger's theory make rationality an important human goal?

The Effects of Initiations

11. Describe what the mild initiation, severe initiation, and the control groups had to do in Aronson and Mills's "initiation" experiment. What was the experimenters' purpose in doing this? What was the psychological inconsistency that the severe initiation group experienced after being allowed to join the group? How was the power of this inconsistency less for the other groups?

The Internalization of Conscience through Dissonance

12. Describe the learning theory account of how children internalize social norms. Aronson and Carlsmith either used a mild or a harsher threat of punishment in order to prevent nursery school children from playing with their second favorite toy for ten minutes. After the ten minutes the experimenters determined if these two types of deterrence had an effect on the children's liking for the prohibited toy. What did they discover for children in the two groups—was one sort of threatened punishment more effective than the other in preventing the children from playing with the forbidden toys? Did one sort of punishment change the liking for the prohibited toys? Would this result be predicted by the theory of cognitive dissonance? Why?

Forced Compliance and Dissonance

13. Describe the tasks that Festinger and Carlsmith had students do for an hour. What were the two experimental groups requested to do after this? One group was paid $1 for doing this, the other was paid $20. How did payment affect how interesting the groups rated the tasks in the first part of the experiment? How does cognitive dissonance theory explain this?

Defining "Psychological Inconsistency"

14. Describe the two central problems of cognitive dissonance theory. What is the problem with defining "inconsistency" as any two cognitions that lead to distortion?

15. Aronson argues that we feel inconsistency when beliefs are unflattering, tainting, to our selves. Goffman proposes three features of acts that relate to whether a person's self will be tainted or not. What are they? Explain each.

Dissonance and Choice

16. Describe the experiment in which students were asked to write an essay that went against their true opinion and then were checked to see if their opinion had changed by writing the essay. What was the importance of making salient the fact that they were free to refuse to write the essay? What was the importance of offering the students $.50 or $2.50 for writing it?

Magnitude of Harm Doing and Dissonance

17. Subjects were induced to write essays favoring the legalization of marijuana when they actually opposed its legalization. They were told that the essays would be shown to a very impressionable group or a unimpressionable group. Did this make a difference in whether the subjects experienced dissonance? The experimenters offered a small or a large reward for writing the essay. According to cognitive dissonance theory, which reward should actually cause a larger change in attitude (toward becoming more favorable to legalizing marijuana)? How does this experiment underline the fact that magnitude of harm affects the action of dissonance?

18. We are responsible for harm doing that we know will follow from our actions, but we are also responsible for consequences that we should be able to foresee even though we did not. Explain. Describe the experiment that demonstrated that foreseen and foreseeable negative consequences produce dissonance but unforeseen negative consequences do not. What is the relation between perceived responsibility and the experience of dissonance?

19. Describe some other things people do to reduce dissonance, other than distorting their attitudes. If a person writes a counterattitudinal essay but then is given the opportunity to "self-affirm," does she still distort her attitudes?

Dissonance Theory Reconsidered

20. Describe how dissonance theory differs from its original formulation. Why does the author argue that cognitive dissonance is just the same as rationalization?

Self-Perception Theory

Inferring Attitudes from Behavior

21. Bem uses as a model for how we know our own attitudes how we know the attitudes of others. Explain.

Self-Perception Theory and the Dissonance Results

22. Describe how Bem reinterpreted the Festinger and Carlsmith dissonance experiment. Remember the Bem interpretation starts with what you would believe about someone else given her behavior and then uses it to explain how the subject thinks about her self.

Self-Perception Theory in Contrast to Dissonance Theory

23. Bem sees the results in the $1 group as a result of a rational inference while cognitive dissonance theory sees it as a distortion. Explain. Dissonance theory postulates unpleasant arousal as a cause of the change in belief, Bem does not. What is the evidence that dissonance in fact produces arousal? What is the effect of arousal-enhancing drugs or sedatives on the extent of dissonance? What different roles could arousal play in the experience of dissonance? How do "misattribution" studies help us distinguish between the different possible functions of arousal? Another way of focusing directly on whether attitude distortion reduces painful arousal is to examine whether subjects are still aroused after their attitude change. Describe an experiment doing this. What were the results? What do the results of this experiment suggest about the relation between dissonance and arousal?

Self-Perception Theory and Intrinsic Motivation

24. Describe what self-perception theory says happens if people are rewarded for doing something they like doing anyway. Describe the Lepper experiment in which some children are rewarded for working on puzzles, an activity that they enjoy. How long did the children play with the puzzles three weeks later as compared to the group of children who had previously been promised no reward?

25. Explain whether rewarding people for doing well on a task they like always saps intrinsic motivation. Describe cognitive evaluation theory and differentiate between the controlling and informational aspects of rewards. Describe an experiment that separates out the informa-

tional and controlling aspects of rewards on intrinsically motivated behavior.

The Foot-in-the-Door Phenomenon and Self-Perception

26. Describe the "foot-in-the-door technique." Give an experimental example. Why should the small request increase compliance with the larger request even though the two requests had almost nothing in common?

Self-Perception and Dissonance: An Assessment

27. Self-perception theory and dissonance theory were first seen as rivals. They are now seen as correct theories applying to different domains. Explain.

Further Challenges to Cognitive Dissonance Theory

Selective Attention

28. Explain what "selective attention" is. Smokers and nonsmokers were given articles both supporting and going against the link between smoking and cancer. What would cognitive dissonance theory predict about the reading choice of smokers? What were the results? Frey has discovered that there is a dissonance-induced selective attention effect under certain circumstances. What are the circumstances?

Dissonance and Self-Presentation

29. Explain Tedeschi's variant on the traditional explanation for cognitive dissonance. Describe the "bogus pipeline" technique. How can using the "bogus pipeline" technique help us to determine whether a person distorts her beliefs or changes them for self-presentational reasons (to impress others)? What were the results of experiments using this technique?

Cognitive Consistency and Schemata

30. Cognitive dissonance theory abandoned the notion that inconsistency in general produces dissonance, but consistency theory does survive in a limited form. Describe how pressure for evaluative consistency will make our attitudes toward things more uniformly positive or negative (closer to our basic attitude). Give an example.

31. Describe what "attitude polarization" is. What should the effect on attitude polarization be of just thinking of something for different lengths of time? According to Tesser what is responsible for attitude polarization? Tesser showed

men and women videotapes of women's fashions and football plays. According to Tesser's theory should the attitudes of men and women polarize equally to football and fashions? Why or why not? What did he find?

PERSUASION

Components of Persuasion
32. Describe what Hovland and his associates considered to be the components of persuasion.

Source Characteristics and Persuasion
33. Describe some characteristics of a person that will make them likely to be effective in persuading you to do something or believe something. Describe the source characteristics that respectively will lead to internalization, identification, and "compliance."
34. Explain what the "sleeper effect" is. How was it discovered? According to Hovland what determines whether there will be a sleeper effect or not? Describe the Hovland and Weiss experiment that demonstrated the effect of credibility on the sleeper effect. Explain how the effect is accounted for by the dissociation of the message from the source.

Fear and Persuasion
35. Describe how arousing fear relates to behavior change. Describe Janis's experiment testing whether fear appeals worked at getting people to go to the dentist. How did Janis explain the results of this experiment? Have Janis's results held up? What are the four conditions that must be met for a fear-inducing appeal to work?

Cognition and Persuasion

Distraction and Persuasion
36. Describe how distraction affects persuasion. Teenagers heard the unpalatable message that teens should not get drivers' licenses. One group

was told to focus on the message and another group focused on the speaker's personality. Which group was influenced most? According to Festinger why? What was his follow-up experiment with a fraternity? Do number of counterarguments produced as well as degree of persuasion vary with distraction?

Central versus Peripheral Routes to Attitude Change
37. Describe the difference between central and peripheral routes to persuasion. Which route requires the most work? What is the difference between algorithms and heuristics? Are algorithms peripheral or central? Are heuristics peripheral or central? Describe the experiment by Chaiken that attempted to vary whether people will use the central or peripheral routes by manipulating degree of subject involvement. What factors other than involvement have been found to affect the likelihood of central vs. peripheral processing?
38. Petty and Cacioppo varied involvement, expertise of persuader, and quality of arguments. Describe this experiment and its results. Are uninvolved people more likely to be affected by the number rather than the quality of the arguments in favor of a position? What about involved people?

Influences of Mode of Information Processing
39. Describe how a good mood will affect whether subjects will be persuaded when there is a limited or unlimited time to process information. How does being a member of a group affect whether an individual will adopt systematic or peripheral information processing? What is the effect of preceding a strong or a weak message with a rhetorical question?

Programmed Exercises

WHAT ARE ATTITUDES?

The Psychological Functions of Attitudes

1. The three functions of attitudes are to define social _____, to establish _____, and to _____ thinking and behavior.

   groups
   identities, guide

2. Attitudes link individual _____ to _____ participation.

   cognition, social

Attitudes as Social Elements: The Bennington Study

3. Bennington was a small, experimental, isolated college whose members, faculty and students, formed a _____.

community

4. Emotional forces relating to belonging in a community affected _____.

attitudes

5. There was a _____ correlation between conservatism on entering Bennington and conservatism on graduating. The students who were the most conservative on entry were the _____ conservative on graduating. But the more conservative students themselves were considerably more _____ by their senior year than when they entered; the class as a whole had become more _____.

high

most

liberal
liberal

6. Newcomb believed that it was the students' attachment to other students that produced the attitude change, but it could also have been due to the attachment of the women students to the young, mainly male _____.

faculty

7. Almost thirty years after graduation, _____ percent of these Bennington graduates voted for Kennedy; this is almost _____ as high as women like them in education, socioeconomic status, and religion.

60
twice

8. Alumnae's political attitudes were strongly _____ with those of their husbands. The reason is that the more liberal women tended to choose more _____ men rather than that they were swayed by the politics of their husbands.

correlated

liberal

9. Lorge asked subjects to rate a pro-revolutionary statement attributed to either Jefferson or Lenin. He found that subjects were much more _____ to the statement if they believed it was made by Jefferson. Lorge believed that this demonstrated subjects' _____ forming political attitudes since they reacted so differently to the same statement depending on who made it.

favorable

blindly

10. Asch argued against Lorge that knowledge of the _____ affects the context in which the subjects judge _____ and that this rational. If authorship affects interpretation, then the interpretation of _____ statements should be most affected by knowledge of authorship, since they are most in need of additional interpretation. This was the case.

author
meaning
ambiguous

11. Asch repeated Lorge's experiment but asked subjects to put down their interpretation of the statement. He found that authorship affected _____.

meaning
(interpretation)

COGNITIVE CONSISTENCY

Balance Theory

12. Heider believed that there is a psychological force that pushes people to make their beliefs about an object _____.

balanced
(consistent)

Cognitive Dissonance Theory

13. According to Festinger's theory of cognitive _____ having two inconsistent beliefs will produce unpleasant _____. When someone experiences this he will try to reduce it by _____ one of the inconsistent beliefs.

dissonance
arousal
altering (changing)

14. Learning theory holds that drive "causes" beliefs, while cognitive dissonance holds that inconsistent beliefs cause _____.

drives (arousal)

15. In Aronson and Mills's "initiation" experiment _____ initiation subjects had to read very sexually embarrassing passages and _____ initiation subjects had to read a mildly embarrassing passage as a screening test for a sex discussion group.

severe
mild

16. The sex discussion group was very boring. The severe initiation group rated it _____ boring, the control group rated it _____ boring, and the mild initiation group rated it in between.

least, most

17. According to Aronson and Mills, believing that we went through unpleasantness to get something worthless is _____ inconsistent, although it is not logically inconsistent.

psychologically

18. In an experiment by Aronson and Carlsmith, children were forbidden to play with a liked toy for ten minutes by either a mild or harsher threat of _____. Both groups of children did not play with the toy but the _____ punishment group subsequently reduced their liking for the forbidden toy; the other group did not.

punishment
mild

19. The belief that "I didn't play with a liked toy although I was hardly threatened with punishment" is _____ inconsistent.

psychologically

20. In the Festinger and Carlsmith study students did very _____ tasks for an hour. Some of the students had to convince another student that the experiment was really _____ and would be paid $1 or $20 for doing so.

boring

interesting

21. Students who were paid _____ later decided that the experiment was really more interesting than either students who were paid _____ or students in a control group who did not have to lie.

$1
$20

22. Aronson claimed that only psychological inconsistency of a certain sort produced arousal that led to distortion when cognitions were inconsistent with a positive _____ - _____.

self-image

23. One way that a person's behavior taints her character occurs when she cannot produce a(n) _____ (a claim that she could not have done otherwise) for a negative behavior.

excuse

24. Another way that a person's character is tainted is when he cannot produce a(n) _____ (a claim that under the circumstances what he did was the right thing to do) for an apparently negative event.

justification

25. The _____ of the harm we have done also affects the extent to which our moral worth is tainted.

magnitude

26. There are three aspects of actions that affect our moral worth: the degree to which we have _____, the degree to which the action was _____, and the magnitude of the _____.

control (choice),
justified, damage
(consequences)

27. Students were asked to write essays against their true opinions. In some cases the fact that the students could refuse was stressed, in other cases it was not. Only when the students believed that they could _____ did they experience a cognitive dissonance effect.

refuse

28. The cognitive dissonance effect in this experiment was that students who had been paid only a small amount of money changed their real opinions (in the direction of what they wrote) _____ than those who were paid a larger sum.

more

29. This effect only occurred when it was made _____ that the subjects were free to refuse.

salient

30. Hence this experiment illustrates the effect of perceived _____, a condition underlying moral judgment (and the assessment of character), on the dissonance effect.

choice

31. Subjects who were against the legalization of marijuana were induced to write essays favoring its legalization. They were either told that the essays would be read by very impressionable or unimpressionable people. Only when the subjects believed that _____ people would read the essay did they subsequently distort their attitudes.

impressionable

32. In the condition where they believed that impressionable people would read their essay the subjects who were offered a large reward for writing the essay distorted their beliefs _____ than those offered a small reward.

less

33. In the condition where the subjects believed that the unimpressionable would read their essay neither the large reward nor small reward group _____ their beliefs.

changed

34. In an experiment subjects who wrote essays supporting their true beliefs were told that the essays caused someone harm. They subsequently _____ their attitudes.

changed

35. Subjects in another experiment who were told that there would be no negative effect and then were informed that there had been one _____ feel dissonance.

didn't

36. Subjects who had an opportunity to _____ their true beliefs after writing a counterattitudinal essay did not distort their attitudes (experience cognitive dissonance).

affirm

37. The original formulation of dissonance theory held that inconsistent beliefs gave rise to dissonance independent of the _____ of the beliefs. The recent formulation of dissonance theory holds that only some specific inconsistent _____ can lead to dissonance, those involving the _____.

content

contents (beliefs)
self (character)

38. We experience dissonance just in those circumstances that we would be said to _____; cognitive dissonance, then, is another name for _____.

rationalize,
rationalization

Self-Perception Theory

39. Bem holds that we know our own attitudes in the same way that we know the attitudes of _____ by observing _____.

others, behavior

40. Bem described to a group of subjects the Festinger and Carlsmith study in which people changed their beliefs more for $1 than for $20. Subjects believed that people doing an experiment for a paltry $1 must find it more interesting than people who have to be paid $20 to do it. They likewise conclude in regard to themselves that if they participated for $1 they must find it _____.

interesting

41. For Bem the results of the above experiment are not due to _____ but to rational _____.

distortion
inference

42. The cognitive dissonance view requires that the subject experience unpleasant _____; the Bem view does not. In fact dissonance circumstances produce _____; drugs that reduce arousal reduce _____; and drugs that increase arousal _____ dissonance.

arousal
arousal, dissonance
increase

43. Arousal might be related to cognitive distortion in two different ways. The arousal of dissonance may be painful and the distortion might relieve the _____, or the arousal might _____ the subject that she has done something wrong.

pain, signal

44. It has been experimentally shown that the circumstances that produce dissonance produce arousal, which acts as a _____ suggesting that the subject has done something wrong. This suggests that the subject realizes that his behavior was _____ with his real beliefs.

cue (signal)

inconsistent

45. According to Bem if you were paid for doing something you like you would wind up liking the activity _____.

less

46. Children who are promised a reward for playing a game they like are likely in the future to play the game _____ than if they hadn't been rewarded. Promising a reward lessened the children's _____ motivation.

less
intrinsic

47. According to cognitive evaluation theory, it is the _____ aspect of rewards that lessens intrinsic motivation. When an experimenter stressed the _____ aspect of her reward, intrinsic motivation was not decreased.

controlling

informational

48. People who had previously agreed to put up a tiny sign supporting safe driving were much _____ likely to agree to putting up a large billboard than those who had not received the first request. This illustrates the _____-_____-_____-_____ technique.

more

foot-in-the-door

49. Complying with the small request affected people's _____-_____, so they saw themselves as "the sort of people who do that sort of thing."

self-perception

Further Challenges to Cognitive Dissonance Theory

50. Frey discovered that dissonance causes _____ _____ under certain circumstances: People do not need to avoid old arguments that they believe that they can _____, but they should experience dissonance with _____, compelling arguments. People should not experience dissonance when they are still deciding and have no fixed position, but once they have have decided they should experience dissonance with information that is _____ their position.

selective exposure

refute
new

against

51. Tedeschi's self-presentational account of why people change their beliefs when they experience cognitive dissonance is that they are worried that they will look sleazy to _____ rather than to themselves as claimed in cognitive dissonance.

others

52. With the "bogus pipeline" technique subjects are made to believe that the experimenter will know when they are _____. If the Tedeschi account of cognitive dissonance is correct, then subjects _____ change their opinions when hooked up to the bogus pipeline. If the standard account of

lying
shouldn't

cognitive dissonance is correct, then subjects _____ change their opinions when hooked up to the bogus pipeline. | should

53. In a bogus pipeline dissonance experiment subjects did _____ their opinions, but they changed them _____ than a control group that was not hooked up to the pipeline. This finding would suggest that the change in belief due to cognitive dissonance is partly due to an attempt to convince oneself and partly due to an attempt to convince _____. | change / less / others

Cognitive Consistency and Schemata

54. Tesser argues that _____ consistency in certain circumstances will make our attitudes more uniformly positive or negative. | evaluative

55. Thinking about our evaluation of an object should produce attitude _____. The longer one thinks about something the more _____ one's attitude becomes about it. This is due to the operation of cognitive _____. | polarization / extreme / schemata

PERSUASION

Components of Persuasion

56. The Hovland group analyzed persuasion into the following components: the _____, a _____, the _____, and the _____ of the message. | source, medium, message, target

57. _____ is a type of persuasion where someone is persuaded because he believes the source. _____ is a type of persuasion where someone is persuaded because he wishes to be like the source. _____ involves being "persuaded" in order to gain a reward or avoid punishment. | Internalization / Identification / Compliance

58. A credible source is important for _____. A powerful source is important for _____. An attractive source is important for _____. | internalization / compliance / identification

59. The sleeper effect is a _____ effect on attitudes of a message from a noncredible source. | delayed

60. Originally a credible source has much more effect on people's beliefs than a noncredible source, but after several weeks the difference in effect will _____ | lessen

61. According to Greenwald, the sleeper effect occurs when subjects are unable to integrate the _____ and its source in memory. | message

62. Janis gave subjects a high, medium, or low fear-inducing message and found that the _____ was most persuasive and the _____ was least persuasive. | low, high

63. Janis argued that the unrelieved _____ in the high fear condition was aversive so the subject ignored the issue. | arousal

64. High fear messages will be effective if the danger is _____, the outcome is_____, the recommended response will _____, and the target is _____ to make the response. | serious / probable, work able

Cognition and Persuasion

65. Both pleasant and unpleasant _____ lead to greater attitude change than does attending to the message, as they prevent the subject from producing _____.

distractions

counterarguments

66. The _____ route to persuasion involves systematic evaluation, consistency checks, and consideration of counterarguments. The _____ route to persuasion is quicker but sketchier.

central

peripheral

67. Peripheral routes to persuasion are likely to involve _____ and central routes are likely to involve _____.

heuristics
algorithms

68. If people are very involved in an issue they are likely to use _____ processing.

central (systematic)

69. Chaiken found that when students were not involved in an issue _____ of the presenter had an effect on attitudes while if the students were involved _____ did not have an effect but number of arguments did.

likability
likability

70. Petty and Cacioppo presented a personally relevant or irrelevant unpleasant message to students from a high or low prestige source using either strong or weak arguments. The subjects who found the message personally relevant were affected by argument _____. The subjects who found the message personally irrelevant were affected by _____ of the source.

quality
prestige

71. Uninvolved subjects are more affected by the _____ of arguments and audience _____, heuristic clues, than are involved subjects.

number
response

72. Subjects in a good mood but with limited time were less likely to use _____ processing than subjects in a more neutral mood.

central

73. Being a member of a group evaluation causes individuals to be more likely to adapt _____ processing.

peripheral

74. Preceding a message with a rhetorical question is a good strategy for inducing attitude change only if the following arguments are _____.

strong

Self-Test

1. Which of the following is not a function of shared attitudes?
   a. defining a social group
   b. establishing identities
   c. requiring us to behave in a particular way
   d. guiding the way we think and feel

2. In Newcomb's Bennington study
   a. there was a shift from conservatism to liberalism during the school years.
   b. the most conservative freshmen generally were the most conservative seniors.

   c. the most conservative group of students were considerably more liberal by senior year than they had been as freshmen.
   d. all of the above

3. Which of the following is the best evidence that attachment to other students or faculty, a feeling of belonging to the community, is responsible for the shift in attitude:
   a. Bennington was an urban school where students had many outside contacts.
   b. Those who wanted to and were able to

become campus leaders shifted their politics most; those who were unable to or unwilling to become leaders were more conservative.

c. Bennington was a large school where students felt anonymous.

d. Being liberal was likely to improve grades.

4. Thirty years after graduation Bennington women
   a. voted in approximately the same way as people of their socioeconomic class.
   b. were likely to be very different politically from their husbands.
   c. were likely to be considerably more liberal than people of their socioeconomic class.
   d. were likely to be unpolitical or anti-political.

5. Lorge asked subjects to rate a pro-revolutionary statement attributed to either Thomas Jefferson or Nikolai Lenin. He found that
   a. subjects rated the same statement much more negatively if it were attributed to Lenin.
   b. subjects rated a statement equally positive or negative if it was the same statement—no matter who wrote it.
   c. subjects rated the same statement more negatively if it were attributed to Jefferson since they felt that he should know better.
   d. subjects became confused and refused to rate the statement.

6. Lorge and Asch disagreed over the interpretation of this experiment. Which statement is *true*?
   a. Lorge believed that the results demonstrated that political beliefs are formed by blind association between attitudes and feelings.
   b. Asch believed that the subjects did not really understand who Lenin was.
   c. Asch believed that authorship of the statement did not really affect the students' interpretation of the experiment and that the results were due to experimental error.
   d. all of the above

7. Asch redid Lorge's experiment, but this time he asked subjects to also put down their interpretation of the statement they agreed or disagreed with. What were the results?
   a. Who made the statement did not affect whether the subjects agreed or disagreed with it.

b. Who made the statement affected the subjects' interpretation of what the statement meant.

c. Who made the statement did not affect the interpretation of what the statement meant.

d. The results demonstrated that context does not affect interpretation.

8. Asch found that subjects used the author of the statement as a clue to what the statement meant. Is this rational?
   a. This is irrational and is rarely done in everyday life.
   b. This is rational and is likely to guarantee a correct judgment.
   c. This is rational but does not guarantee a correct judgment.
   d. This is irrational and guarantees that the judgment will not be correct.

9. Both Lorge and Asch's interpretations of attitudes may be partly correct for different attitudes. Lorge's view would most likely explain
   a. political reasoning.
   b. the success of attitude formation based on a careful assessment of an issue.
   c. the success of advertising associating a famous sports figure with a brand of razor.
   d. why people evaluate the same statement differently if it is attributed to Jefferson or Lenin.

10. Heider believes that there is a psychological force that pushes people to make their beliefs about an object
    a. as different as possible from the beliefs of other people.
    b. interestingly inconsistent.
    c. the best, most intelligent that they possibly can.
    d. consistent and balanced.

11. Sandra likes Joan and hates Adeena yet she knows that Joan likes Adeena. Sandra's attitudes here are
    a. balanced.
    b. consistent.
    c. unbalanced.
    d. neutral.

12. Balanced structures are
    a. easier to learn than unbalanced structures.
    b. are more difficult to learn than unbalanced structures.

c. are difficult to keep in mind.

d. are as easy to learn as unbalanced structures.

13. According to Festinger's theory having two inconsistent beliefs will

a. be unpleasant.

b. produce dissonance.

c. produce arousal.

d. all of the above

14. When two beliefs cause someone to experience cognitive dissonance they will

a. try to reduce the dissonance.

b. try to make the beliefs more consistent.

c. try to reduce the unpleasant arousal caused by having inconsistent beliefs.

d. all of the above

15. In a study by Aronson and Mills subjects who read aloud painfully embarrassing passages as an initiation to a discussion group

a. were less likely to like the boring discussion group than subjects who had a milder initiation.

b. were neither more nor less likely to like the boring discussion group than subjects who had a milder initiation.

c. were more likely to like the boring discussion group than subjects who had a milder initiation.

d. All subjects no matter in which initiation condition liked the discussion group.

16. The results of the Aronson and Mills initiation study imply that

a. fraternity hazing is a very bad idea for producing loyal frat brothers.

b. fraternity hazing is a good idea for producing loyal frat brothers.

c. fraternity hazing should have no effect on loyalty.

d. fraternity hazing is moral.

17. According to Aronson and Mills, believing that we went through unpleasantness to get something worthless

a. is psychologically inconsistent.

b. is psychologically consistent.

c. is logically inconsistent.

d. is psychologically neutral but logically painful.

18. An alternative explanation of why subjects in the "severe" initiation condition liked the dis-

cussion group most was that they were most relieved that the discussion was not embarrassing. There is evidence that this is a weaker explanation than dissonance since

a. if electric shock replaces embarrassment the strong shock group is not more likely to like the discussion more than the other groups.

b. if electric shock replaces embarrassment the severe group still likes the discussion most.

c. if electric shock replaces embarrassment the mild shock group likes the discussion most.

d. the electric shock causes people in all conditions to dislike the discussion intensely.

19. Aronson and Carlsmith forbade children to play with liked toys for ten minutes using harsh or mild threats. Weeks later it was found that

a. children in the harsh threat group reduced their liking for the previously liked toy.

b. children in the mild threat group reduced their liking for the previously liked toy.

c. children in both groups increased their liking for the toy.

d. children in the mild threat group but not the harsh threat group increased their liking for the toy.

20. The reason the children in the mild threat group decreased their liking for the toy in the above experiment is

a. there was a psychological inconsistency between liking a toy and not playing with it just because of a mild threat. Reducing the liking reduced the inconsistency.

b. there was a psychological inconsistency between liking a toy and not playing with it because of a mild threat. Reducing the liking did not reduce the inconsistency but reduced the children's fear about playing with the toy.

c. the children had become bored with the toys after several weeks.

d. children are naturally inconsistent and change their liking for toys quite frequently.

21. Students did a very boring experimental task for an hour. They were then bribed for a smaller or larger amount of money to lie and tell someone else that the experiment was interesting. Their own liking for the boring experiment was measured. What were the results?

a. As learning theory would hold, the larger bribe produced greater liking for the experiment.

b. As cognitive dissonance theory but not learning theory would hold, the larger bribe produced greater liking for the experiment.

c. As cognitive dissonance theory but not learning theory would hold, the smaller bribe produced greater liking for the experiment.

d. As learning theory but not cognitive dissonance theory would hold, the smaller bribe produced greater liking for the experiment.

22. Around 1970 Aronson proposed that not all inconsistent beliefs produced dissonance, only inconsistent beliefs
   a. about physical reality did.
   b. about people in general did.
   c. that tainted a person's character did.
   d. that were logically flawed did.

23. A person performs an act with negative consequences. Then
   a. her character is necessarily tainted.
   b. her character will be tainted unless she finds a successful excuse or justification or can demonstrate that the negative consequences were really very minor.
   c. her character will not be tainted under any circumstances.
   d. her character will be tainted even if she has a successful justification if the consequences were quite negative.

24. An excuse is
   a. a good reason for having done something.
   b. a demonstration that you are too powerful to be punished.
   c. a claim that you could not have done otherwise.
   d. never adequate for a quite negative outcome.

25. A justification is
   a. a claim that under the particular circumstances what was done was actually the right thing to do.
   b. a claim that one could not have done otherwise.
   c. a claim that the damage was actually quite small.
   d. an attempt to get off the hook dishonestly.

26. The magnitude of the harm doing
   a. is irrelevant to the extent to which we are tainted by a wrong action.
   b. affects the degree to which our moral worth is tainted by a wrong action.
   c. is only important as part of an excuse or justification.
   d. is the only thing that enters into whether our characters are tainted by a negative act.

27. Students were asked to write essays against their true opinions. In some cases the fact that the students could refuse was stressed, in other cases it was not. The students subsequently distorted their opinions in the standard dissonance effect only when
   a. they believed that they did not have the freedom to refuse the experimenter.
   b. they were paid a relatively large sum of money.
   c. it was stressed that they could refuse the experimenter's request.
   d. they did not have strong opinions to begin with.

28. The above experiment illustrates the role of _____ in the dissonance effect.
   a. anxiety
   b. logical implications
   c. greed
   d. perceived freedom, choice

29. Subjects were induced to write essays favoring the legalization of marijuana although they actually opposed its legalization. They were either told that the essays would be read by very impressionable or unimpressionable people. When did the basic dissonance effect occur in this experiment?
   a. It occurred only when the subjects believed that impressionable people would read the essay.
   b. It occurred only when the subjects believed that people really favoring marijuana would read the essay.
   c. It occurred only when the students believed that unimpressionable people against the legalization of marijuana would read the essay.
   d. It occurred only when the subjects were paid a relatively large amount.

30. In the condition in which they believed that impressionable people would read their essay,

the subjects who were offered a large reward for writing the essay distorted their beliefs

a. much more than those offered a small reward.
b. slightly more than those offered a small reward.
c. the same as those offered a small reward.
d. less than those offered a small reward.

31. Subjects were asked to write a counter-attitudinal essay and led to believe either that the essay would do harm, might do harm, or would not do harm to the readers of the essay. It was later revealed that there had actually been some harm done. Which of these groups experienced dissonance?

a. all three groups
b. the group that knew there would be harm done but not the group that was told that it "might do harm" or the group that was told that it would not do harm
c. both the group that was told that there would be harm done and the group that was told that there might be harm done but not the group that was told there would be no harm
d. only the group that was told there would be no harm

32. The major difference between the original and the present formulation of dissonance theory is that

a. the original theory saw all inconsistency as leading to dissonance and the present theory sees only inconsistencies involving self-worth as leading to dissonance.
b. the original theory believed that only moral inconsistencies lead to dissonance while the present theory does not believe that moral inconsistencies lead to dissonance.
c. the original theory did not see inconsistencies as involving logical contradictions and the present theory does.
d. none of the above

33. Rationalization

a. is good practical reasoning unlike what happens in cognitive dissonance.
b. is an attempt to make silly or immoral acts look sensible; the distortion in cognitive dissonance is a form of rationalization.
c. is the attempt to teach rationality to schoolchildren.

d. is any bad reasoning, including bad reasoning produced by cognitive dissonance.

34. According to Bem we know what we believe by

a. introspection.
b. intuition.
c. observing our own behavior and generalizing from our observations.
d. our feelings.

35. Bem approached the Festinger and Carlsmith study where subjects changed their beliefs more for $1 than for $20 by asking what an observer would conclude about how interesting someone found a task if he was willing to do it for a $1 or for $20. Bem concluded that

a. an observer would decide that the subject doing it for $20 must like the task more—even if the observer is the subject himself.
b. you can't decide liking from whether a person does an experiment for more or less money.
c. an observer would decide that the subject doing it for $1 must like the task more—even if the observer is the subject himself.
d. an observer would decide that the subject doing it for $1 must really dislike the task.

36. One difference between the Bem and the cognitive dissonance view is that

a. in the dissonance view the subjects' behaviors are rational; in the Bem view they are irrational.
b. the dissonance view requires the subject to experience unpleasant arousal while the Bem view does not.
c. the Bem view requires the subject to experience unpleasant arousal while the dissonance view does not.
d. in the Bem view subjects are upset by an inconsistency while in the dissonance view they notice an inconsistency but are not upset.

37. Drugs that reduce arousal such as alcohol or sedatives

a. reduce the dissonance effect.
b. enhance the dissonance effect.
c. do not reduce or enhance dissonance.
d. serve as distractors that may indirectly increase dissonance.

38. What is the evidence that the role of arousal in dissonance is not a drive that is reduced by distortion but is a signal to the subject that she has done something wrong?
   a. If a subject is misled into believing that a placebo and not dissonance caused the arousal then the dissonance effect will be greater.
   b. If a subject is misled into believing that a placebo and not dissonance caused the arousal then the dissonance effect will at first be greater but then quickly decrease.
   c. If a subject is misled into believing that a placebo and not dissonance caused the arousal then the dissonance effect will not occur.
   d. If a subject is misled into believing that a placebo and not dissonance caused the arousal then the dissonance effect will last for a particularly long time.

39. The above experiment demonstrates that in the dissonance effect
   a. arousal plays a motivating function.
   b. it is not arousal but beliefs about arousal that play a signaling function.
   c. arousal plays both a signaling and motivating function.
   d. arousal has no direct or indirect function.

40. As Bem's theory predicts, children who are promised a reward for playing a game they like for a session are likely in the future to play the game
   a. a little more than if they hadn't been rewarded.
   b. all the time.
   c. less than if they hadn't been rewarded.
   d. the same amount of time as they had previously played it.

41. Promising a reward lessened the children's
   a. extrinsic motivation.
   b. arousal level.
   c. desire for future rewards.
   d. intrinsic motivation.

42. There are two aspects of rewards
   a. a controlling aspect and a motivating aspect.
   b. a pleasant aspect and a status aspect.
   c. an informational aspect and a descriptive aspect.
   d. a controlling aspect and an informational aspect.

43. According to cognitive evaluation theory
   a. all aspects of rewards reduce intrinsic motivation.
   b. it is the controlling aspect of a reward that decreases intrinsic motivation while the informational aspect enhances intrinsic motivation.
   c. it is the informational aspect about competence that decreases intrinsic motivation.
   d. all aspects of rewards increase intrinsic motivation.

44. If people are first asked to put up a tiny sign "Keep California Beautiful" and two weeks later asked to put up a large billboard "Drive Safely" they
   a. are less likely to agree to putting up the billboard than if they hadn't previously received the very different request.
   b. are more likely to agree than if there had not been the previous request but less likely than if the previous request had been on the same topic.
   c. are more likely to agree to putting up the billboard than if they hadn't previously received the very different request.
   d. No one agreed to either request.

45. The above technique is known as
   a. the sabine shuffle.
   b. the persistence ploy.
   c. the foot-in-the-door technique.
   d. procrastination.

46. The reason why complying with the small request affected people's likelihood to comply with a large request is
   a. habit.
   b. people are embarrassed to say no if they had previously said yes.
   c. only people who agree with the cause are asked the second time.
   d. that people identify themselves as the sort of people that will support causes.

47. Smokers and nonsmokers were given articles supporting or refuting the link between smoking and cancer. Smokers were
   a. no less likely than nonsmokers to read anti-smoking articles.
   b. more likely than nonsmokers to read anti-smoking articles.

c. much less likely than nonsmokers to read anti-smoking literature.

d. liable to refuse angrily to read the anti-smoking literature.

48. These findings
a. support cognitive dissonance's prediction that smokers would be more likely to read articles opposing the link between smoking and cancer.
b. support cognitive dissonance's prediction that smokers would be less likely to read articles opposing the link between smoking and cancer.
c. refute cognitive dissonance's prediction that smokers would be more likely to read articles opposing the link between smoking and cancer.
d. do not have any relevance to any of cognitive dissonance's predictions.

49. Frey has shown that dissonance does cause selective exposure when
a. people are not sure they can refute the argument against their position.
b. the material presents new arguments.
c. people have already make up their mind.
d. all of the above

50. Tedeschi's self-presentational interpretation of the dissonance effect sees the person as changing his beliefs as a result of cognitive dissonance because
a. he sees himself as having done something sleazy.
b. he believes that others will see him as having done something sleazy.
c. he sees himself as having done something logically inconsistent.
d. all of the above

51. Subjects who are hooked up to a bogus pipeline and made to believe that the experimenter will know they are lying
a. should experience dissonance and change their opinions if Tedeschi is correct.
b. should experience dissonance and change their opinions if the cognitive dissonance position is correct.
c. should change their opinions on both accounts.
d. should not change their opinion on either account.

52. It was found that subjects hooked up to a bogus pipeline
a. changed their opinions but less than did a group that was not hooked up to the bogus pipeline.
b. did not change their opinions.
c. changed their opinions even more than a group that was not hooked up to the bogus pipeline.
d. became firmer in holding their original beliefs.

53. The above finding suggests
a. that only the cognitive dissonance position is correct.
b. that both the cognitive dissonance and self-presentational positions are partially correct since people are trying to convince themselves as well as others.
c. that the cognitive dissonance position is incorrect.
d. that only Tedeschi's position is correct.

54. According to Tesser, just thinking about something for which we have an attitude will
a. make our thinking more evaluatively consistent.
b. produce attitude polarization.
c. make us more likely to remember things in line with the overall attitude and to forget things contradicting the attitude.
d. all of the above

55. According to Tesser, attitude polarization is due to
a. motivational factors.
b. a feeling of psychological discomfort.
c. the extent to which a subject has a detailed schema for the attitude.
d. a general tendency affecting all attitudes.

56. Which of these findings support Tesser's claims about schemata and attitude polarization?
a. Males, who have a more detailed schema for football than females, showed more attitude polarization than females for football.
b. Females, who have a more detailed schema for fashions than males, showed more attitude polarization than males for fashions.
c. subjects with less well-developed schemata about capital punishment showed less attitude polarization than subjects with more

developed schemata about capital punishment.
d. all of the above

57. The Hovland group analyzed persuasion into
which component(s)?
a. the source
b. a medium
c. the message
d. all of the above

58. Internalization is a type of persuasion where
someone is persuaded because
a. he believes the source.
b. she wishes to be like the source.
c. he wishes to gain a reward or avoid
punishment.
d. she is experiencing dissonance.

59. Identification is a type of persuasion where
someone is persuaded because
a. he believes the source.
b. she wishes to be like the source.
c. he wishes to gain a reward or avoid
punishment.
d. she is experiencing dissonance.

60. Compliance is a type of persuasion where
someone is persuaded because
a. he believes the source.
b. she wishes to be like the source.
c. he wishes to gain a reward or avoid
punishment.
d. she is experiencing dissonance.

61. Which of the following is *true*?
a. A credible source, both expert and
trustworthy, is important for internalization.
b. A powerful source is important for
compliance.
c. An attractive source is important for
identification.
d. all of the above

62. The "sleeper effect" is a delayed effect on
attitudes of a message from a(n)
a. neutral source.
b. a credible source.
c. a noncredible source.
d. inconsistent source.

63. According to Greenwald the sleeper effect only
occurs when
a. the source for the evidence is discredited a
considerable time after the presentation of
the claim.

b. the source of evidence for a claim is
immediately discredited after the
presentation of the claim because people
have difficulty in integrating the claim and
its source in memory.
c. the source of the evidence is first accepted
and then discredited.
d. the source of the evidence is weakly
accepted.

64. Janis gave subjects a high, medium, and low
fear-inducing message and found that the
a. low and high fear-inducing messages were
most persuasive.
b. high fear-inducing message was most
persuasive and the low fear-inducing was
least persuasive.
c. low fear-inducing message was most
persuasive and the high fear-inducing was
least persuasive.
d. there were no major differences in
persuasiveness between the high, medium,
and low fear-inducing messages.

65. High fear messages are sometimes effective
persuaders if
a. the dangerous outcome is probable.
b. the response will be effective.
c. the person being persuaded can make the
response.
d. all of the above

66. Teens heard the unpalatable argument that they
should not get driving licenses. The group that
focused on the message rather than on the
personality of the speaker changed their
attitudes
a. slightly more.
b. considerably more.
c. less.
d. neither more nor less.

67. Distractions
a. lessen attitude change.
b. produce more attitude change only if the
distractions are pleasant.
c. produce more attitude change only if the
distractions are unpleasant.
d. produce more attitude change if the
distractions are pleasant or unpleasant.

68. Brock has argued that distractions convince by
a. putting the subject in a good frame of mind.
b. by inducing dissonance.

c. by preventing the subject from producing counterarguments.

d. all of the above

69. Students heard an argument in favor of raising tuition. They had to at the same time judge different numbers of flashing lights creating a low, high, and medium distraction condition. Students in the high distraction condition produced

a. fewer counterarguments and were more persuaded by the argument.

b. more counterarguments and were more persuaded by the argument.

c. more counterarguments and were less persuaded by the argument.

d. fewer counterarguments and were less persuaded by the argument.

70. Petty and Cacioppo propose that there are two different routes to persuasion

a. the depth route and the surface route.

b. the central and the peripheral route.

c. the camel and the donkey route.

d. the clear and unclear route.

71. The central route to persuasion

a. is faster than the peripheral route.

b. involves heuristics.

c. is sketchier than the peripheral route.

d. involves systematic evaluation, consistency checks, and consideration of counterarguments.

72. The peripheral route to persuasion

a. is quicker than the central route.

b. is sketchier than the central route.

c. involves heuristics rather than algorithms.

d. all of the above

73. If people are very involved in an issue then they are more likely to use

a. heuristics.

b. central processing.

c. peripheral processing.

d. emotional processing.

74. What did Chaiken find about the relation between likability and attitude change?

a. Likability had no effect on attitude change.

b. Likability always had an effect on attitude change.

c. If the student was not involved in the issue then likability had an effect on attitude change.

d. Only if the student was very involved in the issue did likability have an effect on attitude change.

75. Subjects who were put in a good mood and given a limited amount of time were likely to use

a. central processing.

b. peripheral processing.

c. both central and peripheral processing.

d. cognitive dissonance.

76. Subjects who are part of a group making an evaluation are more likely to use

a. central processing.

b. peripheral processing.

c. both central and peripheral processing.

d. algorithms.

Answer Key for Self-Test

1.	c (p. 612)	32.	a (p. 638)
2.	d (p. 615)	33.	b (p. 638)
3.	b (p. 616)	34.	c (p. 639)
4.	c (p. 619)	35.	c (p. 640)
5.	a (p. 622)	36.	b (p. 640)
6.	a (p. 623)	37.	a (p. 641)
7.	b (p. 624)	38.	c (pp. 641-642)
8.	c (pp. 624-625)	39.	b (pp. 642-643)
9.	c (p. 623)	40.	c (p. 644)
10.	d (pp. 625-626)	41.	d (p. 644)
11.	c (p. 626)	42.	d (p. 644)
12.	a (p. 626)	43.	b (p. 645)
13.	d (p. 626)	44.	c (p. 646)
14.	d (p. 626)	45.	c (pp. 645-646)
15.	c (p. 628)	46.	d (p. 646)
16.	b (p. 628)	47.	a (p. 648)
17.	a (p. 628)	48.	c (p. 648)
18.	b (p. 629)	49.	d (pp. 648-649)
19.	b (pp. 630-631)	50.	b (p. 649)
20.	a (pp. 630-631)	51.	b (p. 650)
21.	c (p. 633)	52.	a (p. 650)
22.	c (p. 634)	53.	b (p. 650)
23.	b (pp. 634-635)	54.	d (p. 651)
24.	c (p. 634)	55.	c (p. 651)
25.	a (p. 635)	56.	d (pp. 652-653)
26.	b (p. 635)	57.	d (p. 654)
27.	c (p. 635)	58.	a (p. 655)
28.	d (p. 635)	59.	b (p. 655)
29.	a (p. 636)	60.	c (p. 655)
30.	d (p. 636)	61.	d (p. 655)
31.	c (p. 637)	62.	c (p. 656)

63. b (p. 658)
64. c (p. 659)
65. d (p. 660)
66. c (p. 661)
67. d (pp. 661-662)
68. c (p. 662)
69. a (p. 663)

70. b (p. 663)
71. d (pp. 663-664)
72. d (p. 664)
73. b (p. 664)
74. c (p. 665)
75. b (p. 668)
76. b (p. 668)

Thought Questions and Exercises

1. In the Bennington study it was found that, although the class got much more liberal over the four years at Bennington, the people who were most conservative, center, or on the left in the entering class were still likely to have that same *relative* position on graduation. Can you think of examples in your own experience in which, although the group changed, the relative positions of individuals within the group remained the same?

2. Asch found that people interpret the exact same quote quite differently depending on whether they thought it was from Lenin or Jefferson: "I hold it that a little rebellion, now and then, is a good thing, and as necessary in the political world as storms are in the physical." Use this same quote but attribute it to different people, for instance, Reagan, Gorbachev, the president of your college. Ask for degree of agreement or disagreement and for an interpretation of what it means.

3. Review Heider's notion of balance in relationships. Choose a short story involving love or friendship. See if you can analyze any of the shifts in interpersonal relationships as examples of changes in balance.

4. Now that you know the concept, can you recall ever having experienced dissonance? Looking back, do you think that you altered your beliefs to lessen the dissonance?

5. Aronson modified cognitive dissonance theory. He believed that only cognitions that were unflattering to a person's sense of self should arouse dissonance. Some of the variables that should affect dissonance according to this account involve whether an act was willed or not and whether there was damage caused by the act. Describe several other variables that should increase or reduce dissonance according to this account.

6. What is the difference between an excuse and a justification? How do they each repair the damage to self of a negative act? Give several examples of each.

7. Does the foot-in-the-door technique (see text, p. 645) work when asking for charitable donations? Choose two causes that you would really like to support and that are generally popular. If you live in a dormitory you might have one person canvas for donations for one cause, keeping track of who gave what. The next week have someone else, not known to be a friend of the first, canvas for the other cause. Ask people to give any amount but tell them that a certain amount would be preferred. Make this amount three times the amount that people originally volunteered to give. Your goal is to determine whether having given to a previous cause will make people more or less liable to give. We must rule out an alternative interpretation: that being asked to give a larger amount will make people liable to give more. You will need a control group of people in your dorm who have not as yet been asked for money. Ask them for the same larger amounts as you requested from those who were asked to give a second time.

8. Use a notebook to keep track of all the ways that you are the target of persuasion during the day. By persuasion I mean an attempt to get you to do something that you would not do spontaneously. (If I tell you that you dropped a $20 bill and you pick it up, you have not been "persuaded" to do something since if you had seen the bill you would have spontaneously picked it up. I just provided you with information.)

9. Kelman (see text, p. 655) distinguishes between compliance produced by internalization, identification, and compliance. Give two examples of each from your own experience.

CHAPTER 17

Attitudes and Behavior

Learning Objectives

1. LaPiere toured the United States with a Chinese couple in the early 1930s, a time of great anti-Oriental prejudice. Were they served in the restaurants and hotels they went to? Six months later LaPiere wrote the establishments they had visited and asked whether they served Orientals. What were the results? Why is a breach between attitudes and behavior troublesome for social psychologists?

THE RECONSTRUCTION OF ATTITUDES

2. Fishbein and Ajzen pointed out that attitude measures are usually about a broad class while behavioral measures are about specific responses to a specific stimulus. How might this explain why attitudes and behavior do not appear to be highly correlated? Give some examples.

THE MODEL OF REASONED ACTION

3. According to Fishbein and Ajzen, the immediate psychological determinant of a person's behavior is not her attitude. What is it then? What are some of the limitations on the ability of our intentions to control our behavior? Being greedy is not a behavior but a characterization of a behavior in relation to some standard. Explain.

Attitudes and Intentions

4. According to Fishbein and Ajzen, intentions are the consequences of two elements. What are they? What are "subjective norms"?

The Origins of Attitudes

5. Fishbein and Ajzen hold that a person's attitude toward performing an act is a consequence of two things. What are they?

6. Contrast goals that are ends in themselves with goals that are contingent. Give an example. What are values? In what way are values like biological drives? What produces evaluations?

Subjective Norms

7. Fishbein and Ajzen's model takes into account moral concerns as an independent determinant of action. In what way? According to the model, to what extent are we influenced by our perception of significant others' attitudes toward an act?

Individual Limitations on Reasoned Action

Previous Behavior

8. There are factors (in addition to those that are part of the model of reasoned action) that predict behavior. One is what the person has done previously. Discuss the seat belt study that demonstrated this. Do habits necessarily go against rationality?

Emotions and Rationality

9. Emotions play a rational role within Fishbein and Ajzen's model and an extra-rational role. Give an example of each. What was found about the relation between emotional attitudes toward sex and condom use in sexually active men?

Perceived Behavioral Control and Reasoned Action

10. Ajzen has added an element to his model of reasoned action: whether a person believes that

he is *capable of* carrying out the desired action. Give an example.

Morality and Reasoned Action

11. Describe the two places provided for morality in the model of reasoned action. Even if Mead and Fishbein and Ajzen are right and our moral norms are derived from our parents, it does not mean that what we currently think is moral is what our parents would expect us to think. Explain. If we have moral beliefs independent of our perceptions of others' expectations about us, then moral judgments may be another variable in addition to those proposed by Ajzen and Fishbein. Explain.

Social Influence and Reasoned Action

Modeling and Reasoned Action

12. The model of reasoned action has a place for social influence—what we believe significant others, parents or peers, expect of us. What would Ajzen and Fishbein expect about social influences on whether young people smoke? What was actually found? Explain what it means to say that these young people "modeled" their parents' behavior rather than their parents' expectations?

Cognitive Accounts of Prejudice and Rationality

13. Describe how prejudice might be rational. In the early 1960s Rokeach argued that anti-black prejudice was due to an assumed difference in values between blacks and whites, while Triandis argued that for more intimate connections prejudice is based solely on race. Explain. How has the relation between prejudice based merely on race and prejudice based on assumed values shifted?

Social Influence through Immediate Social Pressure

14. Describe why there is such a large discrepancy between predicted behavior and actual behavior in the Milgram obedience studies. What sort of behavior would the model of reasoned action predict? What is it about the situation that prevents people from acting reasonably?

Cognitive Dissonance and Reasoned Action

15. Explain how the phenomenon of cognitive dissonance presents problems for the model of reasoned action. Dissonance demonstrates that to be rational it is not sufficient for an attitude to be related to perceived consequences and their evaluation. Explain. What else is needed for the attitude to be rational?

WHEN DO ATTITUDES PREDICT BEHAVIOR?

Directly and Indirectly Formed Attitudes

16. Explain how we can have attitudes about things that we have never experienced. What are these attitudes based on?

17. Describe how direct, past experience is likely to be most predictive of future behavior. What is the difference in correlation between attitudes toward research and willingness to participate in research for subjects who have participated in few or no experiments and subjects who have participated in several experiments?

18. Explain how reflecting on behavior can affect attitudes. Subjects reported their attitude toward being religious either before being asked about their previous specific religious behaviors or after being asked. Did the group that had thought about their specific religious behaviors *before* stating their attitudes predict their future behavior better or worse than the group that stated their attitudes before having to think about their behaviors? Why?

19. According to Fazio and Zanna attitudes based on experience are better predictors of behavior because they are stronger than attitudes based on inference. What are the three ways in which they are stronger? What are the information processing differences between directly and indirectly formed attitudes?

Attitude Accessibility as It Affects Behavior

20. Explain how accessibility of an attitude relates to whether the attitude will affect behavior. Describe an experiment to determine whether greater attitude accessibility leads to a tighter correspondence between attitudes and behavior.

21. Direct experience should activate attitudes, make them more accessible, in an *implicit* as well as explicit sense. Explain. How did Fazio attempt to measure an attitude without asking for it? What is "priming"? Describe the experiment that showed that subjects' attitudes toward a person were primed by their attitude toward a directly experienced puzzle, but their attitude toward the person was not primed by an indirectly experienced attitude.

Reflecting on One's Attitudes and Behavior

22. Reflecting on one's attitudes does not always increase the consistency between attitudes and behavior. Describe the experiment involving reflections on relationships that demonstrates this point. What are "cognitively driven" attitudes? How does the difference between cognitively driven and emotional attitudes explain why reflecting on the features of your lover will not be predictive of the endurance of the relationship?

"Mindlessness" and Behavior

23. Explain what Langer means when she says that people often behave "mindlessly" in social interactions? How does the "copying machine" experiment illustrate her point? (Include in your response the effect of a big or little request with no reason attached, a good reason attached, or a "placebic" reason.)

INDIVIDUAL DIFFERENCES

24. Describe the difference between Snyder's high and low self-monitors in their responsiveness to the opinions of others. Under what conditions are low self-monitors more likely to act on their attitudes than high self-monitors?

25. Describe what "private self-consciousness" is. How is it like and how is it unlike high self-monitoring?

26. Subjects' attitudes toward how much they should study and their perceptions of how much others expected them to study were measured. They were correlated with self-monitoring and private self-consciousness. What was the result? Why? Is the difference between high and low self-monitors in the relationship between behavior and intentions or in the likelihood of carrying out intentions once formed?

**ATTITUDES AND BEHAVIOR:
A RECONSIDERATION**

27. How might the research in this chapter explain why LaPiere found such a discrepancy between attitude and behavior in his study?

Programmed Exercises

1. At a time of great prejudice against Orientals LaPiere toured the U.S. with a Chinese couple. They were almost _____ served in the hotels and restaurants visited. Six months later LaPiere wrote the same establishments and asked whether they would serve Orientals. Of those who answered, _____ percent said they would not.

    always

    90

2. This study appears to show that _____ do not predict behavior.

    attitudes

THE RECONSTRUCTION OF ATTITUDES

The Problem of Generality

3. Fishbein and Ajzen pointed out that attitude measures are usually about a _____ class, while behavioral measures are made up of _____ behaviors to a _____ stimulus.

    broad
    specific, specific

4. General attitudes may not predict specific behaviors but _____ attitudes may predict them.

    specific

5. In a study of attitudes toward birth control the correlation between being in favor of birth control and using the pill was very _____, but the correlation of being in favor of the pill and using it was _____.

    low

    high

6. The correlation between favorableness toward religion and church attendance was very _____, but the correlation between attitude toward attending church and actual church attendance was _____.

    low

    high

7. One drawback of reducing the generality of attitudes is that if one attitude does not predict _____ behaviors then the notion of "attitude" is not useful.

many

THE MODEL OF REASONED ACTION

8. According to Fishbein and Ajzen the immediate psychological determinant of a person's behavior is not her attitude but her _____ to perform an act.

intention

9. Intentions only predict _____, not whether it will meet a standard.

behavior

Attitudes and Intentions

10. Intentions are a consequence of _____ toward performing an act, and a person's subjective _____ in regard to the act.

attitudes
norms

11. Subjective norms concern how people _____ to one's life believe one should act.

important

12. According to Fishbein and Ajzen, our attitude toward performing an act is determined by our estimate of the _____ of performing the act and our _____ of them.

consequences
evaluation

13. One source of our attitudes are our _____ drives.

biological

14. Goals that are ends in themselves need no further _____. One example are _____.

justification
values

15. _____ goals are justified by showing that they lead to something else that is desirable.

Contingent

16. A causal account of how one came to have a goal that is an end in itself provides a history but not a _____ for the goal.

justification

17. Values and biological drives are sources of the _____ of particular acts.

evaluation

18. The extent to which you are influenced by the attitudes of significant others depends on your _____ to comply with the wishes of the significant others.

motivation

Individual Limitations on Reasoned Action

19. In addition to the factors presented in the model of reasoned action, what a person usually does in a particular situation, that is, _____, also affects what a person will do.

habit

20. A negative or positive _____ attitude toward sex affected condom use in addition to the factors specified by Fishbein and Ajzen's model of rationality. Males who had a negative emotional attitude toward sex were _____ likely to use condoms than was predicted by the model of rationality.

emotional

less

21. A person might not perform an action that is reasonable because he believes that he is not _____ of performing it.

capable

22. Even if we learn a set of moral norms from significant others, such as our parents, once we have acquired principles we may come to different _____ than our parents do.

conclusions

23. _____ judgments may affect our behavior independently of the variables proposed by Fishbein and Ajzen. In a study of attitudes toward being a transplant donor, subjects indicated both their _____ position on transplants and what _____ others thought of transplants. Both factors independently _____ the subject's attitude toward being a donor. Attitudes correlated with whether the subjects actually _____ or not.

Moral

moral
significant
predicted
donated

Social Influence and Reasoned Action

24. We are not only influenced by the expectations of others but by the _____ they provide.

model

25. In a study of social influences on young people's smoking it was found that parental _____ of smoking had no effect on children's behavior but whether the parents actually _____ or not did have an effect.

approval
smoked

26. Cognitive theories of prejudice maintain that prejudice is rational in the limited sense that it follows from _____ though erroneous beliefs about minorities; these beliefs are called _____.

reasonable
stereotypes

27. In the early 1960s Rokeach argued that anti-black prejudice was due to an assumed difference in _____ between blacks and whites.

values

28. Triandis argued that in addition to an assumed difference in values prejudice is based on _____.

race

29. Exclusion of blacks from distant relationships appeared to be based on an assumed difference in _____ while their exclusion by whites from more intimate relationships was based on _____.

values
race

30. Recent evidence shows that prejudice due to race alone is _____ relative to prejudice based on an assumed difference in values.

declining

31. In the Milgram experiments on obedience to destructive authority people are asked to deliver what they think are extremely dangerous _____ to a protesting victim.

shocks

32. When people are asked what they would do in this experiment, almost _____ _____ said they would go to the end. In fact in the standard experiment _____ people go to the end.

no one
most

33. The Fishbein-Ajzen model of reasoned action predicts what people _____ they would do and not actual _____. Face-to-face _____ brings into play influences that we do not take into account in forming our intentions.

say, behavior
influence

34. The example of cognitive dissonance shows that an attitude might have the right relation to perceived consequences and evaluation and still be _____.

irrational

35. For an attitude to be rational it is not sufficient for it to have the right relations to perceived consequences and evaluations. In addition the perceptions of consequences and evaluations must not be a product of self-deception and _____.

distortion

Reasoned Action and Predicting Behavior

36. Some attitudes are based on direct experience and others on _____ based on similar experiences.

inferences

37. Attitudes based on direct experience are more likely to _____ behavior than attitudes based on inferences.

predict

38. The relationship between attitude toward research and willingness to participate in future experiments was _____ the more experiments people had previously participated in.

stronger

39. Subjects listed the specific religious activities they engaged in and then indicated their attitudes toward religion. Attitude predicted future observance for these subjects more than for those who listed their specific religious activities _____ indicating their attitude toward observance.

after

40. Attitudes based on experience are stronger than indirectly formed attitudes for three reasons: they are _____, held more _____, and are more _____ to attack.

clearer, confidently
resistant

41. Fazio and Zanna argue that directly formed attitudes provide more _____ about their objects, that when we pick up an attitude indirectly from another person then that person may be more _____ than the facts supporting the attitude, and that directly formed attitudes are more _____ from memory than indirectly formed attitudes.

information
salient

accessible

Attitude Accessibility as It Affects Behavior

42. According to Fazio and Zanna _____ formed memories are more accessible than indirectly formed memories.

directly

43. Subjects who solved a puzzle themselves responded to a question about their attitude to the puzzle more _____ than did subjects who saw a video of someone working on the puzzle. Speed of response is a measure of _____.

quickly

accessibility

44. The more frequently an attitude is expressed the more _____ it is. It has been found that greater attitude accessibility leads to a tighter correspondence between attitudes and _____.

accessible

behavior

45. Attitudes may be elicited by a question or by mere _____ to the object of the attitude.

exposure

46. When an attitude is activated the activation spreads to associated ideas. This phenomenon is called _____.

priming

47. Voters with more _____, positive attitudes toward a candidate are more likely to vote for her than voters with less _____, positive attitudes.

accessible
accessible

Reflecting on One's Attitudes and Behavior

48. Reflecting on one's attitudes does not always increase the correspondence between attitudes and _____.

behavior

49. People were asked to make a global assessment of their relationship, or to list the good and bad features of their relationship and then make a global assessment. The list plus global assessment predicted whether the relationship would endure _____ than the global assessment alone.

worse

50. If your attitude is formed by explicit consideration of features then making a list should increase attitude-behavior _____; if your attitude wasn't formed by explicit consideration then making a list should not increase _____.

consistency
(congruence)
consistency

"Mindlessness" and Behavior

51. According to Langer, people in a social interaction act _____, running off a "script" of an interaction without paying attention to details.

mindlessly

52. Subjects asked a favor were as likely to comply if given a useless "placebic" reason as they were to comply if given a good reason but only for _____ favors.

minor

INDIVIDUAL DIFFERENCES

53. _____ self-monitors are very responsive to social pressure, while _____ self-monitors are more responsive to their own attitudes. Snyder demonstrated that low self-monitors acted on their attitudes more than high self-monitors only when the attitudes are made _____.

High
low

salient

54. "Private self-consciousness" involves both attending to one's attitudes and being _____ to act on them.

motivated

55. Subjects' attitudes toward how much they should study and their perception of how much others expected them to study were measured. They were correlated with self-monitoring and private self-consciousness. Only subjects _____ in private self-consciousness and _____ in self-monitoring showed a high attitude-behavior correlation.

high, low

56. The difference between high and low self-monitors acting on their attitudes is not in forming intentions but in _____ them out.

carrying

Self-Test

1. In a period of great prejudice against Orientals LaPiere toured the United States with a Chinese couple. They were almost always served in the hotels they visited; six months later LaPiere wrote these hotels and asked whether they would serve Orientals. Of those who answered
   a. all said they would serve them.
   b. about half said that they would serve them, and half that they would not.
   c. almost all, 90 percent, said they would not serve them.
   d. most, about 60 percent, said that they would serve them.

2. This study appears to show that attitudes
   a. predict behavior.
   b. are essential to understand what people do.
   c. are correlated with behavior.
   d. do not predict behavior.

3. Fishbein and Ajzen believed that attitudes could predict behavior if
   a. the attitude and the behavior were both about sex.
   b. the attitude and the behavior were of the same degree of generality.
   c. the attitude and the behavior were not about race or ethnic groups.
   d. people were sincere.

4. In a study of attitudes toward birth control the correlation between being in favor of birth control and using the pill was
   a. somewhat higher than the correlation between being in favor of the pill and using it.
   b. much lower than the high correlation between being in favor of the pill and using it.
   c. very high.
   d. moderately high.

5. One drawback of reducing the generality of attitudes is that if one attitude does not predict many behaviors then
   a. the notion of "attitude" is not useful.
   b. attitudes will be less likely to predict behavior.
   c. there are no drawbacks to reducing the generality of attitudes.
   d. attitudes will be of too great an interest as compared to behavior.

6. According to Fishbein and Ajzen, the immediate psychological determinant of a person's behavior is
   a. her attitude.
   b. her intention to perform an act.
   c. her stimulus-response system.
   d. her hormones.

7. Intentions predict behavior, but they are not sufficient to predict things that involve standards or behaviors that are partly out of our control, such as:
   a. passing an exam
   b. being greedy
   c. having children
   d. all of the above

8. According to Fishbein and Ajzen "subjective norms" are
   a. how one thinks the central people in one's life would regard an action.
   b. another term for attitudes.
   c. extremely disruptive to behavior
   d. types of reflexes.

9. Intentions are a consequence of
   a. subjective norms alone.
   b. attitudes alone.
   c. attitudes and subjective norms together.
   d. none of the above

10. According to Fishbein and Ajzen, our attitude toward performing an act is determined by
    a. chance.
    b. prejudices.
    c. our estimate of the consequences of performing the act and our evaluation of the consequences.
    d. purely nonrational factors.

11. A causal account of how one has come to have a goal
    a. is the same as a justification for having a goal.

    b. may be entirely different from a justification for having a goal.
    c. involve "ends in themselves."
    d. are not able to be given for human behavior.

12. Goals that are ends in themselves
    a. need no further justification.
    b. are always capable of further justification.
    c. are causal accounts.
    d. are contingent goals.

13. Contingent goals
    a. are causal accounts.
    b. involve ends in themselves.
    c. need no further justification.
    d. are justified by showing that they lead to something else that is desirable.

14. Values are
    a. contingent goals.
    b. goals that are ends in themselves.
    c. are capable of further justification.
    d. are forms of causal analysis.

15. Which of the following are sources of the evaluation of individual acts?
    a. chance
    b. values and biological drives
    c. intentions
    d. attitudes

16. According to Fishbein and Ajzen, in forming an intention to act a person is not only affected by his own attitudes but also
    a. by his perception of the attitudes of people in general.
    b. by his perception of the attitudes of the "upper class."
    c. by his perception of the attitudes of "significant others."
    d. all of the above

17. Studies testing the Fishbein and Ajzen model have found that the likelihood of fulfilling stated intentions varies with
    a. beliefs about and the evaluation of the consequences of the act.
    b. significant others' evaluation of the act.
    c. motivation to please significant others.
    d. all of the above

18. In a study of seat belt use it was found that factors predicted by the Fishbein and Ajzen model predicted the likelihood that a person would use seat belts but that another important

factor also predicted seat belt use. What was this factor?

a. intentions
b. evaluation of the consequences
c. biological drives
d. habit

19. Habits
a. are always opposed to rationality.
b. are never opposed to rationality.
c. sometimes get in the way of doing the rational thing and sometimes do not.
d. are the only source of behavior.

20. Emotional reactions
a. are rooted in values and biological drives and are thus sometimes part of rational action.
b. are always rational.
c. always conflict with rational actions.
d. are never related to values.

21. In a study of condom use and positive and negative attitudes toward sex, it was found that
a. condom use was affected in the way that the Fishbein and Ajzen model specified and in no other way.
b. attitudes did not affect whether people would use condoms or not.
c. males who had a negative emotional attitude toward sex were less likely to use condoms than would be predicted by their measures on the model of rationality.
d. males who had a negative emotional attitude toward sex did not act at all as was predicted by their measures on the model of rationality.

22. According to Ajzen, another reason why a person may not act is because
a. she does not believe that she is capable of successfully completing the action.
b. she is overconfident.
c. she does not really want to act.
d. all of the above

23. The model of reasoned action provides two places for morality as a determinant of action. First, moral concerns enter into our evaluation of consequences; second, moral concerns are part of our perceptions
a. of the evaluations of the act by significant others.
b. of the practical consequences of our actions.

c. of the costs and benefits of our actions.
d. all of the above

24. If our moral principles derive from those of our parents, does this mean that our moral judgments will necessarily be the same as our parents?
a. Yes, since we have the same principles.
b. No, because we may apply those principles to different cases, or be more or less consistent than our parents.
c. No, because moral principles can never justify actions.
d. Yes, because early parental training completely determines our moral outlook.

25. Learning morality is like learning language in that we learn language from our parents but once we learn the principles of language
a. we can correctly create many new sentences that our parents never uttered.
b. we must repeat only the sentences our parents taught us.
c. we only create new sentences when we make a mistake.
d. language allows the creation of new sentences, morality does not.

26. In a study of attitudes toward being a transplant donor, subjects indicated both their moral position on transplants and what their significant others thought of transplants. How did these factors affect behavior?
a. Subjects' moral position on transplants affected whether they would donate, but the attitude of significant others did not.
b. Subjects' moral position on transplants did not affect whether they would donate, but the attitude of significant others did predict whether or not they would donate.
c. Both the subjects' moral position and the attitude of significant others independently predicted whether subjects would donate or not.
d. Neither the subjects' moral position nor the attitude of significant others predicted whether subjects would donate or not.

27. Significant others not only influence our behavior by our taking their expectations into account but also
a. by being models.
b. by what they tell us.

c. by what they write us.

d. Significant others rarely influence behavior.

28. In a study of social influences on young people's smoking it was found that
   a. parental approval or disapproval of smoking had no effect on children's behavior but whether the parents actually smoked did.
   b. parental approval or disapproval of smoking had no effect on children's behavior and neither did whether the parents smoked or not.
   c. parental approval or disapproval of smoking had an effect on children's behavior but whether the parents actually smoked did not.
   d. both parental approval or disapproval of smoking and whether the parents actually smoked had an effect on the behavior of the children.

29. Cognitive theories of prejudice maintain that prejudice is rational in the limited sense that it follows from
   a. irrational, false beliefs about minorities.
   b. irrational, but partly true, beliefs about minorities.
   c. reasonable and correct beliefs about minorities.
   d. reasonable, though incorrect, beliefs about minorities.

30. In the 1960s Rokeach argued that white prejudice against blacks was rational in the above limited sense since
   a. it derived from whites' assumptions that blacks had different values.
   b. it did not extend to blacks who whites believed had the same values as they did.
   c. it would extend to whites with unwholesome values.
   d. all of the above

31. Triandis argued that prejudice derives not only from an assumed difference in values, but also from an irrational prejudice based on race. It was shown that
   a. prejudice based on an assumed difference in values is more important in personal relations while race is more important in work relationships.
   b. prejudice based on an assumed difference in values is more important in distant relationships such as those in the workplace while race is more important for personal relationships.
   c. both prejudice based on a difference in assumed values and prejudice strictly based on race are equally important in all situations.
   d. an assumed difference in values is the only cause of prejudice.

32. How do subjects' predictions and behaviors in the Milgram obedience experiment differ?
   a. Subjects' predictions reflect the variables in the Fishbein-Ajzen model, but their behavior does not.
   b. Subjects' predictions reflect a rational model of action, but their behavior also reflects the Fishbein-Ajzen model of rationality.
   c. Subjects' predictions and behavior are both irrational.
   d. Subjects' predictions do not reflect a model of rational action, if they did they would correctly predict their behavior.

33. Cognitive dissonance poses problems for a theory of rational action since
   a. it shows that people can be induced to act against their better judgment.
   b. it shows that some attitudes, those produced by cognitive dissonance, are distorted and irrational.
   c. it shows that an attitude can be irrational (distorted) even if it is related to perceived consequences and evaluations.
   d. all of the above

34. Attitudes based on direct experience are
   a. more likely to predict behavior than attitudes based on inference.
   b. less likely to predict behavior than attitudes based on inference.
   c. as likely to predict behavior as attitudes based on inference.
   d. likely to be very unstable.

35. The correlation between attitude toward research and stated willingness to participate in future experiments was
   a. stronger the fewer the experiments people had previously participated in.
   b. stronger the more the experiments people had previously participated in.
   c. always negative.
   d. zero.

36. Attitudes based on experience are stronger than indirectly formed attitudes because
    a. they are clearer.
    b. they are more confidently held.
    c. they are more resistant to attack.
    d. all of the above

37. According to Fazio and Zanna, which attitudes are the most accessible from memory?
    a. indirectly formed attitudes
    b. attitudes based on inferences
    c. directly formed attitudes
    d. attitudes derived from information imparted by someone else

38. An attitude is more accessible
    a. when it is expressed more frequently.
    b. when it derives from indirect experience.
    c. if it stands out because it has not been previously expressed.
    d. when it is difficult to retrieve.

39. Greater attitude accessibility leads to
    a. a looser relation between attitudes and behavior.
    b. exaggeration.
    c. a tighter correspondence between attitudes and behavior.
    d. Accessibility of memories has nothing to do with likelihood of behavior.

40. Attitudes when activated spread the activation to associated ideas. This is called
    a. correspondence.
    b. accessibility.
    c. rolfing.
    d. priming.

41. Priming from an attitude to a person associated with the attitude occurs for
    a. directly experienced, accessible attitudes.
    b. all attitudes.
    c. inferentially based attitudes.
    d. attitudes relating to traumatic events experienced in childhood.

42. Voters with less-accessible, positive attitudes toward a candidate in comparison with voters with equally positive but more accessible attitudes are
    a. more likely to believe that the candidate has done well in a debate.
    b. more likely to vote for the candidate.
    c. less likely to vote for the candidate.
    d. likely to develop negative attitudes.

43. An attitude that is "cognitively driven"
    a. results from a global impression of an object.
    b. is the sort of attitude we have toward our friends or lover.
    c. is "obsessive."
    d. is formed by an explicit consideration of the merits of an object.

44. People were asked to make a global assessment of their relationship or to list the good and bad features of their relationship and then make a global assessment. Which better predicted how long the relationship would endure?
    a. the global assessment alone
    b. the list plus the global assessment
    c. the list alone
    d. None predicted how long the relationship would endure.

45. In the above experiment making a list of features
    a. essentially reproduced the way the person first decided to have a relationship.
    b. did not reflect what about the partner had caused the person to enter a relationship.
    c. is always helpful.
    d. is always a distraction.

46. If your attitude is originally formed by an explicit consideration of features then making a list should
    a. decrease the congruence between attitude and behavior.
    b. increase the congruence between attitude and behavior.
    c. have no effect on the relation between attitude and behavior.
    d. increase inconsistency.

47. If one has been involved in a relationship for a short time then explicitly reflecting on it
    a. should be less confusing than if you have been in the relationship for a long time.
    b. should be more confusing or disruptive than if you have been in the relationship for a long time.
    c. is particularly helpful.
    d. clarifies and improves the relationship for men but not for women.

48. Langer argues that people in social interaction often act "mindlessly." She means that
    a. they are typically prejudiced.

b. people often have serious short-term memory deficits.

c. they run off a behavior usually appropriate to an interaction without paying attention to crucial details.

d. they are often unable to run off the general "scripts" of their social interactions.

49. People waiting their turn at a copier were asked if someone could get in line in front of them in order to copy a few or many pages. They were given a good reason or a meaningless "placebic" reason. What happened?

a. For small favors, but not for large, the placebic reason worked as well as the good reason.

b. People were surprised at getting the placebic reason and never gave up their place in line.

c. Placebic reasons worked as well as good reasons for large requests.

d. Very few people yielded their place in line for any request.

50. Which of the following is correct about self-monitors?

a. High self-monitors are very responsive to their own attitudes, and low self-monitors are very responsive to social pressure.

b. High self-monitors are very responsive to social pressure, while low self-monitors are more responsive to their own attitudes.

c. Both high and low self-monitors are particularly responsive to social pressure.

b. Both high and low self-monitors are particularly likely to resist social pressure.

51. Snyder has demonstrated that low self-monitors act on their attitudes more than high self-monitors only

a. when the issue was an important one.

b. when the issue involved political concerns.

c. when the issue was made salient for them.

d. all of the above

52. "Private self-consciousness"

a. involves people only attending to their own attitudes.

b. involves people attending to their own attitudes and being motivated to act on them.

c. is the same thing as self-monitoring.

d. involves people being particularly concerned with privacy.

53. Subjects' attitudes toward how much they should study and their perception of how much others expected them to study were measured. They were correlated with self-monitoring and private self-consciousness. What were the results?

a. Only subjects high in private self-consciousness and low in self-monitoring showed a high attitude-behavior correlation.

b. Only subjects low in private self-consciousness and high in self-monitoring showed a high attitude-behavior correlation.

c. All subjects (no matter what their self-monitoring or private self-consciousness score was) showed a high attitude-behavior correlation.

d. All subjects showed a low attitude-behavior correlation.

54. High self-monitors are

a. as likely as low self-monitors to have their behaviors and intentions in correspondence.

b. less likely than low self-monitors to act on their intentions.

c. more likely than low self-monitors to be distracted by social pressures.

d. all of the above

Answer Key for Self-Test

1.	c (p. 674)	21.	c (p. 684)
2.	d (p. 674)	22.	a (p. 685)
3.	b (p. 675)	23.	a (p. 685)
4.	b (p. 676)	24.	b (pp. 685-686)
5.	a (p. 677)	25.	a (p. 686)
6.	b (p. 677)	26.	c (p. 686)
7.	d (p. 678)	27.	a (p. 687)
8.	a (p. 678)	28.	a (p. 687)
9.	c (p. 678)	29.	d (p. 687)
10.	c (p. 679)	30.	d (pp. 687-688)
11.	b (p. 680)	31.	b (p. 688)
12.	a (p. 680)	32.	a (p. 688)
13.	d (p. 680)	33.	d (p. 689)
14.	b (p. 680)	34.	a (p. 691)
15.	b (p. 680)	35.	b (p. 691)
16.	c (p. 681)	36.	d (p. 691)
17.	d (pp. 681-682)	37.	c (p. 692)
18.	d (p. 683)	38.	a (p. 693)
19.	c (p. 683)	39.	c (p. 694)
20.	a (p. 684)	40.	d (p. 694)

41.	a (p. 695)	48.	c (p. 698)
42.	c (p. 696)	49.	a (p. 699)
43.	d (p. 696)	50.	b (p. 700)
44.	a (p. 696)	51.	c (p. 701)
45.	b (p. 697)	52.	b (pp. 701-702)
46.	b (p. 697)	53.	a (p. 702)
47.	b (p. 698)	54.	d (p. 702)

Thought Questions and Exercises

1. The text presents several reasons why overall attitudes, or stereotypes, may not predict specific behavior. There are more reasons for this than have been presented. Describe various reasons and various circumstances in which you think that your behavior would and would not follow from your general attitudes.

2. According to Fishbein and Ajzen, and common sense, intentions predict behavior. But not always. Sometimes an action—for instance, passing an exam or being greedy—involves living up to, or failing to live up, to standards. For this reason we might not pass an exam despite our intentions and best efforts to do so, or we might be greedy even though we just tried to get more of something we wanted. Our understanding of everyday behaviors often involves seeing people as meeting or failing to meet standards. Give examples of behaviors that involved standards in your life and the life of people you know.

3. The text discusses the difference between justifications for a belief and giving a causal account of why you have a belief (see pp. 680-681). Give three examples of each sort of account of a belief.

4. Parents' approval or disapproval of smoking did not relate to whether their children smoked or not, but parental smoking did. What we do may be a more important influence than what we say. Think of other behaviors for which this might, or might not, be the case—for instance, parental cursing. Have your friends and classmates interview their parents on their attitude toward the behavior, and have them indicate the parents' actual behavior and their actual behavior. Do students imitate behavior and not attitudes? Is this so in all the situations that you have thought of?

5. Usually reflecting on one's attitudes will make behavior more consistent with one's attitudes. But sometimes reflecting on one's own attitudes may reduce attitude-behavior congruence. Romantic relationships are a good example of this. This may be because we don't enter into a romance by going over a list of features of our beloved. What other relationships may this also be true of? What sort of relationships would it not be true of?

6. You may wish to replicate Langer's study of mindlessness (described on pp. 698-699 of the text). Can you design a version of the study using a request for change to use a phone (minor request—change for 25¢; major request—change for $2)? What would be your "placebic request"?